Privacy and Medical Confidentiality in Healthcare

GLOBAL PERSPECTIVES ON MEDICAL LAW

Series Editors: Thierry Vansweevelt, *Faculty of Law, University of Antwerp, Belgium and* Nicola Glover-Thomas, *School of Law, University of Manchester, UK*

The new and exciting Global Perspectives on Medical Law series is an important forum for exploring and examining the most prominent and pressing concerns within medical law from comparative, international and transnational perspectives.

With a strong emphasis on the comparative evaluation and analysis of core legal issues in medicine, Global Perspectives on Medical Law offers a series of books that look at the impact of differing cultural and organizational influences, and in so doing engages with the socio-political landscape of the countries concerned. These differences can be hugely significant in terms of their practical implementation, but also in facilitating our understanding of core concepts within medical law. Topical coverage includes the full spectrum of medico-legal, regulatory and ethical subject matter, ranging from informed consent to medical liability, from the beginning of life to the end of life, and from vulnerability to privacy and patient safety.

With a team representing the 'World Association of Medical Law' network at the helm, books in this series have global relevance as well as strong academic rigour and practical merit.

For a full list of Edward Elgar published titles, including the titles in this series, visit our website at www.e-elgar.com.

Privacy and Medical Confidentiality in Healthcare

A Comparative Analysis

Edited by

Thierry Vansweevelt

Professor of Medical Law, University of Antwerp, Belgium

Nicola Glover-Thomas

Professor of Medical Law, University of Manchester, UK

GLOBAL PERSPECTIVES ON MEDICAL LAW

Cheltenham, UK • Northampton, MA, USA

The second volume in this series

Published by
Edward Elgar Publishing Limited
The Lypiatts
15 Lansdown Road
Cheltenham
Glos GL50 2JA
UK

Edward Elgar Publishing, Inc.
William Pratt House
9 Dewey Court
Northampton
Massachusetts 01060
USA

A catalogue record for this book
is available from the British Library

Library of Congress Control Number: 2023946862

This book is available electronically in the **Elgar**online
Law subject collection
http://dx.doi.org/10.4337/9781035309436

ISBN 978 1 0353 0942 9 (cased)
ISBN 978 1 0353 0943 6 (eBook)
Printed and bound by CPI Group (UK) Ltd, Croydon, CR0 4YY

Contents

Contributors

Emily Baron, Barrister and Solicitor (Ontario) and PhD Candidate, University of Toronto, Canada.

Nils Broeckx, Professor of Health Law, University of Antwerp, Belgium.

Benedikt Buchner, Professor of Civil Law, Liability Law and Law of Digitalization, Faculty of Law, University of Augsburg, Germany.

Sylvester C. Chima, Associate Professor and Head of Programme of Bio & Research Ethics and Medical Law, Nelson R Mandela School of Medicine & SONPH, College of Health Sciences, University of KwaZulu-Natal, Durban, South Africa.

Filip Dewallens, Professor of Health Law, University of Antwerp, Belgium.

Nicola Glover-Thomas, Professor of Medical Law, School of Social Sciences, Department of Law, University of Manchester, United Kingdom.

Mette Hartlev, Professor, Director of the Centre for Legal Studies in Welfare and Market, University of Copenhagen, Denmark.

Trudo Lemmens, Professor, Scholl Chair in Health Law and Policy, Faculty of Law and Dalla Lana School of Public Health, University of Toronto, Canada.

Eiji Maruyama, Professor Emeritus, Kobe University, Japan.

Barry Solaiman, Assistant Professor of Law, Hamad Bin Khalifa University, Qatar; Adjunct Assistant Professor of Medical ethics in clinical medicine, Weill Cornell Medicine, Qatar.

Ferdinand Marcel Temba, Senior Lecturer, Department of Policy Planning and Management, College of Social Sciences and Humanities, Sokoine University of Agriculture, Tanzania.

Stacey A. Tovino, Professor of Law, Director, MLS and LLM in Healthcare Law Programs, The University of Oklahoma College of Law, United States.

Thierry Vansweevelt, Professor of Health Law, University of Antwerp, Belgium.

Foreword

The World Association for Medical Law (WAML) was founded in 1967 with the aim of creating an international academic forum to foster a better understanding of the relevant issues within health law, legal medicine and bioethics. Over the years, the WAML has evolved to become an international peak body in these areas and it serves as a platform which attracts experts from different disciplines, within these three main foci, to better represent a collaborative exchange of ideas. It provides for World Congresses for Medical Law that occur on an annual basis and offer a facility for world experts to meet face-to-face. It provides a venue to discuss ideas and develop international collaboration, such that it can foster potential international research and act as a source of information for all those who are interested in health law, legal medicine and bioethics around the world.

An annual meeting of like-minded people offers a wonderful foundation for the exchange of ideas but such meetings are few and far between and often the cost of travel or extraneous considerations, such as the recent COVID pandemic, greatly restrict their capacity to adequately fulfil the ever growing needs in these rapidly expanding areas of academic endeavour. As the current President of the WAML, I am extremely proud of the initiative, developed by Professors Vansweevelt and Clover-Thomas, the editors of the WAML book series, who, together with the collaboration of world experts, have created a book series to explore various specific topics within health law and to provide a source of information which is available to all those with a special interest in that field. These books are available to young and old and are not restricted by the need to travel to attend international meetings. They provide a perfect complement to such meetings and, while they do not offer the additional social intercourse that accompanies such meetings, they offer immediate access to relevant information in a very timely fashion.

Since 1967, the delivery of medicine has dramatically changed. It has moved from a doctor-centric delivery of service, which was largely based on a paternalistic approach, to become a patient-centric, consumer-based appreciation of the management of health and health services. This WAML book series began in 2020 and emerged coincident with the evolution of the COVID pandemic which greatly restricted world travel and the ability for experts to meet face-to-face. The pandemic resulted in a far greater reliance on telemedicine and telehealth and the remote delivery of patient care, often devoid of direct patient contact. This necessitated a greater dependence on technology, virtual communication platforms and a significant reliance on that which patients reported, often devoid of direct patient scrutiny and examination that is otherwise inherent in direct face-to-face patient contact. With the evolution of virtual telemedicine and remote care there has also emerged a new respect for the need to protect patient confidentiality and privacy.

This, the second book in the WAML book series, is focused on issues of privacy and confidentiality. It encourages a comparison and contrast between different national and international approaches which are designed to protect sensitive patient information. At a time when cyber-security has gained significant prominence, it is both appropriate and imperative to consider and appreciate the whole question of privacy and confidentiality, especially when dealing with patients and their medical records.

There remains an absolute requirement to balance society's needs with those of the individual patient and to achieve a level of equity which accommodates both the needs of the patient and those of the society in which that patient lives while. That balance must, concurrently, demonstrate an acceptable level of mutual respect for both considerations. It must reflect a level of trust that must prevail between therapist and patient to encourage and allow the patient to feel sufficiently comfortable to share intimate and personal details with his/her doctor. The clinician also has a duty of care to both respect the patient's wishes while also being acutely aware of the fine line that may exist between doctor and patient, should the situation prove that the patient has been non-compliant, a situation which could place society at risk. A perfect example of this is found in the field of epilepsy and driving in which the balance required must respect both the needs of the patient while also protecting the safety of society. The recent COVID pandemic which imposed restrictive imposts on patient mobility could also serve to highlight the potential conflict that may have faced the clinician who may have been aware that his/her patient did not respect the restrictions imposed not the use of inoculation to offer herd immunity.

At the heart of patient-centred health care is the ethical consideration of autonomy which represents the expression of a patient's right to control that which he/she is prepared to accept as part of his/her health care, namely that which the patient allows to be done to his/her body. This has direct ramifications for the management of patients, including the management of his/her privacy and confidentiality, to ensure that the trust that exists between patient and therapist is fully respected and maintained.

The production of a book that examines the intricacies of privacy and confidentiality serves as a major contribution to assist doctors, therapists, patients and the healthcare system to fully appreciate that which is required from each member of the team. There are those areas of healthcare in which the privacy of the doctor-patient relationship extends beyond their interpersonal interactions and is controlled by the law. The courts do have the power to subpoena medical records in which case it is up to the lawyers to confirm or dispute questions of privilege that may exist in the preparation of material, specifically designed to be part of a legal action. Litigation in negligible may require discovery of patient information that would otherwise be the subject of privacy and confidentiality. A book, dealing with these issues, is a timely reminder of the complex nature that remains an intricate part of health law, especially in the domain of privacy and confidentiality.

The WAML is delighted to be part of this book series and commends this, the second book in the series on health law, to all those involved in health law, legal medicine and bioethics. As the President of the WAML, I thank all those involved in this project for producing material that will long survive past my presidency and which will serve as a benchmark for future activity and research endeavours.

Roy G Beran
President
The World Association for Medical Law

1. Introduction: privacy and medical confidentiality in healthcare

Thierry Vansweevelt and Nicola Glover-Thomas

Why a book series on health law? That was the crucial question when we began this book series in 2020.

Just as in 2020, it remains the aim of this book series – to bring together the existing and emerging body of research in several important areas of health law, and to provide a comparative, critical and analytical lens from which to view fundamental concepts. Health law, as a distinct discipline and in practice, has gained significant traction over the last 40 years and this is set to continue. Health is something which has global reach – as individuals we are all invested in the notion of good health and the systems in place to support us in reaching and maintaining such health. At a country wide level, all countries are confronted with the same medico-legal problems; yet political and cultural differences often result in very different solutions. Access to these very diverse responses is not always easy: linguistic challenges, the inaccessibility of foreign legal sources, the historical, social, political knowledge gaps and the different jurisprudential contexts, presents a significant challenge when trying to understand how the law operates in practice in a particular country. As global interconnections continue to increase, this is an especially fitting time to publish a comparative view of the field and to provide an international analysis on the different country approaches on a given medico-legal issue.

The editors hope that this book series will serve as a strong reference that presents a comprehensive picture of the field. The books within this series will also provide detailed critical depth when considering current controversies; and will play an important role in moving the field forward. The topics covered by this book series will be enlivened by the cross jurisdictional dialogue by the contributing authors, most of whom are known experts in their part of the world.

This book series is directly linked with the World Association of Medical Law (WAML). Since its inception, the WAML has become the largest international association for medical law and its members include lawyers and healthcare workers across a broad range of specialisms. The WAML was established in 1967 at its first Congress, held in Ghent, Belgium. It now boasts a membership of over 650 associates across 30+ countries. It hosts an international congress annually and is attended by more than 300 participants from all over the world. The WAML provides a large international platform that encourages scholarship and collaborative research endeavours among its members.

Changes in the healthcare landscape have been rapid in many parts of the world. Advances in medical technology and innovation have also provided scope for many people to, at least in theory, access medical interventions that once were not available. At the same time, significant changes have occurred. Medical confidentiality, privacy and health are the focus of book two of the series. These are key foundational concepts in health law and for many people they are the necessary conditions to consult a physician.

At the heart of contemporary medical ethics is the relationship of trust between the patient and the physician. The patient's right to privacy and the duty of medical confidentiality are some of the most basic rights and core principles of health law and ethics. These rights are important for society, for public health and for each patient as an individual. It encourages people to visit their physicians voluntarily, knowing that doctors will protect the confidential nature of the information disclosed. It also encourages people to communicate openly with their doctors, which will help doctors to provide optimal care. The provision of all relevant health information is a prerequisite for making a proper diagnosis and prescribing correct medical treatment. In addition, medical confidentiality ensures that the privacy, autonomy and dignity of the patient are respected. For many, medical confidentiality represents an aggregate social good that must be protected for the benefit of all.

Still, the concepts of privacy and medical confidentiality are similar, but certainly not identical. Privacy is a much broader concept than medical confidentiality. Privacy includes both the 'inner circle', which protects the physical and moral integrity of the person, and the 'external circle', which encompasses the right to establish and develop relationships with other human beings. The right to privacy applies in relation to the government and to other citizens. Medical confidentiality, on the other hand, includes only private data and applies only to medical caregivers.

The concepts of medical confidentiality and the right to privacy have some common characteristics that are shared and recognised around the world. But the way they are interpreted and executed in different parts of the world varies widely.

In this book these critical rights are examined from a variety of country perspectives. Attention is paid, amongst other things, to which healthcare providers are bound by the duty of confidentiality, which information is secret, the exceptions to confidentiality, special cases as genetics and privacy and the liability in case of negligence. Throughout the text, some specific practical cases are discussed. This gives a concrete overview of the similarities and differences between the different jurisdictions.

The importance of privacy is growing, both nationally and internationally. More patients are aware of their rights and are seeking to reinforce them. Furthermore, many countries have established a Data Protection Authority which ensures compliance with the fundamental principles of data protection.

The countries in this book have been chosen to provide an insight across continents, representing a mix of jurisdictions:

1. Jurisdictions from the common law (Canada, except for Quebec, United Kingdom, United States) and civil law (Belgium, Germany, the Nordic countries, South Africa) traditions; and
2. Jurisdictions in which the principle of privacy has been adopted either in the Constitution (Canada, United States, South Africa, Belgium), the Criminal Code (medical confidentiality: Germany, Belgium, Tanzania, Japan), in a Patients' rights Act Code (Nordic countries); or
3. Jurisdictions with rely centrally upon the common law (United Kingdom).

The sample of country coverage, while not offering a comprehensive picture of the way in which medical confidentiality and privacy is both understood and applied, seeks to offer a broad evaluation of the role and versatility of the concept of privacy from a global perspective. In this volume, the contributions focus on the following aspects:

1. *The concept and function of privacy and medical confidentiality*: does it promote self-determination, as an individual right? Is it a family right?
2. *The scope of the duty of medical confidentiality*: to whom applies this duty and which data are concerned?
3. *How is and how should this duty to medical confidentiality be enforced?* What are the problems by enforcing these duties?

THE GOAL OF THE RIGHT TO PRIVACY AND THE DUTY OF MEDICAL CONFIDENTIALITY

What are the objectives of the duty to medical confidentiality? And to what extent is this obligation effective in realising these objectives? The legal recognition of the duty of medical confidentiality is in itself a confirmation of the importance of this principle. It empowers the rights of the patient, and in particular his right to privacy. The courts have an important role to play in enforcing and developing this principle.

While the goal of protecting the privacy of patients is laudable, it is not beyond criticism. In many countries, it has been argued that the obligation to respect patient confidentiality is strict and absolute. Following this point of view there are no exceptions to the duty of medical confidentiality. Breaching this medical confidentiality leads to undesirable results. For example, it could cause patients to lie about their health or specific circumstances of an accident, to become untrustworthy, or – even worse – to avoid seeking advice from physicians, due to fears that they might inform third parties about matters entrusted to them in confidence.

But for other countries, medical confidentiality is seen as an important, but not an absolute value. As a relative value, medical confidentiality can conflict with other values. In such cases, the physician, and perhaps later the judge, must weigh the conflicting interests.

The conflict of interest that is at stake in such situations is the conflict between the duty to maintain confidentiality and the possibility to prevent harm to others. When the life or health of a third party is in serious danger, in some countries it is considered justified for physicians to breach their duty of medical confidentiality. In such a conflict of interest, life and health are valued more highly than medical confidentiality.

In this book it is examined which values are at stake and how absolute the duty of medical confidentiality is interpreted currently. If exceptions to the duty of medical confidentiality are accepted, what are the conditions that must be fulfilled to breach the obligation to respect patient confidentiality?

In the end, the objective of privacy and medical confidentiality is about attaining an effective balance between the patient and medical professionals ensuring the practice of medicine is workable while also ensuring third party rights are properly protected. While medical confidentiality is an aggregate social good that benefits us all, exceptions that justify disclosure will continue to exist in an effort to maintain that often precarious balance between the patient and the public at large.

2. Privacy and health in Belgium

Thierry Vansweevelt, Nils Broeckx and Filip Dewallens

GENERAL INTRODUCTION, ETHICAL BASIS AND KEY SOURCES

The right to privacy is a personality right which is inherent to every person. Personality rights are subjective rights which give rights holders legal control over third parties in relation to the protection and use of intrinsic components or manifestations of their own personality.[1] This privacy right is protected by the European Convention of Human Rights (ECHR), the EU Charter of Fundamental Rights and the Belgian Constitution.[2] Article 8 ECHR contains two kinds of obligations for public authorities: a negative and a positive one. It protects individuals from arbitrary interference by the public authorities with private life and compels the state to abstain from such interference. However, Article 8 can also impose positive obligations on public authorities that effects respect for private life.[3]

In this context, European data protection law is also extremely important. This is because it is applicable to both public authorities and citizens, and because it further shapes the content of the general privacy right. According to the General Data Protection Regulation (GDPR), the processing of personal data is subject to several conditions. Health data fall under a specific regime. In principle, the processing of health data is prohibited, unless one of the criteria set out in article 9(2) GDPR applies.

---

[1] *Cf* J.-L. Renchon (ed), *Les droits de la personnalité* (Brussels, Bruylant, 2009), 3–4.

[2] Art. 8 European Convention of Human Rights; art. 3 EU Charter of Fundamental Rights; art. 22 Belgian Constitution.

[3] ECRM 26 March 1985, nr. 8978/80, X and Y/The Netherlands.

In addition, some other legal provisions specifically impose certain privacy obligations on physicians and other healthcare providers. For example, article 10 of the Law on Patients' Rights stipulates:

> The patient has the right to protection of his privacy with each intervention of a health care provider and in particular concerning the information related to his health.
>
> The patient has the right to intimacy. Subject to the patient's agreement, only the persons whose presence is professionally justified may be present during examinations or treatment.
>
> There shall be no interference with the exercise of this right except such as is in accordance with the law and is necessary for the protection of health or for the protection of the rights and freedoms of others.[4]

Specifically, in relation to the patient's informational privacy, article 458 of the Penal Code also prohibits physicians and other healthcare workers to divulge secrets or confidential information (health data or other patient information). This legal provision is still the basis of the medical secrecy. Moreover, medical confidentiality is also a rule of professional ethics.[5]

The patient's right to privacy and the duty of medical confidentiality are some of the most basic rights and core principles of health law in Belgium. This right is important for society, for public health and for each patient as an individual. It encourages people to visit their physicians voluntarily, knowing that doctors will protect the confidential nature of the information disclosed.[6] It also encourages people to communicate openly with their doctors, which will help doctors to provide optimal care. The provision of all relevant health information is a prerequisite for making a proper diagnosis and prescribing correct medical treatment. In addition, medical confidentiality ensures that the privacy, autonomy and dignity of the patient are respected. The importance of the right to privacy and the duty of medical confidentiality is demonstrated by the fact that these rights are included in specific legislation. Infringements of these rights are punishable by fine and/or imprisonment.[7]

---

[4]   Belgian Law on Patients' Rights, 22 August 2002, *Belgian Official Gazette*, 26 September 2002.

[5]   Art. 25 Code of Medical Deontology, www.ordomedic.be.

[6]   American Medical Association, Patient Confidentiality, www.ama-ass.org.

[7]   Art. 458 Penal Code; art. 222 Law of 30 July 2018 on the protection of natural persons with regard to the processing of personal data, *Belgian Official Gazette*, 5 September 2018.

PERSONS BOUND BY THE DUTY OF CONFIDENTIALITY

Article 458 of the Penal Code explicitly mentions physicians, pharmacists and midwives as being bound to secrecy. But this requirement is not limited to those professions alone. Each person who, by state or by profession is entrusted with secrets, is bound by confidentiality.

The reference to 'by state or by profession' is a vague formulation and has required further clarification. The Court of Cassation has specified that article 458 of the Penal Code is applicable to people who are necessary confidants according to the law, the uses and customs.[8]

In the medical context, this means that everyone who has knowledge of personal data because of his professional activities is necessarily bound by professional confidentiality. Clearly, the duty of confidentiality is applicable to healthcare workers, including physicians,[9] dentists,[10] pharmacists,[11] nurses,[12] midwives,[13] physiotherapists and paramedics.[14]

However, the duty of confidentiality is not limited to those who provide health services. It is also applicable to other people whose work is necessary to provide these healthcare services, such as the administrative and operational staff. In this way, people holding the following types of roles are also subject to confidentiality: the hospital director,[15] the head doctor,[16] the ombudsperson,[17] administrative[18] and operational staff[19] and social assistants.[20]

---

[8] Court of Cassation 20 February 1905, *Pasicrisie* 1905, I, 141, conclusions Janssens.

[9] Art. 458 Penal Code.

[10] Y. Vermylen and C. Contreras, *Tandarts & Recht* (Acco, 2008), 93.

[11] Art. 458 Penal Code.

[12] KI Antwerp 2 November 2000, *Limburgs Rechtsleven* 2002, 192.

[13] Art. 458 Penal Code.

[14] F. Blockx, *Beroepsgeheim* (Antwerp, Intersentia, 2013), 78–79; A. Dierickx, J. Buelens and A. Vijverman, 'The Right to Privacy' in *Handbook on Health Law (Handboek Gezondheidsrecht)* (Antwerp, Intersentia, 2014), 613.

[15] Court of Cassation 30 October 1978, *Arr.Cass.* 1978-79, n° 235.

[16] Court of Appeal Antwerp 14 June 2001, *Belgian Journal of Health Law (Tijdschrift voor Gezondheidsrecht)*, 2004-05, 128, comment T. Balthazar.

[17] Art. 3 Royal Decree of 8 July 2003 concerning ombudsperson in hospitals, *Belgian Official Gazette*, 26 August 2003.

[18] F. Blockx, *Beroepsgeheim* (Antwerp, Intersentia, 2013), 80.

[19] Court of Appeal Antwerp 14 June 2001, *Belgian Journal of Health Law (Tijdschrift voor Gezondheidsrecht)*, 2004-05, 128, comment T. Balthazar.

[20] Art. 189 Flemish decree 22 December 2017 on Local government, *Belgian Official Gazette*, 15 February 2018; T. Vansweevelt and N. Broeckx, 'Het patiënten-dossier en de toegang tot en doorstroming van gezondheidsgegevens tussen gezond-

Not everyone working in the healthcare sector is a necessary confidant. Hence, such ancillary staff would not be bound by medical confidentiality. However, they can be bound by an obligation of discretion. Violation of this obligation is not a criminal offence but can lead to an entitlement to compensation of harm. It is a legal, disciplinary or contractual duty for people who are not a necessary confidant. Examples of staff in a medical context that are affected by this obligation would be cleaning staff and handymen.

The line between the duty of confidentiality and the duty of discretion is not always clear. For instance, there is controversy about the obligations of members of an ethics committee. Some authors think the committee members are bound by medical confidentiality,[21] but according to others it is merely an obligation of discretion.[22]

LEGAL DUTIES OF CONFIDENTIALITY/INTIMACY/ PRIVACY

Medical confidentiality is a broad concept which covers a very wide area. The duty of medical confidentiality leads to several other duties, such as the right to intimacy. These obligations apply from birth and even after death and will be discussed below.

From Birth and After Death

The healthcare worker is bound by his duty of confidentiality even after the death of the patient. This is important in the light of the goal of confidentiality, which does not only relate to the protection of the privacy. This duty also ensures that people can consult a physician without having to fear that confidential information would be divulged to third parties, during life or after death. In this regard, the scope of the duty of medical confidentiality is broader than the scope of the GDPR, since the GDPR and the related data protection law only applies to information relating to living individuals.[23]

---

heidszorgbeoefenaars in het raam van de Kwaliteitswet', The Quality Act (*De Kwaliteitswet*) (Antwerp, Intersentia, 2020), 138.

[21] A. Dierickx, J. Buelens and A. Vijverman, 'The Right to Privacy' in *Handbook on Health Law (Handboek Gezondheidsrecht)* (Antwerp, Intersentia, 2014), 620–21.

[22] T. Vansweevelt, 'Verplichte ethische comités in ziekenhuizen: Who Watches the Doctor Watchers?', *Liber Amicorum A. Prims* (Ghent, Mys&Breesch, 1995), 398–99.

[23] Consideration 27 GDPR.

The Scope of Medical Confidentiality

The healthcare worker is bound to medical confidentiality which means he/ she may not divulge secrets, according to article 458 of the Penal Code. This criminal offence requires the fulfilment of three conditions: a piece of secret information, the divulgation of the secret to a third party and the disclosure being made by a person bound by confidentiality.

Secret information

Medical confidentiality is limited to secret information. In determining the secret character of information, the judge will take into account the nature of the information, the private character of the information, the importance of the task and the necessity of the confidentiality.[24]

The secret information can cover not only facts, decisions, opinions and judgments, but also everything the physician discovers while examining the patient. The following type of information is considered to be secret: the identity of the patient,[25] his/her telephone number,[26] his/her hospital admission,[27] his/her address, his/her marital or family status, his/her disease or health condition[28] and his/her treatment or medication.[29]

Of course, when the information is public or generally known, the information is not secret anymore. When the patient has publicly announced his/ her disease, his/her hospital admission or his/her treatment, there can be no medical confidentiality about these facts.

The secret information must be linked to a person. When a physician divulges information about an anonymous person, no one's privacy is violated. It is sufficient that the secret information can be linked to a person. His identification must be possible based on the divulged information. For example, by

---

[24] S. Carval and R. Sefton-Green, 'Medical Liability in France' in B. Koch (ed), *Medical Liability in Europe* (Berlin, De Gruyter, 2011), 225.

[25] Corr. Ghent 2 december 2013, *Belgian Journal of Health Law* (*Tijdschrift voor Gezondheidsrecht*), 2014–15, 108, comment F. Blockx.

[26] Corr. Ghent 2 december 2013, *Belgian Journal of Health Law* (*Tijdschrift voor Gezondheidsrecht*), 2014–15, 108, comment F. Blockx.

[27] National Council of Physicians, Advice about Medical confidentiality of 16 March 1991, www.ordomedic.be.

[28] Court of Appeal Antwerp 14 June 2001, *Belgian Journal of Health Law* (*Tijdschrift voor Gezondheidsrecht*), 2004–05, 128, comment T. Balthazar.

[29] Court of Appeal Antwerp 14 June 2001, *Belgian Journal of Health Law* (*Tijdschrift voor Gezondheidsrecht*), 2004–05, 128, comment T. Balthazar.

giving the initials and the date of birth, the identity of the patient is sufficiently clear, and identification is possible. [30]

The disclosure to a third party

The criminal offence of violation of medical confidentiality implies the secret information has been divulged to a third party. The disclosure of secret information can be done either orally or in writing. No damage or publicity is required. It is sufficient that the secret information has been told to one person,[31] which is a third party. Divulging information about a health condition to the patient himself or herself is logically no violation of the medical confidentiality. The healthcare provider must inform the patient about his/her health condition and about everything that is needed for the patient to give informed consent.

The duty to medical confidentiality is a duty of the healthcare provider. The patient is free to reveal health information about himself of herself. He can also reveal information about the healthcare worker and record a conversation with his healthcare worker, because he is a party to the communication, and when this is for private purposes or to file a complaint.[32]

It happens sometimes that private detectives working for an insurance company make a video recording of a patient in a liability case, to prove his/her damage is not that serious as claimed. This would be a processing of personal data and should be in line with the GDPR. It would be justified as long as the video is a recording of public appearance of the patient[33] and the processing is necessary for the establishment, exercise or defence of legal claims.[34]

When the patient is not considered legally capable, the information can be given to a legal representative or a person of trust. This person is the legal representative of the patient, and he/she acts in the name and on behalf of the patient. Hence, the legal representative is not a third party.

Other than the patient or his/her legal representative, everyone else is a third party, including the government.[35] For example, a pharmaceutical company is a third party. In one case, a surgeon that specialised in knee surgery passed information about every patient to a pharmaceutical company. This information included patients' names and telephone numbers. The purpose of the

---

[30] Court of Appeal Antwerp 14 June 2001, *Belgian Journal of Health Law* (*Tijdschrift voor Gezondheidsrecht*), 2004–05, 128, comment T. Balthazar.

[31] F. Blockx, *Confidentiality (Beroepsgeheim)* (Antwerp, Intersentia, 2013), 112.

[32] Court of Cassation 17 November 2015, AR.P.15.0880.N.

[33] Art. 5 Law of 19 July 1991 regulating the profession of private detective, *Belgian Official Gazette*, 2 October 1991.

[34] Art. 9(2)(f) GDPR.

[35] But see *infra* the exceptions.

disclosure was so that the pharmaceutical company could offer the patient some food supplements to facilitate a better rehabilitation. The surgeon was convicted of violating medical confidentiality.[36]

In principle, the partner and relatives of the patient are also third parties. When a physician asks a relative to bring the patient's HIV-medicine to the clinic, where the relative does not know about the patient being HIV-positive, the duty of medical confidentiality is violated.[37] When the partner, relative or friend is the confidant or representative of the patient, confidential information about the patient can be disclosed.

The media also naturally counts as a third party. A head doctor who wanted to reply to allegations of patients in the press, and issued a press release with the initials, illness, and treatment of the patient, was found to have violated his duty of confidentiality.[38]

The Right of Intimacy

The right of intimacy has been recognised as a full and independent patient right.[39] The concept of intimacy can be defined here as the right to 'spatial privacy'. The examination and treatment rooms must guarantee the necessary intimacy for the patient. Moreover, only healthcare workers whose presence is necessary may be present when the treating physician intervenes. Article 10 Law on Patients' Rights stipulates that subject to the patient's agreement, only the persons whose presence is professionally justified may be present during examinations or treatment. This means that a trainee doctor may be present because it is the only way they can learn from these practical experiences. However, the patient has the right to oppose the presence of a trainee doctor. In any event, the patient has the right to be informed in advanced of the possible presence of a trainee doctor.

Of course, this right to oppose concerns not only trainee doctors, but every other healthcare worker or other third party. The patient is entitled to limit their consultation to the presence of his/her treating physician. This rule is important and justified. During a medical consultation delicate and confidential information is exchanged, and intimate medical examinations are carried out. The

---

[36]   Corr. Ghent 2 december 2013, *Belgian Journal of Health Law (Tijdschrift voor Gezondheidsrecht)*, 2014–15, 108, comment F. Blockx.

[37]   Labour Court 14 June 2021, *Belgian Journal of Health Law (Tijdschrift voor Gezondheidsrecht)*, 2022–23, 34, comment T. Vansweevelt.

[38]   Court of Appeal Antwerp 14 June 2001, *Belgian Journal of Health Law (Tijdschrift voor Gezondheidsrecht)*, 2004–05, 128, comment T. Balthazar.

[39]   Art. 10 Belgian Law on Patients' Rights.

patient must have the right to limit the discussion of this intimate information to his treating physician, with whom he/she has a relation of trust.

DATA PROTECTION LAW

Like in any other country, the General Data Protection Regulation[40] or GDPR applies in Belgium. The GDPR framework protects the privacy of the patient by restricting the use of the patient's personal health data (and other personal data). This means that physicians, hospitals and other data controllers cannot process health data except under specific criteria within the meaning of articles 6 and 9 GDPR, and if all other GDPR requirements (transparency, security, etc.) are complied with. Although the GDPR framework is directly binding, there is nevertheless some margin for national legislatures to add some country specific rules and limitations with regard to the processing of health data (article 9(4) GDPR). The Belgian legislature makes use of this margin, most notably through the legislation detailed below.

The Belgian Framework of Data Protection Law

The Belgian Law of 30 July 2018 on the protection of natural persons with regard to the processing of personal data[41] further specifies the security obligation under article 32 GDPR. The Belgian law states that each data controller (e.g. hospital) must keep a list of categories of persons who will have access to health data (including an accurate description of their role) and that such persons must be bound by a legal or equivalent contractual obligation of confidentiality.[42] This law furthermore also contains an entire chapter on processing of data, including patient data, for statistical and scientific research.

Since article 9(4) GDPR allows for other specific rules to be made, the various data processing provisions in the specific laws on physicians, hospitals, and others also remain in effect. This will be explained further throughout the rest of this country report.

The Information Security Committee
For every transfer of health data from one data controller (e.g., a hospital) to another data controller (e.g., a biotech company) the Belgian Law of 13 December 2006 requires a prior authorisation[43] from the Belgian Information

---

[40]   Regulation (EU) 2016/679.
[41]   *Belgian Official Gazette*, 5 September 2018.
[42]   Art. 9 Law of 30 July 2018.
[43]   In line with art. 87 GDPR, a similar system of authorisation from the Belgian the Ministry of internal affairs exists for the use of the National Identification Number

Security Committee (ISC).[44] This committee exists alongside the Belgian Data Protection Authority 'Gegevensbeschermingsautoriteit'/'Autorité de protection des données'), which is Belgium's official supervisory authority under the GDPR.

The data controller must initiate a request for authorisation for a health data transfer, upon which the ISC will perform a basic assessment of compliance with the main GDPR principles. There are nevertheless some exceptions to this authorisation requirement. For example, an ISC authorisation is not required for transfers between physicians for diagnostic or therapeutic purposes nor for health data transfers which take place based on a specific legal framework (e.g., under the Belgian Law of 7 May 2004 on human experiments). Also, there are no sanctions provided by law in case the data transfer takes place without authorisation. Unlike the Belgian Data Protection Authority, the ISC does not have the power to impose fines or other sanctions. This begs the question of whether the ISC still makes sense considering the GDPR.

The ISC is not to be confused with the Belgian eHealth-platform. This is a government agency established by law with a mission to create (not directly binding) standards and guidance for the sharing of health-related data between HCPs within and outside medical facilities, as well as to create certain systems that facilitate the sharing of patient data.[45] Physicians in Belgium have a deontological obligation to only use systems which are provided or validated by the Belgian government (i.e., the eHealth-platform).[46] In Flanders, it is actually a legal obligation for health care providers and healthcare institutions to use the services of the eHealth-platform for sharing data with other health care providers and healthcare institutions.[47]

EXCEPTIONS TO CONFIDENTIALITY

In principle, every healthcare worker has a duty of confidentiality. A violation of this duty is an offence and will normally lead to criminal liability. However, in some circumstances, the healthcare worker can invoke a ground

---

or NIN (*'Rijksregisternummer'*/*'numéro de Registre national'*). See: Law of 8 August 1983 on the organisation of a national register of natural persons, *Belgian Official Gazette*, 21 April 1984.

[44] Art. 42 Law of 13 December 2006 on various provisions regarding health, *Belgian Official Gazette*, 22 December 2006.

[45] Art. 5 Law of 21 August 2008 on the establishment and organisation of the eHealth-platform and various provisions, *Belgian Official Gazette*, 13 October 2008.

[46] Art. 40 Code of Medical Deontology, to be consulted at www.ordomedic.be.

[47] Art. 6–8 Flemish Decree of 25 April 2014 regarding the organisation of the network for data sharing between actors in healthcare, *B. Off. J.*, 20 August 2014.

of justification to escape liability. Legal doctrine in Belgium recognises several exceptions to the rule of medical confidentiality. According to article 458 of the Penal Code there is no violation of medical confidentiality where the healthcare worker was obliged or permitted to divulgate the confidential information. Other exceptions are based on case law. We will explain some of the most important exceptions below.

A Testimony for a Judge or a Parliamentary Investigation Committee

According to article 458 of the Penal Code there is no criminal act when the physician gives evidence before a judge or a parliamentary investigation committee. The physician is not obliged to testify – he/she has the right, but not the obligation.

Police Investigation

A statement before the police or public prosecutor does not count as a testimony before a judge, so there is no general rule which allows physicians to share patient information with the police or a prosecutor.[48] For example, a physician who administered first aid after a car accident, assessed the driver and then spontaneously told a police officer that the driver was drunk, was found to have violated his duty of medical confidentiality.[49] The same principle applies to, for example, a nursing home: when staff report a disappearance of an elderly inhabitant, they are generally not allowed to communicate to the police the entire medical history of that inhabitant, even if the police explicitly asks for this information.[50]

This does not mean that a healthcare worker may never share patient information with the police during an investigation. The Belgian legislature has allowed multidisciplinary information sharing between the likes of police, physicians and social workers for the purposes of preventing certain crimes (e.g. terrorism, domestic violence). However, the public prosecutor must have given consent for such information sharing.[51] This gives the healthcare worker the possibility, without any obligation, to share certain patient information. Apart from this, the healthcare worker may also share patient information to

---

[48]　A. Dierickx, J. Buelens and A. Vijverman, 'The Right to Privacy' in *Handbook on Health Law (Handboek Gezondheidsrecht)* (Antwerp, Intersentia, 2014), 627.

[49]　Police court of Namur 27 February 1981, *RGAR* 1982, n° 10.542. See however: Cass. 3 September 2014, AR P.13.1966.F, www.cass.be.

[50]　Sectoral Committee on health, consultation nr. 12/024 of 20 March 2012 and nr. 13/066 of 18 June 2013, https://www.ksz-bcss.fgov.be.

[51]　Art. 458*ter* Penal Code.

the police during an investigation in exercise of the right of defence, or in case of emergency. A physician may furthermore be obliged to allow access to patient data during an investigation, provided that a representative of the Order of Physicians has been notified.[52]

A Court Injunction

According to article 877 of the Judicial Code, a judge can order any person (e.g., a physician) to transmit any document (e.g., the patient file) when there are serious, certain and convergent presumptions that this document contains the evidence of any relevant fact.

Offences Towards a Minor or Vulnerable Person

According to article 458*bis* of the Penal Code, the physician or any other person bound by professional secrecy can inform the public prosecutor of an offence against a minor or vulnerable person. The same principle applies when there is serious and imminent danger to the physical or mental integrity of minors and vulnerable persons. Vulnerability can result from various causes, such as age, pregnancy, partner violence and the use of violence due to cultural motives, customs, traditions, religion or the so-called honour, a disease, a physical or mental impairment or deficiency. These circumstances might involve such matters including child abuse, sexual abuse and crimes of honour.

This legal provision has been introduced because of the uncertainties surrounding the application of the state of necessity as a possible justification to breach medical confidentiality. A specific legal provision as a justification ground would give greater legal certainty. It should be noted that the legal provision gives the physician the right to speak and to inform the public prosecutor but does not involve an obligation to speak or to breach medical confidentiality.

The Obligation to Provide Assistance

According to article 422*bis* of the Penal Code every citizen has the duty to give assistance to a person in great danger. Violation of this duty is a criminal offence. The physician is confronted with two values: the value of privacy and the value of personal integrity of the patient/ a third person. These two values must be balanced against each other. One might assume that the personal integrity of a person has a higher weight than the right to privacy.

---

[52]   Art. *39bis*, §9 Code of Criminal Procedure.

Thus, the physician should give priority to his duty to give assistance. For instance, the physician has the obligation to inform the partner of a HIV-seropositive patient, when the patient refuses to inform his/her partner. Indeed, the life or health of the partner would be at that moment in danger.[53]

The Rights of Defence

It is generally accepted that the healthcare worker can breach his duty to confidentiality to defend himself or herself in court.[54] The right to defence has priority over medical confidentiality. The legal justification for this principle lies in article 6 European Convention of Human Rights. The breach of medical confidentiality is limited to the information that is necessary for the defence in court.

A Study or Examination Ordered by a Judge or a Public Prosecutor

In technical matters, it is common for the judge to order a report by a suitable technical expert. A court expert is not bound by professional secrecy towards the judge and the litigants. It is his/her legal duty to give advice to the judge. Based on this legal exception, the court expert does not violate professional secrecy when he/she reveals medical data about the patient to the judge.[55] The investigating judge or the public prosecutor can appoint an expert to take blood, hair follicles or mouth swabs to carry out a DNA-examination.[56] The expert may transmit the research results of this DNA-examination to the investigating judge or public prosecutor, without violating the duty to medical confidentiality, because the law is a valid ground of justification.

National Institute for Sickness and Disability Insurance (RIZIV/INAMI)

According to article 150 of the Law on compulsory insurance for medical care and benefits, physicians must provide all necessary information and documents to the inspectors and auditors of the RIZIV/INAMI. This legal exception to medical confidentiality is logical. The inspectors and auditors need these documents and information to do their work. The obligation for physicians

---

[53]   T. Vansweevelt, *Aids en Recht. Een aansprakelijkheids- en verzekeringsrechteli-jke studie* (Antwerp, Maklu, 1989), 55–56.

[54]   Court of Cassation 5 February 1985, *Arr.Cass.* 1984–85, 749.

[55]   Court of Cassation 24 May 2005, T.Gez./Rev.dr.santé 2006–07, 174, comments F. Blockx.

[56]   Art. 44*quinquies* and following and art. 90*undecies* Code of Criminal Procedure.

to hand over the documents is therefore limited to what is necessary for the inspectors and auditors to fulfil their control tasks.[57]

Legal and Administrative Tasks in Healthcare and Public Health

Physicians play an important role in the organisation of healthcare and public health. In carrying out these specific tasks they are sometimes obliged to reveal secrets. This breach of medical confidentiality is justified, because of the legal ground and because of the importance of healthcare.

In this way, physicians may reveal the following secrets to the government:

— a declaration to a physician-inspector of the government of biotic factors which are a potential danger to public health. These biotic factors include infections and transmissible diseases such as cholera, diphtheria and, in an epidemic situation, diseases such as yellow fever, gonorrhoea, hepatitis A and B, malaria, SARS, poliomyelitis and tuberculosis.[58]
— a declaration of a birth: the hospital informs the civil registrar of the birth of a child, the names of the parents and of the child. When the delivery was not in a hospital, the parents can declare the birth of the child with a certificate of a physician or a midwife. A stillbirth can also be declared to the civil registrar with a medical certificate.[59]
— a declaration of death: the physician who has confirmed the death of a person must prepare a certificate of death which will be transmitted to the civil registrar.[60]
— a certificate of mental illness: the compulsory admission of a mentally ill person requires, except in an emergency situation, a detailed medical report prepared by a physician who has examined the patient.[61]

Certificate for Insurance Matters

According to article 61, paragraph 1 of the Insurance Law 2014[62] the physician is obliged to transmit to an insurance physician a declaration about the cause of a person's death if the insured party has given his prior consent to do so. By

---

[57] Court of Cassation 7 September 1989, *Rechtskundig Weekblad* 1989–90, 404.
[58] Flemish Decree 21 November 2003 on the preventive health policy, *Belgian Official Gazette*, 3 February 2004.
[59] Art. 58 Civil Code.
[60] Art. 55 Civil Code.
[61] Art. 2 Law of 26 June 1990 concerning the protection of the person of the mentally ill, *Belgian Official Gazette*, 27 July 1990.
[62] *Belgian Official Gazette*, 30 April 2014.

transmitting such a post-mortem declaration, the physician *prima facie* violates his duty to medical confidentiality. In the past these declarations were found to be void, because the insured could not release his physician from his obligation of professional secrecy. Article 61, paragraph 1 of the Insurance Law 2014 no longer prohibits these post-mortem declarations. The rationale behind this is that the patient/insured party is the authority over his/her confidentiality. Medical confidentiality cannot be used or misused to mask any fraud.[63]

A State of Emergency

Medical confidentiality can conflict with other values. In such cases, a physician, and perhaps later a judge, must balance the conflicting interests. The conflict of interest that is at stake in such situations is the conflict between the duty to maintain confidentiality and the possibility to prevent harm to others. When the life and/or health of a third party is in danger, most would consider it justified for physicians to breach their duty of medical confidentiality. In such a conflict of interest, life and health are valued more highly than medical confidentiality. When physicians are confronted with matters of urgency, they may breach their duty to confidentiality without fearing criminal prosecution or liability. For example:

- a physician confronted with a case of possible child abuse has the legal right to inform the competent authorities such as the public prosecutor or a specific administrative authority (e.g., a child abuse medical counselling centre).[64]
- the physician was allowed to reveal the hiding place of gang members whom he tread, because the prevention of other crimes was seen as more important than the value of medical confidentiality.[65]

But, as has been noted already, the breach of medical confidentiality is only justified in light of a higher value being present. In contrast, no state of emergency exists when, for example, a head doctor replies to patient allegations in the press. In that case, an unlawful violation resulted from the use of a press

---

[63]   T. Vansweevelt and B. Weyts, 'Medical Declarations', in T. Vansweevelt and B. Weyts (eds), *Handbook on Insurance Law (Handboek Verzekeringsrecht)* (Antwerp, Intersentia, 2016), 429.
[64]   T. Vansweevelt, 'Liabilities of a Physician Confronted with Child Abuse', *European Journal of Health Law* 2013, 271–88.
[65]   Court of Cassation 13 May 1987, *Arr.Cass.* 1987, 1203.

release with information about the patient, in order to defend the honour and dignity of the doctor's hospital.[66]

Shared Professional Confidentiality

Healthcare is increasingly provided by a team, and healthcare providers need to share their findings with each other. To resolve potential confidentiality problems that may arise between healthcare providers, the law has developed the theory of shared confidentiality.

The Court of Cassation accepted this theory in 2012 in a landmark decision.[67] The theory of shared confidentiality is subject to two conditions:

- the confidential information holder shares his or her information with someone who acts for the same purpose and towards the same patient.
- the communication must be necessary and pertinent for the task of the information holder.

Based on this theory, we can justify circumstances such as surgeons sharing medical information about the patient with other healthcare providers involved in the medical treatment, such as anaesthesiologists, nurses and paramedics. The shared professional confidentiality of healthcare providers regarding patient health data has even been codified in articles 36–38 of the so-called Quality Act[68] regarding qualitative practice in healthcare but is now subject to the condition of patient consent and to a strict condition of necessity for healthcare. It is however accepted that this consent is a broad consent (i.e., the patient can consent to all information sharing within a hospital)[69] and the law moreover states that such consent is not required in case of emergency (article 39 of the Quality Act).

Research and Teaching

In Belgium, a distinction is generally made between prospective and purely retrospective medical research. Prospective research on patients, including the

---

[66] Court of Appeal Antwerp 14 June 2001, *Belgian Journal of Health Law* (*Tijdschrift voor Gezondheidsrecht*), 2004–05, 128, comment T. Balthazar.

[67] Court of Cassation 13 March 13 May 1987, *Arr.Cass.* 1987, 1203.

[68] Law of 22 April 2019 regarding qualitative practice in healthcare, *Belgian Official Gazette*, 14 May 2019.

[69] T. Vansweevelt and N. Broeckx, 'Het patiëntendossier en de toegang tot en doorstroming van gezondheidsgegevens tussen gezondheidszorgbeoefenaars in het raam van de Kwaliteitswet' in T. Vansweevelt et al., *The Quality Act* (*De Kwaliteitswet*) (Antwerpen, Intersentia, 2020), 142–43.

collection and sharing of their health data for medical study purposes, is only allowed if the patient has given a written informed consent, if a competent ethics committee has approved the study and if certain other conditions are met (e.g., the study sponsor has an insurance policy specifically for harm caused to the patient by the study).[70] Patient data processing in the context of purely retrospective medical research (i.e., studies that only rely on data collected in the past, for example in the patient's health record) is allowed without patient consent, but still requires compliance with the GDPR requirements (e.g., adequate information being provided to patients) and with the Belgian Law of 30 July (e.g., pseudonymisation), as well as an authorisation from the Belgian Information Security Committee. It is however possible to anonymise the data first (most notably through high level aggregation), in which case the GDPR requirements and the authorisation requirement no longer apply.

Regarding teaching, article 10 of the Law on Patients' Rights requires the patient's consent before any student can perform observations: 'The patient has the right to intimacy. Subject to the patient's agreement, only the persons whose presence is professionally justified may be present during examinations or treatment'. It can be argued that this covers all necessary patient information communicated during such examinations or treatments. The same principle applies to sharing patient information for teaching purposes without direct observation (e.g., showing patient x-rays during lectures). Either this information must be anonymised within the meaning of the GDPR, or the patient must give his/her free, informed consent in advance (article 6(1)(a) and article 9(2)(a) GDPR).

Audits

It can be argued that the use of patient data for audits is allowed on the basis of either article 6(4) GDPR or on the basis of the need to manage healthcare services as referred to article 6(1)(f) and 9(2)(h) GDPR, provided of course that all other GDPR requirements (e.g., transparency towards patients, data security) are met. This is especially true in case of general quality audits, specific medical audits and accreditation procedures in hospitals.[71] For the accreditation of Flemish hospitals, the law has approved the possibility to

---

[70]   Law of 7 May 2004 on human experiments, Belgian Official Gazette 18 May 2004; Clinical Trial Regulation (EU) 536/2014.

[71]   See also: art. 20 Coordinated Law of 10 July 2008 on hospitals and other care institutions, Belgian Official Gazette 7 November 2008; art. 6/1 Royal Decree of 15 December 1987 regarding the implementation of arts 13 to 17 of the law on hospitals, Belgian Official Gazette 15 December 1987; Sectoral Committee on health, consultation nr. 17/024 of 21 March 2017 on NIAZ accreditation, www.ksz-bcss.fgov.be.

share patient information (and even copies thereof) with certain accreditation organisations, but only if this is necessary.[72]

Press Freedom

Given the fundamental nature of the freedom of expression (article 10 European Convention of Human Rights; articles 19 and 25 Belgian Constitution), journalists have a rather large margin of freedom to report on matters relating healthcare in the media, provided they abide by the deontological rules of journalism. In line with article 85 GDPR, they are exempt from several GDPR requirements such as those under articles 7 to 10, 11(2), 13 to 16, 18 to 20 and 21(1).[73] This exemption means that journalists can report on the health of patients if this information serves a legitimate interest (e.g., matters of state security or public health) which outweighs the individual interests of the patient in a particular case,[74] without informing that patient beforehand. In the same vein, they can also report on alleged malpractice cases, even if such malpractice was not (yet) established before a competent court.[75]

This does not mean that the freedom of journalists regarding health matters is absolute. It is argued that patients and healthcare workers can still prevent press releases (or claim damages afterwards) if such releases are unnecessarily harmful, plainly incorrect, or unproven to the point of slander or defamation. For example, it has been considered illegal to publish a statement on a website – without any evidence – that a physician is a 'learned quack' who cunningly makes a lot of money to the detriment of desperate people, suggesting that his medical practice is not far from criminal.[76] Healthcare workers must of course take care to respect their duty of medical confidentiality, and should ask the patient's informed consent[77] as well as respect the GDPR requirements before saying anything in public regarding that patient.[78]

---

[72] Art. 108 Flemish Decree of 15 July 2016 on various provisions regarding welfare, Healthcare and families, Belgian Official Gazette 19 August 2016.

[73] Art. 24 Law of 30 July 2018.

[74] On the basis of art. 6(1)(f) GDPR.

[75] European Court of Human Rights, 29 March 2011, Case of *R.T.B.F. v. Belgium*, n° 50084/06, https://hudoc.echr.coe.int.

[76] Court of Appeal of Antwerp 23 June 2010, NJW 2010, p. 790, comment E. Brewaeys.

[77] Arts 6(1)(a) and 9(2)(a) GDPR.

[78] See also: Advice of 7 February 2015 of the National Council of the Order of Physicians on physicians and digital media, www.ordomedic.be; Advice of 16 July 2011 of the National Council of the Order of Physicians on the participation of physicians on television show, docusoaps and press articles, www.ordomedic.be.

CONFIDENTIALITY AND GENETICS

In principle, only the patient has the right to be informed about his/her diagnosis. Medical confidentiality prohibits the physician from informing third parties. Genetic information is medical information and falls thus under the scope of medical confidentiality. Thus, in principle, no other party can be informed about a genetic disorder. However, genetic information has a specific character. Information about a genetic disorder is also important for relatives of the patient. The fact of a higher risk of developing breast cancer (BRCA) or a cardiac arrest (Brugada syndrome), is important knowledge for everyone in the family who carries that gene. In most cases, the patient will inform his/her relatives so they eventually can take appropriate measures. The physician will also try to convince the patient to inform his/her relatives about this genetic disorder. The patient might also ask his/her physician to inform his/her relatives. However, the patient may not always be willing to inform family members, because of disrupted relationships, social or emotional obstacles.[79]

Therefore, this raises the question of whether the physician has the right to inform the relatives when the patient refuses to do so. As has been said before, a state of emergency could be a legal basis to inform relatives. In balancing the conflict of interest, the physician may give greater priority to safeguarding the life or health of a third party than to respecting medical confidentiality. C. Cornelis has pointed out the danger to life and health does not to have to be imminent. There are not many genetic diseases which pose an imminent risk. The condition of 'imminent risk' would make the state of emergency useless in genetics. It is sufficient that a genetic disorder poses a serious risk to life or health.[80] Disclosure can be justified even when no treatment is available, for example, for Huntington's disease. The information can be relevant for other decisions such as life planning and reproductive choices.

CHALLENGES, CONTROVERSIES AND REMEDIES

The duty of medical confidentiality has long been considered the basic Belgian rule regarding patient information and privacy. This rule has been modified over the years by several exceptions, either by case law or specific legislation. In today's data-driven society, a fundamental debate on the sharing and use

---

[79] C. Cornelis, 'Medical Confidentiality and Disclosing Genetic Information to Family Members', *Medicine and Law* 2020, 420.

[80] C. Cornelis, 'Medical Confidentiality and Disclosing Genetic Information to Family Members', *Medicine and Law* 2020, 444.

of health data is urgently required to streamline the current rules on patient information and privacy.

With regard to the therapeutical context, there is still a lot of discussion on the role of patient consent. A patient should no doubt give informed consent (either in writing or otherwise) before any healthcare intervention is performed on that patient. The Belgian legislature is now steering towards the requirement of a second, additional consent of the patient for the use of that patient's information in the context of such intervention. We do not believe this double consent approach is a meaningful solution for preventing abuse of patient information. A medical intervention and the use of patient data for such intervention go hand in hand. The one is not possible without the other. It would be better to put more focus on clear and specific rules for transparency towards patients and for the security of patient data to prevent information abuse.

Within the research context, the requirement of prior authorisation of the Belgian Information Security Committee acts as a major source of legal uncertainty in practice. To facilitate the scientific use of patient data, we suggest abolishing or at least reforming this system of prior authorisation.

3. Privacy and health in Canada

Emily Baron and Trudo Lemmens

The collection, use and sharing of personal information related to an individual's physical and mental health and access to health care services plays an important role in health care. The accuracy and completeness of personal health information (hereinafter referred to as "PHI" and defined according to legislation in section 2 of this chapter) is critical to the proper provision of health care services. But PHI is also often uniquely sensitive and imbued with privacy interests. As set out in *McInerney v MacDonald*, the information given by an individual for treatment by a physician "goes to the personal integrity and autonomy of the patient".[1] Proper protection of privacy is therefore critical to ensuring that necessary information can be comfortably shared between patients and health care professionals.[2] As noted by the Canadian Medical Association ("CMA"), "the protection of privacy and the concomitant duty of confidentiality are essential to foster trust in the patient-physician-relationship, the delivery of good patient care and a positive patient care experience".[3]

In Canada, the right to privacy and/or the duty of confidentiality arises from a variety of sources, including health professions ethical codes, the common law, the Canadian Charter of Rights and Freedoms ("the Charter"), which is part of the Constitution, and federal and provincial/territorial legislation.[4] Privacy is difficult to clearly define and Canadian privacy law tends to be constructed around a narrow concept of privacy as control over information, which may not offer the best and most comprehensive protection of privacy interests. Much of Canadian privacy law may be understood as protecting an

---

[1] *McInerney v MacDonald*, [1992], 2 SCR 138 at para 18 (*McInerney*).

[2] See for instance *M(A) v Ryan*, [1997] 1 SCR 157 at paras 25–26 (*Ryan*).

[3] Canadian Medical Association, "Principles for the Protection of Patient Privacy" (2017), online (pdf): <www.cma.ca/sites/default/files/2018-11/PD18-02.pdf.>

[4] The Charter does not explicitly refer to privacy rights or the protection of personal information. Privacy protections are afforded, however, under sections 7 and 8 of the Charter, which concern the right to life, liberty and the security of the person and the right to be secure against unreasonable search or seizure, respectively. See Canadian Charter of Rights and Freedoms, Part 1 of the Constitution Act, 1982, being Schedule B to the Canada Act 1982 (UK), c 11; Reference re Genetic Non-Discrimination Act, 2020 SCC 17.

individual's right to determine for themselves "when, how, and to what extent" they will release personal information.[5] But for many legal scholars, this picture, as well as the emphasis on individual consent being the primary means of protecting privacy, is an oversimplified and/or misdirected view of what privacy protects.[6] As noted by Barbara Tigerstrom, while control over information is central to the right to privacy, it "also extends beyond information to protect our identities, our personal space, and even our bodies from outside scrutiny and interference".[7]

In recent years, Canada's privacy statutes have expanded, responding to the changing landscape of technology and health innovations, such as in the area of genetic testing. These changes pose new and large-scale privacy challenges for personal information arising in the context of health care.

Importantly, the right to privacy is not absolute.[8] As exceptions in both legislation and common law recognize, there are competing interests that sometimes override a patient's expectation that information will be kept confidential. For example, common law or statute may oblige or permit health care providers to disclose information in instances where disclosure may avert or minimize imminent danger to the health or safety of others.[9] Such balancing of individual privacy interests with other competing values is not without controversy, as this chapter will explore.

The aim of this chapter is to overview the source and content of the right to privacy and duty of confidentiality pertaining to PHI. Even though there is relevant constitutional and federal statutory law related to privacy, the delivery of most health care services, and thus also issues related to PHI, falls within provincial jurisdiction.[10] This chapter focuses mostly on the law and health care policy in Canada's most populated province, Ontario, but also highlights

---

[5]   *R v Duarte*, [1990] 1 SCR 30.

[6]   See Lisa M. Austin, "Enough About Me: Why Privacy is About Power, Not Consent (or Harm)" in Austin Sarat, ed., *A World Without Privacy?: What Can/Should Law Do* (Cambridge, 2014) for a critique of consent-based privacy models; Lisa M. Austin, "Re-Reading Westin" (2019) 20 *Theoretical Inquiries in Law* 53.

[7]   Barbara von Tigerstrom, *Information and Privacy Law in Canada* (Toronto, ON: Irwin Law Inc, 2020) at 1.

[8]   *Halls v Mitchel*, [1928] SCR 125 at 136.

[9]   See, for example, (ON) Health Protection and Promotion Act, RSO 1990, c H 7 at s 77.6 (HPPA).

[10]   It is important to note, however, that the Federal government has responsibilities regarding health and, among other things, determines national standards for the health care system under the Canada Health Act, RSC, 1985, c C-6. For a short overview of jurisdiction over health care in Canada, see Trudo Lemmens, Jennifer Bergman, Kanksha Mahadevia Ghimire and Maryam Shahid, *Medical Law in Canada*, 2nd ed. (Alphen aan den Rijn: Kluwer Law International BV, 2020) at 28-30 (Lemmens et al. 2020).

similarities and differences across other Canadian common-law provinces. In contrast with Canada's common-law jurisdictions, the province of Quebec operates under civil law and was the first to develop a strong statutory privacy regime for the governmental sector in 1982,[11] and for the private sector in 1993.[12] It has stricter provisions related to penalties for violations of the act and arguably a less "compliance" based legal regime. This chapter will focus on the federal law and the common law jurisdictions in Canada.

This chapter overviews six topics central to understanding Canadian health privacy law. First, it provides an overview of the source of the duty of confidentiality, which arises from common law and ethical codes of self-regulating professions. Second, it outlines the federal and provincial/territorial privacy legislation that applies to PHI. Third, this chapter discusses various exceptions to confidentiality. Fourth, it addresses the growing privacy concerns arising from technological advancements as well as the growing reliance on technology in the provision of health care services and tracking of PHI during the COVID-19 pandemic. Fifth, it overviews the unique privacy challenges that arise in the context of genetic testing and research. Sixth, it discusses the need to recognize Indigenous Peoples' unique perspective on privacy and information management in discussions respecting health information privacy.

THE DUTY OF CONFIDENTIALITY

The sharing of personal information with health care professionals is part and parcel of health care practice. Within the health care context, health care providers have special obligations. One of their key duties is the duty of confidentiality, which is the duty to safeguard personal information. This duty arises from both an ethical and common law basis.

First, the duty of confidentiality arises within the ethical codes of self-regulating professions. Most of the health care professions in Canada are self-regulating and determine standards of conduct for their profession. Under provincial and territorial legislation, self-regulating professions have powers such as undertaking disciplinary proceedings and sanctioning members who fail to comply with the profession's standards.

Under the ethical code of the CMA, for instance, confidentiality is defined as an obligation that flows from respect for patient autonomy, seen as people's right to "conduct and control their lives as they choose".[13] The CMA Code of

---

[11] See Act Respecting Access to Documents Held by Public Bodies and the Protection of Personal Information, CQLR c A-2.1.

[12] Act Respecting the Protection of Personal Information in the Private Sector, CQLR, c P-39.1.

[13] CMA, Principles for the Protection of Patient Privacy, supra note 3.

Ethics and Professionalism indicates that physicians' duty of confidentiality includes: "keeping identifiable patient information confidential; collecting, using, and disclosing only as much health information as necessary to benefit the patient; and sharing information only to benefit the patient and within the patient's circle of care."[14]

Duties of confidentiality are also set out in the ethical codes of various other health professions, such as psychology, nursing and chiropractic. The Canadian Psychological Association, for example, outlines confidentiality obligations under the heading of "Respect for the Dignity of Persons and Peoples" in its Canadian Code of Ethics for Psychologists.[15]

Second, the duties imposed on physicians by the law of equity, which frames physician-patient relationships as archetypal fiduciary relationships,[16] also incorporate confidentiality obligations.[17] A fiduciary relationship is a relationship whereby one party bestows special trust and reliance on the other party, who has a duty to act in good faith and for the benefit of the other party. These relationships tend to be characterized by special knowledge and expertise held by the fiduciary. As set out in *McInerney*, this special relationship obligates a physician to "act with utmost good faith and loyalty, and to hold information received from or about a patient in confidence".[18]

PRIVACY AND HEALTH LEGISLATION

PHI is protected under general privacy legislation, as well as legislation specific to the health care context. Legislation concerning personal information privacy is available at both the federal and provincial/territorial level across Canada's 10 provinces and 3 territories.[19] Under federal legislation, the Privacy Act and Access to Information Act apply to information under federal

---

[14]   Canadian Medical Association, CMA Code of Ethics and Professionalism, CMA, 2018 at para 18, online (pdf): <policybase.cma.ca/viewer?file=%2Fmedia %2FPolicyPDF%2FPD19-03.pdf#page=1>.

[15]   Canadian Psychological Association, Canadian Code of Ethics for Psychologists, CPA, 2017, online: <cpa.ca/docs/File/Ethics/CPA_Code_2017_4thEd.pdf> at 16–17.

[16]   That is, at least with respect to some of the relationships resulting from the health care context—it does not apply, for example, to the relation between a medical doctor assessing a patient for an insurance contract.

[17]   *McInerney*, supra note 1; *Norberg v Wynrib*, [1992] 2 SCR 226.

[18]   *McInerney*, ibid at para 20.

[19]   Canada's provinces are Alberta (AB), British Columbia (BC), Manitoba (MB), New Brunswick (NB), Newfoundland and Labrador (NL), Nova Scotia (NS), Ontario (ON), Quebec (QC), Prince Edward Island (PE), Saskatchewan (SK), and its territories are Northwest Territories (NT), Nunavut (NU), and Yukon (YT).

public institutions, such as Health Canada.[20] The federal Personal Information Protection and Electronic Documents Act ("PIPEDA"),[21] introduced in 2000, is inspired by the Fair Information Principles embedded in the Organization of Economic Cooperation and Development privacy guidelines.[22] These grounding principles are: accountability, identifying purposes, consent, limiting collection, limiting use, disclosure, and retention, accuracy, safeguards, openness, individual access, and challenging compliance. PIPEDA has been influential in promoting greater coherency in privacy rules across the country.[23] The federal statute applies to information in the private, commercial sector and in instances where information crosses provincial boundaries, but its application is suspended in those provinces or territories that develop their own privacy law governing commercial activities to the extent that the provincial privacy laws are substantially similar.[24] Many provinces and territories have legislation governing privacy of personal information but variations exist across jurisdiction regarding which public bodies or private actors engaged in commercial activities they apply to. Some provinces' general privacy statutes have been deemed substantially similar to PIPEDA.[25]

There is also legislation specific to health information privacy in most provinces/territories.[26] This legislation varies across jurisdiction, but typically applies to health information held by custodians or trustees, which include a variety of individuals and organizations who have access to PHI. Where this legislation is deemed substantially similar to the provisions under PIPEDA, it is taken to apply in the place of PIPEDA.[27]

---

[20]   Privacy Act, RSC 1985, c P-21; Access to Information Act, RSC 1985, c A-1.

[21]   Personal Information Protection and Electronic Documents Act, SC 2000, c 5. (PIPEDA).

[22]   Organization for Economic Cooperation and Development (OECD), "OECD Guidelines on the Protection of Privacy and Transborder Flows of Personal Data" (2001), online: <www.oecd-ilibrary.org/docserver/9789264196391 -en.pdf?expires=1677460057&id=id&accname=guest&checksum=02 186D795F9B2EDBE4145349CCA218DD>.

[23]   See von Tigerstrom, supra note 7 at 291–97.

[24]   Alberta, British Columbia and Quebec have provincial privacy laws equivalent to PIPEDA. See (AB) Personal Information Protection Act, SA 2003, c P-6.5; (BC) Personal Information Protection Act, SBC 2003, c 63; (QC) Act Respecting the Protection of Personal Information in the Private Sector, CQRL, c P-39.1.

[25]   Organizations in the Province of Alberta Exemption Order, SOR/2004-220, Organizations in the Province of British Columbia Exemption Order, SOR/2004-220, Organizations in the Province of Quebec Exemption Order, SOR/2003-374.

[26]   Nunavut being the exception.

[27]   See Health Information Custodians in the Province of Ontario Exemption Order, SOR/2005-399; Personal Health Information Custodians in New Brunswick Exemption Order, SOR/2011-265; Personal Health Information Custodians in Newfoundland and

Across provincial and territorial borders, public health legislation provides that identifying PHI must be kept confidential. For example, under Ontario's Health Protection and Promotion Act ("HPPA"), section 39(1) prohibits the disclosure of identifying information in the course of activities concerning the prevention of the spread of disease.[28]

Provincial and territorial privacy legislation sets out broader protections of confidentiality and applies to a wide variety of individuals and organizations, known as health information "custodians" or "trustees". The persons or organizations who qualify as custodians or trustees include both governmental and non-governmental bodies but vary by jurisdiction. An example of a provincial privacy statute is Ontario's Personal Health Information Protection Act ("PHIPA"), which, among other purposes, aims to protect the confidentiality of PHI and the privacy of individuals.[29] In Ontario, PHIPA stipulates that regulated health care practitioners, hospital and psychiatric facility operators, ambulance services, pharmacies and long-term care and retirement homes, to name a few, are considered health information custodians.[30]

PHI is broadly defined across federal and provincial/territorial legislation. Per section 2(1), PIPEDA defines PHI as information respecting a living or deceased individual that includes:

(a)   information concerning the physical or mental health of the individual;

(b)   information concerning any health service provided to the individual;

(c)   information concerning the donation by the individual of any body part or any bodily substance of the individual or information derived from the testing or examination of a body part or bodily substance of the individual;

(d)   information that is collected in the course of providing health services to the individual; or

(e)   information that is collected incidentally to the provision of health services to the individual.

Labrador Exemption Order, SI/2012-72; Personal Health Information Custodians in Nova Scotia Exemption Order, SOR/2-16-62.

[28]   HPPA, supra note 9 at s 39(1).

[29]   Personal Health Information Protection Act, 2004, S O 2004, c. 3, Sch A, at s 1 ((ON) PHIPA).

[30]   Ibid at s 3.

Section 4 of Ontario's PHIPA notes that "personal health information" under the Act includes:[31]

> ... identifying information about an individual in oral or recorded form, if the information,
>
> (a)   relates to the physical or mental health of the individual, including informa-tion that consists of the health history of the individual's family,
>
> (b)   relates to the providing of health care to the individual, including the identifi-cation of a person as a provider of health care to the individual ...
>
> (c.1) is a plan that sets out the home and community care services for the individual to be provided by a health service provider or Ontario Health Team pursuant to funding under section 21 of the Connecting Care Act, 2019,
>
> (d)   relates to payments or eligibility for health care, or eligibility for coverage for health care, in respect of the individual,
>
> (e)   relates to the donation by the individual of any body part or bodily substance of the individual or is derived from the testing or examination of any such body part or bodily substance,
>
> (f)   is the individual's health number, or
>
> (g)   identifies an individual's substitute decision-maker

As will be discussed in a later section of this chapter, unless provided for under common law or statute, custodians or trustees of PHI are generally prohibited from disclosing it to others. Custodians and trustees must also take reasonable care that the information is accurate, complete and up to date as necessary before using or sharing it.[32] Many jurisdictions also include specific provisions regarding notification requirements where confidentiality has been breached, which include notifying either the individual whose information is in question and/or the relevant Information and Privacy Commissioner of that province.[33]

In addition, custodians and trustees have an obligation to make reasonable efforts to safeguard personal information against loss and theft, as well as unauthorized use or disclosure.[34] The content of these obligations depends on the sensitivity of the information in question, and involves engaging in administrative, technical and physical measures to ensure its security. Most

---

[31]   Ibid at s 4(1). Note that this definition is subject to subsections (3) and (4), which concern mixed records and exceptions.

[32]   For example, as set out in s 11 of (ON) PHIPA, supra note 29. This is also a prin-ciple of PIPEDA.

[33]   E.g., (NB) Personal Health Information Privacy and Access Act, SNB 2009, c P-7.05, s 49(1)(c); (NL) Personal Health Information Act, SNL 2008, c P-7.01, ss 15(3), (4), (7); (NS) Personal Health Information Act, SNS 2010, c 41, s 69; (ON) PHIPA, supra note 29 at s 12(2) and (3); (NT) Health Information Act, SNWT 2014, c 2, s 87; (YT) Health Information Privacy and Management Act, SY 2013, s 16, s 30(1).

[34]   See for instance (ON) PHIPA, supra note 29 at s 12(1); (NS) Personal Health Information Act, supra note 33, s 69.

legislation also includes the requirement that custodians and trustees establish information retention and disposal policies.[35]

To ensure compliance with privacy legislation, the Office of the Privacy Commissioner of Canada ("OPC") was established in 1983 to govern federal agencies and departments' handling of personal information, as well as private sector businesses under PIPEDA.[36] The OPC, whose duties are to protect and promote individual's privacy rights and oversee compliance with the Privacy Act and PIPEDA, is independent of government, and reports to Parliament. Provinces and territories also have their own Privacy Commissioner or Ombudsman[37] whose duty it is to enforce the provincial or territorial privacy statutes.

OWNERSHIP, ACCESS AND CORRECTION OF PERSONAL HEALTH INFORMATION

Ownership of health records rests with the individual or institution that recorded the information. Patients have a qualified right of access to their own records and a right to the correction of their records under PIPEDA, or applicable provincial or territorial legislation. Custodians may deny a patient access to their medical records in some cases, such as where access to the information would pose a risk to the patient or another person's health and safety. Custodians denying access bear the burden of justifying the refusal. For instance, in Ontario, to deny a patient access to their medical records, a physician must reasonably expect that access to the information would pose either a risk of serious harm to the treatment or recovery of the patient, or a risk of serious bodily harm to the patient or another person.[38]

ELECTRONIC HEALTH RECORDS

Electronic health records ("EHRs") are comprehensive personal health records stored in electronic form.[39] These records amalgamate information from

---

[35] (ON) PHIPA, supra note 29 at s 13(1). In Quebec, personal information held by public bodies must be destroyed once the purpose for which the information was collected or used was achieved, subject to the Archives Act or Professional Code. See Act Respecting Access to Documents Held by Public Bodies and the Protection of Personal Information, 1982, RSQ, c A-21, supra note 11 at s 73.

[36] Office of the Privacy Commissioner of Canada, "Who we are", online: <www.priv.gc.ca/en/about-the-opc/who-we-are/>.

[37] As is the case in Manitoba.

[38] (ON) PHIPA, supra note 29 at s 52(1)(e)(i).

[39] See Nola M Ries, "Patient Privacy in a Wired (and Wireless) World: Consent in the Context of Electronic Health Records" (2006) 43:4 *Alberta Law Review* 681.

a wide array of sources, such as hospitals, physicians, and laboratories. The facilitation and development of appropriate EHR systems across the provinces and territories has been aided by Canada Health Infoway, a non-profit national organization created in 2001. EHR systems facilitate efficient access to patient information for the purposes of providing care, but they also increase the risk that PHI will be improperly accessed or shared.[40]

LIABILITY FOR BREACH OF CONFIDENTIALITY UNDER COMMON LAW AND STATUTE

Wrongful disclosure of PHI may, depending on the particular circumstances of the case, give rise to one or more causes of action, such as breach of fiduciary duty, defamation, negligence, breach of confidence and breach of contract.[41] The Ontario Court of Appeal has also recognized a tort of "intrusion upon seclusion" for serious invasion of personal privacy in the 2012 case of *Jones v Tsige*.[42] To prove this tort, a plaintiff must show that (1) the defendant's conduct was intentional or reckless, (2) the defendant invaded the plaintiff's private affairs or concerns without lawful justification and (3) a reasonable person would regard the invasion as highly offensive causing distress, humiliation, or anguish.[43] In *Hopkins v Kay* (2015), the Ontario Court of Appeal held that the existence of a separate legal regime which can be used to challenge a violation of privacy through *PHIPA* does not preclude the use of this tort remedy.[44] Recently in *Broutzas v Rouge Valley Health System*, the Ontario Superior Court clarified that this tort will only apply to privacy intrusions involving PHI that can be considered very serious.[45] In this case, three hospital employees breached PHIPA and PIPEDA by accessing the hospital records of patients who had recently given birth. One employee used the information to elicit sales, while the other two sold the patients' contact information to salespeople. Finding that only contact information was ultimately shared for the purposes of eliciting sales, the Court of Appeal upheld the motion judge's dismissal of the plaintiff's certification motions, finding that a tort of intrusion

---

[40] See Noela J Inions, Leanne E Tran and Lorne E Rozovsky, "Electronic Communications and Health Information" in *Canadian Health Information: A Practical Legal and Risk Management Guide*, 4th ed. (Toronto: LexisNexis 2018) at 145–57.

[41] See von Tigerstrom, supra note 7 at 447–50; Lemmens et al. 2020, supra note 10 at 103–04 for an overview of these causes of action.

[42] *Jones v Tsige*, 2012 ONCA 32 (*Tsige*).

[43] Ibid at para 71.

[44] *Hopkins v Kay*, 2015 ONCA 112, leave to appeal to SCC refused, 2015 CanLII 69422 (SCC).

[45] 2023 ONSC 540. See also *Stewart v Demme*, 2022 ONSC 1790.

upon seclusion could not succeed; the information shared was personal but not private and so no serious invasion of privacy occurred.[46]

Health information legislation also contains a number of offences and penalties related to the unjustified disclosure or use of personal information by custodians or trustees. For instance, in Ontario, section 72(2) of PHIPA outlines 11 offences, including the offences of wilfully collecting, using or disclosing PHI "in contravention of the Act or its regulations" and making "a request under the Act under false pretences ...".[47] Most provinces and territories set out that an individual found to have contravened these acts may be liable of a fine and/or imprisonment. Variation exists, however, across jurisdictions depending on the details and perpetrator of the offence. In Ontario, individuals may be fined up to $200,000 and/or subject to up to one-year imprisonment whereas non-natural persons may be subject to a fine of up to a maximum of $1,000,000.[48] While most provincial and territorial legislation is limited to compliance mechanisms that impose penalties on custodians and trustees, some provinces set out a civil cause of action by which an individual may seek damages for a breach of their privacy.[49]

Exceptions to Confidentiality

The general rule that health care professionals may not share confidential patient information is not without exceptions. Confidentiality may be expressly or implicitly waived by the patient, and both common law and statute set out several exceptions based on competing interests, such as the prevention of harm to third parties.

Patient consent, waiver and emergency situations
Medical professionals may share confidential information in cases where there is either express or implicit patient consent to do so.[50] Typically, the sharing of PHI between health care providers who require it to treat a patient—sometimes referred to as a patient's "circle of care"—is taken to be consented to implicit-

---

[46] Ibid at paras 30–35.
[47] (ON) PHIPA, supra note 29 at s 72(1).
[48] Ibid at s 72(2)(a)–(b).
[49] Ibid at s 65.
[50] Canadian Medical Association, CMA Code of Ethics and Professionalism (2018), supra note 14 at para 18; *Hay v University of Alberta Hospital*, (1990) AJ No 333, 69 DLR (4th) 755 at 757–58 (Alta QB) (Hay); (ON) PHIPA, supra note 29 at s 18(2).

ly.[51] Caregivers do not typically obtain express consent before sharing patient information with another health care professional, for example, in cases where a patient agrees to a referral to another health care provider or when a caregiver consults with other professionals. Outside of the circle of care, explicit consent from the patient is generally required, unless an exception is provided for under common law or statute. In some cases, individually identifying diagnostic, treatment and care information may be shared in the absence of consent. For instance, if not contrary to an express request of the individual, under sections 35(1)(c), (d) and (d.1), of Alberta's Health Information Act, a custodian may disclose this information:[52]

> (c)   to family members of the individual or to another person with whom the individual is believed to have a close personal relationship, if the information is given in general terms and concerns the presence, location, condition, diagnosis, progress and prognosis of the individual on the day on which the information is disclosed ...
> (d)   where an individual is injured, ill or deceased, so that family members of the individual or another person with whom the individual is believed to have a close personal relationship or a friend of the individual can be contacted ...
> (d.1) where an individual is deceased, to family members of the individual or to another person with whom the individual is believed to have had a close personal relationship, if the information relates to circumstances surrounding the death of the individual or to health services recently received by the individual ...

Consent is not required where an individual is found incapable of consenting to the collection, use, or disclosure of their PHI. In such a case, PHI may be shared with a relative or guardian of the individual so that they may make the decision on the patient's behalf.[53] In cases of an emergency, health care providers are permitted to provide necessary PHI where this information is imminently required for the patient's health or safety.

In the context of civil litigation, a patient may be understood to have waived their right to confidentiality where their legal claims implicate their health.[54] Specifically, where a patient puts their health at issue by commencing a lawsuit, relevant information regarding the plaintiff's health is *prima facie*

---

[51]   Information and Privacy Commissioner of Ontario, "Circle of Care: Sharing Personal Health Information for Health-Care Purposes" (2015), online (pdf): <www.ipc .on.ca/wp-content/uploads/resources/circle-of-care.pdf>; see also *Stebner v Canadian Broadcasting Corporation*, 2019 SKQB 91 at 44–45, which highlights that a caregiver must require the information, not merely classify as being in the "circle of care".
[52]   RSA 2000, c H-5 ("HIA").
[53]   See e.g., PHIPA, supra note 29 at s 26(1).
[54]   *Cook v Ip*, (1985) 52 OR (2d) 289.

admissible.[55] Permission is not required where a patient wishes to record a medical professional's provision of care to them.[56] Further, these recordings may be admissible in legal proceedings.[57] In criminal contexts, trustees and custodians should be provided with express consent from a patient before disclosing personal information to the patient's defence counsel.[58]

Teaching, research, management and audit

Privacy law also recognizes that in addition to other permitted "public interest" uses of identifiable information, some of which are discussed later on in this chapter, PHI can be collected, stored and used for the proper administration of health care, including for quality assurance and auditing by health authorities. Provincial and territorial legislation explicitly permits the collection, storage and use of PHI for the administration of the health care system and to organize payment for care.[59] The sharing of PHI within the provincial health care systems for these purposes is permissible without explicit informed consent.

Use of information originally gathered for the purpose of providing health care for research purposes is governed by provincial and territorial legislation; by research ethics guidelines, particularly the Tri-Council Policy Statement ("TCPS"), which is developed by the major federal funding agencies;[60] and in some provinces, also by ethics guidelines and policies developed by provincial entities.[61] Research undertaken with the goal of obtaining data for the approval of drugs and medical devices is submitted to a regulatory regime organized by the federal health authorities, but even in that context, the TCPS is treated as an authoritative research ethics guideline. The TCPS is to be followed by all

---

[55] *Hay*, supra note 50 at para 84.

[56] In Canada, recordings of a private conversation are permitted where the recording is taken by one of the participants to the recording. Criminal Code s 184(2)(a).

[57] See e.g., *JW v CAD*, 2017 CanLII 60317 (ON HPARB).

[58] As a general rule, PHI should not be disclosed without patient consent to those who are not custodians and for a purpose other than the provision of health care services.

[59] See for instance, (ON) PHIPA, supra note 29 at ss 37(1)(d), (e), (f), and (i) and 45(1).

[60] Canadian Institutes of Health Research, Natural Sciences and Engineering Research Council of Canada, and Social Sciences and Humanities Research Council, Tri-Council Policy Statement: Ethical Conduct for Research Involving Humans – TCPS 2, December 2022, online: <ethics.gc.ca/eng/documents/tcps2-2022-en.pdf> (TCPS).

[61] See e.g., the Quebec guidelines on biobanking: Unité de la recherche, Guide d'élaboration de la recherche des cadres de gestion des banques de données et de matériel biologique constituées à des fins de recherche (Ministère de la santé et des services sociaux, Québec), October 2012 online: <publications.msss.gouv.qc.ca/msss/fichiers/2012/12-727-02W.pdf>.

researchers who engage in research in institutions funded by federal funding agencies. As a guideline emanating from funding agencies, failure to respect the guidelines can result in suspension of funding to the researchers and institutions in which the research takes place.[62]

The TCPS has a special chapter devoted to privacy and confidentiality. It embraces a "proportionate approach" to privacy and confidentiality, which emphasizes identifiability (risk of re-identification), sensitivity and likelihood of harm resulting from disclosure of information.[63] It contains various rules about the duty of confidentiality, consent and secondary use of data, safeguarding information and confidentiality measures.

Research ethics boards play a crucial role in the determination of the respect for privacy and confidentiality standards in research. They conduct a prior review of research protocols and determine, for example, whether sufficient privacy protection is in place, whether informed consent procedures are adequate, and whether the research will not result in disproportionate privacy risks.

In some Canadian provinces, the only strict legal framework for these research ethics boards is contained in privacy legislation, even though the research ethics boards do much more than reviewing the privacy issues in research. In Ontario, for example, it is *PHIPA* that specifies the composition of these research ethics boards and requires involvement of these boards when research uses PHI.[64]

Detailed rules about the collection, storage and use of health information in the context of research are to be found in the research ethics guidelines, but provincial privacy statutes also have overlapping provisions.

In general, privacy laws only concern information that would reasonably identify an individual, and so information that has no reasonable prospect of doing so is not within the scope of provincial and territorial legislation. However, as has been pointed out by commentators, new technologies make it increasingly hard to ensure that health information and biological samples containing such information are completely unidentifiable.[65] Whether information could "reasonably" be de-identified may therefore evolve over time.

---

[62]   See the discussion in Lemmens et al. 2020, supra note 10 at 160–62 and references there.

[63]   See Chapter 5, TCPS, supra note 60 at 77–91.

[64]   (ON) PHIPA, supra note 29 at s 44.

[65]   Trudo Lemmens and Lisa Austin, "The End of Individual Control Over Health Information: Governing Biobanks and Promoting Fair Information Practices" in Jane Kaye and Mark Stranger, eds, *Governing Biobanks* (Farnham (UK): Ashgate, 2009) 243, in particular at 248–50; see also The Expert Panel on Timely Access to Health and Social Data for Health Research and Health Systems Innovation,

Privacy statutes are relatively flexible with respect to the use of health information for research. In several statutes, consistent use provisions appear to facilitate research and can be seen to reflect an acceptance of broad consent for secondary use of data.[66] The provisions with respect to use of health data for research in Ontario's PHIPA, for example, are explicitly only illustrative of the "relevant matters" that research ethics boards should evaluate, leaving much room for appreciation.[67] Its article 44(3) suggests a number of issues that the boards should "consider" when determining if data can be used for research without consent: whether the research can reasonably be accomplished without access to the data; the public interest in the research and the public interest in protecting the privacy of individuals (without explicitly requiring that the public interest must clearly outweigh the privacy interests, a requirement some other privacy statutes have); and whether obtaining consent is impractical.[68]

This appears more flexible than the provisions of the TCPS. The TCPS allows researchers to access identifiable health data for secondary use only if the research ethics board agrees, for example, that: (1) access to the data is essential; (2) it is unlikely it will adversely impact their welfare; (3) the researchers will comply with any known preferences of people whose information is to be used; (4) it is impossible or impractical to obtain consent.[69] In theory, a situation could thus arise that research ethics boards allow secondary use of data that respects provincial legislation but that violates the funding agency guidelines.

The TCPS also requires researchers to obtain permission from research ethics boards to create data linkages. Researchers have to indicate whether it will result in identifiable data, implement adequate safety measures, and show why data linkage is "essential".[70] Some provincial privacy statutes[71]

Accessing Health and Health-Related Data in Canada, (Ottawa: Council of Canadian Academies, 2015), online: <cca-reports.ca/wp-content/uploads/2018/10/healthdatafullreporten.pdf> at p 79, which states that "it is difficult to be sure whether a data set qualifies as non-identifiable".

[66] See Tom Archibald and Trudo Lemmens, "Data Collection from Legally Incompetent Subjects: A Paradigm Legal and Ethical Challenge for Population Databases" (2008) Special Edition: Visions *Health Law Journal* 145 at 161–62; Adrian Thorogood, "Canada: Will Privacy Rules Continue to Favour Open Science?" (2018) 137 *Human Genetics* 595 at 599.

[67] (ON) PHIPA supra note 29 at s 44(3).

[68] Ibid at s 44(3).

[69] TCPS, supra note 60 at article 5.5A.

[70] Ibid at article 5.

[71] E.g., British Columbia. See Freedom of Information and Protection of Privacy Act, RSBC 1996, c 165 at s 33(1)(iii).

and a directive of Statistics Canada[72] also contain data linkage provisions for research.

Prevention of harm

Both common law and statute give rise to confidentiality exceptions based on prevention of harm, including both allowable disclosures and mandatory reporting obligations. There are a number of scenarios in which a custodian who believes on reasonable grounds that disclosure will avert or minimize imminent danger to the health or safety of any person is either allowed or obliged to break confidentiality.

Under provincial and territorial legislation, care providers must report reasonably suspected child abuse, including physical injury, sexual abuse and emotional abuse.[73] Health care professionals are also required to report suspected abuse of adults in care facilities. For example, in Alberta, providers must report in cases where they have reasonable grounds to believe that a client has been abused.[74]

The federal Quarantine Act as well as all provinces and territories have legislation that obligates the reporting of communicable diseases.[75] This legislation, however, varies in respect to who it applies to and what information it concerns. Under Ontario's HPPA, health professionals and administrators who form an opinion that an individual has or may have a communicable disease are required to report it to the medical officer of health of the applicable unit.[76] This requirement applies to physicians and registered nurses, a variety of health practitioners such as chiropractors and naturopaths, hospital administrators, superintendents of institutions, school principals and laboratory operators.[77]

Mandatory reporting requirements for designated communicable diseases have led to special concern due to the harms that may arise because of disclosure, such as the harm of stigmatization, which has been a particularly salient concern in cases of HIV/AIDS diagnoses.[78] Due to the risk posed by the reporting of a diagnosis, concern has also arisen that mandatory reporting require-

---

[72] Statistics Canada, "Directive on Microdata Linkage", (2017), online: <www .statcan.gc.ca/eng/record/policy4-1>.

[73] See for instance, (SK) Children and Family Services Act, SS 1989-90, c C-7.2, s 12; (ON) Children, Youth, and Family Services Act, 2017, SO 2017, c 14, Sched 1 at s. 124.

[74] (AB) Protection for Persons in Care Act, SA 2009, c P-29.1.

[75] Quarantine Act, SC 2005, c 20.

[76] (ON) HPPA, supra note 9 at s 25(1).

[77] Ibid at ss 25–29.

[78] See *Canadian AIDS Society v Ontario*, (1995) 25 OR (3d) 388 (Sup ct J), Aff'd (1996), 31 OR.

ments ultimately lead to a reduction in individuals seeking testing. In response to this worry, some jurisdictions offer anonymous HIV/AIDS testing.[79]

Beyond the aforementioned categories, a common law reporting obligation purposed with preventing harm to others is not firmly developed in Canadian common law, but case law supports an option to warn and an obligation under limited circumstances. While the reasoning found in US jurisprudence, which supports an obligation to warn, has not been directly applied in a Canadian context, the case law has had some influence. In the US case of *Tarasoff v the Regent of the University of California*, the Court found that the defendant therapist breached the duty of care owed to the victim of one of his patients by not warning her of the threat to her life.[80] This case was cited in the Supreme Court of Canada case of *Smith v Jones*, which concerns solicitor-client privilege and was brought by a psychiatrist acting as an expert witness for a defendant accused of the aggravated assault of a sex worker.[81] In this case, the psychiatrist sought to warn the court of his patient's intentions to kidnap, rape and murder sex workers upon his release. While maintaining that there is no express duty to do so, the Court held that there is an option to warn where three factors are met: (1) imminent risk of (2) serious bodily harm or death to (3) an identifiable person or group of persons.[82]

The courts have also held that it may be open for a health care provider to disclose personal information, where doing so might prevent a miscarriage of justice. For instance, the court has held that a health professional who has reason to believe that a witness in a criminal case is unreliable may be entitled to disclose this information to the Crown and/or defence.[83]

Limited case law exists that deals directly with a health care provider's option or duty to disclose patient health information relevant to other family members (e.g., genetic information).[84] The only Canadian case on the topic of the duty to inform family members of genetic risks and the existence of

---

[79] See Public Health Agency of Canada (PHAC), "HIV/AIDS Epi Updates, Chapter 3, HIV Testing and Surveillance Systems in Canada" (July 2010), online: <www .canada.ca/en/public-health/services/hiv-aids/publications/epi-updates/chapter-3-hiv -testing-surveillance-systems-canada.html>.

[80] *Tarasoff v Regents of the University of California*, 17 Cal 3d 425 (Sup ct, 1976).

[81] *Smith v Jones*, [1999] 1 SCR 455.

[82] Ibid at paras 77–78.

[83] *R v Ross*, [1993] NSJ no 18, 79 CCC (3d) 253.

[84] See Adrian Thorogood, Alexander Bernier, Ma'n H. Zawati and Bartha Maria Knoppers, "A Legal Duty of Genetic Recontact in Canada" (2019) 40(2) *Health Law in Canada* 58–78; Trudo Lemmens, Lori Luther and Michael Hoy, "Genetic Information Access, a Legal Perspective: A Duty to Know or a Right Not to Know, and a Duty or Option to Warn?" in *Encyclopedia of Life Sciences* (Chichester: John Willey & Sons, Ltd, 2015).

a potential duty to warn of genetic risks[85] is the Quebec Court of Appeal case, *Watters v White*, which was decided under civil rather than common law. In this case, the Court of Appeal, reversing the trial decision to find the defendant doctor liable for failing to warn the family members of a patient born with a serious genetic disorder, held that the defendant doctor could not have warned his patient's family members without breaching his duty of confidentiality towards his patients.[86] While the Court recognized the importance of knowing this diagnosis for the family members of the patient, it concluded that this circumstance did not meet the imminence requirement in order to justify a breach of patient confidentiality.[87] As Justice Kasirer noted, writing for the Court, "care must be taken not to overstate the exceptions to the fundamental duty of confidentiality a physician owes to his patient. There is a narrow category of exception whereby non-consensual disclosure is justified by considerations of public health, urgency or imminent danger".[88]

It should be noted that the circumstances of the case were such that it was difficult to establish a causal link between what the plaintiffs argued to be a failure to directly inform the mother of a child identified with a genetic condition, and the fact that remote family members gave birth to a child with the same genetic condition three decades later. In this case, the physician had informed the father, who shortly thereafter divorced the mother and never told her about the hereditary nature of the condition. Furthermore, the Court of Appeal also mentioned the prevailing professional standards at the time when the alleged failure to warn took place (1970). The case therefore does not necessarily reflect what Canadian courts would decide in a case of a failure to inform a family member in the context of a serious risk of preventable harm identified as a result of a genetic test result (for example a case of hypertrophic cardiomyopathy). In the 2021 Ontario case of *Bonenfant v Ponesse*, the Ontario Superior Court noted that if determined under common law, the claim in *Watters* "would likely have fallen at the hurdle of proximity, long before policy considerations came into play".[89]

---

[85] On the difference between the duty to inform and the duty to warn, see Ma'n H. Zawati and Adrian Thorogood, "The Physician Who Knew Too Much: A Comment on Watters v White" (2014) 21 *Health Law Journal* 1 at 18–20 (Zawati and Thorogood, "The Physician").

[86] *Watters v White*, 2012 QCCA 257 [*Watters*].

[87] Ibid.

[88] Ibid at para 111.

[89] 2021 ONSC 8544 at para 76.

POLICE INVESTIGATION

There is no obligation to fulfil police requests for PHI unless there is a legal authority requiring disclosure.[90] Under common law, unless expressly required/granted by statute, a physician who discloses PHI without patient consent breaches their duty of confidentiality.[91] Whether or not an unjustified breach of confidentiality will lead to a successful claim against the physician or bar use of information by the police, however, is another matter.[92]

Where police seek disclosure of PHI and have a warrant available, caregivers should co-operate with the demands of the warrant. Caregivers are not, however, required to provide information orally or provide pre-trial testimony. In some instances, compliance with a warrant requires the exercise of professional opinion. For example, per section 320.29(1) of the Canadian Criminal Code, in complying with a warrant, the medical professional must believe the individual is unable to consent and that taking a blood sample will not endanger the health of the individual.[93]

PUBLIC INTEREST

In response to requests for information in criminal contexts, health professionals should only provide information where there is an explicit legal requirement to do so. Health professionals should comply with court orders and are permitted to share otherwise confidential information in their role as a witness for a preliminary inquiry or criminal trial.[94] Health professionals may act as witnesses in a voluntary capacity or be compelled to do so. The Supreme Court of Canada, however, has recognized that privilege may exist for communications made in the context of a physician and patient relationship in some instances, as assessed on a case-by-case basis.[95] The test to determine privilege on a case-by-case basis is that of the four-part "Wigmore test":

1. The communications must originate in a confidence that they will not be disclosed;

---

[90]   The Criminal Code, however, requires citizens not to obstruct or omit to assist without reasonable excuse police acting in the course of their duties. See Criminal Code of Canada, RSC 1985, c C46, s 129.

[91]   *R v Dersch* [1993] 3 SCR 768, 85 CCC (3d) 1.

[92]   See Gilbert Sharpe, *The Law & Medicine in Canada*, 2nd ed. (Toronto: Butterworths, 1987) at 187–91.

[93]   Canadian Criminal Code, RSC 1985, c C-46, s 320.29(1).

[94]   Ibid at ss 697–700.1; *Ogden v Simon Fraser University* [1998] BCJ No 2288 (BC prov Ct (sm Cl Div).

[95]   *Ryan*, supra note 2.

2. This element of confidentiality must be essential to the full and satisfactory maintenance of the relationship between the parties;

3. The relation must be one which in the opinion of the community ought to be sedulously fostered; and

4. The injury that would injure to the relation by the disclosure of the communications must be greater than the benefit thereby gained for the correct disposal of litigation.[96]

Some provincial laws require that health facilities report gunshot and/or stab wound injuries to the police.[97] This legislation is not, however, without controversy. As noted by Andrew Martin, it is unclear whether the underlying aim of such legislation is public health and safety or law enforcement.[98] Moreover, this legislation may inhibit individuals from obtaining medical care for these injuries, due to concerns about police investigations.[99]

PRIVACY AND DATA PROTECTION IN THE AGE OF TECHNOLOGY AND THE COVID-19 PANDEMIC

The growing use of technology for both the provision of health care services and storage of health information poses significant privacy and data security challenges. As noted, the electronic storage of health records, while increasing efficiency of access, also increases the risk of unauthorized access and security breaches. This is evidenced by the recent and extensive cyber-attacks on

---

[96] John Henry Wigmore, *Evidence in Trials at Common Law*, vol 8, McNaughton Revision (Boston: Little, Brown & Co, 1961) as cited in *R v Gruenke* [1991] 3 SCR 263.

[97] (AB) Gunshot and Stab Wound Mandatory Disclosure Act, SA 2009, c. G-12; (BC) Gunshot and Stab Wound Disclosure Act, SBC 2010, c. 7; (MB) Gunshot and Stab Wounds Mandatory Reporting Act, CCSM c G125; (NL) Gunshot and Stab Wound Reporting Act, SNL 2011, c G-7.1; (SK) Gunshot and Stab Wounds Mandatory Reporting Act, SS 2007, c G-9.1; (NT) Gunshot and Stab Wound Mandatory Disclosure Act, SNWT 2013, c 19; (NS) Gunshot Wounds Mandatory Reporting Act, SNS 2007, c 30, (ON) Mandatory Gunshot Wounds Reporting Act, 2005, SO 2005, c 9, s 2.

[98] See Andrew Flavelle Martin, "The Adoption of Mandatory Gunshot Wound Reporting Legislation in Canada: A Decade of Tension in Lawmaking at the Intersection of Law Enforcement and Public Health" (2016) 9:2 *McGill Journal of Law & Health* 175, online: <papers.ssrn.com/abstract=2811953>.

[99] See Merril A Pauls and Jocelyn Downie, "Shooting Ourselves in the Foot: Why Mandatory Reporting of Gunshot Wounds Is a Bad Idea" (2004) 170 *Canadian Medical Association Journal* 1255.

a number of health systems across Canada, which have impacted millions of patient files.[100]

The provision of virtual care services also raises privacy and data security concerns based on risks associated with technology, which have been particularly salient since the start of the COVID-19 pandemic. While virtual health care is not a recent development in Canada, the COVID-19 pandemic significantly increased its use.[101] Risks associated with virtual health care services include breaches of personal information by technical and configuration errors, hacking and software exploitation, and "electronic eavesdropping".[102] The use of virtual platforms also raises privacy risks in the commercial collection, use, and sharing of health information.[103]

In the early days of the pandemic, limited guidance was available to health care providers regarding the appropriate level of technological security for the provision of virtual health care services, leaving many decisions relevant to information security to the discretion of individual care providers. The prioritization of making virtual health services available thus resulted in health care professionals use of a broad range of technology platforms with varied security risks, including email, video calling platforms such as FaceTime

---

[100] See for instance, Office of the Saskatchewan Information and Privacy Commissioner, "Saskatchewan IPC finds ransomware attack results in one of the largest privacy breaches in this province involving citizens' most sensitive data" (2021), online: <oipc.sk.ca/saskatchewan-ipc-finds-ransomware-attack-results-in-one-of-the-largest-privacy-breaches-in-this-province-involving-citizens-most-sensitive-data/>.

[101] Office of the Privacy Commissioner of Canada, "Privacy in a pandemic", (8 October, 2020), online: <www.priv.gc.ca/en/opc-actions-and-decisions/ar_index/201920/ar_201920/>; see Patrick B. Patterson, Jenna Roddick, Candice A. Pollack and Daniel J. Dutton, "Virtual Care and the Influence of a Pandemic: Necessary Policy Shifts to Drive Digital Innovation in Healthcare" (2022) 35(5) *Healthcare Management Forum* 272.

[102] Information and Privacy Commissioner of Ontario, "privacy and virtual health care", online: <www.ipc.on.ca/covid-19-information-and-resources/privacy-and-virtual-health-care/>.

[103] Sheryl Spithoff, Brenda McPhail, Quinn Grundy, Robyn K Rowe, Matthew Herder, Beatrice Allard, and Leslie Schumacher, "Commercial Virtual Healthcare Services in Canada: Digital Trails, De-Identified Data and Privacy Implications" (2023) Health Tech and Society Lab. Toronto, online: <static1.squarespace.com/static/61803ca0424ab062d9625e2d/t/640799d52430852f868b06a1/1678219738649/Commercial+Virtual+Healthcare+Services+in+Canada+Digital+Trails%2C+De-Identified+Data+and+Privacy+Implications+3.0.pdf>; Tracey L Adams and Kathleen Leslie, "Regulating for-profit virtual care in Canada: Implications for medical profession regulators and policy-makers" (2023) *Healthcare Management Forum* 36(2), online: <www.ncbi.nlm.nih.gov/pmc/articles/PMC9975815/#bibr1-08404704221134872>.

or Zoom, and various for-profit health care specific "apps".[104] Adoption of health care apps to provide health care services has been widespread in some provinces. Following a partnership between Telus Health and Babylon,[105] for instance, Ontario, British Columbia, and Alberta started providing virtual walk-in services through the Babylon app.[106] On April 21, 2020 the Office of the Information and Privacy Commissioner of Alberta announced that it had launched investigations into this app, following concerns raised in privacy impact assessments by both a physician and Babylon Health Canada Limited.[107] Two reports by the Privacy Commissioner revealed that Telus Health did not comply with Alberta's Health Information Act or PIPEDA by, among other things, collecting information that was not essential to the provision of health care services.[108]

In response to the growing use of virtual care services, various authorities, including Information and Privacy Commissioners, provincial and federal working groups, self-regulating health professions and Health Canada, have developed virtual care guidelines. For instance, the Information and Privacy Commissioner of Ontario released "Privacy and security considerations for virtual health care visits: Guidelines for the Health Sector" in February 2021.[109] This guideline describes key requirements of PHIPA and outlines safeguards

---

[104] Doctors Manitoba, "Advice on Video Visit Apps", online: <doctorsmanitoba.ca/managing-your-practice/covid-19/virtual-care/advice-on-video-visit-apps>; Doctors Technology Office, "DTO Frequently Asked Questions: Virtual Care for Physicians and MOAs" (2 February, 2021), online, <www.doctorsofbc.ca/sites/default/files/dto_virtual_care_faq_for_physicians_and_moas.pdf>; College of Physicians & Surgeons of Alberta, "COVID-19: Virtual Care", (March 2020, updated November 2020), online: <cpsa.ca/wp-content/uploads/2020/06/AP_COVID-19-Virtual-Care.pdf>; see Maria Jogova, James Shaw and Trevor Jamieson, "The Regulatory Challenge of Mobile Health: Lessons for Canada" (2019) 14:3 *Healthcare Policy* 19; Bill Marczak and John Scott-Railton, "Zoom's Waiting Room Vulnerability" (8 April 2020), online: <citizenlab.ca/2020/04/zooms-waiting-room-vulnerability/>.
[105] TELUS Health, "New app from TELUS health and Babylon enables Canadians to visit a doctor through their smartphone", online: <www.telus.com/en/health/press-releases/new-app-telus-health-babylon-enables-canadians-visit-doctor-smartphone>.
[106] Lorian Hardcastle and Ubaka Ogbogu, "Virtual Care: Enhancing Access or Harming Care?" (2020) 336 *Healthcare Management Forum* 288.
[107] Office of the Information and Privacy Commissioner of Alberta, News Release, "Commissioner Investigating Babylon by Telus Health App" (21 April 2020), online: <www.oipc.ab.ca/news-and-events/news-releases/2020/commissioner-investigating-babylon-by-telus-health-app.aspx>.
[108] Office of the Information and Privacy Commissioner of Alberta, "Commissioner Releases Babylon by Telus Health Investigation Reports" (29 July 2021), online: <oipc.ab.ca/p2021-ir-02-h2021-ir-01/>.
[109] Online: <www.ipc.on.ca/wp-content/uploads/2021/02/virtual-health-care-visits.pdf>.

Privacy and health in Canada   45

to enhance privacy and security in virtual health care. On a national level, the College of Family Physicians of Canada, Royal College of Physicians and Surgeons of Canada and the Canadian Medical Association have jointly produced a "Virtual Care Playbook", released in 2020 and updated in 2021, which includes some guidance related to technology use and security standards in the provision of virtual health services.[110] Over the past two years, further standards for the provision of virtual care have developed, including those touching on technological requirements. For instance, in 2022, Ontario Health released the Virtual Visit Verification Standard, which requires virtual care services to use secure platforms for video and messaging communication.[111]

Technological advancements have also enhanced the Canadian government's ability to respond to and monitor public health emergencies, by enabling wide-spread data collection and tracking capabilities. In turn, measures responding to the COVID-19 pandemic have triggered further privacy concerns, including the fear that the deployment of contact tracing apps would result in significant privacy incursions by the government that would outlast the current pandemic.[112] In July 2020, a national COVID-19 exposure notification mobile app, originally developed in Ontario, was released to assist in the notification of users of exposure to individuals who tested positive for COVID-19.[113] Despite initial concerns, contract tracing in Canada has, according to official reports, not resulted in privacy incursions related to PHI. In June 2022, the Office of Audit and Evaluation Health Canada and the Public Health Agency of Canada released an evaluation of the app, which included an assessment of its adherence to privacy principles.[114] This report found that the

---

[110] The College of Family Physicians of Canada, Royal College of Physicians and Surgeons of Canada, and the Canadian Medical Association, Virtual Care Playbook (2021), online: <www.cma.ca/sites/default/files/pdf/Virtual-Care-Playbook_mar2020_E.pdf>.

[111] Ontario Health, "Virtual Visits Verification Standard" (June 29, 2023), online: <www.ontariohealth.ca/system-planning/digital-standards/virtual-visits-verification.

[112] See Lisa M. Austin, Vincent Chiao, Beth Coleman, David Lie, Martha Shaffer, Andrea Slane and François Tanguay-Renaud, "Test, Trace, and Isolate: COVID-19 and the Canadian Constitution" (2020) Osgoode Legal Studies Research Paper; Canadian Civil Liberties Association, "Canadian Rights During COVID-19: CCLA's Interim Report on COVID's First Wave" (2020), online: <ccla.org/wp-content/uploads/2021/06/2nd-Interim-Report-Working-Document-August-2020-1.pdf>.

[113] Prime Minister of Canada, "Prime minister announces new mobile app to help notify Canadians of COVID-10 exposure" (2020), online: <pm.gc.ca/en/news/news-releases/2020/07/31/new-mobile-app-help-notify-canadians-potential-covid-19-exposure-now#:~:text=The%20Prime%20Minister%2C%20Justin%20Trudeau,tested%20positive%20for%20COVID%2D19>.

[114] Office of Audit and Evaluation Health Canada and the Public Health Agency of Canada, "Evaluation of the National COVID-10 Exposure Notification App" (June

app included appropriate privacy protections and that the app did not collect health information or lead to the sharing of personal information.[115] Effective June 17, 2022, this app has now been decommissioned.[116]

As the pandemic developed, privacy concerns arose in the context of other measures that involved the collection of or disclosure of PHI.[117] For example, in Ontario, vaccine passports were introduced in September 2021 to restrict access to non-essential businesses such as gyms, indoor restaurants, movie theatres and concert halls.[118] Businesses were requested to ask for proof of vaccination or an officially recognized exemption. The province introduced a system of QR code, available on cell phones. Yet, initially, while this new system was being implemented, full copies of official vaccination status had to be shown at the entry of businesses, while those with a medical exemption had to produce the letter of a health practitioner, explaining the exemption, with potential details of medical conditions that justified the exemption. At the federal level, measures were also introduced by airline companies and railway companies, imposing the sharing of vaccination status.[119] Some airline companies conducted their own review of those with an official medical exemption, approved by the provincial authorities. This involved requesting those with an officially approved medical exemption to share detailed health information, which would be assessed by the airline companies' own health evaluators.

2022), online: <www.canada.ca/content/dam/hc-sc/documents/corporate/transparency/corporate-management-reporting/evaluation/results-covid-alert-national-covid-19-exposure-notification-app/covid-alert-app-evaluation-en.pdf>.

[115] Ibid at 13, 16.

[116] Health Canada, "Statement from Health Canada on Decommissioning COVID Alert" (2022), online: <www.canada.ca/en/health-canada/news/2022/06/statement-from-health-canada-on-decommissioning-covid-alert.html>.

[117] See Privacy and COVID-19 Vaccine Passports - Office of the Privacy Commissioner of Canada; Canadian Civil Liberties Association, "FAQ: Vaccine Passports" (2021), online: <ccla.org/privacy/surveillance-technology/faq-vaccine-passports/>.

[118] Miriam Katawzi, "Ontario reveals vaccine passport system for restauarants, gyms and theatres. Here's what you need to know" (September 1, 2021) CTV News, online: <toronto.ctvnews.ca/ontario-reveals-vaccine-passport-system-for-restaurants-gyms-and-theatres-here-s-what-you-need-to-know-1.5569198>; Ontario, "Ontario to Require Proof of Vaccination in Select Settings" (September 1, 2021) News Release, online: <news.ontario.ca/en/release/1000779/ontario-to-require-proof-of-vaccination-in-select-settings>.

[119] Government of Canada, "Mandatory COVID-19 vaccination requirements for federally regulated transportation employees and travelers", online: <www.canada.ca/en/transport-canada/news/2021/10/mandatory-covid-19-vaccination-requirements-for-federally-regulated-transportation-employees-and-travellers.html>.

Sharing of medical information about vaccine status or medical exemptions was also introduced by many employers. The Ontario government did not introduce double vaccination as a legal requirement, but as a recommendation. In response, many employers, including all educational institutions, imposed double vaccination with a threat of sanctions, including suspension without pay or even dismissal for employees, and suspension from attending classes for students, for failure to produce such information.

A discussion of the reasonableness of these policies exceeds the scope of this chapter, but it is worth pointing out that in all Canadian provinces, except Quebec, and at the federal level, double vaccination was introduced as a requirement (either by government or by employers), even for those previously infected. Although most courts, human rights commissions, including the Ontario Human Rights Commission, and labour arbitrators explicitly accepted the reasonableness of this approach, questions have been asked about the proportionality of such imposition.[120] This has privacy implications. Indeed, if imposing the production of detailed health information to employers, or private businesses, was disproportionate, it constituted a violation of privacy. A clear example, arguably, is the imposition of the production of detailed health information about vaccination or the basis of an exemption, for persons working remotely, or on leave.[121] In several colleges and universities, booster shots following a second vaccination have also been imposed as a requirement for students residing in university residences, the reasonableness of which can be questioned in light of waning immunity and the specific risk/benefit balance for adolescents and young adults.[122] Again, imposing such requirement and the production of evidence of it arguably constitutes a violation of privacy because of a lack of justification and proportionality.

Other steps taken by the government have been subject to strong criticism that such measures constituted unjustified violation of citizens' privacy rights. A further example includes Ontario Regulation 120/20 under the Emergency Management and Civil Protection Act, which allowed first-responders, including members of the police force, firefighters, and paramedics, access to individual's "COVID-19 status information", which included the individual's name, address, date of birth and, if applicable, their positive COVID-19 test

---

[120] Kevin Bardosh et al., "The unintended consequences of COVID-19 vaccine policy: why mandates, passports and restrictions may cause more harm than good" 7 (2022) *BMJ Global Health*, online: <gh.bmj.com/content/7/5/e008684>.

[121] Ibid.

[122] Kevin Bardosh et al., "COVID-19 vaccine boosters for young adults: a risk benefit assessment and ethical analysis of mandate policies at universities" (2022) *Journal of Medical Ethics*, online: <jme.bmj.com/content/early/2022/12/05/jme-2022 -108449>.

results.[123] This regulation's stated purpose was to help "first responders to take appropriate safety precautions to protect themselves and the communities they serve".[124] This regulation was vehemently opposed by a number of human rights groups, including Aboriginal Legal Services, Black Legal Action Centre, the Canadian Civil Liberties Association and the HIV & AIDS Legal Clinic Ontario, who were concerned about the utility of this regulation, as well as the legality of sharing PHI under these circumstances.[125] It was repealed on July 22, 2020.

In June 2022, the federal government proposed an overhaul of the current private sector privacy legislation under PIPEDA by introducing Bill C-27. Bill C-27, known by its short title as the Digital Charter Implementation Act, 2022, is an updated version of Bill C-11 of the same name proposed in November 2020[126] that seeks to repeal the privacy provisions under PIPEDA and replace them with the Consumer Privacy Protection Act ("CPPA"). Changes under the CPPA would include greater fines for non-compliance and new legal claims for breaches of privacy. Bill C-27 passed its second reading in the House of Commons on April 24, 2023, and is being considered by the Standing Committee on Industry and Technology.

Bill C-27 also proposes two additional pieces of legislation: the Personal Information and Data Protection Act and the Artificial Intelligence and Data Act. The Personal Information and Data Protection Tribunal Act would establish an administrative tribunal purposed with hearing appeals from the Privacy Commissioner's decisions and administering the CPPA. The proposed Artificial Intelligence and Data Act, if passed, would constitute the federal government's first comprehensive regulation of artificial intelligence.

CONFIDENTIALITY AND GENETICS

Advancements in the area of genetics pose special privacy challenges arising from the uniquely identifying nature of genetic information and the type of information genetic testing makes available. As genomic technology develops

---

[123] Order under Subsection 7.0.2(4) of the Act – Access to COVID-19 Status Information by Specified Persons, O Reg 120/20.

[124] Ontario, News Release, "Ontario Takes Additional Measures to Protect First Responders During the COVID-19 Outbreak" (6 April 2020), online: <news.ontario .ca/en/statement/56590/ontario-takes-additional-measures-to-protect-first-responders -during-the-covid-19-outbreak>.

[125] Canadian Civil Liberties Association, "Ontario Government Agrees to Human Rights Groups' Demands to End Police Access to COVID Database" (2021), online: <ccla.org/press-release/ontario-government-agrees-to-human-rights-groups-demands -to-end-police-access-to-covid-database-2/>.

[126] Bill C-11 died on the order paper as a result of the 2021 Federal election.

to make it feasible to obtain even more sequence data from individuals, so risk and privacy concerns increase.[127]

One such privacy challenge arises from the fact that individual genetic information is of a familial nature and so is relevant to an individual's family members.[128] The relational nature of this information raises difficult questions regarding what duties or options flow from this relationship regarding the sharing of personal genetic information with family members.[129] Canadian law, however, does not currently impose a duty or option to warn family members of serious genetic conditions as such scenarios do not meet the requisite test set out in *Smith v Jones*. As discussed previously, this test allows for an exception to confidentiality in cases where there is an *imminent* threat of serious harm to an identifiable person or group. The leading case in this area is *Watters v White* as discussed above, in which the Quebec Court of Appeal held that the defendant physician could not have warned family members of his patient's serious genetic condition without breaching his duty of confidentiality towards his patient.[130] As noted, there is little Canadian case law concerning privacy and genetics and the *Watters v White* case may, due to the circumstances of the case, not represent how other courts may decide in other cases of imminent, preventable harm identified through genetic testing.

The disclosure of genetic information is also an area of particular concern given the concerns about genetic discrimination.[131] In response to these concerns, Parliament enacted the Genetic Non-Discrimination Act in 2017. This act established prohibitions against individuals and corporations requiring genetic tests "as a condition of obtaining access to goods, services and contracts" or using genetic test results without written consent in these contexts.[132]

---

[127] See Kelly E Ormond and Mildred K. Cho, "Translating Personalized Medicine Using New Genetic Technologies in Clinical Practice: The Ethical Issues" (2014) 11:2 *Personalized Medicine* 211.

[128] See Lemmens, Luther and Hoy, supra note 84.

[129] See ibid; Katie M Saulnier et al., "Communication of Genetic Information in the Palliative Care Context: Ethical and Legal Issues" (2018) 18:4 *Medical Law International* 219.

[130] *Watters*, supra note 86; see also Zawati and Thorogood, "The Physician", supra note 85.

[131] See Annet Wauters and Ine Van Hoyweghen, "Global Trends on Fears and Concerns of Genetic Discrimination: A Systematic Literature Review" (2016) 61:4 *Journal of Human Genetics* 275–82.

[132] Genetic Non-Discrimination Act, SC 2017, c 3. Whether this act added much to the protection already offered by other human rights legislation in Canada was contested: the concept of 'disability' has been interpreted so broadly that it already encompasses genetic risk factors. For a detailed discussion, see Kathleen Hammond, "Unnecessary and Redundant? Evaluating Canada's Genetic Non-Discrimination Act, 2017" (2020) 98(3) *Canadian Bar Review* 480–511, who supports the law but

The constitutionality of this act was recently affirmed by the Supreme Court of Canada in Reference re Genetic Non-Discrimination Act.[133]

HEALTH INFORMATION GOVERNANCE AND INDIGENOUS PEOPLE

In the last several decades, there is a growing emphasis in Canada on the need to come to terms with the historical injustice done to Indigenous Peoples since the beginning of colonization, to renew the relationship with the three Indigenous groups (First Nations, Inuit and Métis Nation),[134] and to recognize Indigenous self-governance. This also involves a recognition of the unique interests of Indigenous Peoples, including in relation to privacy.

Commentators have pointed out that there is a clear interest among Indigenous communities in the gathering of information focusing on long-term health, recognizing a more holistic concept of health (general health and well-being within a broader collective level), as well as the importance of public health surveillance.[135] However, Indigenous Peoples are historically suspicious about the reason behind governmental collection of personal, familial and community-related information. One of the reasons is that governmental data have in the past been used, for example, for the forced removal of Indigenous children from their families for forced acculturation in residential schools, where many were submitted to abuse, malnutrition and rampant infectious diseases. In the context of research, there have also been instances of collection of information and biological samples from Indigenous Peoples without individual and/or community consent.[136] Questions about who can collect information and for what purpose are therefore very sensitive. But the development of health information practices records has also faced challenges

---

admits there is some redundancy. For a stronger endorsement, see Yvonne Bombard, Ronald Cohn and Stephen Scherer, "Why we need a law to prevent genetic discrimination" *The Globe and Mail* (19 September 2016), online: <www.theglobeandmail.com/opinion/why-we-need-a-law-to-prevent-genetic-discrimination/article31936476/>. For an earlier discussion, see Trudo Lemmens, "Selective Justice, Genetic Discrimination and Insurance: Should We Single Out Genes in Our Laws?" (2000) 45 *McGill Law Journal* 347–412.

[133] Reference re Genetic Non-Discrimination Act, supra note 4.

[134] Indigenous People constitute about 5 percent of the population or 1.8 million people. For a short discussion of health issues faced by Indigenous People, see Lemmens et al. 2020, supra note 10 at 73–81 and references there.

[135] See James Williams, Megan Vis-Dunbar and Jens Webber, "First Nations Privacy and Modern Health Care Delivery" (2011) 10:1 *Indigenous Law Journal* 101 at 113–14.

[136] Ibid at 115.

because of jurisdictional issues and a failure to accommodate Indigenous views of health care and privacy.[137]

Already in 2007, First Nations people embraced a framework for dealing with information, the so-called Ownership, Control, Access, and Possession (OCAP) principles, a high-level framework that guides First Nations approaches to information management.[138] The principles reflect overall a more communal view of information management, in contrast with the strong individual-rights focus of Canada's privacy law.[139] The ownership principle refers to cultural knowledge of First Nations and the collective ownership of certain forms of information. The control principle emphasizes self-governance in information management, including with respect to policy making and data management.[140] The access principle affirms the right of First Nations to obtain access to information wherever it is stored and the possession principle helps to assert ownership over the data by First Nations.[141]

In 2010, major funding agencies included a separate Chapter on research involving Indigenous people in the federal research ethics guidelines (i.e., the TCPS).[142] This Chapter is not intended to replace ethical guidance developed by Indigenous peoples' themselves; instead, it calls for an explicit recognition of Indigenous Peoples' knowledge systems, distinct world views, and communal interests of Indigenous people in the design, implementation, analysis and publication of research. It replaced earlier guidelines by the health research funding agency, the "CIHR Guidelines for Health Research Involving Aboriginal People" which existed between 2007 and 2010.[143]

The special Chapter functions as a framework for ethical standards in research involving Indigenous people.[144] The provisions reflect a recognition of the need for community engagement at the various stages of the research

---

[137] See in general the discussion in ibid, and in particular at 115–16.

[138] First Nations Centre, OCAP: Ownership, Control, Access and Possession, First Nations Information Governance Committee, Assembly of First Nations (Ottawa: National Aboriginal Health Organization, 2007). See First Nations Information Governance Centre website: <fnigc.ca/ocap-training/#:~:text=The%20First%20Nations %20principles%20of%20ownership%2C%20control%2C%20access%2C%20and,this %20information%20can%20be%20used>.

[139] A point emphasized also by Williams, Vis-Dunbar and Webber, supra note 35 at 120.

[140] See the discussion in ibid at 117.

[141] Ibid.

[142] See Chapter 9, TCPS, supra note 60.

[143] Canadian Institutes of Health Research, "CIHR Guidelines for Health Research Involving Aboriginal People (2007-2010)" (27 June 2013), online: <cihr-irsc.gc.ca/e/ 29134.html>.

[144] See Chapter 9, TCPS, supra note 60 at 107–32.

process, and also of Indigenous self-governance and unique governance structures. The guidelines require, for example, that researchers work with the community to identify "Elders and other Knowledge Holders" and to meaningfully
involve them in the design, the conduct and the interpretation of findings. The
guidelines specifically refer to the need to identify early on the privacy and
confidentiality interests of "communities and individuals".[145]

There are also specific provisions for secondary use of data. Researchers
who want to access data or biological samples "identifiable as originating from
an Indigenous community or peoples" have an obligation to "engage" with the
community if the data is not publicly available or legally accessible and there
is no research plan or the research plan does not explicitly allow secondary use
and people did not explicitly consent.[146] The research ethics board can impose
an obligation to engage the Indigenous community with respect to the secondary use of data. Researchers also need to obtain approval for research linking
two anonymous data sets when "there is a reasonable prospect that this could
generate information identifiable as originating from a specific Indigenous
community or a segment of the Indigenous community at large."[147]

In addition to explicit guidance already introduced in research ethics guidelines, Canada's federal department of Justice has announced its intention to
integrate the perspectives of Indigenous people in its modernization of the
federal privacy act. A discussion paper reflects the same ideas of the need to
respect self-governance and the more collective interests of Indigenous people
in information.[148]

What we thus witness in Canada is a growing demand for self-governance
and self-determination of Indigenous Peoples when it comes to information
governance, including in relation to health information. This takes place within
a context of complex jurisdictional issues with respect to the application of
federal or provincial law to Indigenous people living on and off reserves.
Indigenous self-governance of health may be accompanied in the future by
the development of Indigenous privacy law initiatives that may raise tension
with provincial health information infrastructures and legal provisions in
privacy statutes. There are also specific initiatives aimed at the implementa-

---

[145]   Ibid at art. 9.16.
[146]   Ibid at art. 9.20.
[147]   Ibid at art. 9.22.
[148]   See Department of Justice Canada, "Privacy Act Modernization: A Discussion
Paper: 5. Modernizing the Privacy Act's relationship with Indigenous peoples in
Canada" (2020), online (pdf): <www.justice.gc.ca/eng/csj-sjc/pa-lprp/dp-dd/pdf/dp-5
.pdf>.

tion of Indigenous perspectives on health information.[149] It will be interesting to see whether the modernization of Canada's privacy statutes at the federal and provincial level will also provide an occasion for a formal integration of Indigenous perspectives in federal or provincial privacy law. Indigenous leaders have expressed frustration about the lack of adequate consultation in the context of various federal privacy initiatives, including the modernization of the federal Privacy Act and Access to Information Act.[150]

CONCLUSION

The law in relation to privacy and confidentiality is governed in Canada by a complex interaction of common law, constitutional law and statutory law at both the federal and provincial level. Common law has long recognized strong confidentiality obligations of physicians and health care providers, including through a recognition of the fiduciary nature of the doctor-patient relationship. In 2012, the Ontario Court of Appeal has confirmed a common law remedy for invasion of privacy, known as "intrusion upon seclusion".[151] This court-based remedy is available in addition to regulatory interventions that may be undertaken by provincial or federal privacy commissioners under provincial and federal privacy statutes. In most provinces, the majority of privacy related remedies are of a soft-governance nature, although some penalties can be imposed under privacy law. With respect to health information, provincial statutory law is most important, although the federal privacy statute PIPEDA, enacted in 2000, has been influential through the recognition of substantially similar provincial legislation. Under this system, provincial privacy statutes apply in lieu of the federal statute even in areas of federal jurisdiction (e.g., commercial transactions) when the federal privacy commission has accepted the provincial statute as substantially similar.

In the last couple of years, provincial and federal privacy officers have launched initiatives to modernize the various privacy acts and to address new privacy concerns raised by new information technology and artificial intelligence. Canadian federal and provincial governments are under pressure

---

[149] See the discussion by Williams, Vis-Dunbar and Webber, supra note 135 at 121–23.

[150] See, for example, National Claims Research Directors and Union of BC Indian Chiefs, "The Impacts of Bill C-58 on First Nations Access to Information: A Discussion Paper Following the Review of Bill C-58 by the Senate Committee on Legal and Constitutional Affairs" (20 March 2019) online: <d3n8a8pro7vhmx.cloudfront.net/ubcic/pages/1440/attachments/original/1559070680/C-58DiscussionPaperFINAL.pdf ?1559070680>.

[151] *Tsige*, supra note 42.

to change their privacy regime in order to continue to benefit from the free exchange of data granted in the past by the European Union, which granted Canadian privacy law "adequacy" status with respect to protection of privacy.[152] If passed, Bill-27 would move Canada's privacy law closer to the General Data Protection Regulations in the European Union.

Canada's federal and provincial governments are also recognizing the unique status of Indigenous People's in Canada and their specific demands with respect to health information privacy. There is growing pressure to acknowledge Indigenous self-governance, including in the health and health information context, which is already reflected in adjustments that have been made to research ethics guidelines and is now being considered in the context of the renewal of privacy legislation. As discussed, Indigenous people have put forward specific claims to self-governance of health information and also indicated their demand for a recognition of more collective interests in health information privacy. Problems with meaningful involvement of Indigenous Peoples in the design of privacy law and the recognition of their different interests in relation to health information remain a challenge that provincial and federal governments will have to address in the modernization of Canadian privacy law, in close collaboration with Indigenous communities.

ACKNOWLEDGEMENT

The authors would like to acknowledge Max Levy for his suggestions and assistance with references, Talia Wolfe for suggestions of sources about Indigenous approaches to privacy, Erin Lee for relevant case law research, and Erica McLachlan for her feedback on an earlier draft of this chapter.

---

[152] Government of Canada, Sixth Update Report on Developments in Data Protection Law in Canada: Report to the European Commission (Ottawa: Innovation, Science and Economic Development Canada, 2019) online: <publications.gc.ca/collections/collection_2020/isde-ised/Iu37-8-6-2020-eng.pdf>.

4. Privacy and health in Germany

Benedikt Buchner

GENERAL INTRODUCTION[1]

Privacy in the health sector has two main foundations in German law: data protection law and medical confidentiality. The former is regulated primarily by the GDPR, supplemented by national Federal and State data protection acts as well as sector-specific data protection regulations, while the latter (medical confidentiality) is based first on medical professional law and § 203 StGB (Criminal Code). The potential parallel applicability of data protection law and medical confidentiality remains unchanged under the GDPR. Although the GDPR – as a regulation in accordance with Article 288 TFEU – pursues an immediate and comprehensive regulatory approach, due to many relevant opening clauses, the regulation of health data protection is still largely left to the national legislator.[2]

The relationship of general data protection law and medical confidentiality has always been controversial – before the GDPR came into force and still today. Sometimes it is argued that medical confidentiality takes precedence over data protection regulations. According to another point of view, both regulatory systems apply independently so that any processing of data is subject to data protection law as well as medical confidentiality. In practice, these different views on the relationship of data protection and medical confidentiality are frequently irrelevant since purpose and basic design of data protection law and medical confidentiality largely coincide. Occasionally, however, depth and content of regulation differ, for example where the requirements for consent to data processing are concerned, so that it will become necessary to determine the relationship of the two regulatory frameworks.

---

[1]   The author would like to thank Petra Wilkins (University of Bremen Institute for Information, Health and Medical Law) for her help with the translation.
[2]   Cf Art. 9 (3) and (4) GDPR; see Thilo Weichert in Jürgen Kühling and Benedikt Buchner (eds), *DS-GVO/BDSG* (3rd edn, C. H. Beck 2020), Art. 9 DS-GVO No 139 and 150.

THE ETHICAL BASIS OF CONFIDENTIALITY

The confidentiality of the doctor-patient relationship is not an end in itself, but the core prerequisite for successful medical treatment and thus also for a functioning healthcare system. As early as in 1972, the German Federal Constitutional Court noted in its decision on the seizure of a doctor's patient record that anyone who seeks medical treatment must and can expect

> that anything the physician learns about his state of health remains confidential and will not become known to any third parties. Only when this is ensured, the trust between patient and physician can be built, which is one of the basic prerequisites of medical treatment as it increases the chances of recovery and overall serves to maintain effective healthcare.[3]

The comprehensive protection of confidentiality is indispensable for a relationship of trust between physician and patient. Patients will only trust their physicians if they are assured that their secrets are safe. This protection of confidentiality must apply comprehensively, in particular, there must be no distinction between secrets more or less worthy of protection. The Federal Constitutional Court has adopted a clear position in the above-cited decision of 1972 insofar, too. According to this, patient confidentiality does not only cover records relating to

> diseases, conditions or complaints, the disclosure of which would place those concerned under suspicion of a criminal offence, be embarrassing for them in other respects or damaging to their social standing. Rather, it is the wish of the individual to protect personal matters such as the physician's assessment of his or her state of health from disclosure to third parties that must be respected.[4]

In principle, it is the patient's self-determination that is at the centre of the doctor-patient relationship, not only as the guiding principle for whether and how medical treatment is to take place, but also with regard to the confidentiality of treatment. The will of the patient is paramount even when this is neither "reasonable" nor "beneficial" from a medical or healthcare perspective.[5] The example of the electronic patient file may illustrate this point: from a medical or healthcare point of view it would be more than advisable to store all available patient data in the electronic patient file, not only diagnostic and

---

[3]   BVerfG, Jdg of 8 March 1972 – 2 BvR 28/71, NJW 1972, 1123, 1124.
[4]   BVerfG, Jdg of 8 March 1972 – 2 BvR 28/71, NJW 1972, 1123, 1124.
[5]   Cf Benedikt Buchner, 'Die Vertraulichkeit der Arzt-Patienten-Beziehung – Doppelt geschützt hält besser?' in Christian Katzenmeier (ed), *Festschrift für Dieter Hart* (Springer 2020), 49, 53.

therapy data but also medication plan and emergency information. However, the legal starting point in this (and similar constellations) is always the will of the patient, and it is the patient who decides whether or not to accept this kind of data processing.[6]

MEDICAL CONFIDENTIALITY

The very first basis in German law for privacy in the health sector is medical confidentiality as a core element of professional ethics.

Key Sources of the Duty of Medical Confidentiality

In German law, the duty of medical confidentiality has its legal basis in medical professional law on the one hand, and in criminal law on the other.

In professional law, medical confidentiality is regulated by § 9 (1) sent. 1 of the Professional Code of Conduct (MBO-Ä) in the version of the Codes of Conduct of the respective State Medical Associations. According to this, doctors must "keep confidential anything that has been revealed or become known to them in their capacity as physicians – even after the decease of the patient".

In addition, medical confidentiality is protected by the Criminal Code. According to § 203 (1) No. 1 StGB

> whoever unlawfully discloses another's secret, in particular a secret relating to that person's personal sphere of life or a business or trade secret which was revealed or otherwise made known to them in their capacity as a physician, dentist, veterinarian, pharmacist or member of another healthcare profession which requires state-regulated training to engage in the profession or to use the professional title ... incurs a penalty of imprisonment for a term not exceeding one year or a fine.

Persons Bound by the Duty of Confidentiality

The duty of medical confidentiality applies first of all to doctors in private practices and employed doctors.[7] However, § 203 (1) No. 1 StGB also refers to members of other healthcare professions which require state-regulated training to engage in the profession or to use the professional title, such as psychotherapists, midwifes, masseurs or physiotherapists.[8] Medical assistants such

---

[6] For the electronic patient file see § 344 SGB V.

[7] Bert-Sebastian Dörfer in Carsten Dochow et al, *Datenschutz in der ärztlichen Praxis* (1st edn, Deutscher Ärzteverlag 2019), chapter 11.4.

[8] Christoph Knauer and Johannes Brose in Andreas Spickhoff (ed), *Medizinrecht* (4th edn, C. H. Beck 2022), StGB § 203 No 12.

as doctor's receptionists, medical-technical assistants or persons employed by doctors for vocational preparation purposes, for example trainees or medical students, are also bound by medical confidentiality (§ 203 (4) sent. 1, § 203 (3) sent. 1 StGB).[9] Last but not least, § 203 (4) sent. 1, § 203 (3) sent. 2 StGB also cover persons involved in the work of doctors by providing external services, such as accounting, file archiving and in particular IT services.

Legal Duties of Confidentiality

Medical confidentiality is on principle comprehensively applicable, for example also with respect to relatives of the physician or after the decease of the patient. Private secrets as defined by § 203 StGB include all particulars which are only known to a certain, restricted number of persons and which the person concerned has a legitimate interest not to disclose. These include in particular:

- the identity of the patient
- the fact that the patient is undergoing medical treatment
- specific information about the treatment or
- the personal, professional or financial circumstances of the patient.

The information must have been disclosed to the doctor in his or her capacity as a physician; there must be an inherent connection between the information and the provision of medical care.[10] Already the attempt of a patient to contact a physician is subject to medical confidentiality, even if a treatment relationship has not been established.[11]

§ 9 (1) sent. 2 MBO-Ä lists as examples of sources of information which are subject to medical confidentiality "written communications from the patient, records concerning patients, X-ray images and other examination findings".

Medical confidentiality is procedurally protected by a right to refuse testimony under § 53 (1) no. 3 StPO (Code of Criminal Procedure) and a prohibition of seizure under § 97 StPO. In accordance with these provisions, physicians are entitled to refuse to testify about facts falling under § 203 StGB and documents relating to the doctor-patient relationship may not be seized from a physician.

---

[9]   Knauer and Brose (n 8), StGB § 203 No 21.
[10]   Klaus Ulsenheimer in Adolf Laufs and Bernd-Rüdiger Kern/Martin Rehborn (eds), *Handbuch des Arztrechts* (5th ed, C. H. Beck 2019), § 140 No 8.
[11]   Dörfer (n 7) chapter 11.3.

DATA PROTECTION LAW

The second key source of privacy in the health sector, besides medical confidentiality, is data protection law. The legal starting point for any data processing and thus also data processing in healthcare is the GDPR. However, the comprehensive applicability of the GDPR is limited by numerous opening clauses in the field of health data protection, in particular in Article 9 (2) lit. h and lit. I, and Article 9 (4) GDPR, which leave a wide scope for national regulation, and which the German legislator has made extensive use of in national law.

The Relationship of Data Protection Law and Medical Confidentiality

As has already been mentioned above, the relationship of data protection law and medical confidentiality in German law has still not been conclusively determined. According to § 1 (2) sent. 2 BDSG (Federal Data Protection Act) the "duty to observe the legal obligation of maintaining secrecy or professional or special official confidentiality not based on legal provisions shall remain unaffected". One such "duty to maintain professional confidentiality" is medical confidentiality, which thus remains "unaffected" by data protection regulations.

The specific meaning of this is interpreted in different ways by academic literature and case law. Sometimes, a "precedence" of medical confidentiality over data protection regulations is referred to, leading to the conclusion that compliance with medical confidentiality equals compliance with the requirements of data protection.[12] According to another point of view, the interaction of data protection and medical confidentiality falls under the so-called two-barriers-principle, which means that both regulatory systems apply independently so that any processing of data is subject to data protection law as well as medical confidentiality.[13] A two-stage examination is thus required and the processing of data will only be deemed lawful if both the requirements of

---

[12] See for example Hans-Dieter Lippert in Rudolf Ratzel, Hans-Dieter Lippert and Jens Prütting, *Kommentar zur (Muster-)Berufsordnung für die in Deutschland tätigen Ärztinnen und Ärzte – MBO-Ä 1997* (7th edn, Springer 2018), § 9 No 82; Christoph Gusy/Johannes Eichenhofer in Heinrich Amadeus Wolff/Stefan Brink (eds), *BeckOK Datenschutzrecht* (42th edn, C. H. Beck 2021), BDSG § 1 No 83; Wronka, 'Datenschutzrechtliche Aspekte des 'neuen' § 203 StGB' (2017), RDV 129, 131.

[13] As has been argued, for example, by Carsten Dochow, 'Unterscheidung und Verhältnis von Gesundheitsdatenschutz und ärztlicher Schweigepflicht (Teil 2)' (2019), MedR 363, 366; Jürgen Kühling, 'Datenschutz im Gesundheitswesen' (2019), MedR 611, 619; Weichert (n 2) DS-GVO Art. 9 No 146.

data protection law and those based on the principles of medical confidentiality are complied with.

Common Features of Data Protection Law and Medical Confidentiality

In many cases, the coexistence of data protection law and medical confidentiality does not cause any problems since the protective purpose and basic regulatory approach of the two regulatory regimes are essentially the same.[14]

As a common starting point, the basic principle of data protection as well as medical confidentiality is that patient data may not be freely communicated. Medical professional law obliges doctors to "remain silent" about anything that has become known to them in their capacity as physicians and, similarly, the processing of personal data is in principle prohibited by data protection law (Article 6 (1) GDPR and Article 9 (1) GDPR). However, under both legal regimes, this principle of prohibition is only a starting point since the disclosure of patient data is generally permitted if provided for by law or if the patient has consented to it. As a general guidance which applies irrespective of the regulatory regime, it may be noted that any communication required for the successful treatment outcome aimed at in the specific case is permitted and does not require the explicit consent of the respective patient. In general, this will either be provided for by a statutory exemption or the disclosure may at least be legitimated by the implied or presumed consent of the patient.[15]

Differences Between Data Protection Law and Medical Confidentiality – The Example of Consent

The parallels between data protection law and medical confidentiality continue with regard to consent as a legitimate basis for the disclosure of data. The consent of the person concerned has always been of central importance under both regulatory regimes. In data protection law, consent is the primary basis for the lawful processing of data as provided by Article 6 (1) lit. a and Article 9 (2) lit. a GDPR. With regard to medical confidentiality, § 9 (2) MBO-Ä expressly provides that a physician is entitled to disclose patient data insofar as he or she has been released from the obligation of medical confidentiality. The underlying concept in both cases is that the will of the patient should determine how his or her data is handled.

Differences between data protection law and medical confidentiality become apparent, however, where the specific requirements of valid consent

---

[14]   Cf Buchner (n 5) 51.
[15]   Buchner (n 5) 55.

are concerned. According to data protection law standards, consent must be given "explicitly" in order to be valid, as provided by Article 9 (2) lit. a GDPR. In contrast, the principles of medical confidentiality provide that valid consent can also be implied. If one presumes, in accordance with the two-barriers-principle, that both the requirements of data protection law as well as the requirements of medical confidentiality have to be complied with,[16] the stricter requirement, that is, the "explicitness" required by the principles of data protection law, would take precedence.

It appears more convincing, however, at least where patient data is processed exclusively for purposes of medical treatment, to primarily base the effectiveness of consent only on the principles of medical confidentiality. This means that the consent of a patient to the processing of data does not always have to be explicit, as required by the stricter provisions of data protection law but may be implied or presumed in accordance with the principles of medical confidentiality, where data is passed from one physician to another. Insofar, a strict two-barriers-principle is ultimately not applied.

EXCEPTIONS TO CONFIDENTIALITY

As noted before, the starting point for data protection law as well as medical confidentiality is the requirement that patient data must not be freely communicated. The disclosure of patient data in accordance with the principles of medical confidentiality is only permissible if provided for by law or if the patient has consented to it. The same basic principle applies with regard to data protection law.

Statutory Exceptions

A violation of the duty of medical confidentiality is generally excluded if the physician is required to disclose the patient data. § 9 (2) sent. 2 MBO-Ä explicitly states that statutory obligations of disclosure and notification are exempt from the duty of confidentiality.

Provisions which stipulate a duty of the physician to disclose patient data can be found in various laws and regulations, from specific health-related laws such as the Infection Protection Act, to social law provisions, up to general law such as criminal law. Since the beginning of the COVID-19 pandemic, in particular the provisions of the Infection Protection Act (IfSG), which provide reporting requirements for certain diseases and the detection of pathogens, inter alia COVID-19, have become of central importance in this respect. In

---

[16] See Weichert (n 2) DS-GVO Art. 9 No 49; Dochow (n 13) 365.

statutory health insurance law, the requirement to notify health insurance funds about the causes of diseases and injuries to health caused by third parties (§ 294a SGB V) or the requirement of data transmission for accounting purposes to Associations of Statutory Health Insurance Physicians (§ 295 SGB V) are relevant examples. A further example for reporting requirements can be found in §§ 138, 139 StGB, which stipulate an obligation of the physician to report the risk of an impending criminal offence of a particularly serious nature.

Specific provisions which do not require but allow doctors to disclose patient data can be found in the State Hospital Acts of the individual Federal States. Most Federal States have adopted more or less detailed specific provisions on data protection in hospitals. The Cancer Registry Acts of the individual Federal States also allow for or require the reporting of tumour diseases to so-called trust centres (Vertrauensstellen), which then record pseudonymised patient data in the cancer registries. Moreover, some State laws contain provisions enabling registered psychiatrists and psychologists to pass on patient data without consent, for purposes of support and protection in cases of mental illness, to third parties such as courts or road traffic authorities.

Although the GDPR takes precedence over national legislation, the national exemptions for data processing continue to apply, as provided for by the opening clauses of Article 9 (2) lit. h and lit. I, and Article 9 (4) GDPR. Provisions of the State Hospital Acts for example, which provide for a processing of patient data for the fulfilment of the treatment contract, including documentation requirements, social assistance, and advice to caregivers of patients, and accounting purposes, come under the opening clause of Article 9 (2) lit. h GDPR. Exemptions of State Hospital Acts providing for data processing for purposes of quality assurance in inpatient care or the detection, prevention or control of hospital infections can fall under Article 9 (2) lit. h as well as lit. i GDPR. Within the framework of exemptions for Member State legislation, the principle of necessity must always be observed to comply with the requirements of the GDPR. If the purposes listed in Article 9 (2) lit. h and lit. I GDPR can be achieved with pseudonymised or even anonymised data, the processing of personal data is not permitted to this extent. The State hospital acts, for example, have already taken these requirements into account, either by explicitly providing for the anonymisation and pseudonymisation of patient data or, at least, by establishing the principle of necessity.[17]

According to the predominant view, the churches' right to self-administration guaranteed by Article 140 Basic Law (GG) in conjunction with Article

---

[17]   Benedikt Buchner and Simon Schwichtenberg, 'Gesundheitsdatenschutz unter der Datenschutz-Grundverordnung' (2016), GuP 218, 222.

137 (3) Weimar Constitution (WRV) implies that the Federal and State Data Protection Acts do not apply to church organisations.[18] This constitutional status is also "respected" by the GDPR (Recital 165 GDPR), which stipulates in Article 91 (1) GDPR that churches which apply comprehensive data protection rules at the time of entry into force of the GDPR may continue to apply these rules "provided that they are brought into line with this Regulation". By exercising its right to self-administration, the Protestant Church in Germany has fulfilled the regulatory task set by Article 91 (1) GDPR through the "Data Protection Act of the Protestant Church in Germany" (DSG-EKD) of 15 November 2017, thus bringing its regulations for data processing in the church and diaconal sector into line with the GDPR. The same applies to the Catholic Church, which has also complied with the requirements of the GDPR by adapting existing regulations in the "Church Data Protection Act" (KDG), which came into force in all German (arch)dioceses on 25 May 2018.

Consent

In the absence of a statutory exemption, the lawfulness of a disclosure of patient data depends on whether the patient has consented to such a disclosure by releasing the physician from the duty of confidentiality. According to § 9 (2) MBO-Ä, a physician is entitled to disclose patient data if he or she has been released from medical confidentiality. The consent of the patient is also a justification under § 203 StGB as well as a statutory exemption under data protection law. The underlying general idea is that it should primarily be the patient who decides what is to be done with his or her data.

The consent of the patient is above all of central importance when the disclosure of patient data is not related to the fulfilment of the actual treatment contract, but data is transmitted for other purposes to third parties such as public authorities or companies. If no statutory exemption is applicable, the physician may only disclose data with the consent of the patient concerned. The patient has to consent to the disclosure of his or her data for example in case of requests of private insurance companies according to § 213 VVG (Insurance Contract Act) or disclosure of information about a hospital stay to third parties (e.g. visitors).

Since medical confidentiality is also applicable in the relationship between physicians, the disclosure of patient data from one physician to another – if no statutory exemption applies – depends, again, on the consent of the patient concerned. § 9 (5) MBO-Ä emphasises the central importance of the patient's

---

[18]   Cf. Tobias Herbst in Jürgen Kühling and Benedikt Buchner (eds), *DS-GVO/BDSG* (3rd edn, C. H. Beck 2020), DS-GVO Art. 91 No 22.

wishes: physicians who treat a patient simultaneously or consecutively are only mutually released from the obligation of medical confidentiality "insofar as the patient's informed consent has been given or can be assumed". Frequently, the implicit (tacit) consent of patients is assumed to legitimise the disclosure of data. The patient does not explicitly consent to the disclosure of data, rather, consent is expressed through conclusive behaviour. Such implicit consent to an exchange of data between the physicians involved can generally be assumed if the exchange of data is clearly a prerequisite for successful treatment.[19]

If a patient is unable to give his explicit or implicit (tacit) consent, for example in emergency cases because of unconsciousness, the disclosure of data may be based on the presumed consent of the patient by way of exception. Consent may be presumed if the disclosure of data is in the interest of the patient or if he or she has consented to a similar disclosure of data before. An emergency physician would thus be permitted to disclose date to the physician responsible for subsequent treatment. The disclosure of information to non-medical third parties, in particular close relatives, can also be based on the presumed consent of the patient.

Minors can also effectively consent to the processing of their data and release the physician from the obligation of medical confidentiality if they have the required capacity of understanding. This has to be assessed in the individual case and depends on the minor's ability to act autonomously and responsibly as well as on the kind and purpose of the actual disclosure of data. It has been proposed to base the capacity of understanding on certain age requirements, for example, 14 of 15 years. Such age requirements may provide some orientation; however, they do not release the physician from his or her duty to assess the capacity of understanding of a minor in the individual case.[20]

The very first prerequisite for consent to be considered valid is that it must be freely given. In healthcare, however, patients frequently have no real choice. Whether consent is freely given appears doubtful in emergency situations, but also in underserved rural areas or where highly specialised physicians are consulted. In such cases, the individual concerned will frequently feel, at least subjectively, that he or she is left with no choice and cannot make an autonomous and self-determined decision about consenting to the processing of data.[21]

With regard to a release from the obligation of medical confidentiality vis-à-vis an insurance company, the German Federal Constitutional Court has ruled that such consent will be invalid if it is "virtually non-negotiable"

---

[19] Ulsenheimer (n 10) § 145 No 3.
[20] Benedikt Buchner in Benedikt Buchner (ed), *Datenschutz im Gesundheitswesen* (30th edn, AOK Verlag 2022), chapter A/3.2.7.
[21] This view has also been taken by the Federal Social Court (BSG), Jdg of 10 December 2008 – B 6 KA 37/07 R, MedR 2009, 685.

and the individual concerned is required to consent to the disclosure of his or her personal data to an unreasonable extent.[22] The Federal Constitutional Court makes it clear that a release from confidentiality cannot be seen as an expression of a free and autonomous decision of the individual concerned about the processing of his or her personal data in constellations which are characterised by a considerable "imbalance of negotiating power" between the parties. If, as in this case, the person concerned is dependent on the conclusion of a contract and the conditions are "virtually non-negotiable", the Federal Constitutional Court takes the view that it cannot be reconciled with the right to informational self-determination if the person concerned has to consent to an almost unrestricted processing of sensitive health data of any relevance to the insurance case. The court does not go as far as to question the legitimacy of consent altogether, not even where there is an imbalance of negotiating power between the parties, however, it rightly demands that consent clauses must not be too broad, but that consent to data processing should be restricted to the extent required by the contract.[23]

Other Healthcare Personnel and External Service Providers

The sharing of knowledge with professional assistants such as medical practice or hospital staff (§ 203 (3) sent. 1 StGB) is not deemed disclosure as defined by § 203 StGB. On the contrary, medical confidentiality also applies when patient data is passed from one physician to another since the disclosure of patient data is not lawful simply because the other physician as recipient of the data is also bound by the duty of medical confidentiality.[24] However, frequently, the disclosure of data from one physician to another can be based on the implied or presumed consent of the patient.

When medical practices, hospitals or other healthcare facilities employ an external service provider (for example, for accounting, archiving or IT maintenance purposes), this frequently implies the disclosure of personal data to this external provider. According to the former version of § 203 StGB, such a disclosure of data to external service providers was prohibited, unless the patient concerned had consented to it. With the amendment of § 203 StGB in 2017, physicians may now disclose patients' data without their consent not only to professional assistants under the terms of § 203 (3) StGB, but also to other persons who are involved in the work of physicians, "to the extent that

---

[22]   BVerfG, Jdg of 23 October 2006, 1 BvR 2027/02, MedR 2007, 351.
[23]   See also Benedikt Buchner and Jürgen Kühling in Jürgen Kühling and Benedikt Buchner (eds), *DS-GVO/BDSG* (3rd edn, C. H. Beck 2020), DS-GVO Art. 7 No 42 ff.
[24]   Lippert (n 12) § 9 No 27.

this is necessary in order to be able to use the services rendered by these other involved persons". Services as defined by § 203 (3) sent. 2 StGB include inter alia typing, accounting and telephone answering services, file archiving or IT support.[25] This extension of § 203 StGB has also been translated into medical professional law by § 9 (4) MBO-Ä. Thus, unlike before, the involvement of external service providers does no longer require the consent of the patients concerned.

Likewise, from the point of view of data protection law, the involvement of external service providers does not require the consent of the patient either if the external service provider is classified as a processor in accordance with Article 28 GDPR. This requires (according to the German interpretation of Article 28 GDPR) that the service provider – as a processor – is bound by the instructions of the healthcare provider and is left with no scope of discretion or decision-making in the processing of data.[26]

Research

When patient data is used for research purposes, both the provisions of data protection law and the requirements of medical confidentiality have to be complied with, and insofar, the two-barriers principle is again applicable.

Data processing for research purposes has been accorded a privileged status by data protection law in various respects. Article 9 (2) lit. j GDPR provides for exemptions in national law from the general prohibition of processing sensitive personal data under the terms of Article 9 GDPR if data processing is required for scientific research purposes. The German legislator has made use of this regulatory scope by providing an exemption in § 27 (1) sent. 1 BDSG with a clause aimed at a balancing of interests, which provides for a processing of health data without consent if the processing is necessary for research purposes "and the interests of the controller in processing substantially outweigh those of the data subject in not processing the data". In addition, such a processing of data requires a number of protective measures, which have been regulated under § 27 (1) sent. 2 and § 27 (3) BDSG.

It should be noted that § 27 BDSG – as a kind of basic rule – is not applicable where sector-specific regulations on data processing for research purposes apply, for example social law provisions or medial law provisions such as the Medicinal Products Act (AMG), the Genetic Diagnostics Act (GenDG) or the Transplantation Act (TPG). Sector-specific regulations of the Cancer Registry

---

[25] BT-Dr. 18/11936, p. 22.
[26] Mario Martini in Boris Paal and Daniel Pauly (eds), *DS-GVO/BDSG* (3rd edn, C. H. Beck 2021), DS-GVO Art. 28 No 2.

Acts and the State Hospital Acts also take precedence insofar as they contain specific provisions on data processing for research purposes.

All these sector-specific provisions may also be classified as exemptions in accordance with § 203 StGB, that is, they also legitimate the disclosure of patients' secrets in accordance with the principles of medical confidentiality. The reason for this is that these provisions – unlike the general exemption provided for research data by § 27 BDSG – have been adopted with a view to the confidential nature of data in the doctor-patient relationship and address the processing of data typically protected by medical confidentiality.[27]

Prevention of Harm to Others

Under German law, the physician is also entitled to disclose patient data if there is an immediate danger to life or limb and this danger can only be averted by a violation of medical confidentiality. § 34 StGB assumes a so-called necessity of justification, which can exclude an unlawful violation of medical confidentiality, for such a constellation.

A typical example for a situation where such a necessity of justification can be assumed is the case where a physician informs the life partner of a patient about the latter's life-threatening transmissable disease. In principle, the medical duty of confidentiality also exists vis-à-vis the family or partner of a patient. However, the physician may disregard this duty if this is necessary to protect the life or health of third parties. However, in such constellations, the physician is generally expected first to inform the patient about his or her state of health and the corresponding dangers and to strive to induce the patient to inform his or her life partner. Only if an attempt to persuade the patient is unsuccessful or manifestly pointless due to the unreasonableness of the patient or the nature of the disease, the physician is no longer bound by the duty of confidentiality.

A violation of medical confidentiality is also justified if a paediatrician informs the youth welfare office about serious indications of possible child abuse. The Federal legislator has adopted a regulation providing for advice and the transmission of information in cases where the welfare of a child is endangered: in accordance with § 4 KKG (Child Protection Cooperation Act), the youth welfare office may be informed if harm to the well-being of a child cannot be prevented in any other way (discussion of the situation; encouraging the acceptance of help) and the involvement of the youth welfare office is con-

---

[27] Christian Dierks et al, 'Lösungsvorschläge für ein neues Gesundheitsforschungs-datenschutzrecht in Bund und Ländern', Legal expertise 2019, p. 76; available at www .dierks.company/publications/.

sidered necessary. In such constellations, it is of particular importance that the physician who has observed indications for abuse, neglect or sexual abuse of a child carefully documents if and based on which considerations he or she has decided to report these to the youth welfare office.[28] Some Federal States have also regulated the transmission of information in cases of potential harm to the well-being of children in State acts, for example in Bavaria where physicians who have noticed serious indications of child abuse or neglect are obliged to report their suspicion to the youth welfare office.

Investigating Authorities (Police, Public Prosecutor's Office)

Physicians are also bound by medical confidentiality in policy investigations and preliminary proceedings. The German Code of Criminal Procedure (StPO) provides for a right to refuse testimony and a prohibition of seizure to protect patients' secrets. The mere fact that the police or the public prosecutor's office have instigated investigations cannot justify a breach of medical confidentiality. The disclosure of data may be permissible under exceptional circumstances if there is an immediate danger to life or limb and this danger cannot be averted in any other way.[29] If the Police is looking for a person suspected of having committed a serious crime and likely to commit further acts of violence, a physician may inform the police about the fact that the person has been one of his or her patients and whether certain data are available.

A breach of medical confidentiality is also possible in accordance with §§ 138, 139 StGB, which provide for a duty to report planned crimes which also applies to physicians where particularly serious criminal offences are concerned (e.g. murder, homicide, kidnapping for ransom and hostage-taking).[30]

In accordance with § 32 (1) BMG, there is also a reporting obligation for the admission to a hospital or a care facility if a person has not been registered as resident in Germany and has stayed in the facility for more than three months. Also, these facilities have to provide information to the competent authorities if this is "required in order to avert a substantial and immediate danger, to prosecute criminal offences or to ascertain the fate of missing persons and accident victims in the individual case".

---

[28]   Gert Jacobi et al, 'Misshandlung und Vernachlässigung von Kindern – Diagnose und Vorgehen' (2010), Dtsch Arztebl Int 107(13), 231, 238.

[29]   So-called necessity of justification as defined by § 34 StGB.

[30]   Maren Pollmann in Benedikt Buchner (ed), *Datenschutz im Gesundheitswesen* (30th edn, AOK Verlag 2022), chapter C/3.1.

Media

With respect to media requesting information from healthcare facilities, the challenge lies in balancing the personal rights of patients against the freedom of the press and information. Again, the basic rule is that health data must not be disclosed. Medical confidentiality applies even where general information, such as whether a certain person has been admitted and treated after an accident, is concerned since the identity of the patient and the fact that someone is undergoing medical treatment are also confidential. If the person concerned has not consented, the disclosure of data would be unlawful.

CONFIDENTIALITY AND GENETICS

In German law, the processing of genetic data is regulated by a specific act, the Genetic Diagnostics Act (GenDG). According to § 1 GenDG, the requirements for genetic diagnostics and genetic analyses as well as for the use of genetic samples and data are to be regulated in order to prevent discrimination based of genetic traits. In view of the developments in human genome research, the legislator felt compelled to strengthen the individual's right to self-determination in particular with respect to the processing of genetic data. This intention is based on the conviction that genetic data are particularly sensitive personal data as genetic information obtained through genetic examination retains its importance for long periods of time, is associated with a "high predictive potential" and may also disclose information about third parties (relatives) in the individual case.[31]

§ 4 GenDG stipulates a general prohibition of discrimination according to which nobody may be discriminated because of genetic traits, because he or she has undergone or not undergone a genetic examination or analysis or because of the result of such an examination or analysis. According to § 7 GenDG, genetic examinations and analyses must be performed by physicians. § 8 GenDG stipulates that a genetic examination or analysis can only take place if the person concerned has given his or her explicit written consent. A person who is unable to understand the nature, significance and consequences of the genetic examination, and to make a corresponding decision, may only undergo a genetic examination under very restricted circumstances as defined in detail by § 14 GenDG.

Particularly controversial is the question of whether a physician may inform relatives of his patient, diagnosed with a genetic disease, if the relatives could possibly also be affected by this genetic disease. This question becomes par-

---

[31] BT-Drs. 16/10532, p. 1.

ticularly relevant if early information and treatment could alleviate or even prevent the relatives' disease. In such a constellation, a breach of medical confidentiality under § 34 StGB again might be considered. In connection with genetic data, however, the special provision of § 10 (3) sent. 4 GenDG must then be taken into account. It is argued that the German legislator, when enacting this provision, had precisely the situation described here in mind – and in this respect decided in favour of strict protection of genetic data, even accepting corresponding disadvantages for the patient's relatives. This view is justified primarily by the "special status" of genetic data. In detail, however, much is disputed. For example, an exception to the duty of confidentiality is demanded if the patient manifestly abuses his or her right to confidentiality by refusing to inform relatives whose health is at considerable risk.[32]

RIGHTS OF DATA SUBJECTS, IN PARTICULAR RIGHT OF ACCESS TO INFORMATION

Data protection law, medical professional law and civil law grant patients whose data are processed a number of so-called rights of data subjects, for example rights of access, notification and deletion. These are to ensure that patients are not degraded to mere "objects" of data processing and enable them not only to perceive which of their patient data are being processed, but also, where possible, to effectively control the processing.[33]

The most important right for the patient is the right of access, which is not restricted to access to medical records, but also grants patients the right to obtain a copy of their medical records.[34] According to established case law, the right to self-determination and the personal dignity of patients require that they are given access to their medical records – without having to prove a particular legal interest.[35] This corresponds to the provision of § 630g BGB, which requires the physician to permit the patient on request "to inspect the complete medical records concerning him/her without delay". And also under

---

[32] For details, see Benedikt Kart, Anita Hennig, Susanne A. Schneider and Andreas Spickhoff, 'Information potentiell betroffener Verwandter durch den Arzt im Rahmen der Gendiagnostik' (2021), MedR 775, 778.

[33] Buchner (n 20) chapter A/4.

[34] Christian Katzenmeier in Adolfs Laufs, Christian Katzenmeier and Volker Lipp, *Arztrecht* (8th edn, C. H. Beck 2021), chapter IX No 66; under data protection law, Art. 15(3) sent. 1 GDPR contains a similar provision requiring the controller to "provide a copy of the personal data undergoing processing".

[35] BGH, Jdg of 23 November 1982 – VI ZR 177/81, MedR 1983, 65; BVerfG, Jdg of 16 September 1998 – 1 BvR 1130/98, MedR 1999, 1777.

professional law, the physician is obliged to provide access to medical records in accordance with § 10 Abs. 2 S. 1 MBO-Ä.

General data protection law provides for the right of access under Art. 15 GDPR. This right is perceived as the fundamental data protection right for data subjects. The individual has the right to know "who knows what when and at which occasion about (him)".[36] The right of access is to enable individuals to make use of their right to informational self-determination as a right to control and to request the deletion or correction of their data if necessary.[37]

According to Article 12 (5) GDPR, the patient can in principle exercise his or her right of access – and also obtain a copy of his or her record – free of charge. Under German law, § 630g (2) sent. 2 BGB, however, stipulates that the patient has to "reimburse to the treating party the costs incurred" when electronic copies of the medical record are requested. § 10 (2) sent. 2 MBO-Ä also refers to "copies of the documents in return for reimbursement of the costs".

SANCTIONS

If patient data are disclosed without authorisation, a number of sanctions are possible under German law or European data protection law: claims for damages, fines or even imprisonment, as well as sanctions under professional law.

According to Article 82 GDPR, any person can claim compensation for material or non-material damage suffered as a result of an infringement of the provisions of the GDPR. If the physician has concluded a treatment contract with the patient, contractual claims for damages in accordance with the provisions of BGB may also apply. Moreover, infringements of data protection provisions may also result in the imposition of fines or imprisonment (Article 83 DSGVO, § 42 BDSG).

A violation of medical confidentiality is subject to a fine or imprisonment up to one year in accordance with § 203 (1) StGB. Professional law also provides penalties for infringements of medical confidentiality. The corresponding penalties are laid down in the healthcare professions acts of the Federal States. Depending on the respective State act, penalties may include inter alia fines or even prohibition from practice.

---

[36] See the renowned judgment of the Federal Constitutional Court of 1983: BVerfG, Jdg of 15 December 1983 – 1 BvR 209/83, BVerfGE 65, 1.

[37] Buchner (n 20) chapter A/4.3.1.

5.   Japanese law of privacy and health

Eiji Maruyama

GENERAL INTRODUCTION

The foundation of Japanese law was established on the basis of German and French laws whose reception began in the last quarter of the nineteenth century. Although the impact of American law after the World War II has been significant, Japanese law still belongs to the continental legal system, having the Civil Code that was originally enacted in 1896.

However, the matters of confidentiality and personal data protection are largely regulated by statutes including the Penal Code, the laws regulating the qualification and status of medical personnel and the personal information protection legislation.

THE ETHICAL BASIS OF CONFIDENTIALITY

The Hippocratic Oath proclaimed, "Whatever I see or hear, professionally or privately, which ought not to be divulged, I will keep secret and tell no one."[1] The World Medical Association's Declaration of Geneva contains the statement, "I will respect the secrets that are confided in me, even after the patient has died,"[2] and the Japanese Medical Association affirmatively posts it on its website.[3]

THE PRACTICAL BASIS OF CONFIDENTIALITY

In Japan, like other countries, it is often pointed out that the patient, if ensured the security of confidentiality of her/his communication with doctors, is able to

---

[1]   *Hippocratic Writings*, translated by J. Chadwick and W. N. Mann (Penguin Books 1950).

[2]   See www.wma.net/policies-post/wma-declaration-of-geneva/ (last visited 15 December 2022).

[3]   See www.med.or.jp/doctor/international/wma/geneva.html (last visited 15 December 2022).

visit a clinic or hospital and talk about her/his health problem with the doctor with no concern for unwanted leakage of her/his private physical and mental information.[4]

KEY SOURCES OF THE DUTY OF CONFIDENTIALITY

Section 134 of the Penal Code[5] prohibits a physician, pharmacist, or midwife from disclosing, without justifiable cause, another person's confidential information which has come to be known in the course of her/his service with the penalty of imprisonment with work for not more than six months or a fine of not more than 100,000 yen.

With respect to the other medical personnel, every law regulating their qualification and status has similar provisions prohibiting and penalizing the unjustifiable disclosure of the patient's confidential information. For example, section 19 of the Act on Clinical Laboratory Technicians[6] provides that a clinical laboratory technician must not leak any secrets which the clinical laboratory technician came to know in the course of services without legitimate grounds. Section 23 of the act provides that a person who violated the section 19 is punished by a fine of not more than 500,000 yen.

PERSONS BOUND BY THE DUTY OF CONFIDENTIALITY

All medical professional and personnel must abide by the duty of confidentiality of the patient's confidential information.

LEGAL DUTIES OF CONFIDENTIALITY

See the description in the section "Key sources of the duty of confidentiality," *supra*.

---

4   Y. Noda, *Ijihou Jo* [*Medical Law Part I*] (Seirin Shoin 1984) 193.

5   Its English translation can be found at the following website, although the English translation included in this chapter does not always follow that translation. www.japaneselawtranslation.go.jp/en/laws/view/3581 (last visited 16 December 2022).

6   Its English translation can be found at www.japaneselawtranslation.go.jp/en/laws/view/2956 (last visited 16 December 2022).

DATA PROTECTION LAW

Overview

In Japan, establishment of the personal information protection system started in the local government bodies in the 1970s. With respect to the national government, there had been no general personal information protection legislation until May 2003, when Act on the Protection of Personal Information[7] (hereinafter "APPI"), Act on the Protection of Personal Information Held by Administrative Organs[8] (hereinafter "APPIAO") and Act on the Protection of Personal Information Held by Incorporated Administrative Agencies[9] (hereinafter "APPIIAA") were enacted under the major influence of the 1980 OECD Guidelines governing the Protection of Privacy and Transborder Flows of Personal Data.

After the first three chapters of APPI containing general provisions, the responsibilities of national and local governments and the basic policies of personal information protection were implemented at the time of their promulgation, these three Acts (APPI, APPIAO and APPIIAA) were brought into full force in April 2005. The latter part (chapter 4 through chapter 6) of APPI, when enacted in 2003, provided for the obligations of private business operators processing personal information and penalties for their violations. APPIAO and APPIIAA regulated the processing of personal information in national government bodies and independent national administrative agencies, respectively.

In May 2021, major structural change was made of Japanese personal information protection legislation. This change merged both APPIAO and APPIIAA into the revised APPI in April 2022 (APPIAO and APPIIAA were repealed). Thereafter APPI governs the personal information protection in public as well as private sectors at the national level. In April 2023, the application of APPI will be further extended to local governments and independent local administrative agencies.

Although the revised APPI provides for different sets of rules for private and public sectors, academic institutions like universities and medical institutions like hospitals have come to be regulated similarly, irrespective of whether

---

[7]   The English translation of the Act amended as of 2015 is available at www.japaneselawtranslation.go.jp/en/laws/view/2781 (last visited 16 December 2022). The original 2003 Act seems unable to be read on the Internet.

[8]   The English translation of the Act amended as of 2016 is available at www.japaneselawtranslation.go.jp/en/laws/view/3152 (last visited 16 December 2022).

[9]   The English translation of the Act amended as of 2016 is available at www.japaneselawtranslation.go.jp/en/laws/view/3397 (last visited 16 December 2022).

national, municipal or private, and subject to the same rules provided for the private sector operators. Considering this treatment of all academic and medical institutions as private under the revised APPI, and in view of the fact that legal discussion of medical privacy so far has been centred around APPI, I will write the following explanations with APPI requirements in mind. For convenience, the section numbers of APPI implemented from April 2023 are shown in the following text.

With respect to processing personal information in the medical and nursing care field, the Personal Information Protection Commission and the Ministry of Health, Labor and Welfare issued in 2017 and revised in 2022 and 2023 the Guidance for the Appropriate Processing of Personal Information in the Operators Providing Medical and Nursing Care (hereinafter "MHLW Guidance").[10] This Guidance, like its predecessor entitled "the Guidelines for the Appropriate Processing of Personal Information in the Operators Providing Medical and Nursing Care 2004," was drafted generally based on and following the provisions of APPI.

KEY PROVISIONS OF APPI

Purpose

Section 1 of APPI provides that it aims to protect the rights and interests of the individual (the person who is the subject of personal information) while caring about the utility of personal information. In order to achieve the aim, emphasis is placed on ensuring the transparency and involvement of the individual in the processing of personal information and the purpose of the use of personal information is made a pivotal concept in many of its provisions.

Specification of the Utilization Purpose

Section 17 provides that an operator that processes personal information (either a natural or a legal person, excluding central or local governmental bodies or agencies, that maintains personal information databases, either computerized or not, for business use) (hereinafter "processing operator") shall, in processing personal information, specify the purpose of utilizing the personal information (hereinafter "utilization purpose") as explicitly as possible. Those persons, either natural or legal, that establish and operate clinics or hospitals

---

[10] See www.mhlw.go.jp/content/001120905.pdf (last visited 11 September 2023) (available only in Japanese).

are treated as processing operators as they necessarily maintain databases of, for example, the patients' medical record.

Notice or Publication of the Utilization Purpose

Section 21 provides that a processing operator, having collected personal information, shall promptly inform the individual of or publish its utilization purpose, except where the purpose has already been published.

With respect to processing personal information in medical and nursing care field, the MHLW Guidance states, in comments on sections 18 and 21 of APPI at pp. 25–26, 30, that the medical or nursing care operator shall publish the utilization purposes in such a way as posting a notice within the hospitals, clinics or institutions, and, if practicable, on their website. The purposes suggested by the Guidance, as those having general applicability, includes not only those necessary for providing medical or nursing care to the patient or resident within and without the facility but also those necessary for fees collection (such as sending the bill to third-party payers), prevention and settlement of dispute (such as consulting with or reporting to the insurance company), administration and governance of the facility. The Guidance, in the comment on sections 27 of APPI at pp. 48–49, recommends that the notice should contain the statement that, unless the patient objects and demands the facility obtain her/his express consent, she/he is treated as impliedly assenting to the purposes thus posted.

Limitation by Utilization Purpose

Section 18 provides that a processing operator may not process personal information for purposes unnecessary for achieving the utilization purpose as has been specified under section 17 unless her/his consent has been obtained to the processing. Subsection 3 of section 18 provides that this limitation will not apply to the following cases:

(i)   Where the processing is based on laws or regulations.
(ii)   Where there is a need to protect a human life, body or property and obtaining the individual's consent is difficult.
(iii) Where there is a strong need to promote public health or sound development of children and obtaining the individual's consent is difficult.
(iv)   Where there is a need to cooperate with a national or local governmental body in performing the work stipulated by laws or regulations and obtaining the individual's consent may interfere with its implementation.

(v)   Where the processing operator is an academic institution, and the processing of the personal information is necessary for the purpose of academic research.

(vi) Where the personal data[11] is shared with an academic institution, and processing of the personal data is necessary for the academic institution for the purpose of academic research.

Limitation of Third-Party Sharing

Section 27 provides that a processing operator may not, except in the exempted cases same as those listed in section 18, subsection 3, clauses (i) through (iv) and the additional following clauses (v) through (vii), share personal data with a third-party without obtaining in advance the individual's consent.

(v)   Where the processing operator is an academic institution, and sharing of the personal data is unavoidable for the publication or instruction of the results of academic research (except where the sharing may injure unjustifiably the individual's rights or interests).

(vi) Where the processing operator is an academic institution, and sharing is necessary for the purpose of academic research jointly conducted by the operator and the third-party (same exception as clause vi).

(vii) Where the third-party is an academic institution, and it is necessary for the third party to process the personal data for the purpose of academic research (same exception as clause vi).

Disclosure

Section 33 provides that the individual may demand to a processing operator that it disclose retained personal data that can identify the individual. The processing operator on receiving the demand shall disclose retained personal data to the individual without delay in a way requested by the individual, unless disclosing such data falls under any of the following cases:

(i)   Where there is a possibility that the disclosure may injure the life, body, property or other rights or interests of the individual or the third parties.

(ii) Where there is a possibility that the disclosure may hamper the processing operator from properly conducting of its business.

---

[11]   The term "personal data" is defined in section 16 subsection 3 of APPI, as personal information of which the personal information database consists.

(iii)   Where the disclosure violates laws or regulations.

Correction

Section 34 provides that, when the contents of retained personal data that can identify the individual are not true, the individual may demand to a processing operator that it make a correction, addition or deletion (hereinafter "correction etc.") of the contents of the data. The processing operator on receiving the demand shall conduct a necessary investigation without delay to the extent necessary to achieve the utilization purpose and, based on the result thereof, make a correction etc. of the contents of the data.

Principal Provisions of APPI Added in the 2015 Amendment

In 2015, APPI was amended to accommodate developments in informational and communication technology, leverage the utilization of big data and establish the Persona Information Protection Commission.

Refinement of the Definition of Personal Information: Individual Identification Code

The amendment introduced three new concepts in the act, one of which is "individual identification code." If the information relating living individual contains an individual identification code, it is treated as personal information, whether the information is identifiable by name, birth date or other identifying descriptions contained in it. There are two kinds of individual identification code: one is the character, letter, number, symbol or other code which one of the bodily characteristics (such as DNA, facial configuration, fingerprint or palmprint) listed in cabinet order is converted into and can identify the individual, the other is the character, letter, number, symbol or other codes which are assigned or issued to an individual as a bearer, recipient, licensee, subject or insured (such as passport number, basic pension number, driver's license number, resident's registration number, my number or health insurance number).

Personal Information Requiring Special Care

"Personal information requiring special care" is another new concept introduced by the amendment. It is defined as personal information that contains the individual's race, creed, social status, medical history, criminal record, record of being a crime victim, or such other descriptions, prescribed by cabinet order, as those the processing of which requires special care so as not to cause unfair discrimination, prejudice or other disadvantages to the individual. In health and medical area, the implementing cabinet order added to medical history set out in the act those descriptions showing (i) the presence of mental or physical disability, (ii) the results of health checkups or other medical tests or (iii) the provision of health consultation, medical care or prescription filling, as the descriptions requiring special care. In effect, all medical and health information became to be characterized as personal data requiring special care.

Subsection 2 of section 20, in effect, provides that collecting personal information requiring special care is allowed only where the advance consent of the individual is obtained except in the exempted cases similar to those listed in section 18.

Anonymized Information

"Anonymized information" is the third new concept introduced by the 2015 amendment. It is defined as information that has been created by processing personal information to make it neither individually identifiable nor restorable to any personal information by taking one of the following actions:

(i)   Deleting all those descriptions in the said personal information identifying the individual, or
(ii) Deleting all individual identification codes in the said personal information.

Establishment of the Personal Information Protection Commission

The 2015 amendment established the Personal Information Protection Commission as an independent governmental authority supervising a whole area of personal information protection in private sector (after the 2021 revision has been fully implemented, its jurisdiction covers whole area, both private and public, and national and municipal).

THE ENACTMENT OF THE NEXT-GENERATION MEDICAL INFRASTRUCTURE ACT

In April 2017, the Japanese Parliament passed the so-called Next-Generation Medical Infrastructure Act.[12] Its aim was to create the scheme in which hos-

---

[12]   Its Official name is translated as the Act on Anonymized Medical Data That Are Meant to Contribute to Research and Development in the Medical Field. Its English

pitals and other institutions using medical and health database can provide patients' or subjects' data to governmentally accredited private companies skilled in data processing and data security. It will be operated on voluntary basis. Hospitals, clinics, schools and employers are free to take part in the scheme. Patients or other subjects (such as students or employees) of participating institutions are given the written notice of it and offered the opportunity to opt out of it.

The data company will collect and pool patients' and subjects' data, consolidating the data of the same individual, and create a database of anonymized medical data. The anonymized database will be provided for a fee to pharmaceutical companies, research institutions and government agencies for research, development or public health promotion.

EXCEPTIONS TO CONFIDENTIALITY

Statutory Exceptions

As stated in the section on 'Key sources of the duty of confidentiality', the Penal Code and every law regulating the qualification and status of medical personnel, while generally prohibiting disclosure of the patient's confidential information, provide for exemption when justifiable cause exists for the disclosure. The patient's consent (next subsection *infra*) and legislation allowing or requiring the disclosure are most common cause justifying the disclosure. For example, the Act on the Prevention of Infectious Diseases and Medical Care for Patients with Infectious Diseases,[13] in section 12, subsection 1, provides as follows:

> Where a physician has diagnosed either of the following persons, the physician must file a notification with the prefectural governor via the chief of the nearest public health center, except in the cases specified by the Order of the Ministry of Health, Labor and Welfare, of the person's name, age, gender and other matters specified by the Ministry Order immediately if the person is the one set forth in clause (i), or of the person's age, gender and other matters specified by the Ministry Order within seven days if the person is the one set forth in clause (ii):
> (i)   A patient of Class I Infectious Disease, a patient or asymptomatic carrier of Class II, Class III or Class IV Infectious Disease, a patient of any of the Class V Infectious Diseases specified by the Ministry Order or a Novel Influenza

---

translation can be found at www.japaneselawtranslation.go.jp/ja/laws/view/3441 (last visited 19 December 2022).

[13]   English translation can be found at www.japaneselawtranslation.go.jp/ja/laws/view/2830 (last visited 19 December 2022).

Infection etc.,[14] or a person suspected to be infected with a New Infectious Disease, or

(ii) a patient of any of the Class V Infectious Diseases specified by the Ministry Order (including asymptomatic Carriers of any of the Class V Infectious Diseases specified by the Ministry Order).

As stated in "Limitation of Third-Party Sharing," *supra*, section 27 of APPI, while generally prohibiting a processing operator from sharing personal data with the third parties without the individual's consent, provides for exemption for the specified cases listed in the same section.

Explicit and Implicit Consent

Where the patient's consent is secured to the disclosure of her/his confidential medical information to the third-party, its sharing will be allowed. Conversely, unconsented third-party disclosure of the confidential medical information is basically unlawful, and the consent must generally be explicit for its validity. This basic principle is exemplified in the case shown in the next section.

Explicit consent

In a civil case, a company employee who was injured while working for the company brought suit against the hospital and physician that provided medical care to him for the breach of confidentiality by unlawfully disclosing without his consent his medical information to the employer, that was the defendant of another suit brought by him for damages caused by the industrial accident. The court awarded damages to the plaintiff against the defendants for the mental suffering caused by the doctor in destroying the plaintiff's confidence in the doctor by the leakage.[15]

Another example of the requirement of explicit consent can be found in the notice often posted on the website of hospitals in Japan stating that the insurance company employee who wants to have a meeting with or otherwise obtain information from a physician about the patient receiving care at the hospital (insured or beneficiary etc.) must in advance obtain written consent of his/her to the sharing of the information.

---

[14] COVID-19 infectious disease was made a Designated Infectious Disease in February 2020 and has been included in "Novel Influenza Infection etc." since February 2021. It has been treated in effect like a Class II infectious disease under the Act.

[15] Saitama Chiho Saibansho [Saitama Dist. Ct.] March 4, 2010, Hei 19 (wa) no. 256, 2083 Hanrei Jihou [Hanji] 112 (Japan).

Implicit consent

The MHLW Guidance states that the third-party disclosure that is included in the utilization purposes shown on the notice displayed in the facility is, unless objected to by the patient, treated as impliedly assented by her/him.

In a case involving damage claims by the victims of the adverse side-effect of a drug against its manufacturer, the court dismissed a doctor's refusal to submit their medical records on the basis of non-disclosure duty of the patient's confidential information, saying that "As the victim patients are seeking damages from the manufacturer disclosing their confidential information including their disease's name, symptoms and conditions, the issue of breach of confidentiality will not arise with respect to the records ordered to be submit in this case."[16]

Other Healthcare Personnel

As described *supra*, the same rules as those applicable to the physician will generally be applied to the other healthcare personnel except for the provisions, like the section 12 of Act on the Prevention of Infectious Diseases and Medical Care for Patients with Infectious Diseases, that apply only to the physician.

Teaching, Research, and Audit

With respect to teaching and audit (except for audit/monitoring in research), there is no specific provision exempting these cases from the general rule discussed above, except that teaching or audit may be regarded as justifiable cause for disclosure in applying section 134 of the Penal Code.

With respect to medical research, promotion of "public health" provided in subsection 1, clause iii of section 27 of APPI, quoted *supra*, is now interpreted to include advancement of medicine through medical research and accords the basis of exemption from the general prohibition of sharing information with third parties. In addition, before the revision in 2021, APPI, in section 76, exempted the press, writing professionals, academic institutions, religious organizations and political organizations that use personal information for their primary purpose from the obligations imposed by it. Accordingly, limitation of third-party sharing provision of APPI did not apply to academic research conducted by academic institutions. However, although the EU and Japan entered into mutual adequacy arrangement about each other's personal

---

[16]   Fukuoka Koto Saibansho [Fukuoka High Court] Sept. 17, 1977, Sho 52 (ra) no. 59, 28(9–12) Kaminshu 969, 973 (Japan).

data protection system in January 2019 under article 45 of the EU General Data Protection Regulation and section 24 (after 2021 revision, section 28) of APPI, those processing of personal information that was categorically exempted from the duty requirements provided by APPI were not covered the arrangement. In order to redress this situation with respect to academic institutions, Japanese government, when preparing the bill for revised APPI in 2021, removed the academic institution from the category of operators granted general exemption of APPI's duties, and added new exemptive provisions for academic institutions with respect to utilization purpose limitation (section 18, subsection 3) and third-party sharing limitation (section 27, subsection 1) (both are explained *supra*) as well as consent requirement for collection of personal information requiring special care (section 20, subsection 2). The result of this change in the EU adequacy determination is to be seen.

Regulation of Medical Research by Legislation and Guidelines

Japanese government and its ministries have promulgated several sets of ethical guidelines for medical research and legislation governing medical research including:

– Ethical Guidelines for Life Science and Medical Research Involving Human Subject (promulgated in 2021, last revised in 2023)
– The Act on the Safety of Regenerative Medicine (enacted in 2013)
– The Clinical Research Act (enacted in 2017)
– Ministry Orders on Good Clinical Practice issued under the Act on Securing Quality, Efficacy and Safety of Products Including Pharmaceuticals and Medical Devices (originally enacted in 1960 under the name of the Pharmaceutical Affairs Act and revised and renamed in 2013).[17]

These sets of guidelines and legislation provide for the requirement of informed consent for the processing of personally identifiable information and specimens of the research subjects. So far, these guidelines and legislation have been drafted with the principles embodied in APPI in mind, and every medical research, in effect, is governed by one of these guidelines or legislation.

Generally speaking, under these guidelines or legislation, written informed consent must be secured before a research subject is enrolled in invasive medical research, while collection of those specimens and information generated not for the research purpose (existing material) for the purpose of conducting research can be allowed if appropriate schemes for notification or

---

[17]   English translation can be found at www.japaneselawtranslation.go.jp/en/laws/view/3213 (last visited 21 December 2022).

publication about their research use and the opportunity to opt out of being the participant are properly provided.

Prevention of Harm to Others

Prevention of harm to others usually amounts to the protection of the lives, bodies or properties of others that are included in APPI section 27, subsection 1, clause (ii) as exempting reasons for the third party sharing of personal information. Accordingly, with respect to personal information legislation, prevention of harm to others will unquestionably be recognized as exception to confidentiality.

With respect to the duty of confidentiality in the Penal Code and other laws on the qualification and status of medical personnel, prevention of harm to others can be interpreted as falling within the scope of justifiable cause.

Additionally, it can be pointed out that prevention of harm to others is the main ground for the statutory provision requiring physicians to report cases of infectious diseases, one example of which is discussed *supra*.

Police Investigation

With respect to police investigation, section 197, subsection 2 of the Code of Criminal Procedure[18] provides that public offices or public or private organizations may be requested to make a report on necessary matters relating to the investigation. Judging from the opinion submitted by the cabinet to the parliament in 2004, when a medical institution discloses the personal information to the police answering the request for disclosure, the disclosure seems to be made based on a provision of legislation, which is allowed under the section 27, subsection 1, clause (i) of APPI.[19]

With respect to the duty of confidentiality in the Penal Code and other laws on the qualification and status of medical personnel, police investigation can be interpreted as falling within the scope of justifiable cause.

Public Interest

Subsection 1 of section 27 of APPI provides that the third-party data sharing is allowed where there is a strong need to promote public health and obtain-

---

[18]   English translation can be found at www.japaneselawtranslation.go.jp/en/laws/view/3739 (last visited 22 December 2022).

[19]   Uga Katsuya, *Shin Kojinjyohohogoho no Chikujyokaisetsu* [*New Commentaries on the Act on the Protection of Personal Information*] (Yuhikaku 2021) 250.

ing the individual's consent is difficult (clause 3) or where there is a need to cooperate with a national or local governmental body (clause 4). Promotion of public health and cooperation with public bodies can be characterized as public interest.

The MHLW Guidance *supra* sets out the examples of data sharing with population-based cancer registries and the Statistics Bureau of Government (at p. 47).

Press Freedom

Section 57, subsection 1, clauses 1 and 2 of APPI exempted the press and writing professionals that use personal information for reporting or writing purpose from the obligations and penalties provided for by APPI. On the other hand, disclosure of personal information to the press or writers will not be justified with regard to the confidentiality duty of the physician imposed by section 134 of the Penal Code. In a case where a psychiatrist, who was ordered to write an expert opinion in a juvenile case and given the copy of the materials about the juvenile, disclosed to a free-lance journalist the materials and the written results of psychiatric test and investigation conducted by him. The Supreme Court affirmed the conviction of the psychiatrist saying that he violated the duty of confidentiality imposed by section 134 of the Penal Code.[20]

Other Grounds: Prevention and Correction of Child Abuse and Neglect

Subsection 1, clause (iii) of section 27 of APPI provides that the third-party data sharing is allowed where there is a strong need to promote sound development of children and obtaining the individual's consent is difficult. This provision aims to prevent and correct the child abuse or neglect through enabling prompt exchange of personal data of the subject child with child protective agencies.

CONFIDENTIALITY AND GENETICS

DNA Data as Individual Identification Code

With respect to the genetic information in the context of personal information protection, the 2015 amendment to APPI introduced the concept of individual identification code and the cabinet order provided that DNA data identifiable

---

[20]   Saiko Saibansho [Sup. Ct.] Feb. 13, 2012, Hei 22 (a) no. 126, 66 Saiko Saibansho Keiji Hanreishu [Keishu] 405 (Japan).

to the individual is treated as the code if it is whole genome sequence data, whole exome sequence data, whole SNP data, sequence data consisting of 40 or more SNPs independent of each other, or short tandem repeat of four bases of nine or more loci.[21]

Genetic Data in Clinical Medicine

The Japanese Association of Medical Sciences, that now consists of 142 medical societies for various specialty fields in medicine, issued in 2011 and revised in 2022 the Guidelines for Genetic Tests and Diagnoses in Medical Practice (hereinafter JAMS Guidelines).[22] JAMS Guidelines emphasize that "genetic information must be handled with particular attention because it remains as it is throughout the individual's lifetime, can be used to predict diseases, and could also affect their biological relatives. Genetic information should be handled confidentially and in accordance with the personal information protection laws."[23]

---

[21]   Personal Information Protection Commission, Guidelines for the Act on the Protection of Personal Information (General Rules) 9 (2016).

[22]   Its English translation can be found at the following website, although the English translation included in this paper does not always follow that translation, https://jams .med.or.jp/guideline/genetics-diagnosis_e_2022.pdf (last visited 22 December 2022).

[23]   JAMS Guidelines lists the following characteristics of genetic information.
  •   It does not change throughout the individual's lifetime.
  •   It is partially shared with biological relatives.
  •   The genotype or phenotype of biological relatives can be predicted with a relatively accurate probability.
  •   It is possible to make a diagnosis of asymptomatic carriers (who have almost no chances of developing the disease related to the pathogenic variant [mutation] in the future but possess the variant [mutation] and can pass it onto the next generation).
  •   It is possible to almost certainly predict the likelihood of future onset of a disease before it develops.
  •   It may be used for prenatal or preimplantation genetic testing.
  •   Inappropriate handling of genetic information can cause social disadvantages to the examinees and their relatives.
  •   Uncertainty is inherent in genetic testing. Uncertainty refers to possible changes in significance and individual variations to the onset, timing of onset, symptoms or severity of the disease predicted by a pathogenic variant (mutation) and that their clinical utility may change with the advancement of medical care and research.

JAMS Guidelines, in section 4 entitled "Handling personal information and personal genetic information," provide as follows:

(1)   Protection of personal information
       Healthcare professionals who have access to an examinee's genetic information are required to fully understand the characteristics of genetic information and handle personal genetic information appropriately in accordance with this guideline and conform to personal information protection laws.
(2)   Documentation on medical records
       Germline genetic information stays constant throughout one's lifetime (static information), but it is simultaneously cross-organic information, which is shared by all the cells of the body. It is also shared not only by current biological relatives but also by future biological relatives. As such, genetic information must be shared between clinical departments and between physicians and co-medicals and stored for a long term to ensure sufficient protection of the patient's privacy. The results of genetic testing and content of genetic counseling should likewise generally be documented in medical records, similar to other clinical data.
(3)   Education and training of medical staff
       ...
(4)   Confidentiality obligations to the examinee and explanation of results to biological relatives
       All personal genetic information obtained from genetic tests, as any other medical information, is subject to confidentiality and should not be disclosed to any third party, including the examinee's relatives without the consent of the examinee. However, when the genetic diagnosis of an examinee is considered beneficial for the health management of the relatives of the examinee, disclosure of the genetic information to the relatives may be considered if it is impossible to implement effective prevention and treatment without such information. In doing so, the consent of the examinee would be necessary before disclosing the results to the biological relatives. However, considering the best interest of the examinee's relatives, genetic information of the examinee may be disclosed to their biological relatives to prevent disbenefits to them, even if the consent of the examinee cannot be obtained. In such cases, disclosure to the examinee's relative(s) should be performed not just based on the sole judgment of the attending doctor but through consultation with the ethics committee of the relevant medical institution.
(5)   Consideration for preventing social disadvantages and discrimination
       ...

Genetic Tests of Children or Other Incompetent Persons

With respect to the genetic testing of children or other incompetent persons, the JAMS Guidelines, in section 3-3, provide as follows:

In the case of genetic testing of a disease that has developed in a minor or a person incapable of consent, it is necessary to obtain the consent of an individual standing as a surrogate representative. In this case, the surrogate should decide after a careful consideration of the examinee's beneficence in his/her health care. It is desirable to obtain assent from the examinee after giving the explanation of the test at a level corresponding to the patient's ability.

The same should be applied for genetic testing of diseases that develop before adulthood if their presymptomatic diagnoses are useful in the management of the examinee's healthcare.

Meanwhile, asymptomatic carrier diagnosis or presymptomatic testing for diseases that develop in and after adulthood in a minor should generally not be performed by the consent of the examinee's surrogate, but should generally be postponed until the minor reaches adulthood and is capable of taking autonomous decisions.

COMMENTS TO THE FOUR SPECIFIC CASES FROM THE PERSPECTIVE OF JAPANESE LAW, GUIDELINES AND PRACTICE

Case 1: Is there a duty of confidentiality towards the family/the partner of the patient? Example: partner of the patient calls the nurse in the hospital to ask for some news about his partner/the patient. Nurse asks the partner to bring his HIV medication to the hospital. The partner was not aware of his HIV-status. The nurse is fired, because of breach of the duty of confidentiality.

In principle, confidential health information of a patient may not be disclosed even to the patient's family or partner. On the other hand, where the patient is in a condition that made her/him unable to make medical decision, the family member or partner usually become a proxy decisionmaker and as such hear the patient's medical information. However, in this case, the patient does not seem unable to make her/his medical decision. Accordingly, when a nurse asks the partner to bring his HIV medication, she should have obtained the patient's consent to reveal her/his HIV condition to the partner. The nurse's request to bring HIV medication contains the presupposition that the patient is HIV positive, and that information is sensitive. Accordingly, the request, if made without the patient's consent, will amount to leakage of the patient's confidential information. Whether the firing of the nurse is defendable depends on the consideration of the actual situation regarding the urgency of its necessity, its availability within the hospital, her status under the employment contract and work record as well as employment practice of the hospital.

Case 2: What is the status of audio and video recordings and the use of a private detective: can a patient make an audio recording of his conversation with the physician and use this recording in court? Can an insurance company use a private detective who makes a video recording of a patient/the claimant in a liability case, to prove the claimant is not that paralyzed as he pretends?

With respect to the use of audio and video recording, there is no problem as long as the recording is concerned with her/his own conversation. In fact, it is often suggested or recommended as a good way to prevent dispute to make an audio or video record of the conversation between the patient and the physician and other medical personnel with the consent of both sides secured.

Using a private detective for recording of a patient/the claimant's condition seems allowable as long as the information gathering and use is not against the law, as in the case that observation and recording of her/his public appearance is conducted for the limited purpose of insurance claim settlement.

Case 3: Family treatment: a child shows signs of child abuse: can the physician report this to the competent authorities, even when the parents are also a patient and are entitled to confidentiality.

Under section 27, subsection 1, clause (iii) of APPI, third-party data sharing is allowed where there is a strong need to promote sound development of children and obtaining the individual's (i.e., the parent's) consent is difficult. This provision aims to prevent and correct the child abuse or neglect. Accordingly, the physician can report the case to the appropriate child protective agency without the concern of breaching confidentiality.

Case 4: Confidentiality of genetic information and blood relatives' right to know: [Although the email from Professor Thierry Vansweevelt on July 22, 2022 15:44 cited *ABC v St George's NHS Hospital Trust* [2017] EWCA Civ 336, on 28 February 2020, the High Court (Justice Yip) entered judgment on the merit after remand in 2017 by the Court of Appeal. As Mrs. Yip's opinion is more informative about factual circumstances and comprehensive in analysis, I took the liberty of writing the following part with Justice Yip's judgment in mind. The paragraph numbers refer to the numbers shown in the Justice Yip's opinion.]

Regarding the case *ABC v St George's Healthcare NHS Trust*, I think Justice Yip's judgment in the High Court ([2020] EWHC 455 (QB)), entered on the merit after remand by the Court of Appeal ([2017] EWCA Civ 336), dismissing the claim for damages by the claimant, was appropriately decided. Her opinion impressed me with her exhaustive analysis and sympathetic treatment of the claimant's case.

A Japanese court faced with the same factual situation, I am convinced, will similarly deny remedy to the plaintiff as there is no disclosure obligation on the part of hospital personnel and causation does not exist between non-disclosure and the injury allegedly sustained by the claimant. The Japanese court may not follow the intricate line of reasoning of first finding a duty of care owed the claimant on the part of the second defendant to balance her interest in being informed of her genetic risk against her father's interest and the public interest in maintaining confidentiality and to act in accordance with its outcome (paras 259–260) then denying any actionable breach of that duty (para 263), but write an opinion directly denying the duty on the part of second defendant to alert the claimant to her genetic risk referring to the absence of causation that she would terminate her pregnancy had the risk been disclosed to her.

As to hospital personnel's obligation to disclose the examinee's information, JAMS Guideline *supra*, in section 4, clause 4) on "confidentiality obligations to the examinee and explanation of results to biological relatives," provides that when the genetic diagnosis of an examinee is considered beneficial for the health management of the relatives of the examinee, disclosure of the genetic information to the relatives may be considered if otherwise it is impossible to implement effective prevention and treatment, and while obtaining the consent of the examinee is generally necessary, in the case where the consideration of the best interests of the examinee's relatives make the disclosure necessary, genetic information of the examinee may be disclosed to their biological relatives even without the examinee's consent. In such cases, JAMS Guideline recommends the consultation with the ethics committee, the procedure taken for the disclosure to the claimant's sister in the ABC case.

With respect to the disclosure obligation of the part of hospital personnel in the scenario of the ABC case, I think the unswerving refusal of the proband patient is crucial to the determination of its denial. If the disclosure is obligated or allowed on the part of medical staff in spite of his strong refusal of disclosure many patients will shy away from seeing doctors from the concern for unwanted divulgement of her/his sensitive medical and genetic information. Accordingly, the conclusion of the ABC case should be supported specifically by this policy reason.

From a legal point of view, it seems to me that the injury alleged to be sustained by the claimant might not be so substantial as to justify the claimed remedy of damages. However, the court did not pursue this matter, as the parties agreed that if the requirements of breach of duty and causation were established, the claimant should recover damages in the sum of £345,000 (para 1).

With respect to the moral obligation, I think the same obligation should be morally recognized that was described by Justice Yip in the ABC case to be legally imposed on the hospital trust to balance the claimant's interest in being informed of her genetic risk against her father's interest and the public interest in maintaining confidentiality and to act in accordance with its outcome following the guidelines issued by organizations of medical profession. Implementation of this obligation will be secured by ethical guidelines, institutional ethics committees and finally the judicial court.

6. Privacy and health in the Nordic countries

Mette Hartlev

GENERAL INTRODUCTION

The Nordic countries – also referred to as the Scandinavian[1] countries – consist of five smaller[2] autonomous states: Denmark, Finland, Iceland, Norway and Sweden. They are *welfare states* with a publicly funded universal healthcare system, which is sometimes characterized as a special 'Nordic model'.[3] Running the Nordic welfare state model requires comprehensive redistribution of economic resources. Taxes must be collected from citizens and businesses and distributed to various public and private entities responsible for healthcare, social security, education, care for children and elderly, and allocated further on to beneficiaries within the population. To enable this 'circular economy' personal data are of crucial importance. Hence, all the Nordic countries have quite early introduced personal identification numbers for citizens to facilitate a correct tax collection and distribution of various public benefits. In fact, Sweden is the first country in the world to introduce a nation-wide personal identification number as early as 1947.[4] Iceland followed in 1954, Finland and

---

[1]   'Scandinavia' is normally used as the term to define the three kingdoms of Denmark, Norway and Sweden; whereas 'Nordic countries' refers to the countries on the Scandinavian peninsula, which include Finland, as well as Iceland.
[2]   These are small populations – in total, the Scandinavian population amounts to approximately 25 million.
[3]   G. Esping Andersen, *The Three Worlds of Welfare Capitalism* (Cambridge: Polity Press, 2002); and J. Magnusson, K. Vrangbæk, R.B. Saltmann and P.E. Martinussen, 'Introduction: The Nordic Model of Health Care' in J. Magnusson, K. Vrangbæk and R.B. Saltmann, *Nordic Health Care Systems: Recent Reforms and Current Policy Challenges*, European Observatory on Health Systems and Policies Series (Buckingham: Open University Press, 2009), 3–20.
[4]   J.F. Ludvigsson, P. Otterblad-Olausson, B.U. Pettersson and A. Ekbom, 'The Swedish Personal Identity Number: Possibilities and Pitfalls in Healthcare and Medical Research' (2009) 24(11) *European Journal of Epidemiology* 659.

Norway ten years later (1964) and Denmark in 1968.[5] The personal identification number has been crucial for building up comprehensive registers and for collection and sharing of personal data in the public (and private sector), including the healthcare services.

The Nordic countries have traditionally been strong promoters of human rights, which is reflected in the status of patients' rights in the Nordic legal systems. Finland was the first country in the world to introduce a special Act on Patients' Rights, in 1992. This was soon followed by Iceland (1997), Denmark (1998) and Norway (1999). Sweden took somewhat longer in this regard, first adopting a Patients' Rights Act in 2014.[6]

All Nordic countries now have separate Acts (Finland,[7] Iceland,[8] Norway[9] and Sweden),[10] or separate chapters in a more comprehensive Act (Denmark),[11] outlining the rights of patients, including the right to protection of privacy. Both the character and the justiciability of these rights differ from country to country. The special patients' rights legislation should further be seen as part of a more comprehensive cluster of legislation, in which the rights of patients are intertwined with both the duties of healthcare professionals and patient safety and quality regulations, as well as data protection legislation. Thus, patients' rights in the Nordic countries are positioned within a complex legal landscape which may make it difficult to navigate and find clear lines of demarcation.

The duty of confidentiality is an illustrative example of how various professional and public regulations interact. Confidentiality has for long been a fundamental principle in medical ethics, dating back to the Hippocratic Oath. It is stipulated in both professional codes of ethics, and in special laws *regulating*

---

[5]   See for Iceland, I. Watson, 'A Short History of National Identification Numbering in Iceland' (2010) (4) *Bifröst Journal of Social Science* 51, for Finland, Norway and Denmark, see S. Bauer, 'From Administrative Infrastructure to Biomedical Resource: Danish Population Registries, the "Scandinavian Laboratory", and the "Epidemiologist's Dream"' (2014) 27(2) *Science in Context* 187.

[6]   The reasons and implications of a delayed legislative development in Sweden are discussed in E. Rynning, 'Still No Patients' Act in Sweden. Reasons and Implications' in E. Rynning and M. Hartlev (eds), *Nordic Health Law in a European Context. Welfare State Perspectives on Patients' Rights and Biomedicine* (Malmö/Leiden: Liber/Martinus Nijhoff Publishers, 2012), 122–36.

[7]   The Act on the Status and Rights of Patients (*Laki potilaan asemasta ja oikeudesta*) 785/1992, which came into force in 1993.

[8]   Patients' Rights Act (74/1997).

[9]   Act on Patients' and Users' Rights (*Lov om pasient- og brukerrettigheter*), 63 of 2 July 1999. The Act came into force in 2001.

[10]   Patient Act (*Patientlag*), 2014:821, 19 June 2014.

[11]   Consolidated Act 1011 of 17 June 2023 – Health Act (*Sundhedsloven*). The original Act 428 of 1 July 1998 on Legal Status of Patients (*lov om patienters retsstilling*) was merged with a number of other Acts into the Health Act in 2005.

the medical profession in all the Nordic countries. With *patients' rights acts*, and national and EU *data protection regulation*, the principle of confidentiality has been supplemented with other regulatory instruments focusing on how to balance patient's right to privacy and autonomy with various other interests in the processing of health data. Confidentiality and privacy in Nordic health care is thus embedded in a more complex legal landscape mitigating various – and partly conflicting – interests in collecting and using health data for treatment and other purposes.

In general, there is a strong protection of personal liberty in the Constitutions of the Nordic countries, including the right to privacy and family life, and freedom of information. As discussed in this chapter, there are obviously some restrictions on privacy rights, based on consideration for the interests and rights of others, as well as vital public interests, including public health interests. The balancing of these interests, and the attention of the entire legislative framework in the individual Nordic countries presents some variations, and each country has its own characteristics. Finland is known for its strong focus on data-driven innovation which is reflected in recent legislation promoting use of health data for innovation. Sweden was the first country in the world to introduce freedom of information as a constitutional principle (in 1766), which provides a special framework for application of the confidentiality principle in Sweden. Norway has a long tradition for comprehensive protection of confidentiality and data protection through legislation on data protection and ethics assessment of use of health data. Iceland is known for the efforts of a private company (DeCode) to create a genealogical data base and build up a population-wide genetic database based on voluntary donations. Finally, Denmark is known for its high-quality information resources and digitalized register practices, and – in a Nordic context – liberal legislation regarding use of health data for a variety of purposes.

In the following sections selected characteristics of protection of privacy in the Nordic healthcare services are outlined. The focus will be on Danish[12] law, which will be related to the legal situations in the other Nordic countries where this is of particular interest.

It should be noted that all Nordic countries belong to the civil law family, and case law does not have the same prominent position as in common law countries. There are a few, but not many court cases concerned with confi-

---

[12] The author of this chapter is from Denmark. Although there are similarities in the legislation (based on a long tradition of legal collaboration), and Danish, Norwegian and Swedish are – to some extent – mutually understandable, there are also some distinct differences in terms of language, organization of health care services and legal regulation. As a result, a comprehensive comparative analysis of all Nordic countries is beyond the scope of this chapter.

dentiality and privacy in health care. Still, there are various administrative complaint or disciplinary mechanisms in all the Nordic countries which can address cases and complaints regarding violation of confidentiality and other patients' rights as well as violations of data protection laws.

KEY ETHICAL AND LEGAL SOURCES OF CONFIDENTIALITY

As mentioned in the introduction, there are various sources of confidentiality in the Nordic countries. Taking a historical perspective on the introduction of the principle of confidentiality in Danish law, it takes its point of departure in *legal regulation* dating back to 1672 where a royal executive decree for 'Doctors and Pharmacists' stipulated a duty of confidentiality stating that pharmacists (and their assistants) could not 'enunciate or reveal' information about the medical condition of patients unless concealment might cause danger.[13] A particularly strong commitment to secrecy was expected of midwifes working at the Danish Royal Birth Clinic where women could give birth in secret (clandestine birth). This was introduced in the eighteenth century, prohibiting a midwife to 'misuse the confidence demonstrated to her by a pregnant woman in an unfortunate situation'.[14] While the secrecy of pharmacists primarily was meant to ensure patients' interest in not having sensitive information exposed, the confidentiality obligations of midwifes rather served the purpose of avoiding amoral practices of infanticide. For doctors, confidentiality became part of 'official' medical ethics in 1815 where a medical oath for medical graduates – based on the Hippocratic oath – was introduced at the University of Copenhagen. This oath is still in place but has nowadays mostly a ceremonial function.

From the beginning of the twentieth century special legislation for various health care professionals was introduced in Denmark. First a special Act on Pharmacists (1913), followed by an Act on Midwifes (1914), Act on Dentists (2016), Act on Nurses (1933) and Act on Medical Doctors (1934). All these acts included a duty of confidentiality. The Act on Medical Doctors is of special interest because the preparatory work discusses in detail why confidentiality is important. A dual concern for the individual and for population health is highlighted, and the white paper preceding the Act states, that

> If the medical doctors were entitled to speak of everything they might learn about the illnesses or other conditions of their patients, it is to be feared that people, for

---

[13]   Kongelig forordning af 4. december 1672 om Medicis og Apothekere, section 24. At that time, Norway was a part of the Kingdom Denmark-Norway.

[14]   Reskript af 13. marts 1750 and Reskript af 6. januar 1764.

this reason, would refrain from consulting a doctor or omit to provide complete information, which would go against the interests of the individual as well as public health interests.[15]

Consequently, confidentiality was seen as a precondition to build trust with patients, and thereby to encourage them to seek medical attention and convey information that was necessary to diagnose and treat diseases.

The preparatory work is still used as point of reference for interpretation of current legislation, because of the clarity provided regarding the underlying rationale. The Criminal Code was also amended in 1930 with a provision regarding criminal sanction for violating a duty of confidentiality by any person who performed professional activities based on a public authorization or license (e.g. doctors, pharmacists, midwifes etc) and any person who assisted a licensed person in their professional activities.[16]

Nowadays, a mix of legislative acts has an impact on the regulation of confidentiality in the Nordic countries. First of all, there are in all country's legislation regulating the *health care professionals' rights and duties*, and in all countries, this is now a general regulation of all health care professionals and not – as previously – separate acts for each group of health care professionals (doctors, nurses, midwifes etc). Apart from Denmark, the acts on health professionals' rights and duties includes a separate provision stipulating a duty of confidentiality.[17] In Denmark[18] this was seen as unnecessary when the Act was revised almost 20 years ago, because a duty of confidentiality already follows from the Criminal Code, and also from the rights and duties regarding processing of medical data laid down in the patients' rights section of the Health Act.[19] *Criminal Codes* in the other Nordic countries also include provisions regarding

---

[15]   Ministry of Internal Affairs, 1931. White paper submitted by the commission regarding the legal status of medical doctors (*Betænkning afgivet af Kommissionen Angaaende Lægers Retsstilling*) (Copenhagen: J.H. Schultz A.-S, 1931), 27.

[16]   For a description of the legislative development in Denmark, including the interaction of the principle of confidentiality and data protection law see S. Wadmann, M. Hartlev and K. Hoeyer, 'The Life and Death of Confidentiality: A Historical Analysis of the Flows of Patient Information' (2023) BioSocieties. https://doi.org/10.1057/s41292-021-00269-x (last accessed 28 August 2023).

[17]   See the Finish Healthcare Professionals Act (Laki terveydenhuollon ammattihenkilöistä) no. 559 of 28 June 1994, section 17, the Icelandic Healthcare Practitioners Act (Lög um heilbrigðisstarfsmenn) no. 34/2012, article 17, the Norwegian Healthcare Personnel Act (Helsepersonelloven) no. 64 of 2 July 1999, section 21, and the Swedish Patient Safety Act (Patientsäkkerhetslagen) no. 659 of 17 June 2010, section 12.

[18]   Consolidated Act on Authorization of Healthcare Professionals and Health Services (Lov om autorisation af sundhedspersoner og om sundhedsfaglig virksomhed), no. 122 of 24 January 2023.

[19]   Consolidated Act no. 1011 of 17 June 2023 – Health Act.

sanctions for violation of duties of confidentiality. A duty of confidentiality may also rely on *contractual obligations*, for example in an employment contract. General *administrative law* also regulates a duty of confidentiality for public employees, which is of special relevance in the Nordic countries due to the universal and (widely) publicly funded healthcare services. Finally, *patients' rights*, *research ethics* and *data protection* legislation as well as special regulation on health registries, health data and biobanks also have an impact on confidentiality and use of health data in the Nordic countries.[20]

Regardless of being established as a *legal duty*, confidentiality is also laid down in special codes of *ethics*, passed by associations of healthcare professionals. Despite the superiority of the formal legislation, ethical obligations are also important sources as they inspire the practices of health care professionals.

PERSONS BOUND BY A DUTY OF CONFIDENTIALITY

In general, the duty of confidentiality applies to licensed health care professionals and their assistants. It differs a bit between the Nordic countries for which kind of professional activity a public license is necessary. In Denmark a wide range of professionals are covered by a requirement of public license (e.g. doctors, nurses, midwifes, dentists, chiropractors, physiotherapists, psychologist, health care assistants, radiologists). In total 28 groups of health care professionals are covered by the license system in Denmark. In some of the other Nordic countries, license requirement applies to fewer (Sweden) or more (Finland, Iceland and Norway) groups of health professionals.[21] In addition, a duty of confidentiality also applies to all public employees and may also follow from a contractual obligation.

LEGAL DUTIES OF CONFIDENTIALITY

In all Nordic countries the legal duty of confidentiality applies to all pieces of *confidential* information revealed to an *unauthorised person* in a *professional relation* between the patient and the health care professional. Consequently, three criteria – all open to interpretation – must be in place.

---

[20]   For a comprehensive general overview see Nordic Innovation, Bridging Nordic Data. Legal overview of possibilities and obstacles for secondary use of health data for innovation and development (Oslo, 2020) available at https://www.nordicinnovation .org/2020/bridging-nordic-data. (last accessed 28 August 2023).

[21]   Nordisk Ministerråd, Håndbok over regulerte helsepersonelgrupper i Norden (Handbook on regulated groups of health care professionals in the Nordic countries) (København, 2016) available here http://norden.diva-portal.org/smash/get/diva2: 941436/FULLTEXT03.pdf (last accessed 28 August 2023).

In a Danish context *confidential data* are normally defined as data an individual would not like to have revealed to others. Based on this definition it has been considered whether all health information (from a twisted ankle to a serious cancer condition) should be considered confidential or whether confidentiality only applies to more sensitive health data, for example related to a serious health condition or to reproductive or mental health. However, there is general agreement that it is impossible to make clear distinctions between sensitive and non-sensitive health data, as trivial health data in a specific context or to individual persons may be considered sensitive. Consequently, any kind of health data is confidential, irrespective of whether it is concerned with trivial health problems or more sensitive issues. This is in conformity with the definition of health data in the EU General Data Protection Regulation (Article 4.15) where health data are defined broadly as any data related directly or indirectly to a person's physical or mental health status. It should be noted that tissue samples, which can be linked to an individual, is also considered health data in a Danish context and regulated as other personal data. In the other Nordic countries, there are separate acts for regulation of biobanks.[22]

The duty of confidentiality in healthcare law is not restricted to health data, but covers all sorts of confidential data, including data regarding family issues, employment and financial issues. The mere fact that a patient is sick (without revealing the diagnosis) or has been in contact with the healthcare services is also considered confidential information, irrespective of whether more specific medical information about the patient is revealed or not. This was already established in a court case dating back to 1963[23] where the police were investigating a burglary and could see that the burglar had cut himself when falling through a roof window. When contacting the emergency ward at the nearby local hospital, the ward confirmed that they had treated patients with cuts but refused to reveal the names. The police asked for a Court order to have access to the identities of patients, but the court concluded that the mere identity of persons who had been at the ward should be considered confidential information, and that there was no justification of derogating from the principle of confidentiality.

The duty of confidentiality only applies vis-à-vis 'unauthorised' persons, which means persons without a legitimate legal access to the information. Legitimate access is delineated in the legislation regulating access to or right to pass on or receive information about specific patients. It can also

---

[22]   Finland: Biobank Act 688/2012, Iceland: Act no. 110/2000 on Biobanks and health-data banks, amended by Act no. 45/2014, Norway: Act no. 12 of 21 February 2003 related to treatment biobanks, and Sweden: Act no. 297 of 23 May 2002 on Biobanks in healthcare.

[23]   U 1963.1045 Ø.

rely on patient consent, or a power of attorney. As a main rule, health care professionals involved in providing care for the patient are normally not considered 'unauthorised', whereas employers, family members and close relatives should be treated as unauthorised persons (see more in 'Exemptions to Confidentiality').

Finally, the duty of confidentiality is limited to knowledge about the patient obtained in a *professional relationship between the patient and the health care professional*. If a patient has a private conversation with a neighbour, who happens to be a nurse, this will normally not be considered a professional relationship unless the patient approaches the nurse to get medical advice. In this case, it could be argued that a professional relationship has been established. The question of distinction between a professional or private relationship has been discussed in a patient complaint case, where the patient was working as a dental assistant at a local medical centre, where she was a patient of one of the GPs. She told the GP about some personal problems and when she learned that the GP had told other colleagues at the centre about her problems, she filed a complaint. The Patient Complaint Board concluded that her communication to the GP was not part of a doctor-patient relationship, and that no violation of confidentiality had occurred.[24] The duty of confidentiality in the patient-health care professional relationship is a one-way duty. Accordingly, the patient has no duty of confidentiality vis-à-vis the health care professional. This means that a patient is free to reveal information about the health care professional, and they are also entitled to, for example, record a conversation they have with a health care professional without prior consent, if this is only used for private purposes (e.g. to remember what was said during the conversation). In contrast, if the recorded conversation is used for other than private purposes, for example in a complaints case, it is important to ensure compliance with the GDPR and national data protection legislation. It should also be noted that information regarding a patient's health condition, which is visible when the person is in the public realm, is also outside the scope of the patient-health care professional relationship. Here the collection and disclosure of health and other personal information could be covered by the GDPR, national data protection or penal law, and human rights regulation. If, for example, a private detective working for an insurance company is following and video recording a patient/claimant in a liability case, to prove the claimant is not that paralyzed

---

[24] Patient complaint no. 0229601, available (in Danish) here https://stpk.dk/afgorelser-og-domme/afgorelser-fra-sundhedsvaesenets-disciplinaernaevn/0229601/ (accessed latest 28 August 2023).

which she claims to be, this would be a processing of personal data, but would normally be justified as long as the video is not made publicly available.[25]

In Danish law, the legal duty of confidentiality has a rights-based counterpart, which is a *patient's right to confidentiality*. It follows from section 40 of the Health Act that a patient is entitled to a healthcare professional observing silence about what they experience during the exercise of their profession regarding health conditions and other confidential information. This right of confidentiality is also reflected in the self-determination rights granted to patients in the Health Act regarding control of health data (see more in 'Explicit and Implicit Consent').

DATA PROTECTION LAW

All the Nordic countries are either members of the European Union (Denmark, Finland and Sweden) or of the European Economic Area (EEA) (Iceland and Norway). This means that national data protection legislation must comply with the EU General Data Protection Regulation (GDPR).[26] The GDPR is complemented by separate national data protection acts to provide a legal basis for application of some of the GDPR provisions and/or to profit from provisions leaving room for national variations (e.g. regarding use of data for research purposes, GDPR Article 89). Data protection rules may also be included in other acts than the national data protection act. For example, in Denmark, the Health Act and the Act on Research Ethics Assessment of Health Research and Health Data Research Projects[27] includes provisions which takes precedence over the Danish Data Protection Act (DPA).[28] In the other Nordic countries supplementary special health regulation taking precedence is also common. The Danish Health Act primarily differs from the GDPR and the DPA in giving patients more influence on the use of data within the healthcare services; partly through consent requirements and partly through opt-out-possibilities. This will be touched upon in more details in 'Explicit and Implicit Consent'.

---

[25] Information obtained about the patient or a health care professional through secret observations or recordings could be used as evidence in court cases, if the Court assesses that the evidence has crucial importance for the case.

[26] Regulation (EU) 2016/679 of the European Parliament and of the Council of 27 April 2016 on the protection of natural persons with regard to the processing of personal data and on the free movement of such data, and repealing EU Directive 95/46/EC (General Data Protection Regulation), OJ L 119/1.

[27] Consolidated Act no. 1338 of 1 September 2020 on Research Ethics Review of Health Research Projects and Health Data Research Projects.

[28] Act no. 502 of 23 May 2018 on supplementary provisions to the regulation on the protection of natural persons with regard to the processing of personal data and on the free movement of such data – Data Protection Act.

EXEMPTIONS TO CONFIDENTIALITY

The duty of confidentiality is not absolute and the legislation in all Nordic countries rely on a number of derogations from confidentiality, with some variations of the criteria for derogations. In some situations, derogations follow from statutory provisions explicitly designated as exemptions. In other situations, derogations follow from other statutory provisions, for example when the GDPR and national data protection laws enable processing of data for scientific purposes. Furthermore, derogations may in some situations require an order of the Court, for example in situations where the police require access to patient data for forensic investigation purposes.

Statutory

In some situations, a duty of confidentiality collides with other statutory duties. In Danish legislation, the statutory principle of confidentiality does not apply in situations where – according to other statutory obligations – there is a *duty to report or provide information* to other public authorities (see e.g. the Health Act, section 43.2.2). This could apply in a variety of situations. Healthcare professionals are for example required to report information to various registries regarding specific diseases, incidents (e.g. birth and death), vaccinations, prescriptions and side effects of pharmaceuticals. The obligation to report infectious diseases represents an interesting case in a Danish context. Like in other countries, it is for surveillance purposes an obligation to report cases of several infectious diseases to the health authorities, spanning from more common diseases like flue, COVID and meningitis to rarer diseases like cholera, measles, polio and Monkeypox. The report should include the patient's personal identification number, and in some situations also their phone number. Whereas this has previously not been much debated, the COVID pandemic provoked increased attention to both collection of samples and data, and secondary use of data for research and other purposes. It came somehow as a surprise that collection and use of data and samples during COVID could be a challenge to the general public's trust in the health care services. This is interesting, as the public health authorities in the context of reporting cases of HIV/AIDS has paid specific attention to install trust in being tested. In this situation, there is a right of individuals to be tested anonymously, which implies that reports will not include the tested person's ID (see more in 'Prevention of harm to others').

Health care professionals are also obliged to inform the social security services in situations where a child has been exposed to abuse or parents do not pay sufficient attention to the medical needs of the child. This obligation also applies in situations where the parents are patients and entitled to confidentiality, if for example the parents for medical reasons are not capable of taking sufficient care of the child. In these situations, no balancing of interest is taking place, but it should be assessed whether the information provided is of importance for the receiving public authority. The duty to report has priority over the duty of confidentiality.

The Danish Criminal Code (section 164a) also requires everyone (including healthcare professionals) to contact the police, if they have knowledge about an innocent person who is accused of or convicted for a crime. This could be relevant for healthcare professionals in situations where they have treated a patient who has revealed they have committed a crime or whom they for good reasons suspect to have committed a crime, and where another innocent person is at risk of being accused or convicted for the crime.

Explicit and Implicit Consent

In all the Nordic countries, patient consent can liberate the health care professional from the duty of confidentiality. However, it is important to look closer at the *scope of the consent*, and the *consent requirements*.

Consent to disclosure of health data is the general rule in the Danish Health Act both when information is passed on to other health care professionals (section 41.1 of the Act) or when being disclosed to private persons, or public and private institutions outside the health care services (section 43.1 of the Act). This demonstrates the formal importance attached to patients' rights to informational self-determination in Danish legislation.

When health data are passed on to other health care professionals with the purpose of patient treatment, consent must – generally (but see exceptions immediately below) – be *explicit* and fulfil the consent requirement in Article 4.11 and Article 7 of the GDPR in terms of granularity and clarity.[29] An oral consent suffices, and it can be given to both the healthcare professional providing the information or receiving the information (section 42 of the Act). Consent requirements are stricter in situations where health data are disclosed for other purposes than patient treatment or to actors outside the healthcare services (e.g. to other public authorities, relatives or other private persons, employers or insurance companies). In this situation, an explicit and *written* consent must be provided, and the consent is only valid for a maximum of one year (section 44 of the Act). For children under the age of 15 years and for adults who permanently lack the capacity to consent, the custodial parent(s)

---

[29] See more details in executive order no. 359/2019 regarding information and consent to medical treatment and to processing, disclosure and gaining access to health data.

(children) or close relatives/legal guardians/future representative (adults) are entitled to provide consent.

In addition to explicit consent, the Health Act also makes use of *opt-out solutions*, where patients are provided with information of a *right to object to* disclosure of patient data to other healthcare professionals and to them getting access to their data (section 41.3 and 42a.5 of the Act). The right to object applies in a few situations, for example where various healthcare professionals involved in a specific treatment of the patient are sharing information, or where hospitals as a matter of routine send an epicrisis to the GP about the patient's medical status. In practice, this opt-out option makes the general rule of explicit consent more theoretical than practical. It also applies where health care professionals or students gain access to patient records for the purpose of education and competence development, or to make general analysis of treatment practices for quality assurance purposes. Even though this is not labelled in the Act as 'implicit consent' it is – according to the preparatory work – based on the assumption that patients will be willing to share information in these situations, and if not, they are entitled to object. Consequently, the right to object resembles an *implicit or implied consent*, where a person's non-verbal behaviour, actions or inactions can be interpreted as consent.

Implicit consent cannot be used in Danish law in situations where health data are passed on to actors outside the health care services, and it is also important to note that opt-out options do not fulfil the consent requirement laid down in the GDPR. Consequently, opt-out regulation provided in the Health Act must at the same time have another legal basis in the GDPR (typically Article 9(2) (h–i)).

Other healthcare personnel

Other healthcare professionals involved in the treatment obviously need information about the patient. It is both clear where patients are referred from, for example, a GP to a specialist or/and to a hospital for further diagnostic and treatment, and internally at hospitals where various wards and healthcare professionals are involved in diagnosing and treating the patient. The legislation in all the Nordic countries enables processing of data in these situations without an explicit consent.

According to Danish law, sharing of health data among health professionals for the purpose of providing health care to patients requires – as a rule – the patient's informed consent (Health Act section 41.1). However, there are several exemptions. In situations where it is necessary to *disclose* health data from one health care professional to another for the provision of care in an actual and specific treatment context, this can be done without the patient's explicit consent, provided it is necessary and considered to be in accordance with patient's interests and needs (section 41.2.1). If the other health care professional has *direct access* to the data – for example, through an electronic health record system (EHR) – he/she can have *relevant* access to the data, if this is *necessary* and considered to be in accordance with patient's interests and needs (section 42a.1). The difference between the two situations (disclosure vis-a-vis access) is, that in the disclosure situation, the primary healthcare professional can ensure that only necessary information is disclosed, whereas in the direct access situation, the accessing healthcare professional will inevitably get access to more information than necessary when looking into a patient's EHR. As health data are increasingly accessible from the national health platform sundhed.dk, access is more common than disclosure nowadays.

The Health Act also permits that the patient's medical history (epicrises) can be sent from the hospital to the patient's GP (section 41.2.3–41.2.4), and in case the patient (or a guardian or proxy) is unable to consent to treatment, it is also allowed to disclose or access information if it is of vital interest for the patient (section 41.2.4 and section 42a.2). Furthermore, health care professionals are entitled to access the patients so-called 'Joint Medicine Card', which is a register with information about prescribed medicine which the patient has obtained from the pharmacy. This provides most groups of healthcare professionals (and other non-health related caregivers) with information about medicine prescribed to the patient.

Teaching, research, quality assurance, planning, administration, accreditation and audit

Several activities in the health care services such as teaching and training, medical research, quality assurance and development, planning, administration, accreditation and audit are closely related to patient treatment and are therefore considered to have a special status from a confidentiality perspective. Such activities are sometimes described in Danish law as 'treatment-related activities', which means that use of health data for these activities is considered more as 'primary use' than 'secondary use' of health data.

Students in medicine, nursing and other health professions need to practice as part of their *education*, and when practising they get access to confidential information about the patient. Professors and teachers also regularly use patients or patient cases as part of teaching activities. This is beneficial for future patients but can at the same time be burdensome and intruding for patient subjects. Until a few years ago there was only limited attention to the confidentiality aspects of teaching activities in Danish health legislation. However, it gradually became clear that students were not covered by a duty of confidentiality, when practising in the healthcare services, because the legislation only applied to licensed healthcare professionals and their assistants. In addition, traditional practices among health professionals to 're-visit' health records of patients treated in the past for self-evaluation and learning purposes did not have a legal basis in the Health Act. After an amendment of the Health Act in 2014, this is now explicitly addressed in the Health Act (section 40.2, section 41.2.6–7, section 41.6 and section 42d.2.1) which provides a legal basis for use of patient data for these purposes without an explicit consent – but granting the patient a right to object (see above in 'Explicit and implicit consent').

Medical research is another important area for processing of health data, which is attracting increased attention with big data research, genome sequencing and development of AI-based precision medicine and precision public health initiatives. This development and its impact on confidentiality will be addressed in more details below in 'Confidentiality and genetics'. Most medical research projects rely on health data, both where research subjects are involved, and when research is based on tissue samples or personal data. All the Nordic countries are strongly committed to research, and the legislation in all countries enables in various ways the use of health data and tissue samples for research purposes. However, the legislative framework differs significantly between the five countries, with Denmark and Finland probably being the most research-liberal countries and Norway the country with most restrictions. A complete picture is not possible in this context, but it can briefly be summarized that all countries have exploited the research exemption laid down in Article 89 of GDPR to enable research on personal data, and that the Nordic countries have various research ethics approval mechanisms for research projects dependent on whether individuals are involved as research participants, or projects are exclusively based on tissue samples or personal data. Similarly, there are also countries with special legislation on research projects based on tissue samples and health data.[30]

In Denmark research involving *research participants* will always need an approval from a research ethics committee (REC),[31] and research participants must provide informed consent to participation, which should also address the processing of data in the project. In addition, the researchers must comply with the GDPR and the Danish Data Protection Act (DPA).[32] Where research can

---

[30]   See e.g., Finnish Act no. 552/2019 on the Secondary Use of Health and Social Data, the Icelandic Health records Act (55/2009), the Norwegian Act no. 43 of 20 June 2014 on Health Records and Act no. 44 of 20 June 2008 on Medical and Health Research, and the Swedish Health Data Registries Act and Patient Data Act 2008/355. See for biobanks supra note 20, and separate chapters on each of the Nordic countries (apart from Iceland) in S. Slokenberg, O. Tzortzatou and J. Reichel (eds), *GDPR and Biobanking. Individual Rights, Public Interests and Research Regulation across Europe* (Berlin: Springer, 2020).

[31]   Supra note 27.

[32]   Supra notes 26 and 28.

be carried out *exclusively on personal data or tissue samples*, DPA section 10 'activates' the research exemption in GDPR Article 9(2)(j) and Article 89 and allows the processing of personal data and tissue samples without the data subject's consent for the sole purpose of carrying out statistical or scientific studies. The projects must be *significant to society*, and processing of the data must be *necessary* for the studies. Data should – if possible – be *pseudonymized*, and they may not be used for other purposes than research. Apart from complying with the DPA, these research projects may also need an authorization from a research ethics committee (REC). This is the case for research projects based on tissue samples and for research projects based on sensitive personal data, where there is a risk of generating secondary finding (typically projects using genetic data or advanced imaging). If data are to be *transferred to a third party* outside the geographical scope of the GDPR, a permission from the Danish Data Protection Authority is always needed (DPA section 10.3). This is also the case if transfer involves human tissues samples (also within the scope of the GDPR), or the transfer of data serves the purpose of publication in a recognized scientific journal or similar.

Apart from the DPA, the Health Act also has a few provisions regarding use of health data for research purposes. Section 46.1 of the Health Act, allows for further use of data from *patient records* and registers for scientific purposes, provided the project has been approved by a REC. If the project is not approved by a REC, which will be the case for most projects exclusively based on personal data, the Regional Council (responsible for health care services), must authorize access to the data subject's health records (section 46.2). It is a condition that the project has significant societal interest, and the Regional Council can lay down further conditions for the processing of the data. It is furthermore a condition, that the data subject can only be contacted with the permission of the health care professional, who has provided the treatment (section 46.3). Finally, the data may only be processed for scientific purposes, and any publication of the data must ensure that the data subject is not identifiable (section 48).

Quality-assurance and -development together with *patient safety schemes* are also examples of treatment-related activities. The same goes for *administration, planning, accreditation and audits.* Here again, use of health data typically takes place within a 'circle of confidentiality' where those who get access to data all are under a duty of confidentiality. Consequently, the legislative framework in the Nordic countries enables reporting and sharing of data for such purposes, and normally without the patients' explicit consent. The Danish Health Act includes several reporting duties for quality and patient safety purposes, and allow health authorities access to patient data without patient consent for purposes related to administration, planning and audits (see e.g., section 42d, section 43.2.3–5, and chapter 58–61).

Prevention of harm to others

Confidentiality is a crucial principle not only to protect patients' privacy rights but also to install and sustain trust in the health care services. Consequently, in accordance with article 8 of the European Convention of Human Rights, it is only allowed to disclose information if significant public or private interests are at stake. In situations where there is a significant interest in preventing the harm of others, it may be possible to set aside a duty of confidentiality. In the Danish legislative framework this is clearly reflected in the Health Act (section 43.2.2) which allows for disclosure of information in situations where significant interests of other persons overweight the interest of the patient. Before making use of this option, it is normally necessary having tried to obtain an informed consent from the patient, but if the patient will not consent, it may be justified to pass on information.

Prevention of harm to others is a special concern in situations where the patient has a *contagious disease* or *genetic disorder* (see more in 'CONFIDENTIALITY AND GENETICS'). The public health response to address the HIV infection can be used as an illustrative example of different approaches to confidentiality in situation of *contagious diseases* amongst the Nordic countries.[33] When HIV was at its highest in the 1980s–1990s and treatment options were still limited, the Danish public health policy was to apply the so-called 'cooperation-and-inclusion strategy' and focus on promoting testing by ensuring anonymity and appeal to responsibility within risk groups to prevent the further spread of the disease to others. Only in exceptional cases was it allowed to contact persons at risk and advise them to be tested. The 'cooperation-and-inclusion strategy' was perceived as most suitable for combatting HIV. In Sweden the 'cooperation-and-inclusion strategy' was also endorsed but supplemented with a 'contain-and-control strategy' which ensured registration of HIV patients, tracking of persons, who may have been contaminated, and use of compulsory isolation for persons who did not comply with rules for responsible behavior.[34] Comparing the two strategies it is clear that the Danish approach confirmed the strong commitment in Denmark to perceive confidentiality as an important measure to install trust in the health care services and thereby enable public health policies. It must be added, that after better treatment options for AIDS become available, the assessment of when it is justified to inform persons who might be contaminated may be different, as tracking at-risk individuals today may be lifesaving. The same

---

[33]   See for an interesting comparison Signild Valgårda, 'Problematizations and Path Dependency: HIV/AIDS Policies in Denmark and Sweden' (2007) 51(1) *Medical History* 99–112.

[34]   Compulsory isolation was criticized by the ECtHR in *Enhorn v Sweden*, app. 56527/00 (2005).

considerations could also speak in favour of informing vulnerable persons who have been in contact with COVID-infected persons, if early preventive treatment can impact on the risk of being severely affected. However, it is clear that any non-justified or accidental disclosure of personal medical information or medical history to third parties, including relatives, would be considered a clear violation of the obligation of confidentiality. This could, for example, be the case if the hospital encourages a relative to bring the patient's 'HIV medicine' to the clinic, where the relative does not know about the patient being HIV-positive. A Danish complaints case can also be used as illustration. In this case, the patient, who had an abortion, had instructed the clinic only to send the bill to her private email and not to her home address. Accidentally, the bill was sent to her home address with the result that the partner obtained confidential information. This was considered a clear violation of the duty of confidentiality.[35]

It may also be justified to set aside the duty of confidentiality in other situations where information is necessary to avoid harm to others. In a Danish case from the High Court,[36] a hospital had informed the father of a grown-up patient about her condition, after they had discharged her from the hospital ward. The patient was hospitalized due to somatic health problems, but she was also suffering from a psychiatric condition. When suggesting she would leave the hospital to take her own life, they made a medical assessment but did not find her psychiatric conditions sufficiently severe to justify forcibly keeping her at the hospital. When she was discharged, she explicitly instructed the health care professionals not to inform her father. Despite her own clear refusal to inform the father, the High Court found that it was justified to inform him to avoid exposing him to distress, if she succeeded to take her life.

Police investigations

Disclosure of information for forensic purposes puts the balancing of various interests at the forefront. Police investigations may concern the patient who is suspected of having committed a crime, but can also relate to patients, who are victims of a crime, but for various reasons are not interested in a police inquiry (e.g. in cases of domestic violence). Consequently, several diverging interests are at stake.

The patient has a clear interest in protection of privacy and the right to informational self-determination, either because of the risk of being exposed to criminal investigations or, (as a victim), because a criminal investigation

---

[35] Case no. 16SPS62, available (in Danish) at https://stpk.dk/afgorelser-og-domme/afgorelser-fra-styrelsen-for-patientklager/16sps62/ (last accessed 28 August 2023).

[36] U 1996.1261Ø.

could expose the patient to serious risks. In addition, the health care services have a general interest in sustaining trust in the health care services. On the other hand, there may be substantial interests related to victims of crimes as well as general societal interests in investigating and responding to serious criminal behaviour. The Danish Health Act in combination with the civil and criminal procedure legislation outlines the general principles for the balancing of interest. According to the Health Act, disclosure of information to the police may be justified (but is not obligatory), in cases of *serious* crimes, where the interests of society or private interests clearly has to be given more weight than interests in protecting patient privacy and sustaining trust. A case from the Danish Patients Complaints Board can illustrate this assessment.[37] In the case, a patient at the psychiatric ward had told a physician that he had buried a rifle for later use. He was very distressed and stated he wanted to take his own life. He also said he could be violent and that he was very upset about his girlfriend. The physician didn't assess the patient to be particularly violent, but he nevertheless felt it would be right to inform the police about where the rifle was buried. When asked by the police, he also revealed the identity of the patient. The board agreed that it had been justified to inform the police about the position of the rifle but criticized the disclosure of the patient's identity, as this was not necessary to address the potential threat to others in the case. Normally it is the police who demands information from the health care services. If the health care services refuse to disclose information based on confidentiality concerns, the police will need a Court order, and to issue an order, the Court needs to be convinced that it is a *serious crime*, and that access to patient information is the last resort for investigating the case. Danish Courts have addressed this issue in a number of cases. In an illustrative case the High Court[38] reached the conclusion that there were not sufficiently weighty arguments for forcing a doctor to provide testimony regarding a patient. The case was concerned with arson, which is considered a serious crime, and the police wanted to know whether the patient had signs of burns. However, the Court concluded that even though it was a serious crime, the police had other means of investigating the crime, and that the testimony could not be considered a last resort.

In the Nordic countries there has been a special focus on the use of tissue samples from national neonatal screening biobanks (so-called PKU biobanks), where tissue samples from newborns are stored. In Denmark the PKU biobank has provided access to samples in cases of identifying victims of crimes (e.g.

---

[37]   Case no. 0231702 (available in Danish at https://stpk.dk/afgorelser-og-domme/afgorelser-fra-sundhedsvaesenets-disciplinaernaevn/0231702/ (last accessed 28 August 2023).

[38]   Case U 1995.775V (Western High Court).

a murder case where DNA from victims was found and needed to be identified) and disasters (e.g. a bombing attack on a bar in Bali and victims of the 2004 Indian Ocean tsunami). This is compliant with Danish legislations which allows for derogations from the duty of confidentiality where significant societal interests or interests of private persons need to be acknowledged. In another case, where the police wanted access to a sample from a person suspected of a crime, the High Court refused to issue an order as access to the tissue sample for forensic purposes was considered a violation of both the Danish regulation of a DNA-profile database and ECHR Article 8. In Sweden the use of samples from the PKU-biobank for investigation of the murder of Swedish foreign minister Anna Lindh in 2003 and identification of victims of the 2004 Indian Ocean tsunami has given rise to significant debate. In the Lindh case, the tissue sample from a suspected (and later convicted) person was handed over to the police, which could then check a match with DNA found on the scene of the crime, before they moved on to arrest the person. This was subsequently criticized by several public authorities because no Court order was in place. For the tsunami victims, the Swedish parliament made a temporary amendment to the biobank legislations to enable the use of tissue samples from the PKU biobank for identification of victims. There have subsequently been other incidents where police have requested access to biobank samples for forensic purposes, and the issue has been subject to scrutiny and considerations in two committees. In the white paper from the last committee, it is recommended that there should be a ban on use of biobank samples for forensic purposes, but that use of samples for identification of victims should be allowed.[39]

Public interest
Apart from the societal interest in investigating crimes, there are also several other areas where there is a justified societal interest in having access to health data. Cases where children need care by the social services have already been mentioned (above in 'Exemptions to confidentiality'), and, in general, societies with a universal health- and social care system will often need information to ensure that everybody gets access to the services to which they are entitled, and also that nobody gets more than justified.

The social services can serve as an example. Sickness benefits and social pensions relate to physical and mental health conditions, where access to health data is needed to make an assessment. Generally, this will require the patients consent according to the Danish Health Act, and it is normally also in the patient's own interest to have a positive assessment of an application for social services. It may, however, in some situations be justified to have access

---

[39] *Framtidens biobanker* (Biobanks of the future), SOU 2018.4.

to information based on public interest, for example in cases where there is doubt about whether trustworthy information has been provided. In the *M.S. v Sweden* case,[40] the ECtHR reached the conclusion that it was justified that the Swedish authorities had collected information from the patient record in a case of the industrial insurance compensation. The applicant had a serious back condition which she claimed had been worsened when she accidently slipped and fell at work. The Swedish Social Authority Office had obtained very sensitive health information from her medical files without her consent, and the Court concluded that her application for compensation did not waive her right to privacy, and that an intervention of her right to private life (Article 8.1) had taken place. However, the Court also found that the intervention had been justified and proportionate (Article 8.2). The Social Authority Office needed objective information to assess the application for compensation, and the health data revealed were all relevant for the assessment and was furthermore handed over from one public institution to another.

Freedom of the press
Freedom of information and freedom of the press is protected in the constitution of the Nordic countries. The protection in Sweden dates back to 1766 and in Sweden confidentiality provisions are generally seen as derogations to the constitutional principle of freedom of information and right to access public information. However, freedom of the press must obviously be balanced towards respect for individual's right to privacy, and in this respect the purpose of media coverage of the healthcare services and individual patients' situations is important. There is no protection of gossip journalism trying to reveal health information especially about publicly known persons. On the other hand, media coverage of important informative value (e.g. during the COVID-19 pandemic) or regarding problematic conditions in the healthcare services and maltreatment of patients can serve a legitimate purpose of significant public interest. In a Danish Supreme Court case[41] it was assessed whether a television broadcast of the situation in a psychiatric ward could be banned from being broadcasted. The Regional Council found that the coverage would expose vulnerable patients who – despite their own consent to participate – was not considered able to assess the consequences of participation. The Supreme Court found that most of the patients had been able to provide a valid consent to participation, and for the two patients, who was seen as unable to consent, the Court found that taking the purpose of the broadcast into consideration, a bailiff's ban on the broadcast was unsubstantiated.

---

[40]   *M.S. v Sweden*, ECtHR application no. 20837/92.
[41]   U 1989.726 H.

CONFIDENTIALITY AND GENETICS

There is immense interest in all the Nordic countries in developing precision medicine based on existing health data resources and biobanks, which can provide tissue samples for sequencing and other comprehensive genetic analyses. Iceland has already been moving in this direction for several years, due to initiatives taken by a private company – DeCode – which has also been supported (at least in periods) by the Icelandic government. Denmark has established a National Genome Centre in 2019, and Finland has decided a comprehensive strategy for precision medicine which also includes the establishment of a National Genome Centre. The Danish regulation of the National Genome Centre is not particularly concerned with confidentiality issues and leaves it to be settled by the provisions in the Health Act. However, it does address confidentiality issues related to disclosure of data from the centre for forensic purposes. In this situation data can only be obtained by the police based on a court order and only in cases concerned with investigation of terrorism (and not other serious crimes). In addition the new legislation also acknowledges patients' interest in informational self-determination, when allowing patients to opt-out for secondary use of genetic data stored in the National Genome Centre.

Precision medicine raises some of the same confidentiality issues as genetic testing for health care purposes. In both Norway and Sweden special acts regarding genetic testing and related issues have been in place for several years, and Denmark has regulated the use of genetic information for insurance and employment purposes since 1996 in special employment and insurance acts. Consequently, there is a legal infrastructure available to address the legal and ethical issues affiliated with new genetic and big data technologies, including how this development affects confidentiality in the healthcare services.

There are especially two concerns from a confidentiality perspective; one relates to confidentiality within family relations, the other to confidentiality towards employers, insurance companies and other private entities. The Norwegian Biotechnology Act[42] is the most comprehensive and it addresses both issues. In general, confidentiality issues in family relations are expected to be solved within families, and only in situations where the patient is not keen to inform family members at risk, the healthcare professional may – with the patient's consent – contact genetic relatives with information about a potential risk of having a genetically related disorder. This is also possible in situations where the patient is not able to make a decision. This contact will

---

[42] Act no. 100 of 5 December 2003 relating to the application of biotechnology in biomedicine.

often involve revealing confidential information about the patient to relatives. In the other Nordic countries this issue is dealt with in the general framework for confidentiality and derogations from confidentiality (e.g. to protect the interests of other persons). In a Danish context this issue is normally dealt with as part of the regular genetic counselling taking place in the clinic. Genetic counselling is based on professional ethical principles, according to which it is routine to encourage the tested person to contact relatives, who may also be affected by an identified genetic disorder. In case, the tested person refuses to inform potentially affected relatives, health care professionals must make a proper assessment of whether significant interests of relatives overweight the interest of the patient (Health Act section 43.2.2). This could be the case if the identified genetic disorder could be prevented or alleviated through regular check-ups or early interventions, as could be the case for carriers of the BRAC1 or BRAC2 gene. Unlike other countries,[43] there have not been any Danish court cases testing the scope and limits of relative's right to information and a possible duty of health care professionals to provide such information to relatives ex-officio or on request.

Both the Norwegian Act and the Swedish Act on Genetic Integrity[44] stipulates that no one may as part of an agreement demand another person to have a genetic test or to ask a person to provide genetic information about himself, unless provided for in law. In the Swedish Act insurance companies are, however, entitled to ask for genetic information for insurance sums that exceeds a particular threshold. Danish legislation also prohibits or restricts access to genetic information in both employment and insurance (and pension) relations.[45] In Finland there is only legislation regarding employment[46] and in Iceland legislation[47] is restricted to insurance relations. Consequently, this is an area which clearly needs more legal attention in the Nordic countries.

CONCLUSION

Seen from the perspective of the individual, the legal principles of privacy and confidentiality are situated in a complex landscape where technological developments and societal needs together with private and commercial interests

---

[43]   *ABC v St George's NHS Hospital Trust* [2017] EWCA Civ 336 (On appeal from Nicol J [2015] EWHC 1394 (QB)).

[44]   Act no. 351 of 1 July 2006 on Genetic Integrity.

[45]   Act no. 286 of 24 April 1996 on Health Information in Employment, Consolidated Act no. 1237 of 9 November 2015 on Insurance, and Consolidated Act no. 355 of 2 April 2020 on Company Pension.

[46]   Act on Privacy in Working Life (759/2004).

[47]   Act on Insurance Contracts (30/2004).

for innovation and development are calling for legal and ethical adjustments. The existing ethical and legal framework is not necessarily fit to embrace this development, where individuals are becoming increasingly transparent for society, big tech companies and others, and the idea of a confidential relationship with the family physician seems to be lost in translation. However, the COVID-19 pandemic has clearly demonstrated that the interest in installing and sustaining patients' trust in the health care services is still important. This is also confirmed by important initiatives of the EU Commission to address the ethical and legal challenges affiliated with development and application of AI in the health care services. In a recent white paper, the Commission argued convincingly for the necessity both to develop an ecosystem of excellence (research and development) and an ecosystem of trust (citizens).[48] Key ethical principles for sustaining trust includes transparency, human agency and oversight, non-discrimination and fairness, privacy and data governance and safety and accountability. These principles fit with the Nordic welfare state model and could provide for development of new and more robust ethical and legal avenues.

---

[48]   EU Commission, White Paper – on artificial intelligence. A European approach to excellence and trust, COM (2020) 65 final, 19.02.2020.

7. Data protection, privacy, and confidentiality in Qatar's health system

Barry Solaiman

INTRODUCTION

This chapter examines Qatar, which has exemplified a pivot towards internationalisation, becoming a regionally significant economy wielding major influence globally. These efforts are not merely exampled by hosting major sporting events, international conferences, and creating eye-catching cities and infrastructure, but more fundamentally through institution-building. The onboarding of international legal best practices is resulting in the creation of laws and policies reflecting the standards and norms expected in long-established legal systems. While those norms have yet to be fully realised, they are growing.

This pivot is most tangibly seen with the creation of the Qatar Financial Centre (QFC) which is a business and financial centre.[1] Within the QFC is the Qatar International Court (QIC) that hears disputes arising mainly between QFC entities.[2] Judges from the UK and other established legal systems preside over these courts, applying the general principles of the Common Law. The founding President of the QIC was Lord Phillips, the former President of the UK Supreme Court and Lord Chief Justice. The current President is Lord Thomas, who also served as Lord Chief Justice.[3] Outside the courts, institutions follow the arbitration and mediation rules of leading international

---

[1] See, 'Overview' *QFC*, https://www.qfc.qa/en/about-qfc/overview accessed 10 Sept 2023.
[2] The QIC was established by QFC Law No. 2 of 2009 (Qatar); QICDRC, 'History', www.qicdrc.gov.qa/about-us/history accessed 10 Sept 2023.
[3] Ibid.

organisations. Qatar was the third country in the world to ratify the Singapore Convention on Mediation.[4]

In a region so politically, economically, and culturally diverse, it can be challenging to narrow the choice of country to examine on any legal topic. However, Qatar demonstrates a direct engagement with the international community that warrants closer examination in other spaces of its legal system, such as health.[5] Indeed, while countries in the Middle East lag behind the global GDP average for healthcare spending, there has been increasing investment in local healthcare systems from governmental and private entities.[6] Qatar's spending on health is among the highest in the Middle East per capita.[7]

The application of legal principles in the medical realm is not quite so direct as in the commercial space of the financial courts. Civil disputes are heard in the local courts, which apply civil law principles deriving from the Napoleonic Code. Islamic Sharia Law and criminal law have primacy over civil law in legal disputes involving healthcare professionals. That combination raises certain particularities concerning the legal principles that are examined below. A myriad of norms and influences coalesce within this complex setup when establishing patient rights surrounding privacy and confidentiality.[8] To unpack this complexity, this chapter analyses three broad legal areas and evaluates the

---

[4]   United Nations Convention on International Settlement Agreements Resulting from Mediation Resolution Adopted by the General Assembly on 20 December 2018 (Sixth committee (A/73/496) 73/198); Saudi Arabia was the fourth country to ratify the Singapore Convention.

[5]   Saudi Arabia and the United Arab Emirates have also created financial centres, courts and dispute resolution centres applying English common law. However, it is beyond the scope of this Chapter to examine privacy and confidentiality in all three countries. Future research is certainly needed to fill this void.

[6]   'Current Health Expenditure (% of GDP) – Middle East & North Africa' *The World Bank* (2019) https://data.worldbank.org/indicator/SH.XPD.CHEX.GD.ZS ?locations=ZQ&most_recent_year_desc=true accessed 10 Sept 2023.

[7]   'Qatar's Investment in Healthcare Sector at QR22.7bn' *Peninsula* (22 Sept 2019) https://thepeninsulaqatar.com/article/29/09/2019/Qatar's-investment-in-healthcare -sector-at-QR22.7bn accessed 10 Sept 2023; 'Demand for Health Services in Qatar' *Oxford Business Group* (2020) https://oxfordbusinessgroup.com/overview/keeping-pace -private-sector-set-play-more-important-role-demand-medical-services-continues-rise accessed 10 Sept 2023; There has also been increases in public and private investment in the UAE and Saudi. See, Nitin Mehrotra and others, 'Public Versus Private Investment' *KPMG* (2020) https://assets.kpmg/content/dam/kpmg/ae/pdf-2020/09/public-vs-private -investment.pdf accessed 10 Sept 2023; David Ndichu, 'Private Investment in UAE Healthcare to rise by 9.5% annually: KPMG Report' *Gulf Business* (24 Sept 2020) https:// gulfbusiness.com/private-investment-in-uae-healthcare-to-rise-by-9-5-annually-kpmg -report/ accessed 10 Sept 2023.

[8]   The terms 'Privacy' and 'confidentiality' are used interchangeably in this chapter. Arabic versions of the law take precedence in Qatar over English versions.

relevant implications for privacy. Part 2 examines the ethical and legal basis for confidentiality through religion, the Constitution and general criminal law provisions on privacy. Part 3 explores the specific legislative provisions on confidentiality in medical practice and regulatory protections enabling patient complaints through the Ministry of Public Health (MOPH). Part 4 reveals four areas where specific considerations about confidentiality arise in Qatar. Namely, data protection law, the use of the media to influence behaviour, the social stigma surrounding mental health and the risks of revealing sensitive information through genetic research. Within these sections, this chapter will highlight the applicability of the special cases identified in this book to the law in Qatar. Namely, the duty of confidentiality towards family members (case 1), the status of using audio and video recordings (case 2), family treatment and cases of abuse (case 3), and genetic privacy (case 4).

Overall, the analysis demonstrates that international norms on privacy and confidentiality are prevalent within this system. However, their application differs in certain areas. In many ways, the principles apply as one would expect. Yet, in some respects, privacy is accorded a greater status and almost reverence than systems elsewhere. In other aspects, this chapter reveals that privacy cannot always usurp local social considerations, as well as religious and cultural aspects of life in Qatar. Therefore, a unique balance is maintained between these facets, and the growth of laws premised on international norms raises questions about how this balance will be maintained as Qatar continues to internationalise.

THE OVERARCHING BASIS FOR CONFIDENTIALITY

Qatar is an Arab state, and its religion is Islam. Respecting an individual's 'secrets' or privacy is of great importance in Islam, and it is generally crucial to gain an individual's consent before disclosing confidential matters.[9] This ethical basis is seen in Qatar's Constitution, which states that Islamic Law

---

This chapter relies on official English translations, but there may be discrepancies between the translations.

[9]   World Health Organization, Islamic Code of Medical and Health Ethics, Regional Committee for the Eastern Mediterranean (September 2005) Fifty Second Session, EM/RC52/7; Saeid Nazari Tavaokkoli, Nasrin Nejadsarvari and Ali Ebrahami, 'Analysis of Medical Confidentiality from the Islamic Ethical Perspective' (2015) 54 *Journal of Religion and Health* 427, 430–32.

is the main source of its legislation.[10] Privacy is directly protected in Qatar's Constitution under Article 37, which notes that:

> [T]he sanctity of the individual's privacy shall be inviolable, and therefore interference in a person's privacy, family affairs, home or correspondence, or any other act of interference that may demean or defame a person, shall not be allowed, save as permitted by the provisions stipulated in the Law.[11]

This Article has been relied upon in case law. In the Court of Cassation case QCC 156/2017, a father claimed compensation for the use of his daughter's image (who was a minor) in an exhibition without his permission.[12] The court held that under Article 37, 'it was prohibited to intervene in a person's life and his private affairs or the affairs of their family except through the legal way'.[13] The image was published without the father's permission, and compensation was, therefore, justified.[14] Thus, Article 37 is not merely aspirational. It reflects the ethical basis for confidentiality in Islam and has legal applicability in practice. One also finds a strong manifestation of privacy protections in certain areas of the Penal Code. Invading the privacy of a female is a crime.[15] Defamation is taken very seriously with any photographs, news or comments about any individual or their family (even if those comments are accurate) liable for both fines and imprisonment.[16] Illegally intruding into another's private life without their consent by intercepting letters, telephone calls, recording conversations on any device, and taking photographs of a person in a private place are all punishable with fines and imprisonment.[17] The penalties were increased in 2017 in response to the use of social media. There was concern about photographs being taken of deceased and injured persons in car accidents and those committing traffic violations.[18] The law was also amended to prohibit taking photographs or videos of others in public places for defama-

---

[10] Permanent Constitution of the State of Qatar 2004, Article 1.

[11] Ibid, Article 37.

[12] QCC 156/2017.

[13] Ibid.

[14] Ibid.

[15] Law No. 11 of 2004 Issuing the Penal Code, Article 291 (Penal Code).

[16] Ibid, Article 331.

[17] Ibid, Article 333. The penalties for a violation of Article 333 were increased by Law No. 4 of 2017; See also, Shafeeq Alingal, 'Photography Violating Privacy to Invite Action' *Gulf Times* (2 Feb 2021) www.gulf-times.com/story/683783/Photography-violating-privacy-to-invite-action accessed 10 Sept 2023.

[18] Habib Toumi, 'Qatar Bans Taking Pictures at Accident Sites' *Gulf News* (17 Sept 2015) https://gulfnews.com/world/gulf/qatar/qatar-bans-taking-pictures-at-accident-sites-1.1585446 accessed 10 Sept 2023.

tory purposes.[19] Thus, at a holistic level, privacy is constitutionally and legally protected. Consequently, for Case 2 in this book on the use of audio and video recordings, and private detectives, it is strictly prohibited to record or transmit conversations in public or private places, or to eavesdrop. It would be illegal for a doctor to make such a recording without a patient's consent.

The religious, constitutional, and legal context helps to elucidate the legislative duty of confidentiality as it arises in the healthcare sphere. How that context influences those duties is nuanced. Some laws must balance international best practices with local religious expectations on certain matters. Religious scholars issue legal opinions called *Fatwās*. There is a certain congruence between particular elements in laws and those found in *Fatwās*, such as the limit at which an abortion can be performed or the principle that no financial compensation should be given for a donated organ.[20] The need to find this balance is important but is not pervasive. Religious scholars do consult Western scientific academies for answers where there are conflicting opinions.[21] For privacy, this context is of limited influence in the medical laws themselves that are explored below. It will be seen how those laws tend to replicate the standards of privacy and confidentiality that one would expect in Europe or the US. Nevertheless, the analysis highlights unique aspects of privacy that arise in Qatar's context.

CONFIDENTIALITY AND GENERAL LEGAL DUTIES IN HEALTHCARE

Privacy and confidentiality are strongly protected by legislation in Qatar within the health sphere. Unlike the UK and US, where negligence claims are predominantly brought through the civil courts, claims in Qatar are primarily brought through both the criminal and civil courts. A case will often begin its journey in the criminal court because a conviction can be used as 'conclusive

---

[19]   Law No.4 of 2017; see also, Safwan Moubaydeen and Zaher Nammour, 'Qatar Strengthens Data Protection – Penal Code Amended' *Dentons* (17 May 2017) www .dentons.com/en/insights/alerts/2017/may/17/qatar-strengthens-data-protection#:~:text =4%20of%202017%20was%20published,fine%20not%20exceeding%20QAR%2010 %2C000 accessed 10 Sept 2023.

[20]   Barry Solaiman, 'Medical Liability in Qatar' in Vera Lúcia Raposo and Roy Beran, *Medical Liability in Asia and Australasia* (Springer 2021) 214 and 218; Mohammed Ghaly, *Islam and Disability: Perspectives in Theory and Jurisprudence* (Routledge 2010) 122–23 and 289.

[21]   Mohammed Ghaly, 'Biomedical Scientists as Co-Muftis: Their Contribution to Contemporary Islamic Bioethics' (2015) 55 *Die Welt des Islams* 286, 298.

evidence' in a civil claim.[22] As such, confidentiality breaches arising from the laws explored below are automatically more serious within the Qatari legal environment because of the associated sanctions applied in criminal law.

Article 332 of the Penal Code creates an offence for anyone acting in their official trade or professional capacity who, without consent, illegally divulges a secret entrusted to them.[23] The penalty for such a breach is up to two years in prison and/or a fine.[24] This provision would cover a healthcare professional acting in their capacity who discloses the private and confidential information about a patient without their consent (except where they are entitled to do so for the proper functioning of their job). It should be reiterated that the law applies to any healthcare professional and is not limited to doctors.

Aside from the Penal Code, the primary legislation as it applies to healthcare professionals is Law No. 2 of 1983 (Practice of Medicine), which sets the standard of care expected from a medical professional.[25] Healthcare professionals are expected to provide 'due care' and behave in a 'reasonable and professionally orthodox evidence-based manner' when diagnosing or treating a patient.[26] The standard of care aligns with the English case of *Bolam v Friern Hospital Management*.[27] Breaching a patient's privacy would fall below the standard of care expected of a medical professional. Article 20(1) of the Practice of Medicine Law states that doctors must act with 'professionalism and integrity' and that it is prohibited to disclose 'confidential information about a patient which he discovered on account of his profession, except in those cases permitted by law'. This prohibition is the first of nine stipulated in Article 20 of the law, highlighting how privacy is paramount.

Specific protections for privacy are also articulated in several laws within the health sphere. Law No. 3 of 1983 regulates the pharmacology professions.[28] It similarly requires pharmacists to 'uphold the dignity and honor of the profession and accept its ethical principles'.[29] In that vein, the law prohibits pharmacists from divulging 'confidential information about his customers, save as in those cases authorized by law'.[30] The infectious diseases, organ donation and

---

[22] Law No.13 of 1990 Civil and Commercial Procedure Law, Article 301; Law No. 23 of 2004 Regarding Promulgating the Criminal Procedure Code, Article 319.

[23] Penal Code (n 15) Article 332.

[24] Ibid.

[25] Law No. 2 of 1983 with respect to the Practice of the Profession of Medicine and Dental Medicine and Surgery.

[26] Ibid, Article 18.

[27] *Bolam v Friern Hospital Management* [1957] 1 WLR 582.

[28] Law No. 3 of 1983 with regard to Regulating the Pharmacology Professions, Mediators and Agents of the Drug Factories.

[29] Ibid, Article 8.

[30] Ibid, Article 8(2).

mental health laws also highlight specifics concerning confidentiality. These laws are explored separately below owing to the implications they have for privacy.

Beyond legislation, there are also numerous regulations by the MOPH that reiterate the centrality of privacy and confidentiality. For example, a regulation on the management of acute cholecystitis sets out 'general principles of patient care in Qatar'.[31] It notes that patients must be treated with respect and that their 'privacy is respected, particularly when discussing sensitive, personal issues'.[32] On confidentiality, it states:

> Respect the patient's right to confidentiality and avoid disclosing or sharing patients' information without their informed consent. Students and anyone not directly involved in the delivery of care should first be introduced to the patient before starting consultations or meetings, and let the patient decide if they want them to stay.[33]

These general principles are restated in most of the regulations issued and are often the first principles listed concerning the provision of patient care.[34] They provide further context and detail to what is contained in the law and reiterate the importance of those principles. Some regulations raise specific privacy and confidentiality matters. In Qatar, every resident has an ID card, and one regulation requires that an individual's ID number be used in all documents to avoid mix-ups, cases of mistaken identity and, ultimately, to protect the confidentiality and privacy of patients.[35] Thus, one can find a consistent articulation in Qatar's healthcare laws and regulations on the importance of privacy and confidentiality of patients.

---

[31] MOPH, Assessment & Management of Acute Cholecystitis (19 Sept 2019) V.2 20 Muharram 1441H, p.14.

[32] Ibid.

[33] Ibid.

[34] MOPH, The Assessment & Management of Acute Coronary Syndrome in Adults (20 Aug 2020) V.2, 1 Muharram 1442 H, p.19; MOPH, The Assessment and Management of Chronic Kidney Disease in Adults (15 March 2020) V.2, 20 Rajab 1441 H, p.27; MOPH, The Diagnosis and Management of Depression (5 Feb 2020) V.1, 23 Jumada Al Akhar 1442 H, p.20; MOPH, The Diagnosis and Management of Generalised Anxiety Disorder in Adults (5 Jan 2020) V.1, 10 Jumada Al-Awwal 1441 H, p.16. MOPH, The Management of Lower Back Pain in Adults (22 July 2020) V.1, 1 Dhi Al-Hijjah 1441 H, p.19.

[35] QCHP, The Mandate of Using Patient's QID Personal Number in all Correspondences Related to Him/Her (26 November 2019) Circular No. 2/2019-1.

Confidentiality, Hospital Accreditation and Patient Rights

Additionally, accreditation requirements, hospital, and MOPH policies also govern this area. Patients who have a complaint about privacy and confidentiality can complain to the hospital directly in the first instance. The major hospitals have attained internationally renowned accreditation. For example, Qatar's main public hospital system, Hamad Medical Corporation (HMC), has attained accreditation from Joint Commission International (JCI). HMC is the only hospital system outside the US that achieved corporate Academic Medical Center accreditation in all hospitals simultaneously.[36] This, and other accreditations, create a potential avenue for patients to also complain directly to the accrediting bodies for a breach of accreditation standards such as protecting a patient's rights to privacy and confidentiality.[37]

Further, the MOPH has issued the Patients' Bill of Rights and Responsibilities, which contains privacy and confidentiality provisions.[38] It states that personal information must be kept private and confidential, that patients have a right to nominate a family member or support person to be present during examinations and discussions of their case, and that patients have a right to privacy and respect during physical examinations and treatment.[39] Alongside these rights is a complaints mechanism through the Fitness to Practice department of the MOPH, which falls under the same department responsible for licensing.[40] Those receiving poor standards of clinical care and unethical conduct or behaviour can complain to the relevant department.[41] Such complaints include (but are not limited to) matters protected in the Patients' Bill of Rights and

---

[36] 'HMC Successful in Qatar's Largest International Accreditation Program' *Peninsula* (9 May 2019) https://thepeninsulaqatar.com/article/09/05/2019/HMC -successful-in-Qatar's-largest-international-accreditation-program accessed 10 Sept 2023.

[37] Joint Commission International, Accreditation Standards for Hospitals Including Standards for Academic Medical Center Hospitals (6th edn, 1 July 2017) Rule PFR 1.3, p.10.

[38] MOPH, Patients' Bill of Rights and Responsibilities: Your Health Your Right' Fitness to Practice / Department of Healthcare Professions www.moph.gov.qa/english/ derpartments/policyaffairs/DHP/FTP/Pages/MemosDetails.aspx?ItemId=161 accessed 10 Sept 2023.

[39] Ibid.

[40] MOPH, 'Fitness to Practice Section', www.moph.gov.qa/english/derpartments/ policyaffairs/DHP/FTP/Pages/default.aspx#:~:text=Fitness%20to%20Practice%27s %20responsibility%20is,Public%20Health"%20through%20conducting%20the accessed 10 Sept 2023.

[41] MOPH, 'What Kinds of Complaints Does the Department Deal with?', www .moph.gov.qa/english/derpartments/policyaffairs/DHP/FTP/Pages/tips-details.aspx ?ItemId=4 accessed 10 Sept 2023.

Responsibilities, such as privacy and confidentiality. Compensation cannot be awarded under these procedures.[42] Instead, action would have to be pursued through the court system for such redress. Nevertheless, important sanctions are available to the Fitness to Practice Department of the MOPH, such as giving warnings, suspension, revocation of licenses, and blacklisting practitioners so they cannot obtain work in the Gulf Cooperation Council (GCC) region.[43]

It is also crucial to examine the rights prescribed by Hamad Medical Corporation (HMC) because it is the most essential healthcare provider in the country that sets the relevant standards and attains international accreditation, as noted above. HMC's approach to rights and responsibilities has an important distinction from the rights stated by the MOPH. HMC's document is titled 'Patient and Family Bill of Rights and Responsibilities'.[44] While this appears to equate the rights and responsibilities of both the patient and their family, the document emphasises the patient's 'legal guardian / legal representative', so it may be that the rights of the family technically mean the right of the patient's assigned legal representative.[45] The document covers a range of matters, including access to information and privacy and confidentiality. A patient has the right for their medical record to be read only by individuals directly involved in their care, to have all their records be treated as confidential, and to have a family member notified of his/her emergency admission to hospital. That right to notification does not appear to extend to matters beyond emergency admission, and it is even required that the legal representative 'respect other patient's rights', which likely covers the patient's privacy and confidentiality beyond their relationship.[46]

HMC's electronic health records (EHR) policy is also relevant here.[47] That policy stipulates that patient information must only be accessed by authorised professionals involved in the patient's care (except in cases required by the

---

[42]   Ibid.
[43]   MOPH, 'What are the Outcomes of Investigation Those Complaints?', www.moph.gov.qa/english/derpartments/policyaffairs/DHP/FTP/Pages/tips-details.aspx?ItemId=5 accessed 10 Sept 2023.
[44]   HMC, 'Patient and Family Bill of Rights and Responsibilities', www.hamad.qa/EN/Patient-Information/Documents/Patient%20and%20Family%20Rights%20Poster%20English_2015.pdf accessed 10 Sept 2023.
[45]   Ibid.
[46]   Ibid.
[47]   HMC, 'Electronic Health Record (EHR) Privacy and Confidentiality' (2017) www.hamad.qa/EN/your%20health/Patient%20and%20Family%20Education%20Unit/Publications/For-Health-Practitioners/For%20Health%20Practitioners/Electronic%20Health%20Record%20(EHR)%20Privacy%20and%20Confidentiality%20-%20English.pdf accessed 10 Sept 2023.

law, such as emergencies).[48] Further, healthcare professionals must treat patient health information with confidence and ensure that documentation is stored securely. There are strict security protocols for access to EHRs backed by pin codes and encryption.[49] The EHR policy cites standards set by the Office of the National Coordinator for Health Information Technology (ONC) in the US, the Healthcare Information and Management Systems Society (HIMSS), and the US Department of Health & Human Services.[50]

For Case 1 in this book on whether a nurse would be fired for revealing confidential patient information to a family member, such as their HIV status, that would be a clear breach of confidentiality / privacy under both the MOPH and HMC rules. That information could be shared with the legal representative who would be under the same duty. However, whether the nurse would be fired depends on the case. The most likely sequence of events is that a committee consisting of clinicians and HR and legal representatives will be formed to consider the matter. It may be that other disciplinary action will be taken in the first instance, such as moving the nurse to another role or placement or being given a final written warning before being fired.

Further, a patient's family is often closely involved in their care in Qatar which has strong familial structures. This can be seen in the sections below on mental health, which elucidate these considerations in more detail. The familial approach is not too dissimilar to countries like China, where families are often intimately involved in decision-making.[51] However, different to China, Qatar has a very diverse population that predominantly consists of expats who may be used to strict autonomy of their information in their care. Further studies are required to determine the extent to which the confidentiality provisions are strictly enforced and upheld or whether Qataris would expect their family to know their health information as a practical matter. Studies are also needed on how the differing expectations of Qatar's diverse population affects patients' privacy and confidentiality expectations.

It is also important to consider Case 3 in the book on whether a physician can report cases of child abuse. There are constitutional and legal provisions on protecting children in Qatar and policies and strategies aimed at child abuse,

---

[48]   Ibid 2.
[49]   Ibid 2.
[50]   Ibid 5.
[51]   Barry Solaiman, 'Assessing Healthcare Rights and Responsibilities under the Constitutional Orders of Mainland China and the Special Administrative Regions' in Ngoc Son Bui, Stuart Hargreaves and Ryan Mitchell (eds), *The Handbook of Constitutional Law in Greater China* (Routledge 2022).

neglect and violence.[52] However, there are legal gaps, with authorities recognising the need for a comprehensive legal framework to protect children from abuse.[53] Further, as a cultural matter, it can be a social taboo to report domestic abuse because of the moral damage that might cause to the broader family.[54] Consanguineous marriages are particularly challenging because reporting the abuse may result in 'disgracing' the family, risking family feuds.

For medical professionals, there needs to be more clarity about their legal protection for notifying authorities of such cases.[55] The current process pursued by the major hospitals such as HMC is for the healthcare professional to report cases of abuse to the social services of a hospital which have their own procedures for reporting. Thus, the doctor or nurse will not report a case of abuse directly to the authorities but to a separate division of the hospital that may liaise with relevant external entities. Such entities include the Center for Protection and Social Rehabilitation (AMAN), the Family Consulting Center (Wifaq), government ministries, the Juvenile Police and Community Police Departments, the Public Prosecution Service, and the family courts.[56] A major local hospital called Sidra Medicine has established a Child Advocacy Program offering child abuse protection services.[57] Doctors and nurses can refer individuals to that internal service, which has trained medical professionals and social workers who work in a discrete facility, conducting interviews, undertaking examinations and creating medico-legal reports.[58] In these circumstances, incidences of abuse may be reported to the police.[59] Nevertheless, despite the creation of such services, legal clarity is required about what information physicians can communicate and to whom. A clear child protection

---

[52] Abdulla Saeed Al-Mohannadi and others, 'Addressing Violence Against Children Through a Systems-Strengthening Approach' *Qatar Foundation, WISH & UNICEF* (Nov 2020) UNICEF/UNO144182/RICH, https://www.researchgate.net/publication/355790326_Addressing_Violence_Against_Children_Through_A_Systems-strengthening_Approach accessed 10 Sept 2023, p.10 & 19.

[53] Ibid 20; 'New Law to Protect Children on the Way, QF Webinar' *Qatar Tribune* (19 May 2020) https://www.gulf-times.com/story/663589/New-law-to-protect-children-on-the-way-QF-webinar accessed 10 Sept 2023.

[54] Al-Mohannadi and others (n 52) 19.

[55] Ibid 16.

[56] Ibid 15.

[57] Sidra Medicine, 'Sidra Child Advocacy Program', https://www.sidra.org/clinics-services/childrens-and-young-people/child-safety-and-advocacy/sidra-child-advocacy-program accessed 10 Sept 2023.

[58] Ibid.

[59] Catherine W Gichuki, 'Call Helpline to Report Child Abuse Cases: Ansari' *Qatar Tribune* (16 Feb 2020) www.qatar-tribune.com/article/183230/NATION/Call-helpline-to-report-child-abuse-cases-Ansari accessed 10 Sept 2023.

framework should be enshrined in law as has been recognised by the local authorities.

Overall, there are strong legal confidentiality protections in Qatar. Those protections permeate from religious and ethical expectations to the Constitution, the Penal Code, legislation, and regulations. The threat of sanctions under the criminal law is ever-present, but there are other mechanisms that aggrieved parties can utilise. Despite these legal structures, more research is needed on how those written protections translate into practice. There is also much legal work and clarity needed on the privacy and confidentiality provisions as they apply in situations of child abuse.

SPECIFIC CONSIDERATIONS ON CONFIDENTIALITY IN QATAR

Pioneering Data Protection Standards

Qatar was the first country in the Middle East to introduce a national data privacy law.[60] Spurred on by the General Data Protection Regulation (GDPR), local stakeholders are aiming towards general alignment with European standards. These changes are recent, but it is anticipated that they will have significant implications for privacy and confidentiality in health. The Personal Data Privacy Protection Law of 2016 (PDPPL) created several pertinent provisions on health data.[61] The effect of those provisions remained largely unknown until November 2020. Until then, the Ministry of Transport and Communications (MOTC), responsible for the PDPPL, had yet to issue guidance. This led to questions about the legality of health data processed in the country.[62] However, with the issuance of new guidance, there is now more clarity about the application of the law in practice.

For the general provisions on data protection, the PDPPL states that personal data is 'data of an individual whose identity is defined or can be reasonably defined whether through such Personal Data or through the combination of such data with any other data'.[63] Data is subject to the general principles of transparency and consent. Thus, data can only be processed 'within the

---

[60]   Emma Higham and others, 'New Regulatory Guidelines on the Qatar Personal Data Protection Law' *Clyde&Co* (15 March 2021) www.clydeco.com/en/insights/2021/03/new-regulatory-guidelines-on-the-qatar-persona-1 accessed 10 Sept 2023.

[61]   Law No. 13/2016 on Protecting Personal Data Privacy (PDPPL).

[62]   Barry Solaiman, 'COVID-19 and the Shift Towards Telemedicine: Developing a Regulatory Foundation in a Post-Pandemic World' (2020) 2 *Lexis Nexis Qatar Business Law Review* 7, 13–14.

[63]   PDPPL (n 61) Article 1.

framework of transparency, honesty, and respect of human dignity' and with the individual's consent (unless it is necessary to achieve a lawful purpose defined by the law).[64]

For the specific provisions concerning health data, the PDPPL (much like the GDPR) creates a category for 'Personal Data with Special Nature' under Article 16. This includes data 'related to ethnic origin, children, health, physical or psychological condition, religious creeds, marital relations, and criminal offences, shall be regarded as Personal data with special nature'.[65] Any such data can only be processed after obtaining permission from the Compliance and Data Protection Department (CDP) of the MOTC.[66] Any controller violating this requirement may be subject to a fine not exceeding 5 million Qatari Riyals (approximately 1.3 million USD).[67]

Guidelines were published in November 2020 that clarified the scope and application of these provisions. The guidelines differentiate between 'controllers' and 'processors'. The former is the main decision-maker 'exercising overall control over why and how personal data is processed'.[68] The latter follows the instructions of the controller when processing data.[69] There must be a contract between both entities outlining the responsibilities for the processing and sharing of data.[70] The contract must also require that a duty of confidentiality be imposed on any person processing personal data, including employees, contractors, temporary workers, and third parties.[71] As such, health data is private not only under the law, but also under a separate contract between the parties.

---

[64]   Ibid, Articles 3 and 4. Article 1 PDPPL defines data processing very broadly to include. 'gathering, receipt, registration, organization, storage, preparation, modification, retrieval, usage, disclosure, publication, transfer, withholding, destruction, erasure and cancellation'.

[65]   Ibid, Article 16.

[66]   Ibid; The CDP is entrusted by the MOTC as the Competent Authority for enforcing the law following the Council of Ministers decision (26) of 2018.

[67]   PDPPL (n 61) Article 24.

[68]   Ministry of Transport and Communications, 'Controller and Processor: Guidelines for Regulated Entities' Compliance and Data Protection Department (November 2020) Version 1, PDPPL-02050209E, p.6.

[69]   Ibid. A 'controller' may undertake both functions as a 'joint controller'.

[70]   Ibid, 9.

[71]   Ibid, 14.

For data of a special nature, the guidance emphasises that data may be classified as such where inferences can be made about a person's health (whether physical or mental health).[72] The guidance states that:

> Whether or not this constitutes personal data of special nature depends on how certain that inference is, and whether controllers are intent on drawing that inference. If information can be inferred that relates to one of the categories above with a reasonable degree of certainty, then it's likely to be personal data of special nature.[73]

Accounting for inferences is necessary. There have been arguments that dei-dentification (or anonymisation) of data can be a solution to the threats posed by unauthorised data disclosure.[74] This process involves removing an individual's details such as their name, address, medical record number, and more. That approach can be seen in the US under the Privacy Rule of the Health Insurance Portability and Accountability Act (HIPAA).[75] However, in an environment where technology is powered by big data, and multiple devices are connected by the Internet of Things, de-identification is no longer a panacea. In practice, multiple data points can be combined to draw inferences about health data, including the individual's identity.[76] Drawing inferences can be achieved with non-health data such as occupation, age, marital status, geolocation, and purchases.[77] That reality is why the GDPR and the law in Qatar also protect information that can lead to inferences about a person's health. The GDPR does not permit anonymised data to be used if additional information can be used to attribute the data to a natural person.[78] That is not to say that there are no problems with this approach. It can be difficult to define what is anonymous

---

[72] Ibid, 10.
[73] Ibid. This guidance has echoes with similar advice given for the GDPR. For example, the Information Commissioner's Office (ICO) in the UK, uses the same language concerning whether information can be inferred with a 'reasonable degree of certainty. See, Information Commissioner's Office (UK), 'What is Special Category Data' https://ico.org.uk/for-organisations/guide-to-data-protection/guide-to-the-general-data-protection-regulation-gdpr/special-category-data/what-is-special-category-data/#scd7 accessed 10 Sept 2023.
[74] Beatriz Veyrat and Marco de Morpurgo, 'Digital Therapies: Evolution and Entry into Mainstream Healthcare' *DLA PIPER & The Lawyer* (18 September 2020) 14.
[75] HIPAA, Section 164.514 (United States).
[76] I Glenn Cohen and Michelle M Mello, 'Big Data, Big Tech, and Protecting Patient Privacy' (2019) 322(12) *JAMA* 1141.
[77] 'Health Information Privacy Beyond HIPAA: A 2018 Environmental Scan of Major Trends and Challenges' National Committee on Vital and Health Statistics (NCVHS) (13 Dec 2017) 27, www.ncvhs.hhs.gov/wp-content/uploads/2018/02/NCVHS-Beyond-HIPAA_Report-Final-02-08-18.pdf accessed 10 Sept 2023.
[78] General Data Protection Regulation (GDPR) Recital 26.

and identifiable in practice.[79] Nevertheless, Qatar's approach broadly aligns with international best practices that account for inferences being drawn.

Returning more broadly to the type of data contemplated by the PDPPL, one can see that the law construes 'data of a special nature' widely. To obtain permission from the Compliance and Data Protection Department of the MOTC, controllers and processors need to identify both a 'permitted reason' or purpose and an 'additional condition' for processing the data.[80] On the purpose, the controller will identify the reason for processing the data and that there are 'no other reasonable and less intrusive ways to achieve that purpose'.[81] The controller cannot process data of a special nature without one or more of the noted 'additional conditions'.[82] Where such a condition applies, the data controllers and processors may be permitted to process that data for the reasons laid out in the conditions (as long as other criteria in the law are also fulfilled and permission is granted from the CDP).[83] It is worth unpacking some of the noted conditions because they raise pertinent and topical privacy matters.

First, the condition of 'explicit consent' notes that the controller should obtain consent from an individual to process their data by clearly disclosing the nature and purpose of the processing.[84] This requirement could be simple or complex depending on the context. If the context is straightforward, such as a hospital processing patient data for an administrative function, it would be simple enough to identify the nature and purpose of the processing. However, this paradigm could be far more complex and uncertain where technology is involved. For example, data processing involved in devices using artificial intelligence (AI) may be unclear even to computer scientists developing an algorithm.[85] In such circumstances, the controller may be unable to explain the full nature of data processing. The use of AI in the health context is merely sprouting at present, but this will be a crucial area where further guidance will

---

[79]   Eric Wierda and others, 'Protecting Patient Privacy in Digital Health Technology: The Dutch m-Health Infrastructure of Hartwacht as a Learning Case' (2020) 6 *BMJ Innov* 170, 174–75.

[80]   Ministry of Transport and Communications, 'Special Nature Processing: Guidelines for Regulated Entities' Compliance and Data Protection Department (November 2020) Version 1, PDPPL-02050215E, p.11.

[81]   Ibid, 15.

[82]   Ibid.

[83]   Ibid, 13–14.

[84]   Ibid, 11.

[85]   See, Barry Solaiman and Mark Bloom, 'AI, Explainability, and Safeguarding Patient Safety in Europe: Towards a Science-Focused Regulatory Model' in I. Glenn Cohen, Timo Minssen, W. Nicholson Price II, Christopher Robertson, and Carmel Shachar (eds), *The Future of Medical Device Regulation: Innovation and Protection* (Cambridge University Press 2022) 91.

be required in the future, particularly in Qatar where much research is being conducted on the use of AI in health.[86]

Second, the condition of 'employment' has gained increasing relevance following the COVID-19 pandemic. That condition notes that an employer may need to process an employee's data to fulfil their obligations as an employer as defined in the employment contract.[87] Employers ought to be careful in this realm. They could not, for example, require an employee to obtain a vaccine. Countries in the Middle East did not mandate vaccines (with exceptions for those working in health and other specific areas) and doing so would have arguably violated the principle of patient consent.[88] However, certain employers are subject to specific mandates by public health authorities that could arguably be considered an 'additional condition' under the data protection law. In this regard, the MOPH placed strict requirements on educational institutions such as schools and universities which necessitated those institutions to require staff to declare their COVID-19 status before entering premises.[89] Employees working in education could also avail vaccinations at an accelerated pace compared to some other population sectors.[90] In practice, this required employers to process employee health information to help them avail the vaccine.

Further, it is also simply a requirement of the law that employers must disclose to the relevant health authorities any employee that has tested positive

---

[86]   For an overview of privacy considerations in this context, see Barry Solaiman, 'Addressing Access with Artificial Intelligence: Overcoming the Limitations of Deep Learning to Broaden Remote Care Today' (2021) 51 *The University of Memphis Law Review* 1103, 1121; for an overview of the legal developments of AI in healthcare see, Barry Solaiman, 'From 'AI to Law' in Healthcare: The Proliferation of Global Guidelines in a Void of Legal Uncertainty' (2023) 42(2) *Medicine and Law* 391.

[87]   Ministry of Transport and Communications, 'Special Nature Processing' (n 80) 11.

[88]   Rebecca Ford and others, 'COVID-19 Middle East: Can Employers Require Their Employees to be Vaccinated?' *Lexology* (7 Feb 2021) www.lexology.com/library/detail.aspx?g=e34b0dd0-cbb7-4fa1-b419-844e712ec968/ accessed 10 Sept 2023.

[89]   'Ministry to Make Vaccination Proof or Weekly COVID-19 Test Must All for Educational Staff' *Peninsula* (3 March 2021) https://thepeninsulaqatar.com/article/03/03/2021/Ministry-to-make-vaccination-proof-or-weekly-Covid-19-test-must-for-all-educational-staff accessed 10 Sept 2023.

[90]   'MOPH Includes Teachers and School Staff in COVID-19 Vaccine Priority Group' *Peninsula* (18 Feb 2021) https://thepeninsulaqatar.com/article/18/02/2021/MoPH-includes-teachers-and-school-staff-in-Covid-19-vaccine-priority-group accessed 10 Sept 2023.

for an infectious disease. Article 4 of Law No. 17 of 1990 on the Prevention of Infectious Diseases (as amended by Law No. 9 of 2020) states that:

> It is also the responsibility of the director of the university, institution or school or his representative, as well as the responsibility of the immediate superior if the infection has occurred or suspected to have occurred during work, or the expatriate's recruiter, whether the Infected or Suspected Person is found inside the country or abroad, when such matter has come to the knowledge of either one.

The law, therefore, requires employees to process an employee's health data in this context, and not doing so would be unlawful. The circumstances highlighted by the pandemic also likely fell under two other additional conditions in the data protection guidelines. The first condition is 'public health', which stipulates that the processing is 'necessary for reasons of public interest in the area of public health, such as protecting against serious cross-border threats to health'.[91] The second condition is 'public interest', which states that 'the processing in context is necessary for reasons of substantial public interest with a basis in law'.[92] The COVID-19 pandemic is a good illustration of the application of these conditions. It is in the public interest that educational institutions process certain health data of their employees and doing so comports with their legal obligation, which stems from legislation couched in protecting public health.

Third, the guidance highlights the condition of processing being necessary for 'preventative or occupational medicine'.[93] This includes tasks such as assessing the working capacity of an employee, diagnosing illnesses and providing health care or treatment.[94] The guidance also highlights expected circumstances in which data must be processed where it is in a person's 'vital interests' such as to save their life.[95] Aside from emergencies, the provision of medical care to patients reverts to the discussion earlier in this chapter concerning the legal duty of medical professionals as it pertains to privacy stipulated in other laws. The PDPPL now creates an additional requirement, whereby medical institutions must obtain consent for processing patient data. However, aside from the added administrative load, it appears that these requirements will be easy for controllers to satisfy because the provision of medical care is covered under the PDPPL, and it could be demonstrated that consent obligations are already being fulfilled by compliance with other laws.

---

[91]   Ministry of Transport and Communications, 'Special Nature Processing' (n 80) 11.

[92]   Ibid.

[93]   Ibid.

[94]   Ibid.

[95]   Ibid.

The PDPPL has opened up new legal considerations concerning the privacy and confidentiality of health data in Qatar. The result is that there should be greater checks on the processing of such data and a higher standard of confidentiality than existed before the law.

The Media, Privacy, and Influencing Behaviour

Another notable dimension of privacy in Qatar is the use of the media and publicity to pursue certain aims. Two examples are given here concerning controlling the spread of infectious diseases and organ donations.

During the COVID-19 pandemic, the media frequently published the full names of those violating quarantine restrictions as a means to deter other potential offenders. The headlines were often along the lines of 'Authorities Arrest Five for Violating Home Quarantine', with the articles noting the name of individuals that were referred to prosecutors and that they were 'legally accountable' for their actions.[96] Three laws were relied upon to name and shame individuals. First, Article 253 of the Penal Code states that a person may be imprisoned for up to three years and fined where 'due to his fault, [he] causes the spread of a contagious or an epidemic disease'. Second, Law No. 17 of 1990 on preventing infectious diseases includes several provisions that may justify naming individuals publicly.[97] Article 5 empowers authorities to take 'procedures that it may deem appropriate to avoid the spread of the disease' where there is a confirmed or suspected case of an infectious disease. Article 6 provides that authorities can isolate a person in a designated place for a period deemed necessary. Article 6(bis) requires those isolated to 'stay in the isolation area' and comply with the isolation measures. Third, a law on protecting the community empowers authorities to detain individuals that have committed crimes 'involving state security, honour, decency or public morals'.[98] The provisions are worded broadly, particularly those that empower authorities to take actions that they 'deem appropriate', which could arguably include naming and shaming individuals as a deterrent to breaching quarantine requirements and risk spreading an infectious disease.

Two considerations must be balanced here. First is the individual's privacy as it pertains to their health information. Second, the need to enforce the law and deter potential violators from spreading a harmful disease. A quarantined individual may or may not have had an infectious disease. They could have

---

[96] 'Authorities Arrest Five for Violating Home Quarantine Conditions' *Peninsula* (24 Feb 2021) www.thepeninsulaqatar.com/article/24/02/2021/Authorities-arrest-five-for-violating-home-quarantine-conditions accessed 10 Sept 2023.

[97] Law No. 17 of 1990 on the Prevention of Infectious Diseases.

[98] Law No. 17 of 2002 on Protection of Community, Article 1.

been subject to mandatory home or other quarantine where they tested positive for a disease; they could have been undertaking mandatory quarantine following international travel or where they encountered another person who tested positive. The publication of their name in the media revealed that one of those scenarios was true and was, therefore, a disclosure of confidential information about the individual. That information was particularly sensitive where the individual was infected with a disease. In normal circumstances, this would have been a serious breach of one's health privacy made all the more stark because confidential health information was overtly revealed by authorities legally expected to maintain an individual's privacy.

At the same time, authorities were dealing with a public health crisis, and it was critical that citizens and residents complied with infectious disease laws to lower the spread of a disease to help save lives and protect intensive care units from reaching capacity. The authorities in Qatar deemed privacy to be secondary in this context. Further, it should be emphasised that Qatar (like many other countries) was under an international obligation to prevent the spread of COVID-19 under both the International Covenant on Civil and Political Rights (ICCPR) and the International Covenant on Economic, Social and Cultural Rights (ICESCR).[99] Article 12(1) ICESCR notes the 'right and obligation' of citizens to be inoculated, and Article 12(2) requires that State Parties should take steps to realise that right, which includes the 'prevention, treatment and control of epidemic, endemic, occupational and other diseases'. Further, under Article 12(1) ICCPR, everyone has the liberty to freedom of movement, but that right is qualified under Article 12(3) by allowing restrictions to 'protect national security, public order, public health'. Whether or not one agrees that naming and shaming was a legitimate tool to uphold these international obligations, the COVID-19 pandemic highlighted an exception to the prevailing privacy norms expected in the country. Those exceptions were grounded in vaguely worded provisions of law that gave broad powers to authorities.

In the context of organ donations, the naming of individuals publicly is used both as a carrot and a stick. In the last decade, Qatar has developed a successful organ donation regime premised on encouraging altruism and deterring exploitation. In 2009, almost all patients travelled abroad to receive an organ donation.[100] The opposite was true by 2019, with most patients opting for an

---

[99] International Covenant on Economic, Social and Cultural Rights (adopted 16 December 1966, entered into force 3 January 1976) 993 UNTS 3 (ICESCR); International Covenant on Civil and Political Rights (adopted 16 December 1966, entered into force 23 March 1976) 999 UNTS 171 (ICCPR).

[100] Fazeena Saleem, 'Doha becomes Model for Organ Transplant' *Peninsula* (1 Jan 2019), https://thepeninsulaqatar.com/article/01/01/2019/Doha-becomes-model-for-organ-transplant accessed 10 Sept 2023.

organ donation in Qatar.[101] The principle of privacy has been an important tool in achieving this change. The concern of the Director of the Organ Donation Center revolved around the use of incentive payments to obtain an organ that may exacerbate the risks of coercion and exploitation.[102] Two provisions in the law are designed to combat the distorting effect of money on what should be the 'laudable fulfilment of an ethical responsibility'.[103]

Used as a carrot, Article 16 of Law No.15 of 2015 on Regulating the Human Organs Transfer and Transplantation, makes provision for awarding a 'medal of altruism' to those that have donated (or to the next of kin where it is a deceased donor). The award has been given annually at an awards ceremony attended by leading figures, including the Minister of Health, and royalty.[104] In these circumstances, an individual's decision to donate is publicised and rewarded to encourage altruism rather than keeping the donation private. Used as a stick, Article 24 of the law states that anyone violating the provision of the law, such as purchasing organs, may have their conviction promulgated in 'two daily newspapers at the expense of the convict'. In this manner, naming and shaming (at the financial and reputational expense of the individual) is used as a public means to further the underlying aims of the law. These efforts have clearly been successful, with a reversal in number of those seeking donations abroad. 2022 saw a total of 124 donors, with the largest number of kidney transplant surgeries in the country's history.[105]

Qatar presents an interesting case study of how privacy can be used as a tool to influence the behaviour of individuals. In the cases examined, this aim has always been to achieve some broader public interest either by protecting the spread of a harmful disease or by encouraging altruism in organ donations (a field where there is often a shortage of organs for those in need).

---

[101] 'Over 400,000 Register for Organ Donation' *Gulf Times* (11 Nov 2019), www.gulf-times.com/story/647302/Over-400-000-register-for-organ-donation#: ~:text=Hamad%20Medical%20Corporation%27s%20(HMC)%20Qatar,of%2070 %20recipients%20last%20year accessed 10 Sept 2023.

[102] I Dominique Martin and Riadh AS Fadhil, 'The Doha Model of Organ Donation and Transplantation: Thinking Beyond Citizenship' (2014) 2(2) *Griffith Journal of Law & Human Dignity* 293, 312.

[103] Ibid, 312.

[104] 'Over 400,000 Register for Organ Donation' *Gulf Times* (11 Nov 2019) www.gulf -times.com/story/647302/Over-400-000-register-for-organ-donation accessed 10 Sept 2023; 'HH Sheikha Moza Attends Organ Donation Honouring Ceremony' (4 Sept 2010) www.mozabintnasser.qa/en/news/hh-sheikha-moza-attends-organ-donation-honouring -ceremony accessed 10 Sept 2023.

[105] 'Hamad Medical Corporation Honours 124 Organ Donors and Their Families' *The Peninsula* (12 Nov 2022) https://thepeninsulaqatar.com/article/12/11/2022/hamad -medical-corporation-honours-124-organ-donors-and-their-families accessed 10 Sept 2023.

Mental Health, Secrecy, and Social Stigma

Mental health raises particular challenges for protecting privacy. The need to tackle the stigma associated with mental health conditions remains an ongoing effort in many countries. In the Middle East, those efforts lag behind, and much ground must be covered to improve.[106] Awareness and knowledge of mental disorders is poor, and there remains significant social stigma for those with mental health conditions.[107] Faith healers have been used in the local community instead of mental health services because mental disorders are attributed to supernatural phenomena.[108] Returning to Case 1 in this book on the duty of confidentiality where the patient's family is involved, the individual's interests can be subordinated to those of the family in a region where extended family often live together.[109] Like HMC's Bill of Rights and Responsibilities, Qatar's Mental Health law contemplates the role of the family in its provisions.[110] Where an individual lacks capacity, a legal guardian (usually a family member) will be privy to their information to make applications for admission or discharge on the patient's behalf.[111] The revelation of an individual's admittance to a psychiatric hospital or their receipt of psychiatric care can have a detrimental effect on the individual's standing and that of their family in the local community. Effort is being made in this area by the MOPH and the healthcare community, with new services being introduced into the community.[112] However, those efforts will take time, and this paradigm persists, which creates challenges for patient privacy.

Information about whether a person has a mental health condition will be desirable to some individuals, such as potential marriage partners. This includes the risk of medical professionals working within the system seeking

---

[106]   See, for example, Joelle M. Abi-Rached, 'Psychiatry in the Middle East: The Rebirth of Lunatic Asylums?' (2020) 18(1) *BJPsych International* 5.

[107]   Barry Solaiman and Suhaila Ghuloum, 'Towards Community Care: Qatar's Rapidly Evolving Mental Health Landscape' (2021) 19(1) *BJPsych International* 15; Ovais Wadoo and others, 'Mental Health During COVID-19 in Qatar' (2020) *General Psychiatry* 33:e100313, p.1; Khalid Elzamzamy and others, 'Media and Mental Health' in Suhaila Ghuloum, Amber Haque and Livia L Gilstrap, *Mental Health in Qatar* (Cambridge Scholars Publishing 2020); Khalid Elzamzamy and others, 'Newspaper Depiction of Mental and Physical Health in Qatar' (2020) 23(1) *BJPsych International* 1.

[108]   Wadoo and others (n 107) 1.

[109]   Ibid, 1–2.

[110]   Law No. 16 of 2016 on Mental Health, Article 23.

[111]   Ibid, Article 4.

[112]   Terrance Sharkey, 'Mental Health Strategy and Impact Evaluation in Qatar' (2017) 14(1) *BJPsych International* 18, 20; Elzamzamy and others (n 107) 2–3.

access to information about an individual for their own purposes. The influence of a family can also work both ways. A family generally wants to help their relative. Their support can be imperative to their recovery in a region where family ties are vital. However, the hesitancy surrounding privacy can cause a family to deny a relative the opportunity to receive care in a hospital or clinic when that would be the most beneficial place to be. The family may lack knowledge about mental health, they may refute that a relative has a mental illness, or they may not want to risk a record being made or information about the treatment being disclosed.

Nevertheless, the law on privacy in this area is clear. Not only do the provisions of the Penal Code and the legislation (examined earlier) apply, but so do additional provisions applying specifically under Law No. 16 of 2016 on Mental Health. Article 3 of the law sets out that psychiatric institutions must respect individual rights, including promoting their dignity.[113] There are specific provisions on privacy, including respecting the patient's wishes on accepting or rejecting visitors and protecting:

> [H]is privacy and personal belongings and protect the confidentiality of information related thereto and prohibit any access to such information unless by the members of medical team or the employees in charge of the medical registers, unless by a written permission of the Psychiatric Patient or his Legal Guardian or by an order from the Competent Entity. This commitment shall remain valid even after the Patient's recovery.[114]

A breach of this provision carries a penalty of potential imprisonment and a fine.[115] The law specifically states that anyone who 'discloses any confidential information of the Psychiatric Patient [may be] sentenced to imprisonment' and a fine.[116] For the nurse in Case 1 who might reveal confidential mental health information to a family member, legislation is clear on the importance of patient privacy and carries stringent penalties for those in breach. However, the legal provisions are incongruent with the cultural reality that persists. That is not to say that privacy is being systemically breached, but that legal privacy must navigate a paradigm of complex social and cultural norms. In this environment, greater education and enforcement of the rules are especially necessary to counteract the risks that exist. That is in the first instance. In the long-term, greater investments are required to educate local communities

---

[113] Law No. 16 of 2016 on Mental Health, Article 3(2)(2).
[114] Ibid, Article 3(4)(4).
[115] Ibid, Article 29.
[116] Ibid, Article 29(2).

Privacy and medical confidentiality in healthcare

about mental health and normalise the provision of services throughout the country. Effort is being given to this endeavour, but much work remains.

Genetics, Lineage, and Legitimacy

A final area is that of confidentiality and genetics. Qatar has given significant attention to genetic research, which has led the MOPH to publish several regulations and guidelines. There is the Qatar Genome Programme which is undertaking genome sequencing of the local population, and the Qatar Biobank, which collects samples to study, understand and eventually reduce the number of chronic illnesses.[117] Local universities are also conducting extensive research in this field. The Qatar Biomedical Research Institute (QBRI) under Hamad Bin Khalifa University (HBKU) partnered with the Harvard Stem Cell Institute.[118] Weill Cornell Medicine-Qatar also conducts research in the field of genetics, and there are labs to facilitate such research in a major new hospital called Sidra.[119]

This burgeoning research must be undertaken carefully because of specific Islamic ethical considerations about privacy that involve balancing individual privacy with another's right to access shared genetic information.[120] This implicates Case 4 in the book, which queries whether family members are entitled to know about the genetic test results of a family member that is relevant to their own health. According to Islam, there is an ethical obligation to warn others about life-threatening conditions that may affect them.[121] Genetic research that reveals a serious illness about an individual would require disclosure to others who might be genetically affected by that illness, and not doing so would be

---

[117] 'Qatar Genome Programme', https://qatargenome.org.qa accessed 10 Sept 2023; 'Qatar Biobank: About Us', www.qatarbiobank.org.qa/about-us accessed 10 Sept 2023.

[118] 'QBRI Forms New Partnership with Harvard Stem Cell Institute' (7 Oct 2018) www.hbku.edu.qa/en/qbri/news/qbri-forms-new-partnership-harvard accessed 10 Sept 2023.

[119] 'Genomics' Weill Cornell Medicine-Qatar, https://qatar-weill.cornell.edu/research/core-facilities/genomics accessed 10 Sept 2023; 'Sidra Medicine Opens Three New Core Laboratories' (5 March 2017) www.sidra.org/media/newsroom/2017/march/sidra-opens-three-new-core-laboratories accessed 10 Sept 2023.

[120] Ayman Shabana, 'Living with the Genome, by Angus Clark and Flo Ticehurst, within the Muslim Context' in Mohammed Ghaly (ed), *Islamic Ethics and the Genome Question* (Brill 2018) 247; Mohammed Ghaly (ed), Genomics in the Gulf Region and Islamic Ethics: A Special Report in Collaboration with the Research Center for Islamic Legislation and Ethics, World Innovation Summit for Health (WISH) 27, https://research.moph.gov.qa//DepartmentalDocuments/Genomics-GulfRegion-IslamicEthics.pdf?csrt=6593804482857762924 accessed 10 Sept 2023.

[121] Ghaly (ed), Genomics in the Gulf Region (n 120) 40–41.

a sin.[122] Another consideration is that of misattributed paternity arising from incidental findings.[123] In Islam, having children through legitimate marital relationships affects the rights and duties that follow for the child.[124] Children born out of wedlock may also lose dignity and be subject to stigma.[125] In this context, paternity is automatically established by virtue of marital relations.[126] There has been controversy surrounding the use of DNA testing for checking or verifying an already-established lineage. Such testing must not be used from the perspective of Sharia, a position that led Saudi Arabia to outlaw DNA paternity testing.[127] In this regard, Muslim religious scholars are primarily concerned with safeguarding individuals' privacy and dignity rather than concerns about the efficacy of the technology itself.[128]

Consequently, the extensive research efforts in Qatar have necessitated regulations (specific legislation does not exist). The core guidance in this area by the MOPH emphasises the importance of information security in reducing psychological, privacy, legal and social harms.[129] The ethical basis for protecting the privacy of research subjects is 'respect for persons'.[130] The guidelines state the importance of revealing incidental findings, such as genetic mutations to family members, but note that revealing such information is not required when conducting genomic research. Ultimately, it is up to the investigator whether to withhold such information or not.[131] The guidelines also specifically highlight the legal risks involved in revealing paternity information for individuals, such as questions about their citizenship or their ability to access goods and services.[132] Revealing such information can be both 'traumatic' and 'stigmatizing'.[133] The religious considerations noted above are, therefore, contemplated by the MOPH.

---

[122] Ibid, 41.
[123] Ibid.
[124] Ibid.
[125] Ibid, 42.
[126] Ibid, 43.
[127] Ibid.
[128] Ibid.
[129] MOPH, Guidance for the Design, Ethical Review, and Conduct of Genomic Research in Qatar (2017-2018) 7, https://research.moph.gov.qa//DepartmentalDocuments/Guidance%20for%20the%20Design,%20Ethical%20Review,%20and%20Conduct%20of%20Genomic%20Research%20in%20Qatar.pdf?csrt=6593804482857762924 accessed 10 Sept 2023.
[130] Ibid, 33.
[131] Ibid, 9.
[132] Ibid, 5.
[133] Ibid, 9.

Owing to the risks of disclosing information about an individual's genetics, the guidance emphasises the importance of also keeping test results confidential.[134] Procedures are outlined for limiting access to confidential information such as using passwords, encryption, firewalls, separate access rights, two-factor authentication, proper training, non-disclosure agreements, proper scrutiny of potential hires to determine their likelihood of compliance with private information, the use of data transfer agreements, and more.[135] Overall, there is great emphasis on privacy and confidentiality throughout the guidelines which also contemplate that more stringent measures may be required by an institutional review board (IRB).[136] The importance of privacy in this context is also noted in several other guidelines and sample informed consent forms published by the MOPH.[137]

CONCLUSION

There is much breadth to the privacy protections in Qatar. The centrality of privacy is congruent with religious values, and this is reflected in the country's Constitution. In some respects, confidentiality protections operate in a manner that one would find familiar in Europe and the US, such as doctors adhering to the expected standard of care. Qatar is also rapidly catching up with data protection standards by aligning with the GDPR. It is an outward-looking country seeking to internalise international best practices. Yet, local approaches continue to operate alongside those developments. Punishments for breaching confidentiality under criminal law go beyond those one would find abroad, where cases are predominantly heard in the civil courts. Further, one finds unique applications and deviations from the confidentiality obligations as stipulated in laws and regulations. Future

---

[134]   Ibid, 11.
[135]   Ibid, 7–8.
[136]   Ibid, 34.
[137]   MOPH, Guidelines for Gene Transfer Research in Humans, Department of Research, https://research.moph.gov.qa//DepartmentalDocuments/Guidelines%20for%20Gene %20Transfer%20Research%20in%20Humans.pdf?csrt=6593804482857762924 accessed 10 Sept 2023; MOPH, Template Informed Consent Form – Clinical Trial of Stem Cell Therapy, https://research.moph.gov.qa//DepartmentalDocuments/Consent %20Template%20-%20Clinical%20Trial%20Stem%20Cell%20Therapy-9Jan2019.pdf ?csrt=6593804482857762924 accessed 10 Sept 2023; MOPH, Policies, Regulations and Guidelines for Research Involving Human Research Subjects, Department of Research, https://research.moph.gov.qa//DepartmentalDocuments/Policies,%20Regulations %20and%20Guidelines%20for%20Research%20Involving%20Human.pdf?csrt= 6593804482857762924 accessed 10 Sept 2023.

studies ought to revisit this balance once the data protection standards mature and new laws are promulgated.

8. Privacy, medical confidentiality, and health in Tanzania

Ferdinand Marcel Temba

GENERAL INTRODUCTION

This chapter addresses privacy, medical confidentiality, and health in Tanzania. It starts by explaining the concepts of privacy and confidentiality and how they relate to healthcare systems. The chapter then discusses the health system of Tanzania by describing how it facilitates access to healthcare services. It posits that issues of privacy, medical confidentiality, and health arise when accessing healthcare services within the health system/structure. The nexus between sources of law in Tanzania with privacy, medical confidentiality, and health is expounded.

To start with privacy is generally defined as the claim of individuals, groups, and institutions to determine for themselves when, how, and to what extent information about them is communicated to others.[1] Health professionals define privacy as an individual's claim to control the circumstances in which personal health information is collected, used, stored, and transmitted.[2] It is information produced and stored by healthcare provider organisations and collected from individuals and entities, both passively and actively.[3] Patients have the right to secrecy and the right against the misuse and/or unjustified publication of personal information owned by the healthcare facility within and outside the health field. Privacy and data security of patients form the base of health records in the health facility. Health officials have the responsibility

---

[1]   WW Lowrance, *Privacy, Confidentiality, and Health Research* (Cambridge: Cambridge University Press 2012) 29 citing AF Westin, *Privacy and Freedom* (New York: Atheneum 1967) 7.

[2]   LO Gostin, *Public Health Law: Power, Duty, Restraint* (2nd edn, Berkeley: University of California Press 2009) 316; Lowrance (n 1).

[3]   D McGraw and KD Mandl, 'Privacy Protections to Encourage Use of Health-Relevant Digital Data in A Learning Health System' (2021) 4:2 Digital Medicine 1; available from https://doi.org/10.1038/s41746-020-00362-8, accessed 25 January 2022.

to protect patient privacy held both in hard and electronic files by applying rules governing the collection, handling, and storage of patients' personal data.

On the other hand, confidentiality is the respectful handling of information disclosed within relationships of trust, especially as regards further disclosure.[4] Confidentiality in relation to health professions entails the professional and/or contractual duty of doctors, nurses, midwives, secretaries, medical technicians, paramedical staff, social workers, hospital managers, computer staff, research investigators, in hospitals to safeguard the secrecy of their patient/client information regardless how it is acquired, collected, stored, processed, generated, retrieved, or transmitted in a healthcare institution.[5] Protecting privacy data and confidentiality in doctor-patient relations is important due to existing interaction with information technology companies, government agencies, and healthcare providers. There are increasing activities on the collection, using, and sharing of health personal data which calls for legal intervention to attain privacy and confidentiality in the healthcare system. This chapter addresses whether existing privacy and confidentiality laws in Tanzania provide sufficient protections for health-relevant data.

Health System of Tanzania

The Health system includes activities under the direct control of the Ministry of Health, which are often a relatively limited set of personal curative services.[6] All actors, institutions, and resources that undertake health actions with the primary intent of improving, promoting, restoring, and maintaining health form part of the health system.[7] Thus, the health system includes health services (personal and population-based) and the activities that assist their delivery such as financial resources generation and stewardship functions. In Tanzania, people access healthcare services in the health system structure consisting public health sector, the private health sector which was expanded by the law which allowed private actors other than the Faith Based Organisations to own private hospitals in 1991, and traditional health and alternative health services.

---

[4]   Lowrance (n 1) 29.
[5]   HF Orthner and BI Blum, *Implementing Health Care Information Systems* (George Washington University Medical Center 1986) 226.
[6]   CJL Murray and DB Evans, 'Health Systems Performance Assessment: Goals, Framework and Overview' in CJL Murray and DB Evans (eds), *Health Systems Performance Assessment Debates, Methods and Empiricism* (World Health Organization 2003) 7.
[7]   World Health Organisation, *The World Health Report 2000: Health System Improving Performance* (World Health Organisation 2000) 5.

The structure is set into seven levels in hierarchical order with the national level at the top and the family level at the bottom. The hierarchy includes family level, village level, ward level, district level, regional level, regional level, zonal level, and national level.[8] The structure which is set in a pyramid pattern affects the referral system as it starts from the bottom level to the top level. For instance, at the village level, there are established village health posts and at the ward level, there are established community dispensaries while at the divisional level there are rural health centres. The district councils' level establishes district hospitals or district-designated hospitals, the regional level run the regional referral hospitals and zonal level established zonal consultative referral hospitals and the national level operates national and specialised hospitals.[9] From the structure, a patient will be expected to start seeking healthcare services starting from the lower level and going up the ladder through the referral system. The Dispensaries, Health Centres, and District and/or District Designated Hospitals that form part of Primary Healthcare are regulated by the Local Government Authorities (LGAs). Patients who attend primary healthcare facilities are entitled to be protected on their privacy, medical confidentiality, and health with the same protection upheld to patients who attend Regional Referral Hospitals, Zonal Referral Hospitals, and National Hospitals.

Before independence, the health system was characterised by a public health system governed by the colonial government, private health systems under missionaries, and a traditional health system run by traditional and alternative health practitioners operating in the native health system. After the independence of Tanganyika, the health system took on a different dimension by concentrating resources on developing public health systems. The economic crisis due to the structural adjustment programmes adopted in the 1980s worldwide changed the country's position in the provision of healthcare services by allowing the private health system to flourish. The austerity measures reduced government expenditure on the provision of social services such as healthcare services by allowing private healthcare to operate and complement the government efforts to provide healthcare services. That aside, the traditional health system always plays a great role in healthcare provided provision in Tanzania before and after independence. The provision of healthcare services whether through public health services, private health services, or traditional and alter-

---

[8]   United Republic of Tanzania, *National Health Policy of 2007* (Ministry of Health and Social Welfare 2007) 67.

[9]   G Mtei et al, *An Assessment of the Health Financing System in Tanzania: Implications for Equity and Social Health Insurance: Report on Shield Work Package 1* (Ifakara Health Research and Development Centre - Ministry of Health and Social Welfare Tanzania – London School of Hygiene and Tropical Medicine, 2007) 17.

native health services requires health practitioners within each sector to uphold health ethics by protecting the private and medical confidentiality of patients.

This chapter considers it of vital importance to trace the ethical basis of confidentiality and make analyses of key sources of the right to privacy and the duty of confidentiality in healthcare provisioning.

THE ETHICAL BASIS OF CONFIDENTIALITY

The medical profession involves the transfer of personal information from a patient to a doctor. The sensitive nature of medical details facing patients makes them reluctant to share information with friends and family members worrying that their medical status will be divulged to the general public. The situation becomes more difficult for patients when they meet doctors in health-care facilities. The nature of health information shared between patients and doctors calls for confidentiality to be exercised by a healthcare professional to facilitate trust and open communication between patients and healthcare workers in order to promote efficient diagnosis and effective treatment of disease and management of illness.[10]

In Tanzania, medical confidentiality is one of the least contested areas of medical practice although the doctor-patient relationship remains an essential area in the healthcare system structure. Since the relationship is achieved through the transfer of information from the patient to doctors, upholding medical confidentiality is necessary to achieve the confidence of patients. The history of patient confidentiality can be traced back to at least the Hippocratic Oath of Ancient Greece, which included the statement that 'whatsoever things I see or hear concerning the life of men, in my attendance on the sick or even apart therefrom, which ought not to be noised abroad, I shall keep silence thereon, counting such things as sacred secrets.' The Hippocratic Oath has the longstanding recognition of the importance of professional obligations of confidentiality owed to patients.[11]

Legally, the duty of confidentiality arises from both statute and common law. Statutes have enacted provisions making it an offence for health professionals to disclose patient information to a third party. Common law cases have developed a duty of confidentiality through suits instituted by patients against medical practitioners who have allegedly disclosed confidential information without justification. The foundation of the legal duty of confidentiality can

---

[10]   AH Ferguson, 'The Role of History in Debates Regarding the Boundaries of Medical Confidentiality and Privacy' (2015) 3 Journal of Medical Law and Ethics 65.
[11]   Ibid 68.

further be explained legally on the basis of contract law, equity law, and tort law.

The duty of confidentiality in contracts may exist through an express or implied contractual duty of confidentiality between the medical practitioner and the patient. The contractual duty encourages patients to disclose information so that medical practitioners can provide effective healthcare. A patient has a trust that a doctor will not pass on any information disclosed to him unless prior consent has been granted. This duty nonetheless does not entail keeping all information secret, but rather it is a duty to use the information only for the purposes for which it was provided and not for any other purpose. The usage of information obtained from doctor-patient relationships for other purposes other than treatment of the patient will be made only with the consent of the patient or in accordance with any of the exceptions. In *Parry-Jones v Law Society*,[12] the court dealt with confidential information of solicitor against his client. It stated that: 'the law implies a term into the contract whereby a professional man is to keep his client's affairs secret and not to disclose them to anyone without just cause. Legal advice privilege is a confidence that is created by an implied term in the contract between solicitor and client.' In the health profession, patients have a right of expectation that medical practitioners will not pass on any personal information that they learn in the course of their professional duties unless the patient gives permission.

Equity may equally provide for the duty of confidentiality in doctor-patient relationships. This arises when the patient relies in the good faith on the medical practitioner to keep what has been disclosed between them confidential. In *Breen v Williams*,[13] the court held a relationship between doctor and patient may be fiduciary in nature, but felt that the scope of the duties imposed by such a relationship did not include a duty to allow a patient access to his or her medical file. Equitable intervention in the doctor-patient relationship is only justifiable on the ground that one should not benefit from the information that has been received in confidence.

In tort, the duty of confidentiality is considered part of the medical practitioner's duty of care in the law of negligence. The law of torts imposes a general duty on the medical practitioner not to cause foreseeable harm to another person that may result in damage. In *Furniss v Fitchett*,[14] the plaintiff (Mrs. Furniss) sued her doctor (Dr. Fitchett) for breach of confidentiality. The doctor had disclosed confidential information about the plaintiff to her husband, which was later produced in court against the plaintiff by the hus-

---

[12] [1969] 1 Ch. 1 at 7.
[13] (1996) 138 ALR 259.
[14] [1958] NZLR 396.

band's solicitor. The judge held that 'the doctor ought reasonably to have foreseen that the contents of his certificate were likely to come to the patient's knowledge and he knew that if they did, they would be likely to injure her in her health.'

SOURCES OF THE DUTY OF CONFIDENTIALITY AND PRIVACY IN HEALTH

The sources of the duty of confidentiality and privacy in Tanzania can be explained through sources of law in Tanzania. The sources of law in Tanzania include the constitution, received laws, legislation, precedent/case law, and international law. The analytical explanation of sources of duty of confidentiality and privacy in health can be well explained by starting to focus on how international law through international, regional, and sub-regional instruments influences Tanzania's legal system.

International Law

International law forms part of the sources of law in Tanzania. This chapter focuses on international and regional instruments containing provisions on the duty of confidentiality and privacy. Tanzania is a party to international human rights instruments such as the Universal Declaration of Human Rights (UDHR), the International Covenant on Civil and Political Rights (ICCPR), and the United Nations Convention on the Rights of the Child (CRC). Besides the country subscribes to the regional and sub-regional instruments such as the African Charter on Human and Peoples Rights (ACHPR), the African Charter on the Rights and Welfare of the Child (ACRWC), and the SADC Treaty that protects the right to privacy.

Article 17 (1) of the ICCPR for instance provides that, 'no one shall be subjected to arbitrary or unlawful interference with his privacy, family, home or correspondence, nor to unlawful attacks on his honour and reputation.' Also as per Article 17 (2) of the ICCPR, everyone has the right to the protection of the law against such interference or attacks. State parties to the ICCPR have a positive obligation to 'adopt legislative and other measures to give effect to the prohibition against such interferences and attacks as well as to the protection of this right [privacy].'[15] Article 21 (1) of the SADC Treaty requires the Member States to cooperate in all areas necessary to foster regional development and integration on the basis of balance, equity, and mutual benefits.

---

[15]   General Comment No. 16 (1988), para. 1.

In line with this requirement, Article 21 (3) and (4), the SADC Treaty lists areas of cooperation by member states of the SADC. Although the list does not mention health, it provides an avenue for Member states to have additional areas of cooperation that may be decided by the council. As such, Article 22 (1) of the SADC Treaty states that the Member States are duty-bound to conclude such protocols as may be necessary in each area of cooperation, which shall among others provide the scope and objectives, institutions established and areas of cooperation and integration by the member states. Member States to the SADC agreed to cooperate in the area of health and henceforth adopted the Health Protocol. Article 3 of the SADC Health Protocol requires Member States to cooperate in addressing health problems and challenges facing them through effective regional collaboration and mutual support under the Protocol.

Article 3 (a), (b) of the SADC Health Protocol envisions that cooperation in health challenges facing SADC member states aims at achieving objectives including the identification, promotion, co-ordination and support of activities with the potential in improving the health of the population within the region; and co-ordinating regional efforts on epidemic preparedness, mapping, prevention, control and where possible the eradication of communicable and non-communicable diseases. Also, Article 3 (e) of the SADC Health Protocol has the objective of fostering cooperation and coordination in the area of health with other international organisations and cooperating partners.

Constitution

The Constitution is the fundamental and supreme law of the country. Article 16 of the Constitution provides for the right to privacy. As per Article 16 (1), every person is entitled to respect and protection of his person, the privacy of his own person, his family, and of his matrimonial life, and respect and protection of his residence and private communications. Article 16(2), nonetheless, set limits for the enjoyment of the right by stating that:

> For the purpose of preserving the person's right in accordance with this Article, the state authority shall lay down legal procedures regarding the circumstances, manner, and extent to which the right to privacy, security of the person, his property, and residence may be encroached upon without prejudice to the provisions of this Article.

In conjunction with the right to privacy, Article 18 (c) of the Constitution provides for the right to freedom of expression and protection from interference that every person has the freedom to communicate and a freedom with protection from interference from his communication.[16]

---

[16]　Constitution, Art 18 (1) (c).

Besides, privacy protection conferred under Article 16 and freedom from interference from communication as per Article 18 (c) of the Constitution are subject to the limitations prescribed under Article 30 of the Constitution. Accordingly, Article 30 of the Constitution states that the human rights and freedoms, the principles of which are set out in this Constitution, shall not be exercised by a person in a manner that causes interference with or curtailment of the rights and freedoms of other persons or of the public interest.[17] The basic rights and duties contained in the Constitution shall not be exercised in a manner that renders unlawful any existing law or prohibits the enactment of any law or the doing of any lawful act in accordance with such law for the purposes of ensuring the rights and freedoms of other people or of the interests of the public are not prejudiced by the wrongful exercise of the freedoms and rights of individuals; and ensuring the defence, public safety, public peace, public morality, public health, rural and urban development planning, the exploitation and utilisation of minerals or the increase and development of property of any other interests for the purposes of enhancing the public benefit.[18]

The rights and freedoms provided for in the Constitution do not render unlawful any law or any act done pursuant to such law for the purpose of ensuring the execution of a judgment or order of a court given or made in any civil or criminal matter; and protecting the reputation, rights, and freedoms of others or the privacy of persons involved in any court proceedings, prohibiting the disclosure of confidential information or safeguarding the dignity, authority and independence of the courts; imposing restrictions, supervising and controlling the formation, management and activities of private societies and organisations in the country; or enabling any other thing to be done which promotes or preserves the national interest in general.[19]

Received Laws

These were the laws that were received from England via India in 1920 under Article 17 (2) of the Tanganyika Order in Council on 22 July 1920. They include common law, doctrines of equity, and statutes of general application. After the independence of Tanganyika, Tanganyika Order in Council was repealed and the received laws were incorporated under section 2 (2) of the Judicature and Application of Laws Ordinance, 1961, Cap 453 of the Revised Laws of Tanganyika. In 2002 the existing and applicable laws in Tanzania

---

[17] Ibid, Art 30 (1).
[18] Ibid, Art 30 (2) (a) and (b).
[19] Ibid, Art 30 (2) (c), (d) and (b).

were revised through the Revised Edition and all the Ordinances and Acts were put in the Revised Editions Volumes. The Judicature and Application of Laws Ordinance was renamed as the Judicature and Application of Laws At, Cap 358 R.E 2002. The received laws were re-enacted under section 2 (3) of the Judicature and Application of Laws Act Cap 358 R.E 2002. Since were received under Article 17 (2) of the Tanganyika Order in Council 1920, the received laws are applicable in the Tanzania territory where there is a lacuna/ gap in Tanzania laws or where the circumstances of the country allow. From the foregoing, one of the sources of duty of confidentiality and privacy laws in Tanzania can be deduced from received laws. Common law and doctrines of equity on the duty of confidentiality and privacy in the health profession as developed in commonwealth jurisdictions such as the one stated in *Duchess of Kingston's Case*[20] are applicable in Tanzania as received laws. In the case Lord Mansfield said, 'if a surgeon was voluntarily to reveal these secrets, to be sure he would be guilty of a breach of honour and of great indiscretion; but, to give that information in a court of justice, which by the law of the land he is bound to do, will never be imputed to him as any indiscretion whatever.'[21]

Legislation

The legislation forms another source of law in Tanzania. It is categorised into two parts, that is, principal legislation and subsidiary legislation. Principal legislation/statutes are the Acts of parliament. Subsidiary legislation is the one passed by the authorities' delegated powers by the parliament to enact laws. These authorities include Local Government Authorities (LGAs) which enact bylaws applied in respective local governments, that is, cities, municipalities, and district and town councils. There is subsidiary legislation enacted by sectoral ministries and in this those made by the Ministry of Health and Social Welfare and other bodies which govern healthcare services in Tanzania.

Principal and subsidiary legislation connected with the duty of confidentiality and health in Tanzania include the Electronic and Postal Communication Act, 2010, Tanzania Intelligence and Security Services Act, 1996 and the regulations made thereunder. Others are the Medical, Dental and Allied Health Professionals Act, 2016; Health Laboratory Practitioners Act, 2007; the Environmental Health Practitioners (Registration) Act, 2007; the Medical Radiology and Imaging Professionals Act, 2007; the Optometry Act, 2007; the Nursing and Midwifery Act, 2010; the Pharmacy Act, 2011; the Traditional and Alternative Medicines Act, 2002. Subsidiary legislation regulating privacy

---

[20]   (1776) 20 Howell's State Trials 355.
[21]   Ibid 573.

and confidentiality in Tanzania are the Rules and Regulations such as the Code of Conduct made by the respective councils and boards. For instance, the Medical, Dental, and Allied Health Professionals Act, of 2016 establishes the Medical Council of Tanganyika, and the Nursing and Midwifery Act, of 2010 establishes Tanzania Nursing and Midwifery Council. The Medical Council of Tanganyika has developed the Code of Ethics and Professional Conduct for Medical and Dental Practitioners in Tanzania.

Precedents/Case Laws

Precedents/case laws form part of the sources of laws in Tanzania. Tanzania is a commonwealth country and as such is influenced by the common law doctrines of *stare decisis* and precedent which entails that courts are bound by previous decisions of the superior/courts of authority and set the rules on how the precious decision binds courts. Thus, the decisions of superior courts are binding and they apply through the doctrine of precedent which operates through vertical and horizontal application. The vertical application of the doctrine of precedent entails that the decision of the Court of Appeal which is the highest in the court structure binds all the courts below it and it can depart from its previous decision. This principle was stated in the case of *JUWATA v KIUTA*.[22] Also, the doctrine of precedent entails that previous decisions can apply horizontally and that, the courts of concurrent jurisdiction are persuasive to each other and not binding.

The application of case laws on health-related cases can be drawn from the medical negligence case of *Theodelina Alphaxad a Minor S/T Next Friend v The Medical Officer I/C, Nkinga Hospital*.[23] In the case, one Alphaxad Mirobo, the next friend of Theodelina Alpha, a minor then aged six years, filed this action on her behalf in this Court, against the Medical Officer In Charge of Nkinga Hospital. Five million Tanzanian Shillings were claimed in damages with interests, and costs of the suit, and such further reliefs as may be commensurate to the occasion, for the loss of the left forearm, that was amputated because of the faulty and negligent treatment of the defendant. The defendant objected by stating that the plaintiff's father was negligent in not sending the child back to the hospital. The issues before the court were whether Nkinga hospital was negligent in the medical treatment of Theodelina Alpha which led to limb amputation; and what reliefs, if any, are the parties entitled to.

---

[22]   [1988] TLR 146 (CA).
[23]   [1992] TLR 235 (HC).

In responding to the issues it was held that:

> If a person is admitted as a patient by a hospital, and is, in medical treatment occasioned injury through the negligence of some medical staff, it is unnecessary for him to pick up on any identifiable particular employee for suing purposes. The said hospital was held to be vicariously liable.[24] The hospital is in principle liable due to the negligence of its employee.

PERSONS BOUND BY THE DUTY OF CONFIDENTIALITY IN TANZANIA

Tanzania has developed the use of information and communication technology in health services. Protection of the patient's privacy and confidentiality is implied from the requirement of the law that in the contract between a professional man and his/her client there is an implied duty to keep his client's affairs secret and not to disclose them to anyone without just cause.[25] This contractual duty puts medical practitioners and other healthcare professionals to be bound and observe a duty of confidentiality to their patients.[26] In Tanzania, the regulation of professional conduct for health and medical practitioners in Tanzania is made under the coordination of the office of the Chief Medical Officer (CMO) who oversees the operation of the Professional Councils and Boards established by different Acts of parliament.

The existing health regulatory establishing laws have set up councils which are corporate bodies with perpetual succession and an official seal; capacity to sue or be sued in its corporate name; capable of acquiring, purchasing holding, and disposing of any movable or immovable property; enter into contracts or other transactions and do all other acts and things which a body corporate may lawfully perform; have powers to borrow such sums as it may require for its purpose; and exercise the powers and perform functions conferred upon it by or under the relevant legislation. These councils are autonomous government entities capable of owning, suing, and being sued in their own corporate names.

The councils are advisors to the government on matters pertaining to respective health professional practices. They are also charged with specific functions relating to registration, discipline of the professionals, setting standards and quality of practice for health professionals, training institutions, and health services. The councils are guided by the regulations and/or rules made by the

---

[24]   *Theodelina Alphaxad a Minor S/T Next Friend v The Medical Officer I/C, Nkinga Hospital* [1992] TLR 235 at 240.
[25]   See Lord Denning in *Parry-Jones v Law Society* [1969] 1 Ch 1, p. 7.
[26]   AB Makulilo, 'You Must Take Medical Test' (2010) 34 DuD 571, 575.

minister responsible for health matters and the codes of professional conduct made by the councils themselves. The Regulations prescribe the manner in which the functions are discharged. The health regulatory councils have set Codes of Professional Conduct and Ethics which embody the principles of ethical and behavioural values relevant to the respective health professional. The codes clarify the roles and responsibilities within the profession and embody principles that guide professionals on how to attain acceptable standards as well as how they can interact with their stakeholders and amongst themselves.

Legal Duties of Confidentiality

The issue of confidentiality and privacy of health records are well clarified by specific Codes of Professional Conduct and Ethics of health professionals. The Code of Ethics and Professional Conduct for Medical and Dental Practitioners in Tanzania, 2005 made under the Medical, Dental and Allied Health Professionals Act, 2016 recognise principles of informed consent, that is, the principle of self-determination, privacy, and confidentiality of the patient.

To start with, before treatment, the first principle mandates the client to make informed decisions unrestricted by the values of the practitioner and requires the practitioner to offer treatment and other forms of health intervention to a client only after obtaining the informed consent of the client. The principle requires the practitioner to offer treatment and other forms of health intervention to the client only after getting informed consent from the client; and always give the client sufficient information to enable him to decide whether or not to accept treatment, including the relevant risks, expected benefits, and available alternatives.[27]

The Code of Ethics and Professional Conduct for Medical and Dental Practitioners sets the limitation to access to client's information and obliges the practitioner to access the client's private information under the principle of trust and willingness.[28] As such the practitioner is duty bound to maintain secrecy and security of the client's private information; use professional judgment and responsibility in sharing the client's confidential information among colleagues; and ensure that the subordinate and any other member of staff observe confidentiality.[29] Confidentiality and privacy of patients is equally upheld by other professionals in the healthcare sector such as radiology and

---

[27] The Code of Ethics and Professional Conduct for Medical and Dental Practitioners in Tanzania, 2005, principles 3.1 and 3.2.

[28] Ibid, principle 7.

[29] Ibid, principle s 7.1, 7.2 and 7.3.

imagine professionals, optometry practitioners, nurses, and midwives.[30] There is also legislative protection of privacy and confidentiality of patients such as the ones provided for under the HIV and AIDS (Prevention and Control) Act 2008, and the Tanzanian Human DNA Regulation Act, 2009.

The HIV and AIDS (Prevention and Control) Act was enacted in 2008 to provide for the prevention, treatment, care, support, and control of HIV and AIDS, for the promotion of public health in relation to HIV and AIDS; to provide for appropriate treatment, care and support using available resources to people living with or at risk of HIV and AIDS and to provide for related matters.[31] The Act requires every public healthcare facility, voluntary counselling, and HIV testing centre which are recognised by the National AIDS Control Programme (NACP) to be an HIV testing centre for this Act.[32] It, however, restricts testing by private laboratories by stating that they may only be testing HIV if they are allowed to do so by the order published in the government gazette by the Private Health Laboratory Board.[33] Thus, to maintain privacy and confidentiality HIV testing must only be undertaken in the centres authorised and established under the Act which shall be designated as HIV testing centres.[34] Also, in performing HIV testing, the authorised health practitioners are required by the law to take measures that will ensure that the testing process is carried out promptly and efficiently and further that the result of the HIV test is communicated to the person tested per this Act.[35]

The Act states that HIV test results shall be confidential and shall be released only to the person tested.[36] Medical confidentiality for patients of HIV and AIDS is contained under the Act and Regulations which are made under the Act.[37] A person who received HIV results under the Act shall be obliged to observe confidentiality in respect of the HIV result received by him.[38] The disclosure to a third party of the results of an individual's HIV test without the prior written consent of that individual, or in the case of the minor, the minor's parent, guardian, or legal representative on a form that specifically states

---

[30]   See the Code of Ethics and Professional Conduct for Medical Radiology and Imaging Professionals, principle 2 (b); the Code of Ethics and Professional Conduct for Optometry Practitioners, 2015, principle 4; and the Code of Ethics and Professional Conduct for Nurses and Midwives, principle 7.

[31]   HIV and AIDS (Prevention and Control) Act, 2008, long title.

[32]   Ibid, s 13 (1).

[33]   Ibid, s 13 (2).

[34]   Ibid, s13 (4) and (5).

[35]   Ibid, s13 (3) (a) and (b).

[36]   Ibid, s 16 (1).

[37]   HIV and AIDS (Counselling and testing, use of ARVs and Disclosure) Regulations, 2010.

[38]   HIV and AIDS (Prevention and Control) Act, 2008, s 17 (2).

that HIV tests results may be released is unlawful.[39] Besides, all information and reports pertaining to HIV counselling sessions, testing, and reporting are confidential.[40]

DATA PROTECTION LAW

The past two decades have witnessed the rapid development of information and communications technologies in Africa which has provided an environment for the development of data privacy law in the continent.[41] The development of science and technology brought changes in the management of patient records. However, the incorporation of information and technology in patient data protection and confidentiality has not been smooth due to a shortage of qualified medical practitioners in healthcare facilities, incensement of disease, a large proportion of the population living in rural areas, and a lack of education and primary healthcare.[42] The legislative development on data privacy in Africa has taken place in an environment where knowledge, skills, and literature on data privacy and confidentiality is scant, fragmented, and continued to grow at a snail's pace.[43]

Data are usually collected on remote, distributed databases and their management must be compliant to data privacy laws.[44] This development is faced with problems to protect patients' sensitive data as some statutes are drafted in a way that do not offer effective protection of patients' privacy data. In the earlier case of *Whalen v Roe*[45] the court held that where the statute did not recognise patient data privacy and confidentiality protections, any infringement on patients' privacy would not amount to a violation of constitutional privacy principles as privacy protection must be derived from the statute and not be considered as explicit rights.

The Code of Ethics and Professional Conduct for Medical and Dental Practitioners recognises the principle of privacy as regards records, interests, and affairs relating to the client's health condition are confided to the practitioner only. The principle states that the practitioner shall respect the privacy of

---

[39]   HIV and AIDS (Counselling and testing, use of ARVs and Disclosure) Regulations, 2010, reg.24 (2).

[40]   Ibid, reg. 23 (1).

[41]   AB Makulilo, 'Privacy and Data Protection in Africa: A State of the Art' (2012) 2(3) International Data Privacy Law 163.

[42]   BA Townsend, *Privacy and Data Protection in Ehealth in Africa* (Unpublished PhD Thesis, Faculty of Law University of Cape Town 2017).

[43]   Makulilo (n 41).

[44]   Ibid.

[45]   [1977] 429 U.S. 589.

a client in the course of providing treatment and any other forms of interaction, and shall avoid acts that are degrading, insulting, interfering with, or injuring the self-value of the client.[46] Also, the practitioner shall take into account that touching a client without consent may be construed as trespass to the person, battery, or assault and that the body (corpus) of the client or information of the client is private property.[47]

The law is to the effect that entry of medical records shall be made in the client's file of all services rendered; and the records shall include rendering counselling, informed consent form, investigation requested, test results, and reporting.[48] The law further requires all forms and reports regarding the HIV status of the patients to be maintained in the client's record file, including copies of any referral forms or reports submitted by one health facility to another as part of the plan, and shall be consistent with the requirement of the law.[49] Also, all health practitioners, workers, employers, recruitment agencies, insurance companies, data recorders, sign language interpreters, legal guardians, and other custodians of any medical records, files, data or test results shall observe confidentiality in the handling of all medical information and documents, particularly the identity and status of persons living with HIV and AIDS.[50]

The handling of privacy data records shall be achieved by taking appropriate steps for protection including, keeping records secure at all times and establishing adequate confidentiality to safeguard such records stored in any form whatsoever.[51] Data protection of patient records can be secured by establishing and enforcing reasonable operational guidelines and procedures consistent with confidentiality requirements and training individuals who handle records in security objectives and techniques.[52]

Tanzania Intelligence and Security Services Act, 1996 mandates the Tanzania Intelligence & Security Service (TISS) with the duty to collect information through investigations or otherwise, to the extent that it is strictly necessary. For this position, it is possible for private data contained by healthcare facilities may be divulged to the TISS for what are said to be security

---

[46]   Code of Ethics and Professional Conduct for Medical and Dental Practitioners in Tanzania, 2005, principle 4.1.

[47]   Ibid, principle 4.2.

[48]   HIV and AIDS (Counselling and testing, use of ARVs and Disclosure) Regulations, 2010, reg. 23 (1).

[49]   Ibid, reg. 23 (2).

[50]   HIV and AIDS (Prevention and Control) Act, 2008, s17 (1); HIV and AIDS (Counselling and testing, use of ARVs and Disclosure) Regulations, 2010, reg. 23 (3).

[51]   Ibid, reg. 23 (3) (a).

[52]   Ibid, reg. 23 (3) (b) and (c).

purposes stated under section 14 of the Act which mandates TISS to collect, analyse, and retain information and intelligence respecting activities that may on reasonable grounds be suspected of constituting a threat to the security of the United Republic or any part of it.

Section 18 of the Act further empowers TISS to enter into arrangements with any person, local government or other authority, any police force, or other policing organisations as well as the government of foreign states or an international organisation of states or its institutions for purposes of performing its functions. However, this must be done with the approval of the Minister of Foreign Affairs. Section 5(2) of the Act states that, in exercising the powers, TISS can intercept any communication on the basis of national security but it is barred from instituting surveillance of any person or category of persons by reason only of their involvement in lawful protest, or dissent in respect of any matter affecting the Constitution, laws or the Government of Tanzania.

CONFIDENTIALITY AND GENETICS

Health professionals owe a duty of confidentiality to their patients. The conflict is when one is required to disclose patient confidential information when dealing with genetics. The genetic information of one person may also have implications for their family members. Keeping patient genetic information confidential can be difficult and it is important to alert a family member of the risk of a particular condition. In Tanzanian, Human DNA Regulation Act 2009[53] provide for the management and regulation of the collection, packing, transportation, storage, analysis, and disposal of sample for Human DNA, disclosure of genetic information, and research on Human DNA and provides for related matters.[54] The Act has incorporated provisions governing the collection, authority to collect and analyse, requesting authority, and requirement of written authorisation in dealing with human DNA. The Act further incorporates provisions on packing of samples, transportation of samples, receipt and storage, analysis of samples for Human DNA, recollection, and ownership.[55]

The Act incorporates provisions for the disclosure of genetic information and the destruction of samples for DNA.[56] The law provides that genetic information shall be communicated to the requesting authority who shall disclose the same information to the sample source or parent, guardian, or representative of the sample source.[57] The Regulator or the designated laboratories may,

---

53   Act No. 8 of 2009.
54   Human DNA Regulation Act 2009, long title.
55   Ibid, Part IV.
56   Ibid, Part VIII.
57   Ibid, s 52.

upon written request by the requesting authority, permit the sample source or sample source's representative to access records containing private genetic information and may be provided with a copy of such records at a fee.[58]

Part IV of the Human DNA Regulation Act permits the analysis of the sample for Human DNA. If during the analysis it is determined that a relative of a deceased sample source is at risk of genetic disease which in reasonable medical judgment can be effectively ameliorated, prevented or treated, nothing in this Act shall be construed as prohibiting researchers from contacting such relatives and informing them of such risk.[59]

The law imposes the duty of confidentiality to any person who receives or accesses private genetic information in the performance of his duties or in the cause of his employment. Such private genetic information shall not divulge it to anybody or be used by the person who happened to access it during or after the tenure of employment without the written authorisation of the sample source or the sample source representative.[60] The duty of confidentiality extends to a director of a designated laboratory, a researcher on Human DNA, and a director of a research institution or hospital that conduct Human DNA analysis to take all reasonable measures to ensure that employees and anyone under their supervision maintain confidentiality of the matters brought to their knowledge in the course of discharge of their duties.[61] In Tanzania human DNA is kept in the office of the Regulator of Human DNA Services established within the office of the Chief Government Chemist.[62] By virtue of his office, the Chief Government Chemist shall be the Regulator and responsible for overseeing, regulating, and the administration of Human DNA services and shall not disclose any genetic information obtained and kept under this Act.[63]

EXCEPTION TO OBLIGATIONS OF MEDICAL CONFIDENTIALITY

Confidential information of a patient has exceptions if the disclosure falls within a limited set of permissible disclosures. Health practitioners' laws and codes of ethics and professional conduct contain provisions permitting breach of confidentiality. The common grounds for the breach of confidentiality include statutory exceptions, making a disclosure with the patient's explicit and implicit consent, and disclosures in the public interest. Other grounds

---

[58]   Ibid, s 54.
[59]   Ibid, s 62.
[60]   Ibid, s 64 (1).
[61]   Ibid, s 64 (2).
[62]   Ibid, s 4 (1).
[63]   Ibid, s 65 (1).

for disclosure of confidential information include disclosure for teaching, research, and audit and monitoring and evaluation; disclosure to other health-care personnel; and disclosures to relatives, friends or third parties.

Statutory Exceptions

There are circumstances where medical practitioners may disclose patients' confidential information if the disclosure is in compliance with the requirement of the law.[64] In most cases, this exception is exercised where there is a court order requiring a disclosure. For instance, the health practitioner is required by the law to disclose confidential information of the patient in responding to an order of the court over legal proceedings where the main issue is HIV status of an individual.[65] If a medical practitioner refuses to abide to the court order they may be punished by the judge/magistrate for contempt of court. Statutory exceptions extend to a circumstance where the disclosure of patients' confidential information is given to the appointed member of the deceased's family.[66] From this requirement it seems to end after a patient's death as the legal duty of confidentiality dies with the patient. Regarding the disclosure of genetic confidential information, it may be made responding to the criminal investigation section of police in the course of criminal investigation or proceedings; the person from whom the genetic information was extracted and such genetic information is requested for his defence; and a country making request, which is accepted by the Attorney General for mutual assistance in criminal matters pursuant to the provisions of the Mutual Assistance in Criminal Matters Act.[67]

Making a Disclosure with the Patient's Explicit and Implicit Consent

Disclosure of medical information details may be made if the consent of a client is duly obtained.[68] The patient may expressly consent to the disclosure and once this is done the medical practitioner will be exonerated from liability for the breach of duty of confidence. In other situations, consent to divulge confidential information may be made explicitly or impliedly. Explicit consent is made when the patient enters into an express oral or written agreement with the medical practitioner to reveal confidential medical information. In relying

---

[64]   Code of Ethics and Professional Conduct for Medical and Dental Practitioners in Tanzania, 2005, principle 7.4.

[65]   HIV and AIDS (Prevention and Control) Act, 2008, s 18 (c).

[66]   Ibid, s 18 (d).

[67]   Human DNA Regulation Act 2009, s 65 (1) (a)–(c).

[68]   Code of Ethics and Professional Conduct for Medical and Dental Practitioners in Tanzania, 2005, principle 7.4.

on the disclosure of patient confidential information proof that the patient had the capacity to consent is important. If the patient is suffering from diseases that may impair his capacity to consent it will be a challenge for the medical practitioner to rely on disclosure by consent. Disclosures may equally be made on the presumption of implied consent, in situations where obtaining consent is undesirable or not possible, for example, in a patient in an intensive care unit (ICU).[69] It is important to take note that decisions made on behalf of an individual lacking the capacity to disclose should be done so proportionately and in their best interests.[70]

Disclosures in the Public Interest

Public interest disclosure involves a balancing of the importance of maintaining confidential disclosure with the importance of protecting public health and prevention or detection of serious harm. Medical practitioners have a duty to disclose confidential information of the patient if non-disclosure will expose the public to a serious risk of death or harm. Patient's confidential information likely to cause serious harm are disclosed under the auspices of public interest to protect other member of the community from harm. The case of *X v Y*,[71] where the defendants intended to publish the identities of two HIV-positive doctors who were working in general practice, raised the question of public interest. Those who wanted to publish the names of health practitioners contended that publication was for public interest. The health authority that held their medical records sought an injunction to restrain publication.[72] The question was whether it was in the public interest to publish their names. After hearing evidence the judge held that the risks of HIV transmission by the doctors was extremely small and granted injunction on the basis that the public interest in maintaining confidence and loyalty outweighed the public interest in disclosure by having a free press and informed public debate.

In *Tarasoff v Regents of University of California*,[73] the court found in favour of disclosure for public interest of patient's confidential information. In the case the patient confided to his psychiatrist that he intended to harm the victim. The psychiatrist told the university police, but not the targeted victim. The victim's family successfully sued the psychiatrist and his employer who

---

[69]   K Blightman, SE Griffiths and C Danbury 'Patient Confidentiality: When Can a Breach Be Justified?' (2014) 14(2) Critical Care & Pain 53.

[70]   Ibid.

[71]   [1988] 2 All ER 648.

[72]   N Nicholas, 'Confidentiality, Disclosure and Access to Medical Record' (2007) 9 The Obstetrician & Gynaecologist 257, 263.

[73]   131 Cal. Reporter 14 (Sup. Court 1976).

were held liable for negligence for nondisclosure of the patient's intention to assault a third party, which he did. In Tanzania, the phrase public interest is not explained but the Code of Ethics and Professional Conduct for Medical and Dental Practitioners in Tanzania allows the disclosure of patient's confidential information based on the interest of the public or community.[74]

Teaching, Research, Audit; and Monitoring and Evaluation

Confidential information of the patient may be disclosed based on teaching, research or audit. In Tanzania, medical research are conducted after investigator has obtained Ethical Clearance from the National Health Research Ethics Sub-Committee which is a subcommittee of the Medical Research Coordinating Committee (MRCC) in the National Institute for Medical Research.[75] As such research certificate approval is renewed annually and Principal Investigators are required to submit progress reports biannually.[76] Findings publications is made after the principal investigator has sought permission from the National Institute for Medical Research.[77]

The HIV and AIDS (Prevention and Control) Act states that medical confidentiality shall not be considered breached in complying with reportorial requirements in conjunction with the monitoring and evaluation programmes.[78] The audits are often undertaken under the presumption of implied consent and are therefore acceptable if data are sufficiently anonymised.[79] The use of patient information for teaching in Tanzania is not well captured in the guidelines and regulations but in most cases, it may require ethical clearance from National Institute for Medical Research and the user must maintain the confidentiality and privacy of the patient.

Disclosure to Other Healthcare Personnel

Disclosure of patients' confidential information takes place between members of healthcare professionals. Patients' information is shared with the healthcare professional to achieve the finest patient care. Disclosure will help the fellow health practitioner to have all relevant facts important for the care of the

---

[74] Code of Ethics and Professional Conduct for Medical and Dental Practitioners in Tanzania, 2005, principle 7.4.
[75] Health Research Regulations. Available at www.nimr.or.tz/health-research -regulations/ accessed 30 November 2022.
[76] Ibid.
[77] Ibid.
[78] HIV and AIDS (Prevention and Control) Act, 2008, s 18 (a).
[79] Blightman, Griffiths and Danbury (n 69) 53.

patient. The sharing of patient information with another health practitioner must be made based on professional judgment and responsibility with the assurance that subordinates and any other member of staff observe confidentiality.[80] The HIV and AIDS (Prevention and Control) Act requires health practitioners to share patients' information with other health practitioners directly involved or about to be involved in the treatment or care of a person living with HIV and AIDS.[81]

Disclosures to Relatives, Friends, or Third Parties

There are situations where it is reasonable to disclose confidential information about the patient to a relative or friend. For a patient who is seriously ill, the overall best interests of the patient are to reveal medical information to a spouse, and if a patient is a child, to reveal the information to a parent or guardian. Information may equally be disclosed to third parties for instance when the same is needed by employers under the Employment and Labour Relations Act 2004. The HIV and AIDS (Prevention and Control) Act, 2008 allows the disclosure of results of HIV of a child to parents or recognised guardian.[82] The HIV results of a person with the inability to comprehend the results may be disclosed to a spouse or recognised guardian, and the HIV results may be shared or disclosed to a sexual partner of an HIV-tested person; in other instances, HIV results may be disclosed to the court, if applicable.[83]

The law incorporates the provisions that the genetic information of any person shall not be divulged in compliance with an order for compulsory disclosure in civil proceedings unless the sample source or the sample source's representative is a party to such proceedings and the genetic information is at issue.[84] Also, the law gives power to the court to hear and determine disclosure of genetic information after it has satisfied that no other ways of obtaining private genetic information are available or may be effective; and there is a compelling need for private genetic information which outweighs the potential harm to the privacy of the sample source.[85]

Since the court has the power to hear, determine and order the disclosure of private genetic information, that court is mandatorily required by the law to limit disclosure only to persons whose need for such information is the basis

---

[80]   The Code of Ethics and Professional Conduct for Medical and Dental Practitioners in Tanzania, 2005, principles 7.1, 7.2, and 7.3.
[81]   HIV and AIDS (Prevention and Control) Act, 2008, s 18 (b).
[82]   Ibid, s 16 (2) (a).
[83]   Ibid, s 16 (2) (b)–(d).
[84]   Human DNA Regulation Act 2009, s 55.
[85]   Ibid, s 56 (1) (2) (a) and (b).

of the order; limit the disclosure to those parts of records containing such information which are essential to fulfil the objective of the order; require non-disclosure of names of people in the collection and analysis of the sample of Human DNA from any documents made available to the public, and provide protective measures to the sample source by sealing from public scrutiny the record or any part of the record of any proceedings for which disclosure of the information has been ordered.[86]

CONFIDENTIALITY AND COVID-19

The outbreak of COVID-19 required preventive measures and safe and effective COVID-19 vaccines. In the course of fighting the outbreak, medical institutions and professionals ought to uphold the confidentiality of patient information about COVID-19 status. In Tanzania, the Ministry of Health, Community Development, Gender, Elderly, and Children made the National Guideline of Clinical Management and Infection Prevention and Control of Novel Coronavirus (COVID-19 and Guidelines for COVID-19 Vaccination. The Guideline of Clinical Management and Infection Prevention and Control of COVID-19 requires that health professionals are bound to maintain the confidentiality and privacy of COVID-19 suspected patients and patients.[87] Guidelines for COVID-19 vaccination declared vaccination to be voluntary for eligible individuals and gave a requirement to sign a consent form prior to vaccination.[88]

OFFENCES FOR BREACH OF CONFIDENTIALITY AND DISCLOSURE OF PATIENT INFORMATION

The law in Tanzania prescribes penalties and imposes sanctions on medical practitioners who breach the duty of confidentiality by disclosing confidential information about the patient. For instance, the HIV and AIDS (Prevention and Control) Act, 2008 sets offences for breach of confidentiality by providing that any health practitioner or any person referred to under sections 16 and

---

[86]   Ibid, s 57 (a)–(d).

[87]   Aya ya 9.5 ya Jamhuri ya Muungano wa Tanzania -Wizara ya Afya, Maendeleo ya Jamii, Jinsia Wazee na Watoto, *Mwongozo wa Kinga na Kuzuia Maambukizi Katika Jamii Dhidi ya Ugonjwa wa Corona (Covid 19)*, April 2020 (Unofficial Translation: Para 9.5 of United Republic of Tanzania – Ministry of Health, Community Development, Gender, Elderly and Children, *National Guideline of Clinical Management and Infection Prevention and Control of Novel Coronavirus (COVID-19)* 2020.

[88]   United Republic of Tanzania – Ministry of Health, Community Development, Gender, Elderly and Children, *Guidelines for COVID-19 Vaccination*, 2021 at p. 20.

17 who breaches medical confidentiality, or unlawfully discloses information regarding the HIV and AIDS status of any person, commits an offence, and on conviction shall be liable to a fine of not less than five hundred thousand shillings and not exceeding one million shillings or to imprisonment for a term not less than six months and not exceeding 12 months or both.[89]

Human DNA Regulation Act makes it an offence for any person who discloses any genetic information obtained and kept in the office of the regulator contrary to the provisions of the Act and on conviction is liable to a fine of three million shillings or to imprisonment for a term of two years or to both.[90]

CONCLUSION

This chapter analysed the protection of patient confidential information and privacy in the health sector. It considers the legal framework based on international influences by international instruments and other sources of law in Tanzania from legislative to received laws. From the outset, the chapter finds that the law of confidentiality and privacy in the health sector is underdeveloped. While Tanzania complies with the international legal position on privacy and confidentiality, the customisation of the rules through local legislation has been taking place slowly. There is no general law on protection of patient confidential information only that the health practitioners are guided by a few specific laws such as the HIV and AIDS (Prevention and Control) Act, 2008, and Human DNA Regulation Act 2009. The Codes for Conduct and Ethics for specific health professionals such as medical professionals and dentists, nurses and midwives, radiology and imaging professionals, pharmacists, and optometry provide limited guidelines for the standards of medical confidentiality and privacy as well as the exceptions to medical confidentiality and privacy. Despite these setbacks, the health system is organised and prepared to deal with emerging health challenges although crudely, while maintaining the privacy and confidentiality of patients. For instance, the development of science and technology has led to the enactment of laws to address issues likely to cause difficulties in the day-to-day activities of health professionals and thus laws such as the Human DNA Regulation Act 2009 were enacted to address such changes. The few existing laws, albeit, in summary, set standards of privacy and confidentiality and provide for the grounds for disclosure of confidential information which range from statutory exceptions to disclosure due to public interest. COVID-19 which hit the world in late 2019 made Tanzania to adopt

---

[89]   HIV and AIDS (Prevention and Control) Act, 2008, s 46 (a) and (b).
[90]   Human DNA Regulation Act 2009, s 65 (2).

and customize World Health Organisation COVID-19 standards and set guidelines for the prevention and vaccination of COVID-19.

9. Patient confidentiality rules in South Africa: a legal and ethical perspective

Sylvester C. Chima

GENERAL INTRODUCTION

What is Patient Confidentiality?

Confidentiality may be defined as the right of an individual to have personal, identifiable medical information kept private. Such information should be available only to the physician of record and other health care professionals and insurance personnel as necessary or on a 'need to know' basis. Since 1996, patient confidentiality has been a protected right in South Africa based on some statutes such as the Constitution,[1] the National Health Act (NHA)[2] and more recently the Protection of Personal Information Act (POPIA).[3] Confidentiality remains one of the core tenets of the medical profession since ancient times, as denoted by this excerpt from the ancient Hippocratic Oath:

> Whatever, in connection with my professional practice or not, in connection with it, I see or hear, in the life of men, which ought not to be spoken of abroad, I will not divulge, as reckoning that all such should be kept secret.[4]

Despite this ancient injunction however, medical doctors and other healthcare professionals frequently face challenges to this long-standing obligation to keep all information between physicians and their patients private.

---

[1]   Constitution of the Republic of South Africa, 1996.
[2]   National Health Act 61 of 2003, *Government Gazette* vol. 469 Cape Town, 23 July 2004. No. 26595.
[3]   Protection of Personal Information Act 4 of 2013, *Government Gazette* vol. 581 Cape Town, 26 November 2013, No. 37067, came into full effect July 2021.
[4]   The Hippocratic Oath (Ancient version) (Boston: Harvard Classics Volume 38, P.F. Collier and Son, 1910). Placed in the Public Domain, June 1993; S.C. Chima, *A Primer on Medical Bioethics and Human Rights for African Scholars* (Durban: Chimason Educational Books, 2011) 396–399.

Further, the World Medical Association (WMA) code of medical ethics recommends that, 'A physician shall preserve absolute confidentiality on all he knows about his patient even after the patient has died'. Accordingly, the WMA Declaration on Patients' Rights states that 'all identifiable information about a patient's health status, medical condition diagnosis, prognosis and treatment and all other information of a personal kind must be kept confidential, even after death'. Exceptionally, the patient's relatives may have a right of access to information that would inform them of their health risks. Confidential information can only be disclosed if the patient gives explicit consent or if expressly provided for in the law. Information can be disclosed to other healthcare providers only on a strictly 'need to know' basis unless the patient has given explicit consent. All identifiable patient data must be protected. The protection of the data must be appropriate to the manner of its storage.[5] The WMA declaration also states that human substance from which identifiable data can be derived, for example, human DNA, must be likewise protected.'[6]

A Brief Description of Patient Confidentiality

Patient confidentiality means that personal and medical information given to healthcare providers should not be disclosed to others unless that individual or patient has given specific permission or consent for its release. This is because disclosure of personal information could lead to professional or personal harm. Patients therefore rely on their doctors and other healthcare providers to keep their medical information private. Nevertheless, it has become rare for medical records to remain completely sealed. The most benign breaches of patient confidentiality occur when clinicians share medical information as case studies or case reports. When such information or data is published in professional journals, the identity of patients should never be divulged, and all identifying data should also be eliminated or changed. If this confidentiality is breached in any way, patients may have the right to sue the offending healthcare professional for breach of confidentiality, as illustrated by the landmark South African case of *Jason van Vuuren v Kruger* (also known as the McGeary case).[7] In this case, a medical doctor was successfully sued for breach of confidentiality for

---

[5]   WMA Declaration of Lisbon on the Rights of the Patient. Adopted by the 34th World Medical Assembly, Lisbon, Portugal, September/October 1981, amended by the 47th WMA General Assembly, Bali, Indonesia, September 1995 and editorially revised at the 171st Council Session, Santiago, Chile, October 2005.

[6]   Ibid.

[7]   *Jansen van Vuuren and Another v Kruger* [1993] (4) SA 842.

revealing his patients HIV status to another doctor and a dentist while playing a game of golf.

Facts of the case

Facts: Mr. McGeary wanted to apply for a life assurance policy. The insurance company requested that he should undergo an HIV test. So, Mr McGeary approached his doctor (Dr. Kruger) and asked him to conduct the HIV test. When the doctor received the results of the test, he informed McGeary that he was HIV positive. The next day his doctor was playing golf with another doctor and a dentist. During the course of the game, they discussed HIV-AIDS, and McGeary's doctor told the other doctor and dentist that McGeary had tested positive for HIV. However, Mr. McGeary had asked his doctor not to disclose the information about his HIV status. The other doctor sometimes worked as a locum for Mr. McGeary's doctor, and the dentist had also treated the plaintiff. Within days, the news of McGeary's HIV status had spread throughout his small community. Mr. McGeary then brought a civil claim to get compensation from his doctor for breaching his legal and ethical rights to confidentiality. However, during the trial of the case in court, McGeary died of an AIDS-related illness. But the lawyers representing McGeary's estate continued with the case on his behalf.

Held: the Appellate Division of the Supreme Court (now called the South African Supreme Court of Appeal) decided that:

(a)   A doctor cannot **disclose a patient's** HIV status to other doctors without the consent of the patient unless there is a clear legal duty to do so.
(b)   That Dr. Kruger had not respected McGeary's right to confidentiality.
(c)   Therefore Dr Kruger should thus pay McGeary's estate compensation in the amount of R5000 (Rands), for breaching McGeary's right to confidentiality.[8]

It must be noted that while the monetary award for damages in this case may appear low or insignificant. Nevertheless, it reflects the court's repugnance for the doctor's breach of patient confidentiality. Also, it must be stated that based on such findings, the offending doctor could be reported to the healthcare professionals' regulatory body, such as the Health Professionals Council of South Africa (HPCSA), for additional sanctions for breach of professional ethical rules which may result in additional disciplinary sanctions, such as temporary suspension of a licence to practice, or fines.

However, the greatest threat to medical privacy and confidentiality occurs because most medical bills are now paid through some form of health insur-

---

[8]   Ibid.

ance. This makes it more difficult, or almost impossible, to keep patients' information completely confidential. In addition, health records are routinely viewed not only by doctors and their staffs, but also by employees of insurance companies, medical laboratories, public health departments, researchers, and many others. Also, if an employer provides health insurance, the employer and designated employees may equally have access to employee files, including their health records.

The Purpose of Confidentiality

It has been suggested that confidentiality in medical practice serves two primary purposes:

I.   First, to respect patients' 'privacy' so that they feel no shame and vulnerability.
II. Second, to create an environment for honest communication between doctors or other healthcare professionals and their patients.[9]

During the course of accessing healthcare, patients invariably discuss intimate and personal details about themselves, which they may not even disclose to any other person including their spouses or significant others. Therefore, healthcare users or patients have the right and expectation that such disclosures will remain private and confidential. A breach of such confidence may result in a legal action for invasion of privacy or defamation, as illustrated by the McGeary case.[10] Accordingly, section 14 of the South African Constitution[11] states:

> Everyone has the right to privacy which includes the right not to have the privacy of their communications infringed.[12]

[9]   P.A. Carstens and D. Pearmain, *Foundational Principles of South African Medical Law* (Durban: LexisNexis, 2008) 943–1016; S.C. Chima, *A Primer on Medical Bioethics and Human Rights for African Scholars* (Durban: Chimason Educational Books, 2011) 105–120; J. Saner, *Medical Malpractice in South Africa: A Guide for Medical and Legal Practitioners* (Durban: LexisNexis, 2018).
[10] *van Vuuren v Kruger* (n 8).
[11] The Constitution (n 1) s 14.
[12] Ibid.

According to the World Health Organization (WHO), health:

> is a state of complete physical, mental and social well-being and not merely the absence of disease or infirmity.[13]

Therefore, health remains one of the most sensitive areas for many people when it comes to issues of privacy. The physical examination of a person in a healthcare context is an invasion of privacy, and such examinations can only be lawfully conducted when such a person waives their right to privacy and gives consent for the purpose of medical examination and treatment.[14,15] The NHA[16] provides that all information concerning a healthcare user or patient, including information relating to their health status, treatment, or stay in a health establishment, is confidential. The NHA[17] further provides that such information should not be disclosed unless:

(a)   the healthcare user consents to that disclosure in writing;
(b)   a court order or any law requires that disclosures; or
(c)   where non-disclosure of the information represents a serious threat to public health.

The latter situation was aptly illustrated by the quarantine and disaster management regulations requiring legal disclosure during the recent and ongoing Covid-19 pandemic in some jurisdictions including South Africa.[18]

---

[13]   Constitution of the World Health Organization, 1948, https://www.who.int/about/governance/constitution (last accessed February 25, 2022).

[14]   S.C. Chima, 'An Investigation of Informed Consent in Clinical Practice in South Africa' (LLD Thesis, University of South Africa, 2018).

[15]   S.C. Chima, 'Evaluating the Quality of Informed Consent and Contemporary Clinical Practices by Medical Doctors in South Africa: An Empirical Study' (2013) *BMC Med Ethics* 14 (Suppl 1): S3.

[16]   National Health Act (n 2).

[17]   Ibid.

[18]   S.C. Chima, 'Ethical and legal dilemmas surrounding the Covid-19 pandemic and extremely drug resistant tuberculosis (XDR-TB) in South Africa: Public health versus individual rights' (Hong Kong: *Public Jurist Magazine*, Government and Laws Committee, Hong Kong University, April 2020) 39–44, https://www.researchgate.net/publication/341883223_ETHICAL_AND_LEGAL_DILEMMAS_SURROUNDING_COVID-19_AND_X-DR_TB_IN_SOUTH_AFRICA_PUBLIC_HEALTH_VS_HUMAN_RIGHTS (last accessed September 15, 2023).

Also, based on the common law, there is a professional obligation on medical practitioners and other healthcare professionals to maintain confidentiality, unless:

i.   a court of law orders the doctor or healthcare professional to make such a disclosure;
ii. an Act of Parliament or other relevant laws requires the doctor or healthcare professional to make a disclosure;
iii. where there is a moral or legal obligation on the doctor or healthcare professional to make a disclosure to a person or agency that has a reciprocal moral or legal obligation to receive the information; or
iv. where the patient or healthcare user consents to such disclosures.[19]

While the Hippocratic Oath[20] requires that medical practitioners preserve the confidence of their patient; on the other hand, the law may demand that the doctors breach this confidence under certain circumstances. It has been argued that there is an ethical obligation on doctors not to divulge information about their patients without the patients' consent.[21] According to HPCSA general ethical rules for doctors and other registered healthcare professionals, a breach of confidentiality may be allowed where refusal by a doctor to disclose personal information of a patient could result in prosecution for contempt of court.[22]

What does the Duty of Confidentiality Require from Healthcare Professionals?

The obligation of confidentiality not only prohibits the physician and other healthcare professionals from disclosing information about the patient's case to other interested parties, but also encourages healthcare professionals to take precautions with patients' information to ensure that only authorized access occurs. However, the context of modern medical practice constrains physicians and other healthcare professionals' obligation to protect patient confidentiality. For example, in the course of caring for patients, healthcare professionals will often find themselves exchanging information about

---

[19]   Carstens and Pearmain (n 9); Chima (n 9); Saner (n 9).
[20]   Hippocratic Oath (n 4).
[21]   S.C. Chima, 'Informed consent in South Africa: A Legal, Ethical and Cross-cultural Perspective'. In: T. Vansweevelt and N. Glover-Thomas (eds), *Informed Consent and Health: A Global Analysis*, (Cheltenham: Edward Elgar Publishing, 2020) 83–214; Chima (n 15).
[22]   HPCSA, *Guidelines for Good Practice in the Healthcare Professions: General Ethical Guidelines for the Healthcare Professions* (Booklet 1, HPCSA, 2016).

patients with other healthcare providers, health insurance companies or health maintenance organizations (HMOs).[23] Such discussions are often critical for patient care and are an integral part of the teaching and learning experience in teaching hospitals where most healthcare professionals are trained. Therefore, such inadvertent breaches are justifiable as long as precautions are taken to limit the ability of others who are not a party to patients care, to hear or see such confidential information. Technological advances such as computerized patient records or telemedicine,[24,25] may also pose new and unique challenges to confidentiality. In such circumstances, all healthcare professionals must endeavour to follow prescribed standard operating procedures (SOPs) for computer access and security to provide additional measures designed to enhance and protect patient confidentiality and privacy. One of the methods of general compliance may involve de-identifying personal information, by anonymization of data and removal of any personal identifying information from patients records or case reports to enhance confidentiality.[26,27]

ETHICAL BASIS OR JUSTIFICATIONS FOR THE IMPORTANCE OF CONFIDENTIALITY

Patients or healthcare users share their personal information with physicians and other healthcare professionals every day. Therefore, all healthcare practitioners have a duty of care, to respect the patient's trust and maintain the privacy of patients by keeping such information private. This obligation requires doctors and other healthcare professionals to respect the patient's privacy by restricting access of others to any information disclosed to them. Furthermore, creating a trusting environment by respecting patient privacy will encourage patients to be as honest as possible during the course of the clinical encounter. Ethical principles underlying the importance of confidentiality in medical practice are outlined in the following paragraphs.

---

[23]   S.C. Chima, 'Doctor and healthcare worker strikes. Are they ethical or morally justifiable: Another view' (2020) *Curr Opin Anaesthesiol* 33: 203–210.

[24]   R. Gellman, '*Confidentiality and telemedicine: the need for a federal legislative solution*' (1995) *Telemed J* 3:189–94.

[25]   H Yadav and W.Y. Lin, 'Patient confidentiality, ethics and licensing in telemedicine' (2001) *Asia Pac J Public Health* 13 Suppl: S36–38.

[26]   S.C. Chima, *A Primer on Medical Bioethics and Human Rights for African Scholars* (Durban: Chimason Educational Books, 2011) 104–119.

[27]   US Code of Federal Regulations, Health Insurance Portability and Accountability (HIPAA) Act 1996; UK Data Protection Act 1998.

Fiduciary Relationship

The word *fiduciary* is derived from the Latin word for 'confidence' or 'trust'.[28] The fiduciary duty between doctors and patients is a duty of fidelity or trust between both parties.[29] This bond of trust between the patient and the physician is vital to medical treatment, as well as diagnostic and therapeutic processes. It forms the basis for physician or other healthcare professionals and patients' relationships. Therefore, in order for a doctor or other healthcare practitioner to make accurate diagnoses and provide optimal treatment recommendations, patients must be able to communicate all relevant information about their illness or injury based on the trust and belief that physicians or healthcare professionals are obliged to refrain from divulging any confidential information imparted to them by the patient. This duty is based on accepted codes of professional ethics which recognize the special nature of such relationships between medical doctors and other healthcare practitioners and patients.[30]

Respect for autonomy
The ethical principle of respect for autonomy[31] relates to confidentiality in that personal information about any individual belongs to that individual and should not be made known to others without that person's consent. Furthermore, human beings are deserving of respect and dignity and one way of showing such respect is by preserving the individual's privacy. In terms of South African law, section 14 of the Constitution protects the right to privacy which includes the right not to have the privacy of one's communications infringed.[32] In addition, the NHA[33] states that that all healthcare users or patients have a right to confidentiality which is consistent with the right to

---

[28] Anon, *Oxford South African Concise Dictionary* (2nd edn) (Cape Town: OUP, 2010).

[29] S.C. Chima 'Doctor-Patient Relationship'. In: S.C. Chima, *A Primer on Medical Bioethics and Human Rights for African Scholars* (Durban: Chimason Educational Books, 2011) 121–131.

[30] HPCSA *Guidelines for Good Practice in the Health Care Professions Confidentiality: Protecting and Providing Information* (Booklet 5, HPCSA 2016); Chima (n 26).

[31] S.C. Chima, 'Respect for Autonomy as a Prima Facie Right: Overriding Patient Autonomy in Medical Practice' (2009) *Transactions: Journal of the Colleges of Medicine of South Africa (CMSA)* 53 (1): 38–44; T.L. Beauchamp and J.F. Childress, *Principles of Biomedical Ethics* (5th edn) (New York: OUP, 2001) 80.

[32] The Constitution (n 1).

[33] NHA (n 2).

privacy in the Constitution.[34] Furthermore, ethical rules of the HPCSA state that healthcare practitioners may only divulge information regarding a patient:

(a)   with the express consent of the patient;
(b)   with the written consent of a parent or guardian of a minor under the age of 12 years; or
(c)   in the case of a deceased patient, with the written consent of the next of kin or the executor of the deceased's estate;
(d)   or in exceptional cases based on statutory relations, court order or in the public interest.[35]

Furthermore, HPCSA ethical rules also stipulate that when healthcare practitioners are asked to provide information about patients, they should:

1.   seek the consent of patients before disclosure of information wherever possible and should consider whether or not the patients can be identified from such disclosure. Comprehensive information must be made available to patients with regard to the potential for a breach of confidentiality in reference to ICD-10 coding;[36]
2.   anonymize data where unidentifiable data will serve the purpose; and
3.   keep disclosures to the minimum necessary for the purpose to be achieved.

In addition, healthcare practitioners must always be prepared to justify their decisions in accordance with the laid out ethical guidelines.[37]

Implied promise
Another ethical consideration that is relevant to confidentiality in healthcare is the idea of implied promise.[38] Trust or fidelity is an essential part of the doctor and healthcare practitioner relationship and patient relationship. To be able to access healthcare services, patients or healthcare users are obliged to reveal their private personal information, sometimes to total strangers, such as healthcare practitioners who they maybe meeting for the first time. In such situations, patients should be able to have trust and believe that their caregivers will not divulge such information to others. The basis for this trust or fidelity is the

34   The Constitution (n 1) s 14.
35   HPCSA (n 30).
36   National Department of Health, South Africa, *Technical User Guide compiled by the Ministerial ICD-10 Task Team to define standards and guidelines for ICD-10 coding implementation,* https://www.health.gov.za/wp-content/uploads/2021/02/finaluserguideicd10.pdf (last accessed February 28, 2022).
37   Ibid.
38   T. Hope, J. Savulescu J, and I. Hendrick, *Medical Ethics and Law-The Core Curriculum* (2nd edn) (Edinburgh: Churchill Livingstone, 2008).

ethical and legal standards of confidentiality that are required to be upheld by all healthcare professionals. Without this understanding patients or healthcare users may be reluctant to reveal personal information which may be critical to their care and also inimical to maintaining public health.[39]

Virtue ethics

According to Aristotle '*Virtue, is a state of character concerned with choice, lying in a mean, i.e., the mean relative to us.*'[40] Aristotle thereby described moral virtue as a disposition to behave in the right manner and as a mean between extremes of deficiency and excess, which are vices. One learns moral virtue primarily through habit and practice rather than through reasoning and instruction.[41] By contrast to the ethical principle of respect for autonomy, virtue ethics tends to focus on the physician or healthcare practitioner's' character. One can argue that one of the attributes of a virtuous or conscientious doctor or healthcare practitioner is that he or she is trustworthy and respects patients' confidences and privacy by maintaining patients' confidentiality.[42]

Consequentialism

Finally, another important ethical consideration in relation to confidentiality is consequentialism because it is the consequences of the breach of confidentiality or privacy that determines the seriousness of the breach, and this underlies the need to maintain patients' confidentiality. For example, a patient whose confidence is breached may make a report or complain to other patients, as illustrated by the case of *van Vuuren v Kruger* 1993.[43] Consequently other affected or infected patients may then then refuse to reveal important information to their healthcare practitioners, which may ultimately affect the quality of care that is provided to individual patients or society at large. At common law, confidentiality is important because it is in the public's interest that people should be treated for various diseases because of the consequences of illness for others and the society-at-large, as aptly illustrated by the ongoing Covid-19 pandemic where infected patients who refuse to quarantine, self-isolate, wear prescribed facemasks, and maintain physical distance may pose a serious risk

---

[39]   Ibid; Chima (n 26).
[40]   Aristotle, Nichomachean Ethics (W.D. Ross, Trans), http://classics.mit.edu//Aristotle/nicomachaen.html (last accessed February 15, 2022).
[41]   Aristotle (384–322 BC) Nicomachean Ethics – SparkNotes, https://www.sparknotes.com/philosophy/aristotle/section8/ (last accessed February 15, 2022).
[42]   Hope et al. (n 38); Chima (n 31), Aristotle (nn 40 and 41).
[43]   *van Vuuren v Kruger* (n 7).

(sometimes mortal), to other members of the society at due risk of overburdening and overwhelming the public healthcare system.[44]

KEY SOURCES OF THE DUTY OF CONFIDENTIALITY

In the context of South African law, all legislation derives from the bill of rights within the Constitution. The right to privacy is enshrined in section 14 of the 1996 Constitution[45] which states:

> Everyone has the right to privacy, which includes the right not to have
> a. Their person or home searched
> b. Their property searched
> c. Their possession seized, or
> d. The privacy of their communication infringed

While the Constitution[46] does not define the meaning of 'privacy' *per se*. It has been argued that in the context of healthcare, the physical examination of an individual or his or her property even while in a hospital setting, may represent and invasion of privacy,[47] except where such an individual has waived the right to privacy by providing consent or informed consent.[48] Furthermore, it has been suggested that healthcare workers (HCWs) who search a patients locker while they are in hospital or who may inspect an individual's clothing or person to see what is hidden there, may in fact be violating the person's right to privacy without due consent. Similarly, intercepting messages or any other forms of communication including phone conversations to or by a patient or healthcare user, without appropriate permissions or the users express consent, may broadly constitute an invasion of privacy.[49] While the South African constitution does not define what constitutes 'privacy', the idea or concept of the broad scope of privacy can be surmised by some judgments in the common law such as the dictum of Ackerman J sitting in the Constitutional Court in the

---

[44]   Chima (nn 18 and 26); Hope et al. (n 38); O.J. Kim, 'Ethical Perspectives on the Middle East Respiratory Syndrome Coronavirus Epidemic in Korea' (2016) *J Prev Med* Public Health 49(1): 18–22, https://doi.org/10.3961/jpmph.16.013; E. Agazzi, 'The Coronavirus pandemic and the principle of common good' (2020) *Bioethics Update* 6 (2): 63–66.

[45]   The Constitution (n 1).

[46]   Ibid.

[47]   P. Carstens and D. Pearmain, *Foundational Principles of South African Medical Law* (Durban: LexisNexis, 2010) 943–1016.

[48]   Chima (nn 14 and 15); ibid.

[49]   Carstens and Pearmain (n 47).

case of *National Coalition of Gay and Lesbian Equality v Minister of Justice*[50] where he opined:

> Privacy recognises that we all have a right to a sphere of private intimacy and autonomy which allows us to establish and nurture human relationships without interference from the outside community. The way in which we give expression to our sexuality is at the core of this area of private intimacy. If in expressing our sexuality, we act consensually and without harming one another, invasion of that precinct will be a breach of our privacy.[51]

In a philosophised context, this fragment by Isiah Berlin (1958) when speaking on liberty also pertains to privacy:

> Those who have ever valued liberty for its own sake believed that to be free to choose, and not to be chosen for, is an inalienable ingredient, in what makes human beings human, and that this underlies ... the demand...to be accorded an area... in which one is one's own master, a 'negative' area in which man is not obliged to account for his activities to any man so far as this is compatible with the existence of organized society.[52]

Ultimately, it has been argued that the concept of privacy is closely aligned with the concept of human dignity. Previously the idea of privacy was generally derived from the common law and respect for human rights and dignity. More recently the rules pertaining to privacy and confidentiality have become codified into legal statutes. Similarly in South Africa, arising from the Constitution, the patients' rights to privacy, confidentiality and information protection have been codified in statutory law such as the NHA,[53] where section 14 of this Act stipulates that:

(1)   All information concerning a user, including information relating to his or her health status, treatment or stay in a health establishment, is confidential,

(2)   Subject to section 15, no person may disclose any information contemplated in subsection (1) unless–

   (a)   the user consents to that disclosure in writing;

   (b)   a court order or any law requires that disclosure; or

---

[50]   *National Coalition of Gay and Lesbian Equality v Minister of Justice* 1999 (1) SA 6 (CC).

[51]   Ibid; Carstens and Pearmain (n 47) 961.

[52]   I. Berlin, 'Two Concepts of Liberty'. In: I. Berlin, *Four Essays on Liberty* (Oxford: OUP, 1969); S.C. Chima, A Primer on Medical Bioethics and Human Rights for African Scholars (Durban: Chimason Educational Books, 2011) 80.

[53]   NHA (n 2).

(c)   non-disclosure of the information represents a serious threat to public health.

Whereas section 15 provides access to health records, where–

(1)   A health worker or any health care provider that has access to the health records of a user may disclose such personal information to any other person, healthcare provider or health establishment as is necessary for any legitimate purpose within the ordinary course and scope of his or her duties where such access or disclosure is in the interests of the user.

For the purpose of this section, 'personal information' means personal information as defined in section 1 of the Promotion of Access to Information (PAIA) Act.[54]

With regards to access to health records by healthcare providers, section 16 further stipulates that:

(1)   A health care provider may examine a user's health records for the purposes of–
       (a)   treatment with the authorisation of the user; and
       (b)   study, teaching or research with the authorisation of the user, head of the health establishment concerned and the relevant health research ethics committee.

(2)   If the study, teaching or research contemplated in subsection (1)(b) reflects or obtains no information as to the identity of the user concerned, it is not necessary to obtain the authorisations contemplated in that subsection.

Furthermore, detailed provisions for the protection of health records are laid out in section 17 of the NHA[55] and penalties for failure to adhere to these regulations. These are outlined as follows:

(1)   The person in charge of a health establishment in possession of a user's health records must set up control measures to prevent unauthorised access to those records and to the storage facility in which, or system by which, records are kept.

(2)   Any person who–
       (a)   fails to perform a duty imposed on them in terms of subsection (1);

---

[54]   Promotion of Access to Information Act (PAIA) 2 of 2000.
[55]   NHA (n 2).

(b)   falsifies any record by adding to or deleting or changing any information contained in that record;

(c)   creates, changes or destroys a record without authority to do so;

(d)   fails to create or change a record when properly required to do so;

(e)   provides false information with the intent that it be included in a record;

(f)   without authority, copies any part of a record;

(g)   without authority connects the personal identification elements of a user's with any element of that record that concerns the user's condition, treatment or history;

(h)   gains unauthorised access to a record or record-keeping system, including intercepting information being transmitted from one person, or one part of a record-keeping system, to another;

(i)   without authority, connects any part of a computer or other electronic system on which records are kept to–

      (i)   any other computer or other electronic system; or

      (ii)   any terminal or other installation connected to or forming part of any other computer or other electronic system; or

(j)   without authority, modifies or impairs the operation of–

      (i)   any part of the operating system of a computer or other electronic system on which a user's records are kept; or

      (ii)   any part of the programme used to record, store, retrieve or display information on a computer or other electronic system on which a user's records are kept.

In addition, section 17 of the NHA, stipulates that any person who fails to comply with the above regulations, commits an offence and is liable on conviction to a fine or to imprisonment for a period not exceeding one year or to both a fine and such imprisonment.[56]

Other important statutes that regulate privacy and confidentiality in South Africa include the POPIA Act,[57] which came into full effect in July 2021. This Act was designed to regulate the lawful processing of 'personal information' where '**personal information**' means information relating to an identifiable, living, natural person, and where applicable, to an identifiable, existing juristic person, including, but not limited to–

(a)   information relating to the race, gender, sex, pregnancy, marital status, national, ethnic or social origin, colour, sexual orientation, age, physical

---

[56]   NHA (n 2) ss 14–17.

[57]   POPIA (n 3).

or mental health, well-being, disability, religion, conscience, belief, culture, language and birth of the person;

(b)   information relating to the education or the medical, financial, criminal or employment history of the person;

(c)   any identifying number, symbol, e-mail address, physical address, telephone number, location information, online identifier or other particular assignment to the person;

(d)   the biometric information of the person;

(e)   the personal opinions, views or preferences of the person;

(f)   correspondence sent by the person that is implicitly or explicitly of a private or confidential nature or further correspondence that would reveal the contents of the original correspondence;

(g)   the views or opinions of another individual about the person;and

(h)   the name of the person if it appears with other personal information relating to the person or if the disclosure of the name itself would reveal information about the person.

POPIA[58] regulates the processing of information by a 'private body' where 'processing' means any operation or activity or any set of operations, whether or not by automatic means, concerning personal information, including–

(a)   the collection, receipt, recording, organisation, collation, storage, updating or modification, retrieval, alteration, consultation or use;

(b)   dissemination by means of transmission, distribution or making available in any other form; or

(c)   merging, linking, as well as restriction, degradation, erasure or destruction of information.

In POPIA a 'private body' means–

(a)   a natural person who carries or has carried on any trade, business or profession, but only in such capacity;

(b)   a partnership which carries or has carried on any trade, business or profession; or

(c)   any former or existing juristic person, but excludes a 'public body'.

Whereas the regulation of processing of information by a 'public body' is regulated under the provisions of PAIA, 2000.[59] In this case a 'public body' means–

---

[58]   Ibid.
[59]   PAIA (n 54).

(a)   any department of state or administration in the national or provincial sphere of government or any municipality in the local sphere of government; or

(b)   any other functionary or institution when–

    (i)   exercising a power or performing a duty in terms of the Constitution[60] or a provincial constitution; or

    (ii)   exercising a public power or performing a public function in terms of any legislation.

POPIA[61] further stipulates conditions for the lawful processing of personal information by or for a responsible party which include:

1.   'Accountability', as referred to in section 8;
2.   'Processing limitation', as referred to in sections 9 to 12;
3.   'Purpose specification', as referred to in sections 13 and 14;
4.   'Information quality', as referred to in section 16;
5.   'Openness', as referred to in sections 17 and 18;
6.   'Security safeguards', as referred to in sections 19 to 22; and
7.   'Data subject participation', as referred to in sections 23 to 25.

POPIA[62] further established the office of an 'Information Regulator' who is responsible for regulating lawful processing of information and would be required to give directions in respect of processing of personal information to the extent that such processing is–

i.   excluded, in terms of section 6 or 7, from the operation of this Act; or
ii.   exempted in terms of section 37 or 38, from one or more of the conditions concerned in relation to such processing; or
iii.   where the processing of the special personal information of a data subject is prohibited in terms of section 26 of the POPIA.

For example, the processing of the personal information of a child is prohibited in terms of section 34, unless the–

(a)   provisions of section 35(1) are applicable; or

(b)   the Regulator has granted an authorisation in terms of section 35(2), in which case, subject to section 37, the conditions for the lawful processing

---

[60]   The Constitution (n 1).
[61]   POPIA (n 3).
[62]   Ibid.

of personal information as referred to in Chapter 3 have been complied with.[63]

POPIA also requires that a 'responsible party' must secure the integrity and confidentiality of personal information in its possession or under its control by taking appropriate, reasonable technical and organisational measures to prevent—

I.   loss of, damage to or unauthorised destruction of personal information; and
II. unlawful access to or processing of personal information.

In order to give effect to subsection (1), the responsible party must take reasonable measures to—

III. identify all reasonably foreseeable internal and external risks to personal information in its possession or under its control;
IV. establish and maintain appropriate safeguards against the risks identified;
V.   regularly verify that the safeguards are effectively implemented; and
VI. ensure that the safeguards are continually updated in response to new risks or deficiencies in previously implemented safeguards.

The responsible party must have due regard to generally accepted information security practices and procedures which may apply to it generally or be required in terms of specific industry or professional rules and regulations. In this case a 'responsible party' means a public or private body or any other person which, alone or in conjunction with others, determines the purpose of and means for processing personal information.

POPIA[64] also requires all organizations to appoint an 'Information Officer' which refers to 'information officer' of, or in relation to, a—

(a) public body means an information officer or deputy information officer as contemplated in terms of section 1 or 17 of the Act; or
(b) private body means the head of a private body as contemplated in section 1, of PAIA.[65]

An information officer's responsibilities include—

1.   the encouragement of compliance, by the body, with the conditions for the lawful processing of personal information;

---

[63] POPIA (n 3).
[64] POPIA (n 3).
[65] PAIA (n 54).

2. dealing with requests made to the body pursuant to POPIA;
3. working with the Regulator in relation to investigations conducted pursuant to Chapter 6 in relation to the body;
4. otherwise ensuring compliance by the body with the provisions of this Act; and
5. as may be prescribed.

Information officers must take up their duties in terms of this Act only after the responsible party has registered them with the Regulator.

In addition, POPIA[66] requires that each public and private body must make provision, in the manner prescribed in section 17 of the PAIA,[67]with the necessary changes, for the designation of—

1. such a number of persons, if any, as deputy information officers as is necessary to perform the duties and responsibilities as set out in section 55(1) of this Act; and
2. any power or duty conferred or imposed on an information officer by this Act to a deputy information officer of that public or private body.

Regarding transfer of information from the Republic of South Africa: a responsible party in the Republic may not transfer personal information about a 'data subject' where '**data subject**' means the person to whom personal information relates; to a third party who is in a foreign country unless—

i. the third party who is the recipient of the information is subject to a law, binding corporate rules or binding agreement which provide an adequate level of protection that—
   (a) effectively upholds principles for reasonable processing of the information that are substantially similar to the conditions for the lawful processing of personal information relating to a data subject who is a natural person and, where applicable, a juristic person; and
   (b) includes provisions, that are substantially similar to this section, relating to the further transfer of personal information from the recipient to third parties who are in a foreign country;
   (c) the data subject consents to the transfer;
   (d) the transfer is necessary for the performance of a contract between the data subject and the responsible party, or for the implemen-

---

[66] POPIA (n 3).
[67] PAIA (n 54).

tation of pre-contractual measures taken in response to the data
subject's request;

(e)   the transfer is necessary for the conclusion or performance of
a contract concluded in the interest of the data subject between the
responsible party and a third party; or

(f)   the transfer is for the benefit of the data subject; and

(g)   it is not reasonably practicable to obtain the consent of the data
subject to that transfer; and

(h)   if it were reasonably practicable to obtain such consent, the data
subject would be likely to give it.

For the purpose of the above section—

1.   'binding corporate rules' means personal information processing policies,
within a group of undertakings, which are adhered to by a responsible
party or operator within that group of undertakings when transferring
personal information to a responsible party or operator within that same
group of undertakings in a foreign country; and

2.   'group of undertakings' means a controlling undertaking and its controlled undertakings.

Finally, sections 105–107 of the POPIA[68] set out unlawful acts and penalties
for infringement of the law, while section 109 stipulates some administrative
fines for infringement of aspects of the law.

With regards to penalties, section 107 states that: Any person convicted of
an offence in terms of this Act, is liable, in the case of a contravention of—

1.   sections 100, 103(1), 104(2), 105(1), 106(1), (3) or (4) to a fine or to
imprisonment for a period not exceeding 10 years, or to both a fine and
such imprisonment; or

2.   sections 59, 101, 102, 103(2) or 104(1), to a fine or to imprisonment for
a period not exceeding 12 months, or to both a fine and such imprisonment.

Other, South African legislation which may assist in regulating the privacy and
confidentiality of patients includes the Choice on Termination of Pregnancy
Act, 1996,[69] which states in parts with regards to consent and privacy that:

(a)   The termination of a pregnancy may only take place with the informed
consent of the pregnant woman.

---

[68]   POPIA (n 3).
[69]   Choice on Termination of Pregnancy Act, 1996.

(b) Notwithstanding any other law or the common law, but subject to the provisions of subsections (4) and (5), no consent other than that of the pregnant woman, shall be required for the termination of a pregnancy.

(c) In the case of a pregnant minor, a medical practitioner or a registered midwife who has completed the prescribed training course, as the case may be, shall advise such minor to consult with her parents, guardian, family members or friends before the pregnancy is terminated: provided that the termination of the pregnancy shall not be denied because such minor chooses not to consult them.

It must be noted that in terms of the Choice Act[70] a 'woman' means any female person of any age.

Similarly, the Children's Act, 2005,[71] as amended, protects children's privacy as will be detailed in the last sections of this chapter.

International Legal Instruments Pertaining to Protection of Privacy and Confidentiality in South Africa

It has been argued that patient privacy is a well-recognized principle in international law.[72] Relevant international laws which are also applicable to South Africa include the Universal Declaration of Human Rights,[73] the International Covenant on Civil and Political Rights (ICCPR),[74] the African Charter on Human and Peoples Rights,[75] the United Nations Convention on Migrant Workers,[76] the UN Convention on Protection of the Child[77] and the UN Convention on Elimination of Discrimination Against Women (CEDAW),[78] etc. It has been argued that expression of data protection in various interna-

---

[70]   Ibid.

[71]   Children's Act 38 of 2005.

[72]   Carstens and Pearmain (n 47).

[73]   Universal Declaration of Human Rights (United Nations, 1948).

[74]   United Nations *International Covenant Civil and Political Rights* (United Nations, 1966).

[75]   African Charter on Human and Peoples Rights, adopted in Nairobi 27 June 1981, entered into force 21 October 1986; Chima (n 4).

[76]   The United Nations Convention on Migrant Workers (United Nations, 1990).

[77]   United Nations *Convention on the Rights of the Child* (United Nations, 1989).

[78]   UN Convention on the Elimination of All Forms of Discrimination Against Women (CEDAW) (United Nations 1979); S.C. Chima, 'Legal and Cross-Cultural Issues Regarding the Late Termination of Pregnancy: African Perspectives'. In: Marta Soniewicka (ed.), *The Ethics of Reproductive Genetics - Between Utility, Principles, and Virtues* (New York: Springer Nature, 2018) 241–257.

tional instruments vary only by degree, but require generally that all personal information must:

i.   be obtained fairly and lawfully;
ii. used only for the originally specified purposes;
iii. adequate, relevant and not excessive for the purpose required;
iv. accurate and up to date; and
v.   must be destroyed after the purpose is completed.[79]

Other relevant international instruments protecting patient confidentiality include the World Medical Association (WMA) Declaration of Helsinki[80] and Code of Medical Ethics[81] which state that 'A physician shall preserve absolute confidentiality on all he knows, about his patient even after the patient has died'. The WMA Declaration on the Rights of the Patient[82] summarizes the essential elements of patient confidentiality as detailed in the first section of this chapter.[83]

HPCSA Guidelines on Confidentiality

The HPCSA states in Rule 13 of its ethical rules that health practitioners can only divulge information regarding their patients based on the following conditions:[84]

i.   in terms of a statutory provisions;
ii. based on instructions of a court of law;
iii. when it is in the public's interest;
iv. with the express consent of a patient; or
v.   with the written consent of a parent or guardian of a minor under 12 years of age;
vi. in the case of a deceased patients, with the written consent of the next of kin or the executor of the deceased's estate.[85]

---

[79]   Carstens and Pearmain (n 47).
[80]   World Medical Association *Declaration of Helsinki-Ethical principles for medical research involving human subjects* (Adopted by the 18th WMA General Assembly Helsinki Finland June 1964 as amended by the 64th WMA General Assembly Fortaleza Brazil 2013).
[81]   World Medical Association (WMA), *Manual on Ethics* (3rd edn) (Ferney-Voltaire: WMA, 2015).
[82]   WMA Declaration of Lisbon (n 5).
[83]   Ibid; WMA *Manual on Ethics* (n 81).
[84]   HPCSA (nn 22 and 30).
[85]   Ibid.

Further, disclosures in the public interest would include but are not limited to situations where the patient or other individuals could be subject to harm as a result of risk related contact or exposure.[86]

In addition, HPCSA guidelines prescribe that where healthcare practitioners are asked to provide information about patients, they must:

(a) Seek the consent of patients to disclosure of information wherever possible. And also consider whether or not the patients can be identified from the disclosure. And also ensure that comprehensive information is made available to patients with regard to the potential for a breach of confidentiality especially with regards to ICD-10 coding for healthcare insurance purposes.[87]
(b) Anonymise data where unidentifiable data will serve the purpose requested.
(c) Keep disclosures to the minimum necessary to achieve the desired aim.[88]

Furthermore, healthcare practitioners must always be prepared to justify their decisions in accordance with ethical guidelines.[89]

PERSONS BOUND BY THE DUTY OF CONFIDENTIALITY

The South African NHA[90] requires that all health care providers, which includes all healthcare practitioners registered with professional bodies such as the HPCSA e.g., medical doctors, psychologists, medical laboratory scientists, trainees, etc.[91] It also includes those registered with the South African Nursing Council (SANC),[92] and the South African Pharmacy Council (SAPC).[93] The

---

[86] HPCSA (n 84).
[87] National Department of Health, South Africa (n 36).
[88] HPCSA Guidelines (n 30).
[89] Ibid.
[90] NHA (n 2).
[91] Healthcare practitioners in South Africa are required to be registered with the Health Professions Council of South Africa (HPCSA) in order to practise their profession. A list of professionals and professional boards registered or registrable by the HPCSA are listed here: https://www.hpcsa.co.za/?contentId=0&menuSubId=5&actionName=Core%20Operations (last accessed February 28, 2022).
[92] Categories of nurses and midwives and healthcare professionals registered or registrable with the Nursing council are listed here: https://www.sanc.co.za/wp-content/uploads/2020/06/SANC-Revised-guidelines-Foreign-Registration-2016-05-15.pdf (last accessed February 28, 2022).
[93] All persons registered or registrable with the SAPC are listed here: https://www.pharmcouncil.co.za/registered-persons (last accessed February 28, 2022).

law provides that all healthcare providers are responsible for ensuring that information pertaining to their patients are kept confidential at all times.

The law also stipulates that healthcare establishments are responsible for personal information about their patients and must make sure that such information is effectively protected against improper disclosure at all times. This also means that employees such as clerks, receptionists and other staff must be trained to respect the confidentiality of patients when dealing with personal information.

The NHA[94] provides that this information must not be given to others unless the patient consents or the health care practitioner can justify the disclosure. Practitioners are responsible for ensuring that clerks, receptionists, and other staff respect confidentiality in the performance of their duties.[95]

With regards to the POPIA,[96] all responsible parties are also required to maintain confidentiality of personal information protected by the Act. Where a '**responsible party**' means a public or private body or any other person which, alone or in conjunction with others, determines the purpose of and means for processing personal information.

In this case, **"private body"** means—

(a) a natural person who carries or has carried on any trade, business or profession, but only in such capacity;
(b) a partnership which carries or has carried on any trade, business or profession; or
(c) any former or existing juristic person, but excludes a public body.

While a '**public body**' means—

(a) any department of state or administration in the national or provincial sphere of government or any municipality in the local sphere of government; or
(b) any other functionary or institution when—
    (i) exercising a power or performing a duty in terms of the Constitution or a provincial constitution; or
    (ii) exercising a public power or performing a public function in terms of any legislation.[97]

---

94 NHA (n 2).
95 HPCSA (n 84).
96 POPIA (n 3).
97 Ibid.

LEGAL DUTIES OF CONFIDENTIALITY

It has been suggested that the obligation of confidentiality goes beyond under-taking not to divulge confidential information, but also includes a responsi-bility to make sure that all records containing patient information are kept secure.[98] One could argue that because information pertaining to an individual's health maybe considered very sensitive, personal, and impacts on their privacy and human dignity or *dignitas*.[99] Such information is considered highly confidential and enjoys statutory and common law protection both in South Africa and internationally.

So, What Does the Duty of Confidentiality Require?

The obligation of confidentiality both prohibits the physician or other health-care professional from disclosing information about the patient to other inter-ested parties, but also encourages the physician or healthcare provider to take precautions with the information to ensure that only authorized access occurs. Nevertheless, the context of medical practice constrains physicians or health-care practitioners' obligations to protect patient confidentiality.

Because in the course of caring for patients, healthcare practitioners will usually find themselves having to exchange information about their patients with other healthcare providers, which may be critical to the patients care, or are an integral part of the teaching and learning process in a teaching hospital. Therefore, such disclosures in a professional setting maybe justifiable, so long as precautions are taken to limit the ability of others to hear or see confidential information. Nevertheless, modern biotechnologies such as computerized patient records and DNA analysis may pose new and unique challenges to patients' confidentiality and privacy. It is suggested that healthcare profes-sionals and their employees or assistants should follow prescribed procedures for computer access and security as an added measure to protect patient information.[100]

---

[98]   J-P Rudd, 'Disclosure of Medical confidential information', https://www.golegal .co.za/medical-confidential-information/#:~:text=Common%20law%20protection ,-The%20common%20law&text=The%20obligation%20of%20confidentiality %20goes,patient%20information%20are%20kept%20securely (last accused February 28, 2022).

[99]   Carstens and Pearmain (n 47); Saner (n 9); Rudd (n 98); Chima (n 26).

[100]   Chima (n 26).

Purpose of Confidentiality

Confidentiality in medicine generally serves two purposes:

(a) to respect patients 'privacy' so that they feel no shame and vulnerability; and
(b) to create an environment for honest communication between a doctor or other healthcare practitioner and a patient.

Patients who discuss intimate and personal details about themselves have a right to expect that their disclosures will remain confidential. A breach of such confidence could result in actions for invasion of privacy or defamation in accordance with constitutional and other legal provisions,[101] as demonstrated in the case of *van Vuuren v Kruger.*[102]

It has been posited that the common law right to privacy prevents public disclosure of private facts. And that invasion of privacy is a tort or delict based in the common law, which allows an aggrieved party to bring a lawsuit against another individual or institution who has unlawfully intruded into his or her private affairs, or discloses his or her private information, or publicises him or her in a false light, or misappropriates his or her name or image for personal gain.[103]

The realm of healthcare is one of the most sensitive areas for many people when it comes to issues of privacy. Thus, the physical examination of a person in a healthcare setting is an invasion of privacy and such examination can only be lawfully conducted when an individual waives their right to privacy for the purpose of examination, by providing informed consent or waiver.[104]

In terms of South African laws, section 14 (1) of the NHA[105] provides that all information concerning a health user, including information relating to his or health status, treatment or stay in a health establishment, is confidential.

While section 14(2) of the NHA further provides that such information may not be disclosed unless-

(a) the user consents to that disclosure in writing;
(b) a court order or any law requires that disclosures; or
(c) non-disclosure of the information represents a serious threat to public health.[106]

---

[101]   The Constitution (n 1).
[102]   *van Vuuren v Kruger* (n 7).
[103]   Rudd (n 98).
[104]   Chima (nn 14, 15 and 21).
[105]   NHA (n 2).
[106]   Ibid.

At common law there is a professional duty on medical practitioners or other healthcare professionals to maintain confidentiality unless:

(a) a court of law orders the healthcare practitioner to make a disclosure;

(b) an Act of Parliament or statute requires the doctor or healthcare practitioner to make a disclosure;

(c) where there is a moral or legal obligation on the healthcare practitioner to make a disclosure to a person or agency that has a reciprocal moral or legal obligation to receive the information; or

(d) where the patient or healthcare user consents to the disclosure being made.

Confidentiality in Cases of Physical Injuries or Illness vs Mental Health

It has been suggested that the need for a doctor-patient privilege in respect of physical ailments is usually less than in the case of psychiatrist/psychotherapist-patient relationship. In a few instances in which a patient would desire secrecy for physical ailments, such as where the patient is diagnosed with communicable or sexually transmitted disease (STD), disclosure is usually overwhelmingly in the interest of the public safety. In such circumstances it has been suggested that privileged communications rest on four pillars:

(a)   that the communication must originate in a confidence and that it will not be disclosed;

(b)   that the element of confidentiality must be essential to the relations between the partners;

(c)   that the relation must be one which in the opinion of the community ought to be sedulously fostered; and

(d)   that the injury that would arise to the relationship by disclosure of the communication must be greater than the benefit to be gained for the correct disposal of litigation[107] (*Sulman v Hansa*[108]).

It has been reported that over 90 percent of litigation which concerns the physician-patient relationship in relation to physical injuries involves:

(a)   actions on life policies where the deceased has made misrepresentations concerning his health which are misleading;

---

[107] S.C. Chima, *Lecture Notes in Medical Law, Ethics and Human Rights* (Programme of Bio& Research Ethics and Medical Law (College of Health Sciences, University of KwaZulu-Natal, 2009); D. McQuoid-Mason, *Forensic Medicine: Medical Law and Ethics* (School of Law, University of KwaZulu-Natal, 2006); Chima (n 26).

[108] *Sulman v Hansa* [1971] 4 SA (D).

(b)   actions for damages for bodily injury where the extent of the patients' injuries is the issue.[109]

In life policy and bodily injury cases, medical evidence maybe necessary for the ascertainment of the truth, and there is little need for the patient to conceal the facts. In such cases the patient is usually deemed to have waived the privilege by putting his physical condition at issue. However, sometimes disclosures of peculiarly embarrassing diseases (e.g., STDs) are not always required for public safety, but could still be desirable in the interest of administration of justice as demonstrated in the case of *Parkes v Parkes*.[110] The facts and decision in this case are outlined below:

Facts: A medical practitioner was asked whether he had examined the defendant for venereal disease. The doctor in this case asserted that it was privileged communication protected by doctor-patient confidentiality. Here a wife had sued her husband for adultery and wanted evidence from her husband's doctor regarding STDs which the husband had not contracted from her.

Held: The court in this case ordered the medical practitioner to answer the question. NB: It must be noted that this is an old common law case from South African courts, in terms of current laws a husband and wife as considered as separate entities or separate 'private bodies', and such considerations may no longer apply under current south African laws on confidentiality and constitutional rights.

Confidentiality and Mental Health Care

It has been suggested that unlike the physician-patient privilege in physical injuries and ailments, which have been eroded due to many exceptions and legal requirements, the physiatrist/psychotherapist-patient privilege, has been more often upheld by the courts. This may be due to the fact as has been suggested that secrecy is a *sine qua non* of the practice of psychotherapy and the psychiatrist-patient relationship, as argued in *Zeffert*.[111] The close relationship of trust and confidence required in the psychotherapist-patient relationship makes it somewhat distinguishable from the ordinary physician relationship. For instance, many physical ailments may be treated with the same degree of effectiveness by the healthcare practitioners, whom the patient may not fully trust, but a psychiatrist or psychotherapist requires a patient's full trust and

---

[109]   McQuoid-Mason (n 107).
[110]   *Parkes v Parkes* [1916] CPD 702, 281.
[111]   *Zeffert* 1947 SALJ 435; McQuoid-Mason (n 107).

confidence, or the therapist may not succeed in helping the patient (as demonstrated in the American cases of *Taylor v US*[112] and *Tarasoff*[113]).

This difference is recognized for a number of reasons:

(a)   Psychotherapy requires a patient to divulge his deepest emotions, unfulfilled wishes frustrations and feelings of guilt or fantasies as shown in the *Tarasoff* case.[114]

(b)   Such facts must be freed from conscious or unconscious censorship which is unlikely if the patient fears disclosures.

(c)   Patients are often impelled to visit a psychiatrist because of the nature of the secrets which he or she feels the need to purge, but which cannot be revealed to others.

(d)   A patient experiencing matrimonial difficulties is less likely to speak freely about infidelity, sexual aberration or inadequacy.[115]

It has been suggested that South African courts, similar to recommendations by the English Law Reform Commission, 1967, have decided against an absolute privilege and choose to exercise discretion as to whether they will permit a witness to refuse to give evidence.[116] This is particularly so in criminal matters, as demonstrated in *S v Forbes*[117] The facts of this case are summarized below.

Facts: Here, a general medical practitioner (GP) studying was investigating the mental condition of the accused at a mental health institution. During the investigation the accused made certain statements to the psychiatrist which conflicted with statements made previously to the magistrate during court proceedings. The state wished to lead what was said to the psychiatrist in evidence.

Held: The court agreed that because the prosecution wanted to admit evidence (which did not cast light on the accused's state of mind at the time of the alleged offence) in order to establish certain facts concerning the offence, the

---

[112]   *Taylor v United States* 495 U.S. 575 (1990).

[113]   *Tarasoff v Regents of the University of California* [1976] Cal 425; Chima (n 107); McQuoid-Mason (n 107).

[114]   *Tarasoff* (Ibid).

[115]   McQuoid-Mason (n 107).

[116]   Ibid.

[117]   *S v Forbes* 1970 2 SA 594 (C).

application should be refused. It has been suggested that the application was refused for two reasons:

i.   The provisions of Mental Health Act[118] were designed to obtain expert evidence concerning an accused mental state, not to uncover evidence for the investigation which should be done by the police.
ii. Justice might suffer if persons sent to mental health institutions for observation began to fear that what was told to a psychiatrist by them may be used in court.

It has been suggested that in civil proceedings the courts may also have discretion as to whether to allow the evidence of psychiatrist concerning what transpired with a his or her patient.[119] However, this observation was doubted by the court in *Botha v Botha*.[120] In the *Botha* case, during a custody dispute one of the spouses wished to lead evidence from a psychiatrist who had treated the other spouse. The judge in this case doubted whether he had discretion to exclude the evidence. If he did have such discretion, however, he considered that it was in the child's best interest (who was the subject of the dispute), and in the interest of justice that the evidence should be led. Therefore, one can arrive at the following conclusions based on the judgments outlined above:

i.   In custody disputes psychiatric evidence concerning one or another spouse may be crucial for the wellbeing of children.
ii. The court is the upper guardian of all minors, and the best interests of the child (not the parents) is paramount.
iii. The court maybe, however, conscious of the fact that psychiatric treatment may be inhibited if the psychiatric or mental health patients come to fear disclosures by their psychiatrists/psychotherapists.

Thus, where psychiatric evidence is essential to the administration of justice, it may not be excluded, in cases such as the following:

(a) in proceedings for the hospitalization of the patient in a mental health institution;
(b) where the patient puts his or her mental condition as an issue as part a claim or defence;
(c) where an accused is committed to an institution for forensic observation;
(d) where it is necessary to establish the mental capacity of the testator; and

---

[118] Mental Health Act 18 of 1973; Mental Healthcare Act 17 of 2002.
[119] McQuoid-Mason (n 107).
[120] *Botha v Botha* 1972(2) SA 559.

(e)   in child custody suits as shown in *Sanders.*[121]

Remedies and Defences to Breach of Confidentiality

In South African law, it has been argued that when harm to another person takes the form of an injury to personality, which includes a breach of confidentiality or defamation of character, the appropriate remedy should be based on *actio iniuriarum* – since the *actio iniuriarum* protects a person's dignity or *dignitas,* which embraces the right to privacy or confidentiality.[122] An infringement of an individual's right to privacy in medical practice may take either of two forms

i.   an unlawful intrusion into the personal privacy of another person; or
ii.   the unlawful publication of private facts of or about another person.[123]

As illustrated by the cases of *van Vuuren v Kruger*[124] and *National Coalition of Gay and Lesbian Equality v Minister of Justice,*[125] it has been argued as a general rule and irrespective of the onus of the case, a claimant who relies on an *actio iniuriarum* must allege and prove *animus inuriandi*. It has been suggested that, in practice, the principles formulated in the context of justification of the law of defamation would apply to determine if a *prima facie* case of invasion or breach of privacy is justifiable in the particular case, as alleged.[126]

Defences for Breach of Confidentiality

A healthcare practitioner who has been accused of breach of a patients' confidentiality or privacy may be liable for an action for invasion of privacy, defamation or even breach of contract.[127]

Practitioners Who are Accused of Such Offences May Have Several Defences

I.   Court Order

---

[121] McQuoid-Mason (n 107); Chima (n 107); *Sanders* 1979 NULR 322.
[122] Saner (n 9); Carstens and Pearmain (n 47).
[123] Saner (n 9); Rudd (n 98).
[124] *van Vuuren v Kruger* (n 7).
[125] *National Coalition of Gay and Lesbian Equality v Minister of Justice* (n 50).
[126] Saner (n 9); Carstens and Pearmain (n 47); Rudd (n 98).
[127] Chima (n 107); McQuoid-Mason (n 107), Rudd (n 98); Saner (n 9), Carstens and Pearmain (n 47).

    i.   As demonstrated in the cases of *Parkes v Parkes* and *Botha v Botha*.[128]

II.   Statutory Authority (Acts of Parliament), such as:

    i.   section100 of the Children's Act, 2005[129] (when reporting or disclosing child abuse);

    ii.   Mental Health Care Act, 2002[130] (when reporting or disclosing mental health patients who are dangerous to others, as required by section 13, or reporting exploitation or abuse of mental health users, as required by section 11); or

    iii.   section 47 of the Health Act, 1977[131] or the Disaster Management Act, 2002[132] (in the case of reporting notifiable diseases).

Consent or Waiver to Disclosure

(a)   Where a patient consents to the disclosure of his or her healthcare information, there generally can be no tort or delict action, based on the doctrine of *volenti non fit injuria-* to him who consents no harm can be done.[133]

(b)   Such consent must, however, be to the particular or specific to disclosures made, which means that there must be knowledge, appreciation before consent or agreement. In other words, the consent must be fully informed.[134]

(c)   Consent that is contrary to public policy (*boni mores)*[135], or that is obtained through duress or some form of coercion that undermines the patients' free will or that impacts on the voluntary nature of the consent is unlikely to serve as a good defence against allegations of invasion of privacy.[136]

(d)   Therefore, the defence of consent can only succeed if the *prima facie* wrongful act falls within the limits of consent.

---

[128] *Parkes v Parkes* 1916 CPD 702. 281; *Botha v Botha* 1972(2) SA 559.
[129] Children's Act 38 of 2005 (n 71).
[130] Mental Health Care Act No. 17 of 2002.
[131] Health Act No. 63 of 1977.
[132] Disaster Management Act No. 57 of 2002; Chima (n 18).
[133] Chima (nn 14, 15, 21 and 107); McQuoid-Mason (n 107).
[134] Chima (n 14).
[135] Chima (n 21).
[136] Chima (n 14 and 21).

Furthermore, for consent to operate as a defence the following requirements must be satisfied, among others:

i.   the consenting party 'must have had knowledge and had been aware of the nature and extent of the harm or risk';
ii. the consenting party 'must have appreciated and understood the nature and extent of the harm or risk';
iii. the consenting party 'must have consented to the harm or assumed the risk';
iv. the consent 'must be comprehensive' that is extended to the entire transaction, inclusive of its consequences'.[137]

It must be noted that although these principles were applied in the context of the invasion of a patient's bodily integrity and well being, there is no reason why they cannot be applicable in cases of consent to the disclosure of information or breach thereof.[138]

DATA PROTECTION LAW

Access to Medical Records

In the context of South African laws and regulations, healthcare practitioners such as doctors, healthcare centres, community health clinics, and hospitals own the patients' records held by them. However, this is only a custodial ownership because their rights to use the records are subject to confidentiality rules and subject to relevant legislation such as POPIA[139] and PAIA.[140]

The Constitution[141] provides that everyone has the right of access to information held by the state, as well as information held by private bodies (e.g., private hospitals or healthcare providers). A patient or healthcare user can obtain access to that information where he or she requires such information to exercise or protect any right as stipulated in section 32(1) of the Constitution,[142] and codified in PAIA.[143] Other individuals apart from healthcare practitioners can also access patients' medical records or could be in a position which requires access to confidential patient information from time to time. The question is whether they are ethically obliged to observe patient confiden-

---

137   *Castell v DeGreef* 1994 (4) SA 408 (C); Chima (n 14).
138   Chima (n 14, 21 and 107); McQuoid-Mason (n 107).
139   POPIA (n 3).
140   PAIA (n 54).
141   The Constitution (n 1).
142   Ibid.
143   PAIA (n 54).

tiality rules in the same way as healthcare professionals who work within the same organization or are registered with professional bodies with ethical rules like the HPCSA.[144] This may create a moral dilemma because such healthcare workers are still in the position to make disclosures of confidential information because of their access to health records; while their relationship with patients may not be on the same level of intimacy as that of healthcare professionals who are directly rendering the health services. Nevertheless, the NHA[145] requires all healthcare providers to maintain confidentiality of health-care records and this should be achieved by training of other HCWs apart from healthcare professionals bound by professional ethical rules.

South African courts have held that the HPCSA and similar professional bodies such as the SANC are not organs of state and that a patient may only have access as of right to those parts of medical records held by the councils on behalf of the public hospital that handed them over for inquiry purposes. In such cases the balance of the records should be obtained directly from the public hospital as illustrated by the case of *Korf v HPCSA.*[146]

In terms of the PAIA,[147] an information officer must be appointed by the public and private bodies to provide access to information at reasonable cost.[148] Similarly, the POPIA provides for appointment of information officers and deputy information officers by public and private bodies to assist in protection of personal information.[149]

Section 30 of the PAIA, allows access to medical records to patients, but this may be refused where such access would cause serious harm to the patient's physical or mental well-being.[150]

In addition, section 15 of the NHA[151] provides that a healthcare provider that has access to the health records of a healthcare user may disclose such personal information to any other person, healthcare provider, or health establishment as is necessary, for any legitimate purpose within the ordinary course and scope of his or her duties where such access or disclosure is in the interests of the healthcare user. While section 16 of the NHA[152] provides that a health care provider may examine users' health records for the purposes of:

i.   treatment with the authorization of the user; and

---

144   HPCSA (nn 22 and 30).
145   NHA (n 2).
146   *Korf v Health Professions Council of SA* 2000 1171 (T).
147   PAIA (n 54).
148   Ibid.
149   POPIA (n 3).
150   PAIA (n 54) s 30.
151   NHA (n 2) s 15.
152   NHA (n 2) s 16.

ii. study, teaching or research with the authorization of the user, head of the health establishment concerned. In which case it is not necessary to obtain the above authorizations.

However, the person in charge of a health establishment in possession of a healthcare user's health records, must set up control measures to prevent unauthorized access to those records and the storage facility in which records are kept.

Furthermore, in terms of the PAIA,[153] access of information from a public or private body will not be granted if:

(a) that record is required for the purpose of criminal or civil proceedings;
(b) such records is requested after commencement of the criminal or civil proceedings as the case maybe;
(c) the production of or access to that record for the purpose referred to in paragraph (a) is provided for in any other law.[154]

The PAIA also provides in section 7(1) that any record obtained in a manner that contravenes subsection (1) is not admissible as evidence in civil or criminal proceedings except where the court decides that exclusion of such records would not be in the interest of justice.[155] It has been suggested that based on a judgment in the case of *Unitas Hospital vs Van Wyk*,[156] that the courts will not allow the PAIA to be used for fishing expeditions in civil cases prior to initiation of proceedings.[157]

Confidentiality with Regards to Human Genetic Data, Human Tissues, and DNA

Considering the crucial role that genes play in relation to the identity of human beings, procedures involving gene transfer easily generate controversy. Tough questions need to be answered about the balancing of risks and benefits, equitable access, the cost of interventions and the consequences of the procedures for human evolution. Human genetic data including DNA are critically important to the progress of science and medicine and related non-medical and legal

---

[153] PAIA (n 54).
[154] PAIA (n 55); Saner (n 9).
[155] PAIA (n 54) s 7.
[156] *Unitas Hospital v Van Wyk* [2006] 4 ALL SA 231 (SCA).
[157] Saner (n 9).

purposes. At the same time, the collection, processing, use and storage of such data present potential risks to the people that they pertain to.[158]

Human genetic data are sensitive and problems that may arise from the improper handling of healthcare personal data should not be overlooked. Violations of human rights, fundamental freedoms and human dignity can equally result from the careless and arbitrary use of personal healthcare data. Due care needs to be exercised to prevent stigmatisation, discrimination[159] and other forms of injustice arising from the identification of data with specific individuals or groups. It must be noted that where human tissue samples or related information are gathered in the course of a professional relationship, professional confidentiality must be observed. Identification of samples must be limited to the minimum necessary to achieve the stated objectives of the study. Since it may also produce information relevant to the health and well-being of the person from whom the sample was derived. An ethics committee may request procedures to de-identify participants to facilitate appropriate protection of privacy and confidentiality.[160]

With regards to DNA analysis for DNA profiling, this has been allowed by a South African court in the case of *S v Orrie*.[161] In this case the court allowed the taking of blood for the purpose of conducting a DNA test to solve a double murder case by the police where there was an invasion of the human subject or accused's persons right to privacy and bodily integrity. The court held that the right to privacy was not inviolable, observing that another court in the case of *M v R*[162] had decided that a High Court has the power to order both a minor and an adult to submit to a blood test against their will. In coming to its decision, the *Orrie* court agreed that while the taking of blood from individuals without their consent amounted to a violation of a person's right to bodily integrity. The Constitution allowed the limitation of such rights based on the limitation clause in section 36(1) of the Constitution,[163] which allows the limitation of rights based on a law of general application such as the Criminal Procedure Act.[164] The court held that in such cases the rights of the individual must give way to the public interest. Taking into consideration the factors set

---

[158] S.C. Chima and F. Mamdoo, 'Ethical and Regulatory Issues Surrounding Umbilical Cord Blood Banking in South Africa' (2011) *SAJBL* 4 (2): 79–84; Chima (n 26).

[159] T.O. Famoroti, L. Fernandes, and S.C. Chima, 'Stigmatization of people living with HIV/AIDS by healthcare workers at a tertiary hospital in KwaZulu-Natal, South Africa: A cross-sectional descriptive study' (2013) *BMC Med Ethics* 14(Suppl 1): S6.

[160] Chima (n 107); McQuoid-Mason (n 107); Chima (n 26).

[161] *S v Orrie* 2004 (3) SA 584 (C); Saner (n 9); Carstens and Pearmain (n 47).

[162] *M v R* 1989 (1) SA 416 (O).

[163] The Constitution (n 1) s 36.

[164] Criminal Procedure Act 51 of 1977.

out in section 36(1) of the Constitution,[165] such limitations was necessary and justifiable in an open democratic society, based on human dignity, equality and freedom. In other words, the taking of a blood sample for DNA testing for the purposes of criminal investigation to solve a major crime, was reasonable and necessary to ensure justice is done, while balancing the interests of justice against the individual's right to privacy and dignity.[166]

Similarly in the case of *Minister of Safety and Security v Gaqa*,[167] a South African court allowed the removal of bullet from an accused's leg to be used in criminal proceedings against him. The court held that while this amounted an invasion of the accused's right to bodily integrity. This right was limited by a law of general of application clause, such as the Criminal Procedure Act,[168] as allowed by the Constitution.[169] Based on such considerations as balancing the interests of justice versus individual rights, Desai J allowed the police to conduct a surgical procedure to obtain a bullet from the accused's body to be used in evidence in his criminal proceedings.[170]

Confidentiality and General Patient Data

It must be noted that patient confidentiality and information security are legal obligations. Informed consent requires that the purpose, likely recipients and likely consequences of disclosure or non-disclosure be specified.[171] To maintain continuity of care, diagnosis and procedure information may need to be shared amongst members of the health services team. Data protection procedures are established in the National Health Information System of South Africa (NHISSA), which are enshrined in the ICD-10 diagnosis code.[172]

1. The ICD-10 (International Statistical Classification of Diseases and Related Health Problems) is a diagnostic coding standard owned and maintained by the WHO.
2. The coding standard was adopted by the NHISSA and forms part of the health information strategy of the National Department of Health (NDoH).
3. This standard currently serves as the diagnostic coding standard of choice for both the public and private healthcare sectors for morbidity coding.

---

[165] The Constitution (n 1).
[166] Saner (n 9); Carstens and Pearmain (n 47).
[167] *Minister of Safety and Security v Gaqa* 2002 (1) SACR 654 (C); Chima (n 21); Carstens and Pearmain (n 166).
[168] Criminal Procedure Act (n 164).
[169] The Constitution (n 1) s 36.
[170] Carstens and Pearmain (n 166); Chima (n 21).
[171] Chima (nn 14 and 21).
[172] Technical User Guide compiled by the Ministerial ICD-10 Task Team (n 36).

4. Regulation 5(f) of the Medical Schemes Act[173] prescribes the manner of submission of claims by healthcare providers and determines that all claims must contain 'the relevant diagnostic ... code ... that relates to the health service'.[174]

Confidentiality and Laboratory Records

A laboratory scientist or pathologist can de-identify information by:

(a) providing statistical analysis to show that the said information cannot be used to identify individuals;
(b) eliminating all identifiable information such as names, address, social security number, zip code, health plan membership numbers. For example, a sample is not identifiable if it labelled generically, e.g. 'A 35- year-old black male';
(c) using an arbitrary code and hiding the key so that a third party could not identify the patient

EXCEPTIONS TO CONFIDENTIALITY

The major exceptions to the requirement to confidentiality and privacy are detailed in above sections and include:

I.   Court orders.
II.   Statutory provisions or Acts of Parliament.
III. Consent or waiver by the patient.
IV.   Therapeutic privilege. This was demonstrated in the South African case of *VRM v HPCSA*,[175] where a physician chose not to disclose a diagnosis of HIV positive test to a pregnant woman because of concerns for her vulnerability, psychological integrity and welfare of her unborn baby. He based his decision on the doctrine of therapeutic privilege, which was accepted by the Disciplinary Committee of the HPCSA.[176] This doctrine as an exception is controversial, and it has been argued that it should be used very sparingly and under very specific considerations as discussed by Chima in 2009.[177]

---

[173] Medical Schemes Act 131 of 1998.
[174] Technical User Guide (n 36).
[175] *VRM v HPCSA* [2003] JOL 11944 (T).
[176] Carstens and Pearmain (n 166).
[177] Chima (n 31).

V.   Emergency situations, necessity, and public policy or interest (prevention of harm to others).[178]

VI. Authorisation or waiver provided by Institutional Review Boards (IRBs)/Research Ethics Committees (RECs), such as where the analysis of ancient DNA or where the patient or next of kin cannot be found, or for the purposes of minimal risk research,[179] or audit or educational purposes, or where privacy meets certain standards.[180]

VIII. Police investigation or criminal proceedings as outlined in the South African cases of *S v Orrie*[181] and *Minister of Safety and Security v Gaqa*.[182]

VII. In South Africa, POPIA[183] also excludes the following types of information:

This Act does not apply to the processing of personal information—information generated:

1.   in the course of a purely personal or household activity;

2.   that has been de-identified to the extent that it cannot be re-identified again;

3.   by or on behalf of a public body—

   (a)   which involves national security, including activities that are aimed at assisting in the identification of the financing of terrorist and related activities, defence or public safety; or

   (b)   the purpose of which is the prevention, detection, including assistance in the identification of the proceeds of unlawful activities and the combating of money laundering activities, investigation or proof of offences, the prosecution of offenders or the execution of sentences or security measures, to the extent that adequate safeguards have been established in legislation for the protection of such personal information;

   (c)   by the Cabinet and its committees or the Executive Council of a province; or

---

[178] Carstens and Pearmain (n 47); Chima (nn 18 and 107).

[179] S.C. Chima, C.F. Ryschkewitsch, K.J. Fan, and G. L. Stoner, 'Polyomavirus JC genotypes in an urban US population reflect the history of African origin and genetic admixture in modern African Americans' (2000) *Hum Biol* 72 (5): 837–850.

[180] National Health Act 61 of 2003; US Code of Federal Regulations-Health Insurance Portability and Accountability (HIPAA) Act 1996.

[181] *S v Orrie* (n 161).

[182] *Minister of Safety and Security v Gaqa* (n 167).

[183] POPIA (n 3).

    (d)   relating to the judicial functions of a court referred to in section 166 of the Constitution;[184]

    (e)   'terrorist and related activities', for purposes of subsection (1)(c), means those activities referred to in section 4 of the Protection of Constitutional Democracy against Terrorist and Related Activities Act, 2004.[185]

Furthermore, POPIA[186] provides exclusions for journalistic, literary or artistic purposes as follows:

1.   This Act does not apply to the processing of personal information solely for the purpose of journalistic, literary or artistic expression to the extent that such an exclusion is necessary to reconcile, as a matter of public interest, the right to privacy with the right to freedom of expression.

2.   Where a responsible party who processes personal information for exclusively journalistic purposes is, by virtue of office, employment or profession, subject to a code of ethics that provides adequate safeguards for the protection of personal information, such code will apply to the processing concerned to the exclusion of this Act and any alleged interference with the protection of the personal information of a data subject that may arise as a result of such processing must be adjudicated as provided for in terms of that code.

3.   In the event that a dispute may arise in respect of whether adequate safeguards have been provided for in a code as required in terms of subsection (2) or not, regard may be had to—

    i.   the special importance of the public interest in freedom of expression;

    ii. domestic and international standards balancing the—

        (a) public interest in allowing for the free flow of information to the public through the media in recognition of the right of the public to be informed; and

        (b) public interest in safeguarding the protection of personal information of data subjects;

        (c) the need to secure the integrity of personal information;

        (d) domestic and international standards of professional integrity for journalists. and

        (e) the nature and ambit of self-regulatory forms of supervision provided by the profession.

---

[184] The Constitution (n 1).

[185] Protection of Constitutional Democracy against Terrorist and Related Activities Act, No. 33 of 2004.

[186] POPIA (n 3).

Therefore, while POPIA[187] generally protects personal information held by private and public entities in general, the NHA[188] protects privacy and confidentiality of healthcare and health-related information obtained or processed in the healthcare sphere, including health maintenance organizations (HMOs) and healthcare insurers and their employees. All these while balancing the need for access to information as provided for by PAIA.[189] It has been argued that in terms of promotion of access to information, unreasonable disclosure of personal information pertaining to a third party is also prohibited. This would relate to protection of the right to bodily and psychological integrity, actualized by the right to informed consent as enshrined in the Constitution.[190] Further, the right to privacy, the right to dignity, and the right to life, together imply a wider approach to questions of access to healthcare. Therefore, the right to privacy could be breached by wrongful or unlawful disclosure of personal facts.[191]

CONFIDENTIALITY AND ADULTS LACKING CAPACITY

With regards to adults who lack capacity, HPCSA guidelines observe that problems may arise where health care practitioners consider that a patient is incapable of giving consent to treatment or disclosure due to immaturity, illness or mental incapacity.[192]

In such cases it is suggested that where such patients instruct practitioners not to disclose information to a third party, the healthcare practitioners should try to persuade the patient or healthcare user to allow an appropriate person to be involved in the consultation and healthcare decision-making. If the patient still refuses to give consent and the healthcare practitioner is of the opinion that it is essential to disclose such information in the patients' best interests, they may disclose the relevant information to an appropriate person or authority. However, in such cases the health care practitioner must tell the patient before disclosing any information and seek the consent of the person legally designated to give such consent in terms of the NHA.[193]

---

[187] POPIA (n 3).
[188] NHA (n 2).
[189] PAIA (n 54); Saner (n 9).
[190] Carstens and Pearmain (n 166); Chima (n 14); The Constitution (n 1).
[191] Carstens and Pearmain (n 166); Saner (n 9).
[192] HPCSA (n 30).
[193] HPCSA (n 30); NHA (n 2).

The NHA[194] provides that if no person has been mandated or legally appointed to give consent, then in the following order of precedence, a spouse or partner, parent, grandparent, adult child or adult brother or sister may give consent.[195] In addition, healthcare practitioners should document in the patient's record the steps they took to obtain consent and the reasons for deciding to disclose such information.[196]

CONFIDENTIALITY AND CHILDREN

It has been argued that there is an ethical obligation on healthcare practitioners in South Africa not to divulge information about their patients without the patients' consent if they are over 12 years of age. In the case of minors under 12 years of age, healthcare practitioners require the written consent of their parents or guardians. This is based on the fact that 12 years is the legal age of consent to routine medical procedures in South Africa.[197,198] However, the legal age of consent maybe different in other jurisdictions.

In addition, with regards to children, the paramount consideration when making decisions pertaining to children is based on what is in the best interests of the child.[199] In terms of South African law for example, the Choice on termination of pregnancy Act[200] allows any woman of any age to request the termination of a pregnancy without recourse to disclosure of such information to any adult person or next-of-kin should they not wish to do so.[201] Similarly, section 134 of the Children's Act[202] allows children access to contraceptives without requirement for disclosure to any adult person. In addition, section 133 of the Act allows children to keep a diagnosis of HIV-AIDS confidential.[203] Furthermore, healthcare practitioners are required to breach confidentiality legally in cases suspected of child abuse in accordance with section 100 of the Children's Act.[204] Such disclosures or breach are considered to be in the best interests of the affected child. Finally, the Children's Act, 2005[205] as amended,

[194] Ibid.
[195] NHA (n 2).
[196] HPCSA (n 30).
[197] Children's Act 38 2005; Chima (n 14).
[198] Chima (nn 14, 15 and 21).
[199] Chima (nn 26 and 107); McQuoid-Mason (n 107); *Botha v Botha* (n 120).
[200] Choice Act (n 69); Chima (nn 15 and 21).
[201] Ibid.
[202] Children's Act (n 71) s 134.
[203] Ibid, s 133.
[204] Ibid, s 100.
[205] Children's Act (n 71).

protects children's privacy where it stipulates with regards to information on healthcare that:

(1) Every child has the right to–
    (a) have access to information on health promotion and the prevention and treatment of ill-health and disease, sexuality and reproduction;
    (b) have access to information regarding his or her health status;
    (c) have access to information regarding the causes and treatment of his or her health status; and
    (d) confidentiality regarding his or her health status and the health status of a parent, caregiver or family member, except when main-taining such confidentiality is not in the best interests of the child.

Further with regards confidentiality of information on HIV/AIDS status of children, section 133 of the Children's Act[206] stipulates that:

(1) No person may disclose the fact that a child is HIV-positive without consent given in terms of subsection (2), except–
    (a) within the scope of that person's powers and duties in terms of this Act or any other law;
    (b) when necessary for the purpose of carrying out the provisions of this Act;
    (c) for the purpose of legal proceedings; or
    (d) in terms of an order of a court.

Furthermore, section 134 of the Children's Act[207] stipulates with regards to access to contraceptives: that:

(1) No person may refuse–
    (a) to sell condoms to a child over the age of 12 years; or
    (b) to provide a child over the age of 12 years with condoms on request where such condoms are provided or distributed free of charge.

(2) Contraceptives other than condoms may be provided to a child on request by the child and without the consent of the parent or caregiver of the child if–
    (a) the child is at least 12 years of age;
    (b) proper medical advice is given to the child; and

---

[206] Ibid.
[207] Children's Act (n 71).

(c)   a medical examination is carried out on the child to determine whether there are any medical reasons why a specific contraceptive should not be provided to the child.

(3)   A child who obtains condoms, contraceptives or contraceptive advice in terms of this Act is entitled to confidentiality in this respect, subject to section 110. The latter of which refers to reporting of abused or neglected child and child in need of care and protection.

In terms of the HPCSA ethical guidelines, healthcare practitioners who believe a child or other legally incompetent patient to be a victim of neglect or physical, sexual or emotional abuse and that the patient cannot give or withhold consent to disclosure, should give such information promptly to an appropriate responsible person or statutory agency, where they believe that the disclosure is in the patient's best interests.[208]

In addition, 'healthcare practitioners should inform the patient that they intend to disclose the information before doing so.' Also, where appropriate, healthcare practitioners should inform those with parental responsibility about the disclosure, except where the practitioner believes that disclosure of information to the parents or guardians is not in the best interests of an abused or neglected patient. In this case they should be prepared to justify their decision (e.g., where the parents or guardians are suspected be the child's abuser).[209]

Disclosure After a Patient's Death

HPCSA guidelines suggest that healthcare practitioners still have an obligation to keep personal information confidential after a patient dies, in accordance with WMA guidelines and ethical code.[210] HPCSA guidelines suggest that there are a number of circumstances in which healthcare practitioners may be asked to disclose information about patients who have died, which include:

(a)   to assist in connection with an inquest. In these circumstances, practitioners are required to provide the relevant information;

(b)   as part of a clinical audit or for education or research with the approval of a REC or IRB;

(c)   the publication of properly anonymised case studies;

(d)   on death certificates as stipulated by law which requires healthcare practitioners to complete death certificates honestly and fully;

---

[208]   HPCSA (n 30).
[209]   Ibid.
[210]   HPCSA (n 30); WMA *Manual on Ethics* (n 81).

(e) to obtain information relating to public health surveillance that is approved by a REC or IRB. In this case, anonymised information should be used, unless identifiable data is essential to the study.[211]

However, difficulties or moral dilemmas may arise when there is a conflict of interest between parties affected by the patient's death. For example, if an insurance company seeks information in order to decide whether to make a payment under a life assurance policy, healthcare practitioners should only release information with consent from the next-of-kin of the deceased patient or the executor of the deceased's estate, or if the deceased had consented to it before his or her death.[212]

One can conclude this chapter by addressing some generally issues pertaining to confidentiality and privacy.

Can Confidentiality be Breached?

Confidentiality is not an absolute or inviolable obligation[213] and situations will arise where the harm in maintaining confidentiality is greater than the harm brought about by disclosing confidential information. In general, two such situations that may give rise to exceptions exist. This include where there is risk of great harm to an identifiable individual, or where there is risk of harm to the public in general. In each situation, one should ask – whether lack of this specific information about this patient will put a specific person whom the healthcare practitioner can identify or the public at risk of serious harm? As elaborated above, legal regulations exist that both protect and limit patient's right to privacy.[214] When a healthcare provider is satisfied that information should be released, he or she should act promptly to disclose all relevant information, which maybe essential to protect the best interests of the patient or to safeguard the well-being of others.[215] Release of such information before death in an advance directive or living will is also encouraged.[216]

---

[211] HPCSA (n 30).

[212] Ibid.

[213] Carstens and Pearmain (n 166); Saner (n 9); Chima (nn 26 and 107).

[214] Carstens and Pearmain (n 166); Saner (n 9); Chima (nn 26 and 107); K.A. Edwards 'Confidentiality', http://depts.washington.edu/bioethx/topics/confiden.html (last accessed 2009).

[215] HPCSA (n 30).

[216] HPCSA Guidelines (n 22).

Finally, What Kinds of Disclosure are Inappropriate?

Inappropriate disclosure of information can occur in clinical settings. For example, when healthcare practitioners are pressed for time, the temptation to discuss a clinical case in the elevator may be great, but in such settings, it is very difficult to keep others from hearing such information exchanges. Similarly, extra copies of handouts or clinical notes from teaching conferences that contain identifiable patients should be removed at the conclusion of teaching sessions or case discussions. Other inappropriate breaches include casual breaches for fun or amusement or simply to satisfy another person's curiosity, or to prevent minor crime, or harm to someone. Patients' rights to privacy may not be fully respected in such situations.[217]

CASE STUDIES IN CONFIDENTIALITY

Case Scenario 1

Is there a duty of confidentiality towards the family/the partner of the patient? example: partner of the patient calls the nurse in the hospital to have some news about his partner/the patient. Nurse asks the partner to bring his HIV-medication to the hospital. The partner was not aware of his HIV-status. The nurse is fired, because of breach of the duty of confidentiality.

Answer
There is no legal duty on any healthcare worker (HCW) to tell a patient's family, sexual partners, or caregivers about a patient's HIV status. The patient should ideally decide who to tell. HCWs can only advise the patient on why it may be important to inform family members or sexual partners about the patient's HIV status. It has been suggested that it is unlikely that the courts would expect HCWs to act as police in the HIV/AIDS epidemic by making them responsible for telling all sexual partners of all patients.[218]

A HCW is only under a duty to protect a patient's sexual partner from possible infection where the HCW knows that the sexual partner is in danger, and where the HCW has not followed the general guidelines recommended when dealing with patients with HIV. Ordinarily, patients should decide on who to tell about their HIV status. The HCW is only obliged to give advice to

---

[217] Chima (nn 26 and 107).

[218] S.C. Chima, 'Chapter 5: Confidentiality' in *A Primer on Medical Bioethics and Human Rights for African Scholars* (Durban: Chimason Educational Books, 2011) 104–19.

the patient regarding why it may be useful or important to tell sexual partners or family members about the individual's HIV status. It is generally recommended that HCWs should take the following minimum steps before deciding to inform a person's known sexual partner.

Give in-depth counselling on why it is important to tell a sexual partner. If a HCW is unable to provide this counselling, then the patient should be referred for voluntary counselling and testing (VCT) at a local counselling centre or another suitable facility.

Explain to the patient that the HCW has a duty to warn known sexual partners about their risk of HIV infection.

Explain to the patient that a HCW may be forced to breach the patient's right to confidentiality if the patient refuses to inform their partner by themselves, and also offer the patient an opportunity to inform his/her sexual partner with or without help.

It is only after fulfilling the above conditions that the HCW can make a final decision on whether or not it is necessary to tell the sexual partner that the patient is living with HIV.[219]

When is a healthcare worker obliged to disclose a patient's HIV status to their sexual partner?

Generally, a HCW may only tell a patient's sexual partner about the patient's HIV status when:

i   The sexual partner is clearly known and identifiable – in other words, a specific person, e.g., the patient's wife 'Kate' or husband 'William.'

ii.   Where the sexual partner is at risk of being infected with HIV by the patient, and the patient has refused to inform the partner of their HIV status or has refused to have safer sex.

iii.   After the patient has received appropriate counselling on the need to inform their sexual partner or have safer sex.

iv.   Where the HCW has informed the patient of their duty to protect their known sexual partners.

v.   Finally, after the HCW has warned the patient that if they do not inform your sexual partner or have safe sex, then the HCW may have to breach confidentiality.[220]

Nevertheless, if the patient has been duly warned as above, and the patient informs the doctor or other HCW that their sexual partner is not in danger because they are having 'safe sex', then a HCW concerned must accept this information at face value unless there is clear and convincing evidence to the

---

[219]   Ibid.
[220]   Ibid.

contrary. For example, where the sexual partner falls pregnant while under the care of the same doctor or HCW from their current partner who is known to the doctor. This is based on the understanding that the doctor-patient duty of confidentiality can only be breached under very serious circumstances.[221] Therefore, the patient must be trusted if they say they will be practising 'safer sex' unless there is clear and convincing evidence to the contrary.[222]

Implications of the above information to case scenario 1

In the context of the case scenario above, one would like to argue that since *this* was an accidental or inadvertent disclosure, then the nurse in this case should not have been fired.

The ethical decision-making in this case would be to find out if the patient had been properly counselled on the need to disclose their HIV status to their sexual partner. If so, the onus then lies on the patient to inform their family members or partners about their HIV status. If the patient had not been properly counselled, then this would be an opportunity to counsel both the patient and their partner about the consequences or implications of the patients HIV status. More importantly in the current global context of ready availability of treatments and prophylaxis for HIV/AIDS, both partners should be counselled on the easy availability of Antiretroviral medications (ARVs), both for prevention and treatment of HIV/AIDS. In the current context HIV has simply become another chronic disease, arguably similar to diabetes or hypertension, which can be clinically managed and should invoke no everlasting fear for both the patients and their partners. The issue to be managed in this case would be repairing the trust between the patient and their partner and repairing the HCW-patient or doctor-patient relationship[223] and minimizing the impact of stigmatization due to HIV/AIDS.[224]

Case Scenario 2

What is the status of audio and video recordings and the use of a private detective: Can a patient make an audio recording of his conversation with the physician and use this recording in court? Can an insurance company use a private detective who makes a video recording of a patient/the claimant in a liability case, to prove the claimant is not that paralyzed as he pretends?

---

[221] van Vuuren v Kruger (n 7).
[222] Chima (n 218).
[223] S.C. Chima, *A Primer on Medical Bioethics and Human Rights for African Scholars* (Durban, Chimason Educational Books, 2011) 120–31.
[224] Famoroti et al. (n 159).

To analyze this case scenario in the context of South Africa, one has to consider the implications of section 14 of the Constitution,[225] which enshrines the right to privacy in South African law, in addition to other extant laws such as the Regulation of Interception of Communications and Provision of Communication-Related Information (RICA) Act 2002,[226] as well as the POPIA.[227] In terms of South African law the right to privacy as contained in Section 14 of the Constitution[228] states:

> Everyone has the right to privacy, which shall include the right not to have -
> (a)   their personal homes searched;
> (b)   their property searched;
> (c)   their possessions seized; or
> (d)   the privacy of their communications infringed.[229]

Nevertheless, the rights provided in the South African Constitution and Bill of Rights including the right to privacy are subject to limitations by section 36 of the constitution (the limitation clause), which provides that in order for a right to be lawfully limited, the 'limitation must be reasonable and justifiable in an open and democratic society based on human dignity, equality and freedom …'.[230]

Therefore, the right to privacy guaranteed as by the South African Constitution is not an absolute right and may be limited for just cause. For instance, the South African Constitutional Court in the case of *Bernstein v Bester*[231] discussed the extent to which the right to privacy can be limited. The majority of the Court expressed the opinion that, on the available facts, it was in any event difficult to say how there could be an infringement of the right to privacy.[232] Therefore, there is a legitimate expectation that the right to privacy may not be infringed upon in order to deem the infringement unlawful.

In South Africa, the recordings of communications (both audio and video) are regulated by the 'RICA' Act of 2002.[233] Generally speaking, in terms of RICA, no person may record any conversation without consent. The general rule of RICA is that all intentional interceptions of any sort of communications

---

[225]   The Constitution (s 14).
[226]   Regulation of Interception of Communications and Provision of Communication-Related Information (RICA) Act 70 of 2002.
[227]   POPIA (n 3).
[228]   The Constitution (n 1).
[229]   The Constitution (n 225).
[230]   The Constitution (n 1) s36.
[231]   *Bernstein and Others v Bester NO and Others* (CCT23/95) [1996] ZACC 2.
[232]   Ibid.
[233]   RICA (n 226).

during the course of its occurrence or transmission in South Africa are prohibited. Further, any recording of a conversation that has been done without the consent of a party thereto maybe deemed unlawful, subject to several exceptions. Such exceptions include:

1. Where one is a party to the communication.
2. Where one has received the written consent from one of the parties to the communication.
3. Where the recording has been made for purposes of carrying on of business.

For example, one may be considered a 'party to the communication' if you are the sender, the recipient, or any person included in the communication (such as being copied in on an email). It has been argued that an issue may arise when the content being recorded is deemed 'sensitive.'[234] In such cases it has been suggested that the more sensitive the content is, the less likely it is that all participants would allow the recording of such conversations. Whereas 'some people would only say certain things in a specific moment, and to specific people.'[235] Such types of 'sensitive' information could be considered harmful.[236]

Video and audio recordings

While the RICA Act[237] does not differentiate between video and audio recordings, RICA prohibits all 'intentional interceptions of any communications during the course of its occurrence or transmission in the Republic ...' and states that 'any recordings of conversations that have been done without consent are generally deemed unlawful.'[238]

However, the RICA Act does refer to two categories of communication called 'direct' and 'indirect' communication. Direct communication refers to conversations between any two or more people while 'indirect' communication is a much wider category which pertains to all interactions that are not face-to-face including data, speech and moving images.[239]

As an example, a Skype or Zoom conference call would fall under 'indirect' communication as this would take place by means of an online telecommunication service. As a result, one would need to be either one of the parties to the

---

[234]   Businesstech Online: April 8, 2017. Available from: https://businesstech.co.za/news/trending/167107/__trashed-65/ (accessed January 31, 2023).

[235]   Ibid.

[236]   Op cit (n 234).

[237]   Op cit (n 226).

[238]   G. Keeble, Recording conversations without consent (Schoeman Law Inc, 2021) available from: www.schoemanlaw.co.za.

[239]   Ibid; RICA (n 226).

conversation or have been given consent from one of the parties to record the video. By contrast to a 'direct' communication, such as a recording of an altercation between oneself and a police officer, or the recording of an altercation occurring at a local restaurant.[240] However, if such utterances or conversation are audible to another person in a room, it is likely that one is aware that the other person is there. The question is whether the parties involved have considered your immediate presence. In such cases, Section 4 of the of the RICA Act defines a 'party to the conversation' as a person in whose presence the conversation is taking place, or as a person who is in 'audible presence' of the conversation.[241]

In a situation, such as hiding in a closet to spy on someone else, or a private detective spying on someone, then other considerations would arise such as whether there was criminal intent or the involvement of criminality.[242] It has been noted that while the RICA law was slightly vague on the issue of whether those in altercation may not have necessarily been informed, that they were being filmed. It would still be likely considered as a case of 'direct' communication since the recorder of the conversation would be considered to be within 'audible presence' of the altercation. In such cases the recorder should legally be allowed to film or record within the confines if the RICA law.[243] One can conclude this line of argument by saying that even if the law doesn't require you to get the consent of the other party to the conversation, it would be probably best practice to inform them that you are recording. However, if you are not a 'party to the conversation' at all, it would be unlawful to record such a conversation.

In terms of section 4 (1) of the RICA Act,[244] any person other than a law enforcement officer may intercept any conversation, if he or she is a 'party to the conversation' or communication. So long as the interception was not for the purposes of committing a criminal offence or criminality. Therefore, it is not illegal for anyone to secretly record a conversation where they are a party to that conversation. Furthermore, such intercepted information or conversation obtained through a non-consented recording may also be admissible as evidence in a trial, if the court finds that it is in the interest of justice to do so.[245]

---

[240]   *Bernstein v Bester* (n 231).
[241]   RICA (n 226).
[242]   Ibid.
[243]   Ibid.
[244]   Ibid.
[245]   Eversheds Sutherland and M. Mabaso, Recording of conversations – what does the law say about secretly recording a conversation without the consent of the other party? Available from: www.cofesa.co.za/recording-of-conversations-what -does-the-law-say-about-secretly-recording-a-conversation-without-the-consent-of-the

Can an employer record an employee's phone calls without their consent?

It was established in the South African case of *Protea Technology v Wainer*[246] that an employer cannot intercept an employee's 'private' phone calls. However, where such calls pertain to the employer's business, in such cases the employee would have lost their right to privacy. Further, in the case of *Harvey v Niland*[247] the court held that South African courts have a discretion whether to accept or reject recordings as evidence despite the possibility that such evidence might have been obtained by commission of an offence or violation of a constitutional right.[248] In the case of *Harvey v Niland and Others*,[249] a man was accused of hacking into his former business associate's Facebook® account where he was able to access certain communications made by the ex-associate on his Facebook® account. This act was clearly both criminal and an invasion of privacy. However, the court in this case held that in terms of the common-law principle all relevant evidence which is not inadmissible, because of exclusionary rules, would be considered admissible in a civil court, irrespective of how it was obtained. The court further held that the rights of privacy are not absolute and that the court has the discretion to admit certain evidence even if such evidence was obtained illegally.[250] Despite this judgment however, other commentators have argued that the recording or interception of communications is a complex scenario to navigate, since it is often of a highly sensitive nature. Therefore, complying with at least one of the exceptions listed in RICA,[251] will ensure such recordings are admissible and can be used as evidence in a court of law or disciplinary proceedings.[252]

What does the POPIA Act require in terms of recording of conversations

POPIA,[253] which came into full effect in South Africa on 1 July 2021, prohibits the processing of personal information without the consent of the party or subject. The law creates a civil liability for infringement of the right to privacy. In terms of POPIA, processing of personal information includes collecting,

---

-other-party/#:~:text=What%20does%20POPIA%20provide%20regarding,of%20the %20party%20or%20subject (accessed January 31, 2023).

[246] *Protea Technology Limited v Wainer* (1997) 3 All SA 594 (W).
[247] *Harvey v Niland and Others* (5021/2015) [2015] ZAECGHC 149.
[248] *Bernstein v Bester* (n 231).
[249] Op cit (n 247).
[250] F. Khan, Recording a conversation without permission. Available from: www .findanattorney.co.za/content_recording-conversation-without-consent (accessed January 31, 2023).
[251] RICA (n 226).
[252] Op cit (n 234).
[253] POPIA (n 3).

receiving, recording, transmitting, organizing, distributing, or making such information available to other parties. Personal information relates to information about any identifiable living natural person and where applicable an identifiable existing juristic person. Therefore, in terms of POPIA recording personal information without the consent of the other party is prohibited even if the person recording is a party to the conversation.[254]

Furthermore, POPIA requires that responsible parties obtain prior authorization for certain processing of personal information where the specific processing of certain personal information is likely to cause a higher risk to the data subject. Thus, unless exempted, a responsible party must apply for prior authorization under the following circumstances:

1. **Processing of unique identifiers** – where the responsible party processes a unique identifier for purposes other than those specifically intended at collection of the identifier and with the aim of linking the information with information processed by other responsible parties.

    Such unique identifiers may include data such as account numbers; policy number; identity number; employee number; student number; or any other unique reference numbers.

2. **Criminal, unlawful, or objectionable behaviour** – where the responsible party processes information on criminal behaviour or unlawful or objectionable conduct on behalf of third parties. This would apply, for example, where the responsible party is a company that carries out background check services on behalf of their clients.

3. **Credit reporting** – where the responsible party processes personal information for credit reporting purposes. For example, credit bureaus and other persons processing information for credit reporting purposes.

4. **Cross border transfers of special and children's personal information** – where special or children's personal information is transferred to a third party in a country that does not have adequate data protection laws. The current position is that the Information Regulator requires responsible parties to make a determination as to whether the country in which the third party is located has adequate laws and apply for authorization to transfer the personal information to those countries. Such transfers must be subject to contractual safeguards where the receiving country does not have adequate data protection laws.

5. **As further determined by the regulator** – Here, the Information Regulator may determine that certain categories or types of information processing carries a particular risk for the legitimate interests of the data

---

254 Ibid.

subject, in which case, a responsible party will need to apply for prior authorization in respect of such information processing.

Furthermore, unless a code of conduct has been published by the Information Regulator in respect of specific processing that is subject to prior authorization, a responsible party will need to apply for prior authorization to continue processing personal information that falls within the above categories of information processing. It has been reported that to date, the Credit Bureau Association has applied for a code of conduct for the processing by credit bureaus of personal information for credit reporting purposes.[255]

Nevertheless, it has been argued that for most clients, the categories of processing that may be particularly applicable is the processing of unique identifiers, processing for credit reporting purposes, and the transfer of special and children's personal information cross border. This would apply for example, where medical information is processed for insurance purposes and transferred to countries without adequate data protection laws, most notably, the USA.[256]

It has also been suggested that where a responsible party is required to apply for prior authorization in terms of section 58(1) of POPIA,[257] the Act requires that the responsible party must suspend its processing of the personal information subject to the prior authorization application once the application has been submitted and until the Information Regulator has approved the application or found that prior authorization is not necessary.[258]

One can conclude this section by saying that in South Africa, it may not necessarily be illegal for an individual to secretly record any information to which they are a party to. Further, this information may also be admissible as evidence in a court of law or for disciplinary proceedings regardless of how such information was obtained if it is in the interests of justice to do so. Nevertheless, in terms of POPIA,[259] personal information of another person or data subject cannot be recorded or processed without their express consent.[260] Finally, it has been suggested that by ensuring that one complies with at least one of the exceptions provided by RICA,[261] this will go a long way in ensuring

[255] Dommisse Attorneys Inc. Prior authorization. February 15, 2022. Available from: https://dommisseattorneys.co.za/blog/category/articles/privacy-popi/ (accessed January 31, 2023).

[256] Ibid.

[257] POPIA (n 3).

[258] Op cit (n 255).

[259] Op cit (n 257).

[260] Eversheds and Mabaso (n 245); Dommisse Attorneys (n 255); POPIA (n 3).

[261] RICA (n 226).

that such recordings are admissible and can be used as evidence in a court of law or during disciplinary hearings.[262]

Implications of the above analysis for case scenario 2

Based on the analysis above, in the context of South African law, a patient should be able to use a recording with physician as evidence for proceedings in a court of law, since they will be a party to the conversation in a direct conversation with the physician. Similarly, a private detective may be able to obtain evidence which can be admissible in a South African court, if the court determines that such a recording will serve the best interests of justice, regardless of how such information was obtained, whether directly in conversation with the affected party, or indirectly by any other means. Nonetheless, it would be advisable for a patient to inform the physician that they were recording a conversation and obtain consent for such recording in accordance with POPIA,[263] or comply with one of the exceptions provided for by RICA.[264]

Case Scenario 3

Family treatment: a child shows signs of child abuse: can the physician report this to the competent authorities, even when the parents are also a patient and are entitled to confidentiality.

In South Africa, ethical rules of the HPCSA state that healthcare practitioners may only divulge information regarding a patient:

1. With the express consent of a patient
2. With the written consent of a parent or guardian if the child is less than 12 years of age
3. Or in exceptional cases based on statutory regulations, court order or in the public interest.[265]

---

262 P. Blauw, Consolidated Employers Organization. The admissibility of voice recordings. General comments. January 18, 2022. Available from: https://ceosa.org .za/the-admissibility-of-voice-recordings/#:~:text=Employees%20are%20likewise %20entitled%20to,are%20thus%20admissible%20as%20evidence.
263 POPIA (n 3).
264 RICA (n 226).
265 *HPCSA* (n 30); Chima (n 218).

In terms of statutory authority pertaining to the reporting of child abuse in South Africa, Section 110 of the Children's Act 2005 as amended[266] stipulates as follows:

Reporting of abused or neglected child and child in need of care and protection:
(1)   Any correctional official, dentist, homeopath, immigration official, labour inspector, legal practitioner, medical practitioner, midwife, minister of religion, nurse, occupational therapist, physiotherapist, psychologist, religious leader, social service professional, social worker, speech therapist, teacher, traditional health practitioner, traditional leader or member of staff or volunteer worker at a partial care facility, drop-in centre or child and youth care centre who on reasonable grounds concludes that a child has been abused in a manner causing physical injury, sexually abused or deliberately neglected, must report that conclusion in the prescribed form to a designated child protection organisation, the provincial department of social development or a police official.
(2)   Any person who on reasonable grounds believes that a child is in need of care and protection may report that belief to the provincial department of social development, a designated child protection organisation or a police official.
(3)   A person referred to in subsection (1) or (2)—
      (a)   must substantiate that conclusion or belief to the provincial department of social development, a designated child protection organisation or police official; and
      (b)   who makes a report in good faith is not liable to civil action on the basis of the report.
(4)   A police official to whom a report has been made in terms of subsection (1) or (2) or who becomes aware of a child in need of care and protection must—
      (a)   ensure the safety and well-being of the child concerned if the child's safety or well-being is at risk; and
      (b)   within 24 hours notify the provincial department of social development or a designated child protection organisation of the report and any steps that have been taken with regard to the child.
(5)   The provincial department of social development or designated child protection organisation to whom a report has been made in terms of subsection (1), (2) or (4), must—
      (a)   ensure the safety and well-being of the child concerned, if the child's safety or well-being is at risk;
      (b)   make an initial assessment of the report;
      (c)   unless the report is frivolous or obviously unfounded, investigate the truthfulness of the report or cause it to be investigated;
      (d)   if the report is substantiated by such investigation, without delay initiate proceedings in terms of this Act for the protection of the child; and
      (e)   submit such particulars as may be prescribed to the Director-General for inclusion in Part A of the National Child Protection Register.

---

[266] Children's Amendment Act No. 41 of 2007. Government Gazette No 30884, March 18, 2008.

(6)(a) A designated child protection organisation to whom a report has been made in terms of subsection (1), (2) or (4) must report the matter to the relevant provincial department of social development.

(b) The provincial head of social development must monitor the progress of all matters reported to it in terms of paragraph (a).

(7) The provincial department of social development or designated child protection organisation which has conducted an investigation as contemplated in subsection (5) may—

(a) take measures to assist the child, including counselling, mediation, prevention and early intervention services, family reconstruction and rehabilitation, behaviour modification, problem solving and referral to another suitably qualified person or organisation;

(b) if he or she is satisfied that it is in the best interest of the child not to be removed from his or her home or place where he or she resides, but that the removal of the alleged offender from such home or place would secure the safety and well-being of the child, request a police official in the prescribed manner to take the steps referred to in section 153; or

(c) deal with the child in the manner contemplated in sections 151, 152 or 155.

(8) The provincial department of social development or designated child protection organisation which has conducted an investigation as contemplated in subsection (5) must report the possible commission of an offence to a police official.[267]

Implications of the above analysis for case scenario 3

In light of the detailed regulations regarding the reporting of suspected child abuse in the South African Children's Act as detailed above. It is obvious that there is a statutory obligation on any medical practitioner or other healthcare professional to report a suspected case of child abuse for further investigation and appropriate action. Furthermore, section 110 of the Children's Act, subsection 3(b) states that any person 'who makes a report in good faith is not liable to civil action on the basis of the report.'[268] In view of this, the medical practitioner, or physician or other HCW who makes such a report in good faith, even if they are mistaken, will not be liable for civil action. Nevertheless, the ethical rules of the HPCSA, require medical practitioners to obtain 'parental' consent of minors under the age of 12 before breaching consent.[269] Therefore in such cases, medical professionals should ideally obtain parental consent before reporting the case to appropriate authorities for further investigation. However, if the medical practitioner suspects that the child is in danger because of the

---

[267] Childrens Amendment Act 2007 (s110).
[268] Ibid.
[269] Op cit (n 265).

suspected or severe child abuse, then the physician or other healthcare professional may report the case to the appropriate authorities for further action, without obtaining parental or guardians consent in the best interests of the child. Since the best interests of a child is paramount in terms of the Children's Act 2005.[270]

Case Scenario 4

ABC v St George's NHS Hospital Trust[271] (On appeal from Nicol J EWHC 1394 (QB). This case raises important issues around what information others are entitled to have about another person. Are family members entitled to know about genetic test results that you have had done? Is there a moral obligation to family members? Should a third party be entitled to enforce any such moral obligation?

Excerpts from the court judgment in ABC v St George's *Healthcare* NHS Trust *& Others* [2020] EWHC 455 (QB)[272] [*edited and summarized here for brevity*]

Particulars of claim
This claim was brought against three NHS Trusts. Whereas the claimant contends that the defendants breached a duty of care owed to her, and/or acted contrary to her rights under Article 8 of the European Convention on Human Rights (ECHR)[273] in failing to alert her to the risk that she had inherited the gene for Huntington's Disease (HD) in time for her to terminate her pregnancy. The claimant sought damages for the continuation of her pregnancy, psychiatric damage, and consequential losses. The parties narrowed the issues for the court's determination by agreeing that if the court finds an actionable breach of duty on the part of the defendants (or any of them) and that, but for that breach, the claimant would have terminated her pregnancy, the claimant should recover damages in the sum of £345,000.

The genetic risk had been revealed to the defendants through diagnosis of the claimant's father 'XX', who declined to consent to disclosure of the infor-

---

[270] Children's Act (nn 71 and 266).
[271] *ABC v St George's NHS Hospital Trust* [2017] EWCA Civ 336. On appeal from *ABC v St George's Healthcare NHS trust* [2015] EWHC 1394 (QB).
[272] *ABC v St George's Healthcare NHS Trust & Ors* [2020] EWHC 455 (QB).
[273] Convention for the Protection of Human Rights and Dignity of the Human Being with regard to the Application of Biology and Medicine: Convention on Human Rights and Biomedicine. Oviedo, 4.IV.1997.

mation to the claimant and the defendants' clinicians took the view that they should not override his confidentiality.

The defendants denied that, as a matter of law, they owed any relevant duty of care to the claimant. Even if such a duty was owed, they contended, on the facts of the case, that they did not breach that duty.

Further, they maintain that even if there was a breach of duty, it did not cause the claimant any injury because the evidence did not establish that she would have had a termination (of pregnancy) but for the breach.

The defendants also averred that the claim under the Human Rights Act 1998,[274] fails for the same reasons as the common law claim.

Procedural history of the case

At an early stage in the proceedings, the defendants had applied to strike out the claim earlier on the ground that it disclosed no reasonable cause of action. Nicol J acceded to that application in *ABC v St George's Healthcare and others*.[275] However, the English Court of Appeal overturned his decision and ordered that the matter should proceed to trial in *ABC v St George's Healthcare and others*.[276] The case was then decided at trial in *ABC v St Georges NHS and others*,[277] as excerpted in this chapter.

Facts of the case

> In 2007, the claimant's father killed her mother. He was then convicted of man-slaughter by reason of diminished responsibility and made subject of a restricted hospital order, pursuant to sections 37 and 41 of the Mental Health Act.[278]

'XX' (the claimant's father), was detained at the Shaftsbury Clinic, Springfield Hospital ('Springfield') which is run by the second defendant. He received care and treatment through a multi-disciplinary team, including psychiatrists, psychologists, other therapists, and social workers. XX's responsible clinician was initially Professor Eastman. In 2009, he was transferred into the care of the team headed by Dr Olumoroti, a consultant forensic psychiatrist.

---

[274] United Kingdom, Human Rights Act 1998.

[275] *ABC v St George's Healthcare and others* (n 271).

[276] Ibid.

[277] *ABC v St Georges NHS and others* (QB) (n 272).

[278] UK Mental Health Act 1983; National Collaborating Centre for Mental Health (UK). Service User Experience in Adult Mental Health: Improving the Experience of Care for People Using Adult NHS Mental Health Services. Leicester (UK): British Psychological Society (UK); 2012. (NICE Clinical Guidelines, No. 136.) 11, DETENTION UNDER THE MENTAL HEALTH ACT. Available from: https://www.ncbi.nlm.nih.gov/books/NBK327290/ (last accessed September 20, 2023).

From early in his admission, suspicions were raised that there might be an unspecified organic explanation for some of XX's symptoms. Because of this suspicion, he underwent MRI scans in 2007 and 2008 but no progressive changes were seen in the brain. On 28 April 2009, XX was referred by the psychiatric team to the neurological department at St George's Hospital (which falls within the first defendant's responsibility).

The referral letter stated: 'Our main concern at the moment is that [XX] has gait difficulties. He has a non-progressive choreiform limb movement and an abnormal wide based gait with motor restlessness on sitting still.'

'XX' was seen by Dr Marion, consultant neurologist, on 24 June 2009. She found a clinical picture of hereditary choreic syndrome, which she said was likely to be Huntington's chorea [HD]. She planned to refer 'XX' to Dr McEntagart in the genetics department at St George's hospital.

'XX' apparently agreed to genetic testing at the time. However, it is clear from the medical records that he later became hostile to any suggestion that he had HD and refused to undergo genetic testing. His intransigence about this appears from various entries in his medical records in July and August 2009.

'XX' then made it clear that he did not want the claimant and her sister to know that he was thought to have HD. He was aware that such knowledge could impact on their decision about whether to have children or not. Both daughters were in their 30s; neither had started a family.

Huntington's disease (HD), also known as Huntington's chorea (HC) is a neurodegenerative disorder of genetic origin. […]. It is transmitted as an autosomal dominant trait so that the child of someone with the condition has a 50% chance of being affected. The clinical features of the condition include abnormalities of movement, cognitive problems, and psychiatric symptoms. It is an incurable disease and sufferers have a reduced life expectancy. Symptoms do not appear until adulthood, typically between the ages of 30 and 50 years. [*Further information about HD can be obtained from the following sources - authors addition.*[279]]

In this case, the first defendant's clinical team recognized that the likelihood that 'XX' had Huntington's disease had significant implications for his daughters, who were known to them. Despite struggling to come to terms with their own grief and the devastation of their family, the claimant and her sister continued to support their father. The claimant attended case conferences and

[279] Mayo Clinic, Huntington's Disease. Available from: www.mayoclinic.org/diseases-conditions/huntingtons-disease/symptoms-causes/syc-20356117#:~:text=Huntington's%20disease%20is%20a%20rare,(cognitive)%20and%20psychiatric%20disorders. (accessed February 6, 2023); S. Frank, 'Treatment of Huntington's disease' (2014) 11(1) *Neurotherapeutics* 153-60. doi: 10.1007/s13311-013-0244-z.

planning meetings about 'XX'. Family therapy was proposed, and the claimant commenced attending sessions in March 2009.

The claimant was aware that XX had been referred for a neurological opinion but, given XX's stance, the outcome of the appointment was not shared with her. By August 2009, the second defendant's clinical team had recognized that the situation was very difficult. Their discussions also involved Mary Davies, a social worker in the community team, for whom the third defendant is responsible. On 20 August, Dr Roberts (SHO to Dr Olumoroti) wrote to Dr McEntagart seeking her advice on managing the situation. […] I shall return to consider that letter and Dr McEntagart's response.

By unhappy coincidence, the claimant became pregnant in July 2009, that is around the time that it emerged that XX probably had HD. She was not in a settled relationship and was initially ambivalent about the pregnancy continuing.

A multidisciplinary team meeting took place on 2 September 2009. The claimant attended. Unusually, she was asked to remain outside, and it became apparent that the meeting was proceeding without her. In advance of the meeting, the claimant had told a social worker that she was pregnant but had not decided what to do. When invited into the room, the claimant was asked by Dr Olumoroti whether she had children. She was taken aback and did not share the news of her pregnancy.

However, after the meeting, she did tell her father. He shared the news with his psychologist, Ms. Gill, at a session next day. He remained adamant that he did not want to tell his daughters about the HD diagnosis and 'so jeopardize the pregnancy.' Ms. Gill reported the development to the clinical team.

Having discovered that the claimant was pregnant and following further discussions within the clinical team, Dr Roberts wrote again to Dr McEntagart on 18 September 2009, sending the letter by fax. She acknowledged that a diagnosis of HD would impact on 'his daughter's decision about whether to continue with her pregnancy' and sought urgent advice in view of the pregnancy. Having received that letter, Dr McEntegart discussed XX's case with Dr Olumoroti by telephone and followed up with a letter dated 25 September 2009.

[…] In short, XX continued to insist that his daughters were not told, suggesting that the doctors would be acting illegally if they did so. 'XX' had shared the information about HD with his brother and, in October 2009, the brother attended Springfield for a discussion of the options. After that meeting, 'XX' agreed to be seen by the genetic team. He was seen by Professor Patton at Springfield on 27 October 2009. He gave his consent for genetic testing, having specifically excluded the results going to any member of his family.

The results of XX's genetic testing were reported on 9 November 2009. They confirmed that 'XX' had Huntington's disease (HD).

Professor Patton and a genetic counsellor attended Springfield on 10 December 2009. They informed XX of the results in the presence of Dr Olumoroti. Following the disclosure of the results, Dr Olumoroti called an emergency team meeting to discuss how XX would be supported. It was noted that he might become distressed, depressed or even suicidal.

'XX' continued to maintain that his daughters should not be informed of the diagnosis.

It is notable that by the time 'XX' received the confirmed diagnosis, the claimant was more than 24 weeks pregnant. It is agreed that the last date on which she could have undergone a termination was 6 December 2009.

The claimant had her baby in April 2010. There is no doubt that this was a happy event for her and that she dearly loves her child. On 4 August 2010, a Mental Health Tribunal directed XX's conditional discharge subject to meeting certain requirements. The claimant was concerned about this. In that context, Dr Olumoroti and a social worker visited her at home on 23 August 2010.

It is accepted that Dr Olumoroti breached XX's confidentiality and informed the claimant of XX's diagnosis, although the precise circumstances in which that occurred are in dispute.

The claimant's sister was then in the early stages of her first pregnancy. The claimant informed the clinical team of her sister's pregnancy. The claimant decided that she did not want XX's diagnosis to be disclosed to her sister during her pregnancy. 'XX' also maintained that the sister should not be told. On 7 October 2010, a meeting of the St George's Clinical Ethics Committee took place, chaired by Professor Eastman, to address the question of whether the diagnosis should be disclosed to the claimant's sister.

After discussion of the issues, a vote was taken. The minutes record that the majority supported XX's right to confidentiality and would not disclose the information.

The claimant's sister did not therefore learn of XX's diagnosis until after her baby was born. She has since been tested and has been found not to have the genetic mutation.

The claimant did not undergo genetic testing herself until 2013. When, she sadly tested positive.

Medical evidence confirms that she is likely to develop symptoms within five to ten years.[280] She [the claimant] is greatly distressed by that prospect and is deeply concerned for her child's future, particularly as she is a single parent. She has been engaged in contested family proceedings in which her medical prognosis has featured. That is a further source of distress to her. Given the

---

[280]   Ibid.

agreement the parties have reached as to quantification of the damages, it is unnecessary to comment on the nature and aetiology of the claimant's psychiatric symptoms in any detail. It is worth noting though that the claimant places emphasis on her constant worry that her child may have inherited the HD gene and her concern for her child when the claimant develops symptoms. I stress that it is not the case that the claimant did not want her child. Rather, she feels that it was unfair for her to bring a child into the world in the tragic circumstances I have set out. She complains that she was deprived of the opportunity to make that choice.

The legal basis of claims by the claimant
The claim was brought both in negligence and under the Human Rights Act 1998[281] for breach of Article 8 of the ECHR.[282]

However, in giving judgment in the Court of Appeal in relation to the strike-out application, Irwin LJ said [65]: 'I am unconvinced that the Convention adds anything to the common law or can provide a basis for action if the common law does not do so.'

The claimant was not precluded from maintaining her Article 8 claim at trial and she did so. However, this aspect of the case was not developed in any great detail. In her closing submissions for the claimant, Ms. Gumbel QC (attorney for the claimant), confirmed that the claim under the Human Rights Act ran parallel to the common law claim. In addition to contending that it founded a freestanding claim, Ms. Gumbel argued that the Article 8 obligation was relevant to the issue of whether a duty of care existed.

For practical purposes and given the nature of the agreement as to damages, the claim, however framed, requires the claimant to prove that:

(i)   the defendants ought to have given her sufficient information to put her on notice of the risk that she had inherited the Huntington's gene at a time when it was open to her to terminate her pregnancy;

(ii)   properly advised of that risk, she would have undergone genetic testing and discovered that she had the Huntington's gene in time to terminate her pregnancy; and

(iii)   she would then have had a termination.

Ms. Gumbel confirmed that the court was not asked to consider any alternative basis for an award of damages if the claimant did not establish those essential elements. The issues that arise then are a mix of legal and factual issues. The essential issues the court must determine were summarised as follows:

---

[281]   Op cit (n 274).
[282]   Op cit (n 273).

(i)   Did the defendants (or any of them) owe a relevant duty of care to the claimant?
(ii)   If so, what was the nature and scope of that duty?
(iii)   Did any duty that existed require that the claimant be given sufficient information for her to be aware of the genetic risk at a stage that would have allowed for her to undergo genetic testing and termination of her pregnancy?
(iv)   If a duty of care was owed, did the defendants (or any of them) breach that duty by failing to give her information about the risk that she might have a genetic condition while it was open to her to opt to terminate her pregnancy?
(v)   If there was a breach of duty, did it cause the continuation of the claimant's pregnancy when it would otherwise have been terminated? (This involves consideration of whether the claimant would in fact have had the opportunity to undergo genetic testing and a termination in time but for the breach, and whether she would have chosen to do so.)

The claimant's alternatives as to the existence of a duty of care
As initially pleaded, the claimant's case as to the existence of a duty of care was:

> At all relevant times, the First, Second and Third Defendants knew that the Claimant was the daughter of XX and that a diagnosis of Huntington's Disease would have a direct effect on the health, welfare, and life of the claimant. They each owed to the Claimant a duty of care in respect of any medical information that was relevant to her own welfare. That appeared to encapsulate a broad duty arising through the defendants' possession of information relevant to the claimant's welfare and the knowledge that the information would impact upon her.

At trial, Ms. Gumbel identified three potential routes to a duty of care:

(i)   The claimant was a patient of the defendants (or at least the second defendant) so that the case falls within the scope of the established duty of care arising out of the doctor-patient relationship.
(ii)   The forensic psychiatry unit of the second defendant assumed responsibility for the welfare of the claimant, both in the context of providing family therapy and through her long-standing relationship with the team caring for XX and her involvement in his rehabilitation programme.
(iii)   If neither of the above routes are found to apply, by the application of established principles to the facts of this case by incremental extension

(as explained by *Caparo v Dickman*[283] and *Robinson v Chief Constable of West Yorkshire.*[284]

The defendants' position

The defendants are jointly represented and have stood together in their defence of this claim. The claimant's case was opened on the basis that the three defendants were to be treated as a multidisciplinary team with shared responsibility for the clinicians, therapists and social workers who made up that team.

It is established that the duty of care to an NHS patient is owed by the hospital trust; that such duty must be considered in the round and that it applies to medical and non-medical staff alike (see *Darnley*).[285] The defendants do not invite me to seek to apportion between them if I find that liability is established. However, that does not avoid the need to look at where any duty lay and to consider the scope of any duties owed by the various teams and individuals involved.

For the defendants, Mr. Havers QC (attorney for the defendants), argued that this is plainly a novel claim. The defendants deny that the claimant was their patient, rather she was a third party to the relationship between each of them and 'XX'. Even if she was to be treated as in a relationship equivalent to that of a patient so far as family therapy was concerned, the scope of any duty arising from that could not encompass this case. The defendants also deny that there was any assumption of responsibility. Put simply, the defendants say that this is a novel case involving negligent omission in respect of which no duty has ever previously been recognized by the courts.

Mr. Havers contends that the court should not impose a duty of care in this case. Even if the claimant can establish the necessary proximity and foreseeability of harm (which is not conceded), it would not be fair, just, and reasonable to impose a legal duty in the circumstances of this case. Mr. Havers advances policy reasons for not imposing a duty to the claimant, placing particular reliance on the duty of confidence owed by the defendants to 'XX' and the conflict between that duty and the duty the claimant contends for.

The court's approach to the existence and scope of any duty of care

I must consider (the court) whether a duty was owed to the claimant and, if so, the scope of the duty within the factual matrix of this case. As Lord Woolf MR said in *Kent v Griffiths* 2001: 'In these difficult cases it is necessary to examine

---

[283] *Caparo Industries PLC v Dickman* [1990] ALL ER 568.
[284] *Robinson v Chief Constable of West Yorkshire Police* [2018] UKSC 4.
[285] *Darnley v Croydon Health Services NHS Trust* [2018] UKSC 50.

the facts in detail. ... Before you can apply one case by analogy to another you need to be clear as to the facts to which you are applying it.'[286]

While it may be reasonable to consider the possible wider implications of recognising a duty not previously recognised by the courts, it would not be appropriate for me to attempt to define the limits of any duty of care owed by doctors to those who are not their patients. That is not the way in which the incremental development of the common law operates. I am required only to decide whether, on the facts of this case, a relevant duty was owed to the claimant. If so, I must resolve whether there was an actionable breach of that duty.

Ethical considerations: the duty of confidentiality and professional guidance
It is very well-established, and not in dispute, that medical professionals generally owe a duty to maintain confidence in information about a patient's health and treatment. There is a strong public interest in respecting medical confidentiality which extends beyond the privacy of the individual patient. In *Z v Finland*,[287] the European Court of Human Rights (ECtHR) stated [95]:

> Respecting confidentiality of health data is a vital principle in the legal systems of all the Contracting Parties to the Convention. It is crucial not only to respect the sense of privacy of a patient but also to preserve his or her confidence in the medical profession and in the health services in general. Without such protection, those in need of medical assistance may be deterred from revealing such information of a personal and intimate nature as may be necessary in order to receive appropriate treatment and, even, from seeking such assistance, thereby endangering their own health and, in the case of transmissible diseases, that of the community.

It is equally well-established that the duty of confidence is not absolute. In certain circumstances, the public interest in disclosure may outweigh the public interest in maintaining confidentiality. (See, for example *W v Egdell* 1990 1 Ch. 359,[288] where the Court of Appeal held that the public interest in protecting others against possible violence outweighed the public interest in maintaining confidentiality so as to justify a psychiatrist instructed by a patient subject to a restricted hospital order disclosing his report to the patient's responsible clinician although doing so was contrary to the patient's interests.)

Recognising the competing public interests that may arise in relation to medical confidentiality, the General Medical Council (GMC)[289] have issued guidance for doctors. The GMC guidelines have evolved over time, taking account of developments in medicine and in the law. They are likely to con-

---

[286] *Kent v Griffiths* [2001] QB 36 [37].
[287] *Z v Finland* [1998] 25 EHRR 371.
[288] *W v* Edgell [1990] 1 ALL ER 835.
[289] UK General Medical Council.

tinue to do so. The most recent guidelines ('Confidentiality; good practice in handling patient information')[290] were issued in 2017. They note that the law governing the use and disclosure of personal information is complex but give practical advice on applying ethical and legal principles in practice. It is notable that the 2017 guidelines contain specific guidance about the disclosure of genetic and other shared information, which had not featured in earlier guidelines.

The timeframe with which this case is concerned means that it is necessary to look to two earlier versions of the relevant guidance. That published in 2004 ('Confidentiality: Protecting and Providing Information')[291] was in force until 11 October 2009. New guidelines ('Confidentiality')[292] came into effect on 12 October 2009.

All the guidelines start by acknowledging that patients have a right to expect that information about them will be held in confidence by their doctors but recognise that there will be circumstances where there is a public interest in disclosing information even though the patient does not consent.

The 2004 guidelines stated [22]:

> Personal information may be disclosed in the public interest, without the patient's consent, and in exceptional cases where patients have withheld consent, where the benefit to an individual or to society of the disclosure outweigh the public and the patient's interest in keeping the information confidential. In all cases where you consider disclosing information without consent from the patient, you must weigh the possible harm (both to the patient, and the overall trust between doctors and patients) against the benefits which are likely to arise from the release of information.[293]

Further advice about disclosure where a patient has withheld consent was to be found at [24]: 'In cases where there is a serious risk to the patient or others, disclosures may be justified even where patients have been asked to agree to a disclosure but have withheld consent (for further advice see paragraph 27).'[294]

---

[290] GMC (UK), Confidentiality; good practice in handling patient information, GMC, London, 2017. Available from: www.gmc-uk.org/ethical-guidance/ethical -guidance-for-doctors/confidentiality (accessed February 6, 2023).

[291] GMC (UK), Confidentiality: Protecting and Providing Information, GMC: London; 2004. Available from: www.gmc-uk.org/-/media/documents/confidentiality -2004---2009-55664503.pdf?la=en (accessed February 6, 2023).

[292] GMC (UK), Confidentiality. GMC: 2009. Available from: www.gmc-uk.org/-/ media/documents/confidentiality-2009---2017-74802220.pdf?la=en (accessed February 6, 2023).

[293] Op cit (n 291).

[294] Ibid.

That advice read [27]:

> Disclosure of personal information without consent may be justified in the public
> interest where failure to do so may expose the patient or others to risk of death
> or serious harm. Where the patient or others are exposed to a risk so serious that
> it outweighs the patient's privacy interest, you should seek consent to disclosure
> where practicable ... If you seek consent and the patient withholds it you should
> consider the reasons for this, if any are provided by the patient. If you remain of the
> view that disclosure is necessary to protect a third party from death or serious harm,
> you should disclose information promptly to an appropriate person or authority.
> Such situations arise, for example, where a disclosure may assist in the prevention,
> detection, or prosecution of a serious crime, especially crimes against the person,
> such as abuse of children.[295]

The 2009 guidelines recognised the competing public interests, before stating
[37]:

> Personal information may, therefore, be disclosed in the public interest, without
> patients' consent, and in exceptional cases where patients have withheld consent,
> if the benefits to an individual or society outweigh both the public and the patient's
> interest in keeping the information confidential. You must weigh the harms that are
> likely to arise from non-disclosure of information against the possible harm, both
> to the patient and to the overall trust between doctors and patients, arising from the
> release of that information.[296]

Further guidance about disclosures to protect others was set out at [53]:

> Disclosure of personal information about a patient without consent may be justified
> in the public interest if failure to disclose may expose others to a risk of death or
> serious harm. You should still seek the patient's consent to disclosure if practicable
> and consider any reasons given for refusal.[297]

[In addition] the disciplines with which this case is particularly concerned,
genetics and psychiatry, are areas in which specific guidance has been given
by relevant professional bodies. In the field of genetics, the Royal College
of Physicians, the Royal College of Pathologists, and the British Society
for Human Genetics Guidance published a report of the Joint Committee on
Medical Genetics entitled 'Consent and confidentiality in genetic practice:

---

[295] Ibid.
[296] Op cit (n 292).
[297] Ibid.

Guidance of genetic testing and sharing genetic information'[298] in 2006. That guidance stated [2.5.3]:

> The Human Genetics Commission, the Nuffield Council on Bioethics and the GMC have all expressed the view that the rule of confidentiality is not absolute. In special circumstances it may be justified to break confidence where the aversion of harm by the disclosure substantially outweighs the patient's claim to confidentiality. Examples may include a person declining to inform relatives of a genetic risk of which they may be unaware, or to allow the release of information to allow specific genetic testing to be undertaken. Before disclosure is made in such circumstances, an attempt should have been made to persuade the patient in question to consent to disclosure; the benefit to those at risk should be so considerable as to outweigh any distress which disclosure would cause the patient; and the information should be anonymized and restricted as far as possible to that which is strictly necessary for the communication of risk. We recommend that before disclosure is made when consent has been withheld, the situation should be discussed with experienced professional colleagues and the reason for disclosure documented. Current GMC guidance states that the individual should generally be informed before disclosing the information.[299]

The Royal College of Psychiatrists Guidelines 2006 ('Good Psychiatric Practice: Confidentiality and information sharing')[300] provided guidance to psychiatrists faced with instances where they were required to make a judgment on whether or not the public interest served by disclosure outweighed the duty of confidence. The guidance made it clear that each case must be considered on its merits and continued:

> Decisions to disclose patient-identifiable information apart from the few statutory exceptions ... are matters of judgement – judgement that may be finely balanced. Such balancing would need to take into account the various legal responsibilities at stake, including the duty of confidentiality to the patient and the public interest in the health service maintaining confidentiality. Consideration will need to be given to whether the harm that could result from disclosure (e.g., the possible harm to the relationship of trust or the likelihood of non-concordance with a programme of healthcare intervention in the future) is likely to be outweighed by the possible ben-

---

[298] Royal College of Pathologists, Consent and confidentiality in clinical genetic practice: Guidance on genetic testing and sharing genetic information: A report of the Joint Committee on Medical Genetics. 2nd edition September 2011. Available from: www.rcpath.org/static/f5c7ddc7-7efd-4987-b6b41ee16577f770/consent-and -confidentiality.pdf (accessed February 6, 2023).

[299] Ibid.

[300] Royal College of Psychiatrists, Good Psychiatric Practice Confidentiality and information sharing. Third edition. College Report CR209 November 2017. Available from: www.rcpsych.ac.uk/docs/default-source/improving-care/better-mh -policy/college-reports/college-report-cr209.pdf?sfvrsn=23858153_2 (accessed February 6, 2023).

efits. The potential benefits would need to be soundly grounded in the expectation that disclosure would have the desired effect (e.g., a significant reduction in the risk of harm).[301]

The guidance advises doctors to maintain documentary evidence of the balancing exercise undertaken and, if necessary, to seek legal or other specialist advice. It then continues: 'The doctor must be certain that the disclosure is in the public interest; if he or she cannot be certain of this then the patient's confidentiality must be preserved.'[302]

Events after the claimant learnt of XX's (her fathers) diagnosis
It was decided that the case should be discussed at a Clinical Ethics Committee meeting on 7 October 2010.

The [Clinical ethics] committee decided by a majority vote not to disclose the information to the claimant's sister.

The minutes of the meeting contain details of the discussion that took place about the history, nature of HD and the family dynamics. The family dynamics were thought to be unusual. It was recorded that: 'It is possible that the non-disclosure of the positive test result is either a benevolent act to protect the family or as an act of aggression.'

Before the vote was taken the [Ethics] committee discussed the competing considerations, including:

i)   The harm and benefit in revealing the information to the claimant's sister.
ii)   The pregnancy being grounds for disclosure but that disclosure during pregnancy leads to distress and pressure to make a decision.
iii)   The potential for the claimant's sister to find out inadvertently; the fact that other family members already knew and the fact that XX said he would disclose when the time was right.
iv)   The impact of secrecy on family relationships and the suggestion that the team were colluding in 'secrets and lies.'
v)   The clash between confidentiality and the family therapy aspect.
vi)   Whether Huntington's disease played a part in the offence and whether that provided a reason for disclosure either on the basis of protecting the daughters from a risk of violence and/or reproductive choice.
vii)   Some members of the team felt strongly that XX had a right to confidentiality whereas others thought that the rights of the daughters overrode the patient's right to confidentiality.

---

[301]   Ibid.
[302]   Ibid.

viii)   This was an unusual case but was it exceptional enough 'for there to be deviation from the protocol and for confidentiality to be broken'?

Regarding the policy considerations in this case, the court declared as follows
It is difficult to do justice to the considered views expressed by the experts within a short summary. However, I find the following key points emerge from the genetic evidence as a whole:

i)   Medical confidentiality is a profoundly important principle. Routinely overriding patients' confidentiality would damage the relationship of trust between doctor and patient and may discourage people from coming forward to seek testing and treatment.

ii)   A broad or indiscriminate duty to disclose genetic information to family members against a patient's wishes would cause geneticists very great concern.

iii)   Direct contact of at-risk family members is not a routine part of genetic practice in the UK.

iv)   Clinical geneticists do not consider that they have a professional obligation to warn all relatives of genetic risks. It would be wholly impractical and inappropriate to impose a duty on doctors to trace and inform all relatives about the potential risk to their health.

v)   Geneticists routinely consider the position of relatives and work with patients to encourage the communication of genetic information to family members.

vi)   It is very rare for geneticists to encounter a situation where they need to consider a direct breach of a patient's confidentiality. Even those with a special interest in ethics to whom the most difficult cases are referred, such as Professor Lucassen, will see such cases only very occasionally.

vii)   Usually, a patient's initial refusal to disclose genetic information can be worked around through negotiation. Even if the patient continues to withhold consent, it is often possible to alert relatives without a direct breach of confidence.

viii)   The professional guidelines permit disclosure of genetic information if that would avoid a serious harm to another person.

ix)   None of the professional guidance mandates a particular decision but the relevant guidelines require that clinicians should undertake a proper balancing exercise between the interests of the patient and the at-risk relative.

x)   The decision whether to disclose to the claimant in this case was a difficult and complex one, requiring the exercise of professional judgment.

Furthermore, all the genetic experts agreed that if the claimant had been known to them, they would have tried to alert her to a possible familial risk. Professor Lucassen and Professor Newman suggested that this could have been done without a direct breach of XX's confidentiality. However, when this was explored in cross-examination, they were unable to explain how that could have been done in practice. Professor Lucassen said this:

> I don't know what would have been the ideal setup ... I just envisage there would have been a possible way to do this. It is difficult for me to say quite how it would have happened in the forensic psychiatry setting and that is I think where this is ... a really difficult situation because the clinical geneticists didn't see XX, they only advised about what to do in this situation ... I agree that would have been difficult. But I think it would have been possible.

Professor Newman suggested in cross-examination that Dr Olumoroti could have invited a geneticist to attend Springfield to have a conversation with the claimant.[...] He said he had been thinking through different scenarios since writing his report and while listening to the evidence at trial. He said:

> I absolutely agree that this is extremely complex, challenging counselling. But it is what myself and my colleagues throughout the country train to do, to find ways to express information in a way that is understandable to patients about their inherited risks and about the conditions that may affect them, and then in particular circumstances, very particular circumstances, find ways of sharing information where there is the minimal amount of disclosure of information that others have expressed that they do not want disclosed.

The psychiatric evidence
Again, there was much about which Dr Adshead and Dr McInerny agreed. The following undisputed points emerge from their evidence:

i) The fact that a patient is detained under a court order does not alter the starting point that confidential information should not be disclosed without. consent.

ii) The duty of confidence is not absolute and forensic psychiatrists may be required to disclose confidential information to effect safe clinical care and/or in the public interest.

iii) Forensic psychiatrists face particular ethical challenges in balancing the interests of their patients against the interests of third persons and the public interest.

iv) It is recognised in forensic psychiatry that professional duties are owed to multiple third parties, including victims, potential victims, relatives, the Ministry of Justice, Parole Board, and other organisations within the criminal justice system.

v) The professional guidance to psychiatrists does not mandate disclosure where there is a risk of harm to a third party but does require a balancing exercise to be performed.

vi) A forensic psychiatrist would not have been expected to be aware of the specific guidelines relating to disclosure of genetic information but would have been expected to seek and follow appropriate advice.

vii) This case presented an unusual situation for a forensic psychiatrist and involved a difficult and complex decision.

The psychiatric experts disagreed about whether Dr Olumoroti and the team at Springfield owed a duty of care to the claimant and, if so, whether that duty was breached. Dr McInerny did not think the defendants owed a legal duty to the claimant but in any event thought that Dr Olumoroti and his team had fulfilled their obligations, having regard to the relevant guidelines on confidentiality. Dr Adshead considered that the circumstances of this case mandated telling the claimant about HD. In effect, her evidence was that the balancing exercise could lead to only one outcome.

The court's decision
For the reasons set out in this judgment, I have concluded that the second defendant owed the claimant a duty of care to balance her interest in being informed of her genetic risk against her father's interest and the public interest in maintaining confidentiality. The scope of that duty extended to conducting a balancing exercise and to acting in accordance with its outcome.

This duty arose on the particular facts of this case, which involved a close proximal relationship between the claimant and the second defendant and the foresight that she might suffer harm if not informed.

The duty I have found is not a free-standing duty of disclosure nor is it a broad duty of care owed to all relatives in respect of genetic information. The legal duty recognises and runs parallel to an established professional duty and is to be exercised following the guidance of the GMC and other specialist medical bodies.

I have not found sufficient proximity between the first defendant and the claimant such as to justify the imposition of a duty of care. Further, no sufficient evidential basis arose to maintain a claim against the third defendant.

Although aspects of the process of decision-making and the record-keeping may be subject to criticism, I have not found any actionable breach of duty on the part of the second defendant. The decision not to disclose was supported by a responsible body of medical opinion and was a matter of judgment open to the second defendant after balancing the competing interests.

Having analysed all the available evidence, I have found that the claimant has not established, on a balance of probabilities that she would have been tested and undergone a termination had the risk been disclosed to her during her pregnancy.

In all the circumstances, the common law claim fails on breach of duty and causation.

Further, the alternative human rights claim cannot be maintained on the findings I have made. It follows that, although I have the greatest of sympathy for the tragic circumstances in which the claimant finds herself, this claim must be dismissed.

Comparative analysis of the case

The claimant in this case sued her doctors or healthcare providers for negligence for not having informed her of her father's illness or diagnosis of Huntington's Disease on time, to enable her to terminate her pregnancy and avoid the possibility of transmitting the disease to her own offspring.

In other to prove a claim of negligence, a claimant generally has to prove four things:

1. That the patient was owed a duty of care by the healthcare provider
2. That the healthcare provider breached that duty of care
3. That the breach of the duty of care caused the claimant harm
4. That it was reasonably foreseeable that if the claimant was not provided with the care that was needed (in this case information regarding her father's diagnosis of HD), then she would suffer harm, either now, or in the future.[303]

The defendants in this case (the healthcare providers) through their employer the NHS Trusts that employed the doctors denied her claims. They argued that there was no duty of care between themselves and the claimant since she was not their direct patient. In this case the direct patient was the claimant's father 'XX', who was admitted for mental health problems, and was later was found to be suffering from HD.

The defendants also argued that even if there was a duty of care, they had discharged that duty by informing the claimant about her father's diagnosis, even if this was delayed due to the prevailing circumstances surrounding her family situation. Especially regarding the claimant's father's insistence that his children should not be informed about his diagnosis of HD.

The defendants also argued that even if the claimant was informed of the diagnosis on time, there was no proof that she would have chosen to terminate

---

[303] S.C. Chima, 'Chapter 7: Clinical Negligence and Medical Error' in *A Primer on Medical Bioethics and Human Rights for African Scholars* (Durban: Chimason Educational Books, 2011) 132–50.

her pregnancy. Also, that the period for termination of pregnancy was bound by law, which allowed termination only up to 24 weeks of pregnancy in accordance with English law.

The court in arriving at a decision in this case took great cognizance of the ethical guidelines provided by professional organizations for physicians such as the GMC[304] as well as the Joint Committee on Medical Genetics of the Royal College of Physicians, the Royal College of Pathologists, and the British Society for Human Genetics.[305]

The court also considered the input of the multidisciplinary committee of medical experts as established by the Bolam principle which states that: 'A doctor must act in accordance with a practice which is accepted as proper by a responsible body of men schooled in the particular art' or based on a reasonable doctor standard as established in *Bolam v Friern HMC*[306] and later reaffirmed in *Hills v Potter*[307] where the court held that 'in every case the Court must be satisfied that the standard contended for accords with that upheld by a substantial body of medical opinion ...'[308]

Having considered all the evidence and expert opinions and the history of the case, including the fact that the claimant's father 'XX', had not only delayed in submitting himself for diagnosis; but had also refused to give the doctors permission to breach patient confidentiality and inform his daughters (the claimant and her sister). The court also considered that by the time the claimant inadvertently learnt of her diagnosis it was already too late for her to be eligible for termination of her pregnancy (since termination of pregnancy is only allowed up to 24 weeks of gestation, in accordance with English law).

The court therefore concluded that while one of the defendants (the second defendant) had a duty of care to the claimant, despite the fact that she was not a direct patient in the case. However, the claimant's participation in family therapy because of her father's diagnosis with HD, and the trauma occurring in her family due to her father's murder of her mother, and his subsequent incarceration for that crime, established that one of the NHS Trust involved did owe the clamant a duty of care.

Nevertheless, the court found that there was no breach of duty in this case since she was properly counselled and advised as much as possible, considering her family situation and the refusal of her father to allow the doctors to

---

[304] UK GMC (nn 290, 291 and 292).

[305] Op cit (nn 298 and 299).

[306] *Bolam v Friern Hospital Management Committee* [1957] 1 WLR 582; Chima (n 304).

[307] *Hills v Potter* [1984] 1 WLR 641, QBD.

[308] Ibid.

breach confidentiality and inform her of the diagnosis or suspected diagnosis of HD on time.

Furthermore, there was no evidence, that even if she had been informed, she would have terminated the pregnancy, considering that even after the father's diagnosis was confirmed, and the claimant became aware of it, she was reluctant to inform her own sister regarding the diagnosis during her sister's own pregnancy. In view of these findings, the court dismissed the claim of negligence, against the responsible physicians, and their employers, the NHS Trusts.

Considering the facts of this case in the context of South African law

In the context of South African law, the critical difference in this case would be the time and opportunity the claimant had to be able to terminate her pregnancy to avoid risk of transmission of a hereditary fatal disease such as HD to her offspring. While the time limit for termination of pregnancy in such cases under UK law is 24 weeks, in the case of South Africa, there is no time limit for termination of pregnancy before delivery in cases of severe mental or physical abnormality in the foetus. Accordingly, the Choice on Termination of Pregnancy Act 1996[309] states:

(1) A pregnancy may be terminated:
   (a) upon request of a woman during the first 12 weeks of the gestation period of her pregnancy.
   (b) from the 13th up to and including the 20th week of the gestation period if a medical practitioner, after consultation with the pregnant woman, is of the opinion that:

   (i)   the continued pregnancy would pose a risk of injury to the woman's physical or mental health; or
   (ii) there exists a substantial risk that the fetus would suffer from a severe physical or mental abnormality; or
   (iii) the pregnancy resulted from rape or incest; or
   (iv) the continued pregnancy would significantly affect the social or economic circumstances of the woman.

   (c) after the 20th week of the gestation period if a medical practitioner, after consultation with another medical practitioner or a registered midwife

---

[309] Choice on Termination of Pregnancy Act 92 of 1996.

who has completed the prescribed training, is of the opinion that the continued pregnancy

(i)   would endanger the woman's life; or
(ii) **would result in a severe malformation of the fetus; or**
(iii) **would pose a risk of injury to the fetus.**

Therefore, in terms of South African law, there would have been no hindrance to the claimant's choice regarding termination of the pregnancy at any time based on the diagnosis of HD in her father and herself, and therefore eliminate the 50 percent chance of severe abnormality in her baby or the chance of her baby inheriting HD.

Furthermore, the Choice Act[310] does specify what types of abnormality may be eligible for termination or the level of severity required.

The only other issue that may come into play in the context of South Africa would be the issue of different cultural belief systems. For example, if this patient were a Black South African patient, then other factors including ancestral belief systems may come into play. For example, while average life span of 30–50 years due to inheritance of the HD may be considered unfortunate in other cultures or in a Western-European context. A Black African patient who believes in ancestors and predestination would be quite accepting of such a lifespan and ascribe the 'shortened' life span due to HD to probably be the wish of the ancestors. In such a case, the issue of termination of pregnancy may not even be considered at all, because this, it would be believed, this was the predestined lifespan as conferred on the offspring or child by his or her ancestors, consistent with some African cultural belief systems.[311,312,313]

---

[310] Ibid.

[311] F. Akpa-Inyang and S.C. Chima, South African traditional values and beliefs regarding informed consent and limitations of the principle of respect for autonomy in African communities: a cross-cultural qualitative study. *BMC Med E*thics 2021, *22*(1), 111. https://doi.org/10.1186/s12910-021-00678-4.

[312] S.C. Chima, Evaluating knowledge, practice, and barriers to informed consent among professional and staff nurses in South Africa: An empirical study. *Canadian Journal of Bioethics-Revue Canadienne de Bioéthique*, 2022. DOI: https://doi.org/10.7202/1089785ar.

[313] S. C. Chima and F. Mamdoo, Ethical and legal dilemmas around termination of pregnancy for severe fetal anomalies: A review of two African neonates presenting with ventriculomegaly and holoprosencephaly. *Niger J Clin Pract* 2015, 18: S31-38. DOI: 10.4103/1119-3077.170820.

Summarizing when doctors should or should not breach confidentiality

When doctors should not breach confidentiality – except with patients consent:

1. Casual breaches: for fun or amusement
2. Simply to satisfy another person's curiosity
3. To prevent minor crime
4. To prevent minor harm to someone else
5. In sexually transmitted disease (STD) clinics, no identifying information should be revealed to a third party, except based on a court order, public health, or substantial harm to other known person
6. A doctor should not write a report, or fill out a form, disclosing confidential information except with consent (preferably written consent) of the individual affected

When doctors must breach confidentiality (to specific authorities only):

1. Notifiable diseases
2. Births
3. Deaths
4. To police on request, preferably with a court order
5. Based on a search warrant signed by a judge

When doctors have discretion (regarding whether or not to breach patient confidentiality):

1. When sharing information with other members of the healthcare team for patient care in the interests of the patient
2. In some jurisdiction in accordance with driving laws e.g., legally blind, etc.
3. When a third party is at significant risk of harm e.g., spouse of HIV positive patient (especially if infected spouse refuses to reveal information to their partner or spouse), after due counselling regarding breach.
4. The detection and prevention of serious crime.[314]

---

[314] Chima (nn 107 and 218).

10. Patient privacy and health information confidentiality in the United States of America

Stacey A. Tovino

GENERAL INTRODUCTION

In the United States, patient privacy, health information confidentiality, and data security are governed by a patchwork of federal and state statutes, regulations, judicial opinions, and constitutional provisions. The most well-known federal authorities include the Health Insurance Portability and Accountability Act of 1996 (HIPAA) Privacy, Security, and Breach Notification Rules (Rules), which establish minimum requirements to which certain health industry participants must adhere.[1] Although the HIPAA Rules preempt contrary state laws, states are permitted to enact more stringent laws.[2] State laws in this area vary widely. Some states narrowly regulate the use, disclosure, and protection of health information by traditional health industry participants, such as licensed health care professionals and licensed health care institutions.[3] Other states regulate all persons who comes into possession of health information, regardless of whether they are licensed health care professionals or licensed

---

[1]   *See* Health Insurance Portability and Accountability Act (HIPAA) of 1996, Pub. L. No. 104-191, 110 Stat. 1936 (codified as amended in scattered titles of the U.S Code), *amended by* Health Information Technology for Economic and Clinical Health Act (HITECH), Pub. L. No. 111-5, 123 Stat. 226 (2009) (codified as amended in scattered sections of 42 U.S.C.) [hereinafter HIPAA]. HHS's privacy regulations, which implement section 264(c) of HIPAA, are codified at 45 C.F.R. §§ 164.500–.534 [hereinafter HIPAA Privacy Rule]. The HIPAA Security Rule, which implements section 262(a) of HIPAA (42 U.S.C. § 1320d–2(d)(1)), are codified at 45 C.F.R. §§ 164.302–.318 [hereinafter HIPAA Security Rule]. The HIPAA Breach Notification Rule which implements section 13402 of HITECH (42 U.S.C. § 17932), are codified at 45 C.F.R. §§ 164.400–.414 [hereinafter HIPAA Breach Notification Rule].
[2]   Preemption of State Law: General Rule and Exceptions, 45 C.F.R. § 160.203.
[3]   *See, e.g.*, Oklahoma Hospital Standards, Okla. Admin. Code § 310:667-19-3.

health care institutions.[4] Still other states regulate all persons who conduct business in the state if such persons control or process certain identifiable consumer data, including health data, and if certain data control or data processing thresholds are satisfied.[5] Although this report focuses on the HIPAA Privacy, Security, and Breach Notification Rules—long considered national standards for the US health care industry—other foundational and noteworthy legal authorities are discussed as appropriate.

THE ETHICAL BASIS OF CONFIDENTIALITY

In the United States, patient privacy and health information confidentiality are grounded in basic principles of biomedical ethics, including respect for autonomy.[6] Respect for autonomy is an American norm that requires respect for the decisions—including decisions relating to the use and disclosure of identifiable health information—of adults who have decision-making capacity. Conditions pre-requisite to autonomous behavior include truthful disclosure of material information relevant to patient decision making as well as patient understanding and voluntary choice.[7] In the context of patient privacy and health information confidentiality, an individual's autonomy is considered to be respected when: (1) the individual is informed in advance of a use or disclosure of the individual's identifiable health data;[8] (2) material information regarding such use or disclosure is provided to the individual in plain language that would be understandable by the average person;[9] (3) the individual has the opportunity to authorize or refuse to authorize the information use or disclosure;[10] and (4) the data custodian does not condition the individual's treatment, enrollment in a health plan, or eligibility for health benefits on the individual's authorization.[11] Although important, ethical duties relating to patient privacy

---

[4]   *See, e.g.,* Texas Medical Records Privacy Act, Tex. Health & Safety Code § 181.001(b)(2)(B).

[5]   *See, e.g.,* Virginia Consumer Data Privacy Act, Va. Code §§ 59.1-571–572.

[6]   *See, e.g.,* Tom L. Beauchamp and James F. Childress, Principles of Biomedical Ethics, 8th ed., Part II (Respect for Autonomy) (Oxford University Press 2019).

[7]   *See, e.g.,* American Medical Association, Code of Medical Ethics, Op. 3.2.1 ("In general, patients are entitled to decide whether and to whom their personal health information is disclosed.").

[8]   *See, e.g.,* Notice of Privacy Practices for Protected Health Information, 45 C.F.R. § 164.520.

[9]   *See, e.g.,* Plain Language Requirement, 45 C.F.R. § 164.508(c)(3).

[10]   *See, e.g.,* Uses and Disclosures for Which an Authorization Is Required, 45 C.F.R. § 164.508.

[11]   *See, e.g.,* Prohibition on Conditioning of Authorizations, 45 C.F.R. § 164.508(b)(4).

and health information confidentiality are not absolute and are balanced against the need to use and disclose patient identifiable information for treatment, payment, and health care operations activities as well as a variety of public health, safety, and welfare measures.[12]

KEY SOURCES OF THE DUTY OF CONFIDENTIALITY

In the United States, the duty of confidentiality is sourced in a variety of constitutional, common law, statutory, and regulatory provisions. For example, the Fourteenth Amendment to the United States Constitution, passed by Congress in 1866 and ratified in 1868, provides that, "No State shall make or enforce any law which shall abridge any person of life, liberty, or property, without due process of law; nor deny any person within its jurisdiction the equal protection of the laws."[13] Although the original intent of the Fourteenth Amendment was to grant citizenship rights to African Americans, interests now protected include privacy in decision making, including health-related decision making,[14] as well as a limited interest in the non-disclosure of information.

The limited interest in the non-disclosure of information was addressed by the Supreme Court of the United States in 1977 in *Whalen v. Roe*. In *Whalen*, the Court reviewed a New York statute that required physicians to disclose to the state a copy of every prescription written for drugs with a high potential of abuse.[15] The statute also established security measures for the prescription information once it had been received by the state. Affected patients, physicians, and physician associations argued that the statute violated their constitutionally protected rights of privacy. The district court agreed with the plaintiffs' argument, reasoning that, "[T]he doctor-patient relationship intrudes on one of the zones of privacy accorded constitutional protection' and the patient-identification provisions of the [New York] statute invaded this zone with 'a necessarily broad sweep.'"[16] The Supreme Court came to a different conclusion, placing more weight on the state's interest in gathering the data. However, the Supreme Court did recognize in dicta "the threat to privacy implicit in the accumulation of vast amounts of personal information in

---

[12] *See, e.g.*, American Medical Association, Principles of Medical Ethics, Principle 4 (2016) ("A physician ... shall safeguard patient confidences and privacy *within the constraints of the law*.") (emphasis added).

[13] U.S. Const., amend. XIV.

[14] *See, e.g., Roe v. Wade*, 410 U.S. 113, 153 (1973).

[15] *Whalen v. Roe*, 429 U.S. 589 (1977).

[16] *Id.* at 596.

computerized data banks or other massive government files."[17] The Supreme Court also stated that, "[I]n some circumstances," the duty to avoid unwarranted disclosures of information "arguably had its roots in the Constitution."[18] Some, but not all, state constitutions expressly recognize a right to privacy and some of these states interpret this right to include a limited interest in the non-disclosure of information as well.[19]

In the United States, the duty of confidentiality is also sourced in legal treatises and the common law. In 1890, Samuel Warren and Louis Brandeis published their famous essay ("The Right to Privacy") in the *Harvard Law Review*.[20] In their essay, Warren and Brandeis argued that individuals have a general "right to be let alone," or a "right to privacy," which included an individual's right to determine "to what extent his thoughts, sentiments, and emotions shall be communicated to others."[21] Inspired by Warren and Brandeis' scholarship, a Michigan court declared the very next year that a married woman had a right to privacy during childbirth. This right included the right of the woman: (1) to be informed by her doctor that he proposed to be accompanied by an un-married, un-professional man during her labour and delivery; and (2) to refuse to authorize the second man's involvement in her labour and delivery.[22] The Michigan court ruled in favour of the woman when the doctor did not provide the woman and her husband with accurate information regarding the second man's non-married and non-professional status.

Although the concept of patient privacy, not health information confidentiality, received most of the attention in the late nineteenth and early twentieth century, a Nebraska court upheld a plaintiff's common law breach of confidentiality claim in the medical context in 1920. The Nebraska court stated:

> The relationship of physician and patient is necessarily a highly confidential one. It is often necessary for the patient to give information about himself which would be most embarrassing or harmful to him if given general circulation. This information the physician is bound, not only upon his own professional honor and the ethics of his profession, to keep secret … A wrongful breach of such confidence, and a betrayal of such trust, would give rise to a civil action for the damages naturally flowing from such wrong.[23]

---

[17] *Id.* at 605.
[18] *Id.*
[19] *See, e.g.*, Ala. Const. art. I, § 22; Cal. Const. art. I, § 1; Fla. Const. art. I § 23.
[20] Samuel Warren and Louis Brandeis, *The Right to Privacy*, Harvard L. Rev. (1890).
[21] *Id.*
[22] *DeMay v. Roberts*, 9 N.W. 146 (Mich. 1881).
[23] *Simonsen v. Simonsen*, 177 N.W. 831, 832 (Neb. 1920).

The Nebraska court's right to confidentiality was not absolute, however. For example, the right did not apply if a statute required a physician to disclose the information or if disclosure would protect the health and safety of others.[24]

Today, the common law of torts generally recognizes four basic privacy rights, which were first identified by William Prosser in a seminal 1960 *California Law Review* article and first codified in the mid-1960s in the Restatement (Second) of Torts.[25] These rights include intrusion upon seclusion (seclusion), publication of embarrassing private facts (disclosure), publicly placing a person in false light (false light), and appropriation of name or likeness (appropriation). The first three rights have been asserted in litigation by: (1) patients who desired to keep their physical and mental health conditions private (seclusion); (2) patients who desired to keep their communications with their health care providers and their medical records confidential (disclosure); and (3) individuals who did not want their names or photographs published near an article addressing substance use disorder or another sensitive or stigmatizing physical or mental health conditions (false light). In addition to these privacy torts, today's common law also recognizes a breach of health information confidentiality tort that applies in the medical context. In *McCormick v. England*, for example, the South Carolina Court of Appeals summarized this common law: "A majority of jurisdictions faced with the issue have recognized a cause of action against a physician for the unauthorized disclosure of confidential information unless the disclosure is compelled by law or is in the patient's interest or the public's interest."[26]

In the United States, the duty of confidentiality is also sourced in state health professional practice acts and state health institution licensing laws. For example, the Texas Medical Practice Act, which regulates Texas-licensed physicians, requires both confidential communications ("A communication between a physician and a patient, relative to or in connection with any professional services as a physician to the patient, is confidential and privileged and may not be disclosed") and confidential records ("A record of the identity, diagnosis, evaluation, or treatment of a patient by a physician that is created or maintained by a physician is confidential and privileged and may not be disclosed").[27] By further example, the Texas Hospital Licensing Law forbids hospital employees from disclosing health care information about a patient

---

[24]   *Id.*
[25]   William L. Prosser, *Privacy*, 48 Cal. L. Rev. 389–407 (1960); Restatement (Second) of Torts, §§ 652A–E (1977).
[26]   *McCormick v. England*, 494 S.E.2d 431 (S.C. Ct. App. 1997).
[27]   Tex. Occ. Code § 159.002(a), (b).

without the written authorization of the patient and provides a remedy for patients whose information is disclosed without authorization.[28]

Historically, the duties of confidentiality set forth in state professional practice acts and state institutional licensing laws varied widely, creating an uneven patchwork of state law. To create a federal floor of protections applicable to the health care industry, President William J. Clinton signed the Health Insurance Portability and Accountability Act (HIPAA) into law on August 21, 1996.[29] HIPAA required Congress to enact privacy legislation within three years.[30] If Congress failed to meet its deadline, HIPAA directed the federal Department of Health and Human Services (HHS) to promulgate privacy regulations.[31] When Congress failed to meet its deadline, HHS responded by promulgating the HIPAA Privacy Rule.[32]

PERSONS BOUND BY THE DUTY OF CONFIDENTIALITY

The HIPAA Privacy Rule only applies to covered entities and their business associates.[33] Covered entities include health plans, health care clearinghouses, and certain (but not all) health care providers.[34] A health plan is defined as "any individual or group plan that provides, or pays the cost of, medical care."[35] Health plans include, but are not limited to health insurance issuers, health maintenance organizations, Medicare, issuers of Medicare supplemental policies, Medicaid, the Indian Health Service, the Federal Employees Health Benefits Program, issuers of long-term care policies, and employer-sponsored group health plans that have 50 or more participants or that are administered by a third party administrator.[36] A health care clearinghouse is defined as a "public or private entity, including a billing service, repricing company, community health management information system or community health information system, and value-added networks and switches," that does either of the following functions: (1) processes or facilitates the processing of health information received from another entity in a nonstandard format or containing nonstandard data content into standard data elements or a standard transaction;

---

28   Tex. Health & Safety Code §§ 241.152, 241.156.
29   HIPAA, *supra* note 1.
30   HIPAA § 264(c)(1).
31   HIPAA § 264(c)(1).
32   *See* HIPAA Privacy Rule, *supra* note 1.
33   45 C.F.R. § 164.500(a), (c).
34   45 C.F.R. § 160.103 (defining covered entity).
35   45 C.F.R. § 160.103 (defining health plan).
36   45 C.F.R. § 160.103 (defining group health plan).

or (2) receives a standard transaction from another entity and processes or facilitates the processing of health information into nonstandard format or nonstandard data content for the receiving entity.[37] A health care provider is defined as a "provider of services" (e.g., hospital, critical access hospital, skilled nursing facility, comprehensive outpatient rehabilitation facility, home health agency, hospice), a "provider of medical and other health services" (e.g., physician, nurse-midwife, psychologist, social worker, durable medical equipment, durable medical equipment supplier), and "and any other person or organization who furnishes, bills, or is paid for health care in the normal course of business" (e.g., pharmacist, pharmacy, licensed independent counsellor).[38] Only certain health care providers are covered by the HIPAA Privacy Rule, however. Providers must transmit health information in electronic form in connection with certain standard transactions, such as the health insurance claim transaction, to be covered.[39] Providers who accept only cash, checks, or credit cards for payment, and who do not bill insurance, are not covered by the HIPAA Privacy Rule. Providers who bill insurance but only submit paper (not electronic) bills to such insurers also are not covered by the HIPAA Privacy Rule.

Business associates of covered entities also must comply with the HIPAA Privacy Rule. A business associate is defined as a person who, on behalf of a covered entity, but other than in the capacity of a member of the workforce of the covered entity, creates, receives, maintains, or transmits protected health information (PHI)[40] in order to perform certain regulated activities on behalf of the covered entity.[41] These regulated activities include, but are not limited to, claims processing, claims administration, data analysis, processing or administration, utilization review, quality assurance, certain patient safety activities, billing, benefit management, practice management, and repricing.[42] A business associate also includes a person who provides, other than in the capacity of a member of the workforce of a covered entity, legal, actuarial, accounting, consulting, data aggregation, management, administrative, accreditation, or financial services to or for such covered entity.[43] A business associate further

---

[37]   45 C.F.R. § 160.103 (providing illustrative examples of health plans).
[38]   45 C.F.R. § 160.103 (defining health care provider).
[39]   45 C.F.R. § 160.103 (defining covered entity).
[40]   With four exceptions, protected health information (PHI) is defined as individually identifiable health information (IIHI). 45 C.F.R. § 160.103 (defining PHI and IIHI).
[41]   45 C.F.R. § 160.103 (defining business associate).
[42]   45 C.F.R. § 160.103 (defining business associate).
[43]   45 C.F.R. § 160.103 (defining business associate).

includes a subcontractor that creates, receives, maintains, or transmits PHI on behalf of the business associate.[44]

Due to the limited application of the HIPAA Privacy Rule (as well as the other HIPAA Rules), federal lawmakers have recently introduced to Congress a variety of privacy (and security and breach notification) bills that have broader applicability. Some of these bills are designed to address the privacy and security concerns raised by the collection, use, and disclosure of health data by mobile health applications and other technologies that do not fall within the definition of a covered entity or business associate. Others are designed to respond to the particular privacy and security concerns raised by the collection, use, and disclosure of infectious disease data by non-covered COVID-19 contact tracers and COVID-19 exposure notification services.

In the context of mobile health applications and other technologies, for example, Senator Brian Schatz's (D-HI) Data Care Act of 2018 (DCA) would have established new data protection duties for non-covered online service providers with respect to "individual identifying data," defined in relevant part as data that are "linked, or reasonably linkable" to certain end users and computer devices.[45] By further example, Senator Amy Klobuchar's (D-MN) Protecting Personal Health Data Act of 2019 (PPHDA) would have directed the Secretary of HHS to promulgate regulations that would strengthen privacy and security protections for "personal health data" that are collected, processed, analyzed, or used by non-covered consumer devices, services, applications, or software.[46] Likewise, Senator Ron Wyden's (D-OR) Mind Your Own Business Act of 2019 (MYOBA) would have directed the FTC to promulgate regulations obligating certain non-covered entities to implement reasonable cybersecurity and privacy policies, practices, and procedures to protect "personal information," defined as "any information, regardless of how the information is collected, inferred, or obtained, that is reasonably linkable to a specific consumer or consumer device."[47] As a final illustrative example, Senator Bill Cassidy's (R-LA) Stop Marketing and Revealing the Wearables and Trackers Consumer Health (SMARTWATCH) Data Act would have prohibited certain non-covered entities that collect consumer health information (CHI) from transferring or selling CHI to information brokers who collect or analyze CHI for profit. The SMARTWATCH Data Act defines CHI as "any information about the health status, personal biometric information, or personal kinesthetic information

---

[44]   45 C.F.R. § 160.103 (defining business associate).

[45]   Data Care Act of 2018, S.3744, 115th Cong., 2nd Sess., § 3 (Dec. 12, 2018).

[46]   Protecting Personal Health Data Act, S.1842, 116th Cong., 1st Sess. (June 13, 2019).

[47]   Mind Your Own Business Act of 2019, S.2637, 116th Cong., 1st Sess., § 2(12) (Oct. 17, 2019).

about a specific individual that is created or collected by a personal consumer device, whether detected from sensors or input manually."[48]

To respond to concerns associated with the increase in the collection of infectious disease data by non-covered COVID-19 contact tracers and COVID-19 exposure notification services, Senator Richard Blumenthal's (D-CT) Public Health Emergency Privacy Act of 2020 (PHEPA) would have established certain privacy and security protections for "emergency health data," defined as "data linked or reasonably linkable to an individual or device, including data inferred or derived about the individual or device from other collected data provided such data is still linked or reasonably linkable to the individual or device, that concerns the public COVID–19 health emergency."[49] Similarly, Senator Roger Wicker's (R-MS) COVID-19 Consumer Data Protection Act of 2020 (CCDPA) would have protected "covered data," defined to include "precise geolocation data, proximity data, a persistent identifier, and personal health information."[50] By final illustrative example, Senator Maria Cantwell's (D-WA) Exposure Notification Privacy Act of 2020 (ENPA) would have imposed certain data privacy and security standards on operators of automated infectious disease exposure notification services with respect to "covered data," defined as "information that is: (A) linked or reasonably linkable to any individual or device linked or reasonably linkable to an individual; (B) not aggregate data; and (C) collected, processed, or transferred in connection with an automated exposure notification service."[51] Although Congress has yet to enact any of these federal bills, they illustrate the significant and growing privacy and security concerns raised by Americans' use of mobile health technologies as well as increased efforts to collect, use, and disclose infectious disease data to combat the COVID-19 pandemic.

In addition to the federal authorities discussed above, some states have enacted more general health laws that regulate non-covered entities that "come into possession of protected health information" or "obtain[] or store[] protected health information."[52] As of this writing, five states (California, Colorado, Connecticut, Utah, and Virginia) also have enacted general consumer data protection laws that protect a variety of types of personal data,

---

[48]   Stop Marketing and Revealing the Wearables and Trackers Consumer Health (SMARTWATCH) Data Act, S.2885, 116th Cong., 1st Sess. (Nov. 18, 2019).

[49]   Public Health Emergency Privacy Act, S.3749, 116th Cong., 2nd Sess., § 2(8) (May 14, 2020).

[50]   The COVID-19 Consumer Data Protection Act of 2020, S.3663, 116th Cong., 2nd Sess. (May 7, 2020).

[51]   The Exposure Notification Privacy Act, S.3861, 116th Cong., 2nd Sess., § 2(6) (June 1, 2020).

[52]   Tex. Health & Safety Code 181.001(b)(2)(B), (C).

including health data, that are not protected by the HIPAA Rules.[53] These new laws give data subjects comprehensive privacy rights relating to their personal information.[54] Illustrative rights include the right to know what personal information is being collected, the right to know what personal information is sold and to whom, the right to opt out of the sale or sharing of personal information, the right to limit the use and disclosure of sensitive personal information (including health information), the right to delete personal information, the right to correct inaccurate personal information, the right not to be retaliated against for opting out of the sale of information or the exercise of rights.[55] That said, the five states that have enacted consumer data protection laws require businesses to meet significant financial or data sale thresholds to be regulated. For example, the California Consumer Privacy Act of 2018, the latest revisions to which went into effect January 1, 2023, only applies to businesses that have annual gross revenues in excess of 25 million dollars; or that annually buy, receive, sell, or share the personal information of 50,000 or more consumers; or that derive 50 percent or more of their annual revenues from selling consumers' personal information.[56] Similarly, the Colorado Privacy Act (CPA), effective July 1, 2023, regulates certain data controllers (including certain health data controllers) that conduct business in Colorado or that produce or deliver commercial products or services that are intentionally targeted to residents of Colorado.[57] The CPA regulations only apply, however, if the controller processes the personal data of 100,000 consumers or more during a calendar year or derives revenue or receives a discount on the price of goods or services from the sale of personal data and processes or controls the personal data of 25,000 consumers or more.[58] Along the same lines, the Connecticut Data Privacy Act (CDPA), effective July 1, 2023, also regulates certain businesses and persons

---

[53] *See* California Consumer Privacy Act, *codified at* Cal. Civ. Code §§ 1798.100-.135 (latest revisions eff. January 1, 2023) [hereinafter California Consumer Privacy Act]; Colorado Privacy Act, S.B. 21-190, signed into law on July 7, 2021, *to be codified at* Colo. Rev. Stat. §§ 6-1-1301 - 1313 (eff. July 1, 2023) [hereinafter Colorado Privacy Act]; Connecticut Data Privacy Act, S.B. 6, Pub. Act No. 22-15 (eff. July 1, 2023) [hereinafter Connecticut Data Privacy Act]; Utah Consumer Privacy Act, S.B. 227, 2022 Gen. Sess. (Mar. 24, 2022), *to be codified at* Utah Code Ann. §§ 13-61-101 - 404 [Utah Consumer Privacy Act]; Virginia Consumer Data Protection Act, S.B.1392 (Mar. 2, 2021), *to be codified at* Va. Code Ann. §§ 59.1-571 - .581 (eff. Jan. 1, 2023) [hereinafter Virginia Consumer Data Protection Act].

[54] *See, e.g.,* California Consumer Privacy Act, *supra* note 53, §§ 1798.100-.135 (codifying a number of privacy-related rights).

[55] *See, e.g., id.*

[56] California Consumer Privacy Act, *supra* note 53, § 1798.140.

[57] Colorado Privacy Act, *supra* note 53, § 6-1-1304(1).

[58] *Id.*

that produce products or services that are targeted to residents of Connecticut.[59] However, the CDPA regulations only apply if, during the preceding calendar year, the business or person "controlled or processed the personal data of not less than one hundred thousand consumers, excluding personal data controlled or processed solely for the purpose of completing a payment transaction" or "controlled or processed the personal data of not less than twenty-five thousand consumers and derived more than twenty-five per cent of their gross revenue from the sale of personal data."[60] Utah and Virginia, the fourth and fifth states that have new consumer data protection laws, have similar financial and data thresholds.[61] As of this writing, the US still does not have a national, non-sectoral, consumer data protection law like the European Union's General Data Protection Regulation (GDPR).[62]

LEGAL DUTIES OF CONFIDENTIALITY

The HIPAA Privacy Rule contains three sets of sub-regulations, including the use and disclosure requirements,[63] the individual rights,[64] and the administrative requirements.[65] These three sets of sub-regulations are designed to protect the confidentiality of PHI that is obtained or maintained by covered entities and their business associates. Understanding the definition of PHI is key to understanding the use and disclosure requirements. The definition of PHI is largely based on the definition of individually identifiable health

---

[59]   Connecticut Data Privacy Act, *supra* note 53, § 2.

[60]   *Id.*

[61]   The Utah Consumer Privacy Act, effective December 31, 2023, applies to any controller or processor who conducts business in Utah or produces a product or service that is targeted to Utah resident consumers but only if the controller or processor has: (1) annual revenue of $25,000,000 or more and either (2a) controls or processes personal data of 100,000 or more consumers or (2b) derives over 50% of the entity's gross revenue from the sale of personal data and controls or processes personal data of 25,000 or more consumers. Utah Consumer Privacy Act, *supra* note 53, § 13-61-102. The Virginia Consumer Data Protection Act, effective January 1, 2023, regulates certain businesses that conduct business in Virginia or that produce products or services that are targeted to residents of Virginia but only if, during a calendar year, the business controls or processes the personal data (including health data) of: (1) at least 100,000 consumers or (ii) at least 25,000 consumers and derives over 50 percent of gross revenue from the sale of personal data. Virginia Consumer Data Protection Act, *supra* note 53, § 59.1-572(A).

[62]   Commission Regulation (EU) 2016/679, 2016 O.J. (L 119) (EU) [hereinafter GDPR].

[63]   45 C.F.R. §§ 164.502-.514.

[64]   45 C.F.R. §§ 164.520-.528.

[65]   45 C.F.R. § 164.530.

information (IIHI).[66] IIHI, in turn, is defined as health information that: (1) is created or received by a health care provider, health plan, employer, or health care clearinghouse; and (2) relates to the past, present, or future physical or mental health or condition of an individual; the provision of health care to an individual; or the past, present, or future payment for the provision of health care to an individual; and (i) that identifies the individual; or (ii) with respect to which there is a reasonable basis to believe the information can be used to identify the individual.[67] For example, a physician (i.e., a health care provider) who creates a paper or electronic medical record that documents a patient's diagnosis and treatment plan and that identifies the patient (e.g., contains the patient's name) or that could be used to identify the patient (e.g., contains other identifiers, such as the patient's home address, that could be combined with publicly available property records to identify the patient) has created IIHI. By further example, a health insurer (i.e., a health plan) that creates a paper or electronic claims record documenting the health care claims paid by the insurer also has created IIHI if the claims record identifies the insured or could be used to identify the insured.

PHI is a subset of IIHI. That is, PHI is IIHI that is not: (1) an education record protected under the Family Educational Rights and Privacy Act of 1974 (FERPA); (2) a student treatment record excepted from protection under FERPA; (3) an employment record held by a covered entity in its role as an employer; or (4) individually identifiable health information regarding a person who has been deceased for more than 50 years.[68] With respect to the first two exceptions, HHS did not want to disrupt the regulatory schemes enacted by Congress in 1974 that regulated universities and other educational institutions with respect to their use and disclosure of student-identifiable education records. With respect to the third exception, HHS wanted to draw a line between employment records already protected by federal and state employment and disability non-discrimination laws, such as Title I of the Americans with Disabilities Act (ADA), and health information held by a covered entity in its role as a health care provider, not an employer. The fourth exception relating to persons who have been deceased for more than 50 years was added to the HIPAA Privacy Rule later in time—in 2013—as a way of promoting research on deadly and other diseases and as a method of assisting family members and historians who may seek access to medical records of decedents for personal and public interest reasons.[69]

---

[66] 45 C.F.R. § 160.103 (defining PHI).
[67] 45 C.F.R. § 160.103 (defining IIHI).
[68] 45 C.F.R. § 160.103 (defining PHI).
[69] 78 Fed. Reg. 5566, 5683, 5689 (Jan. 25, 2013).

As discussed above, the HIPAA Privacy Rule only protects PHI, which is based on the definition of IIHI. The HIPAA Privacy Rule does not apply to information that cannot be used to identify an individual. To assist data custodians with their de-identification efforts, the HIPAA Privacy Rule offers two methods (a de-identification safe harbour and an expert determination) by which covered entities and business associates may de-identify information. In its de-identification safe harbour, the HIPAA Privacy Rule identifies eighteen data elements that must be removed from information.[70] If these data elements are removed and the covered entity "does not have actual knowledge that the information could be used alone or in combination with other information to identify an individual who is a subject of the information," the information is considered de-identified and is no longer protected by the HIPAA Privacy Rule.[71] The 18 identifiers that must be removed under the safe harbour include: (1) names, (2) all geographic subdivisions smaller than a state, (3) all elements of dates except for years or dates of birth that are 89 years and younger, (4) telephone numbers, (5) fax numbers, (6) e-mail addresses, (7) social security numbers, (8) medical record numbers, (9) health plan beneficiary numbers, (10) account numbers, (11) certificate and license numbers, (12) vehicle identifiers and license plate numbers, (13) device identifiers, (14) universal resource locators (URLs), (15) internet protocol (IP) address numbers, (16) biometric identifiers, (17) full facial photographs and comparable images, and (18) any other unique identifying number, characteristic, or code.[72]

In an expert determination, a person with "appropriate knowledge of and experience with generally accepted statistical and scientific principles and methods for rendering information not individually identifiable" must apply such principles and methods and determine that "the risk is very small that the information could be used, alone or in combination with other reasonably available information, by an anticipated recipient to identify an individual who is a subject of the information."[73] In theory, an expert could determine that data elements required to be removed by the safe harbour could remain and/or that additional data elements not listed in the safe harbour must be removed.

The Use and Disclosure Requirements

When a covered entity or business associate wishes to use or disclose PHI that has not been de-identified, the HIPAA Privacy Rule requires adherence to one

---

[70] 45 C.F.R. § 164.514(b)(2)(i).
[71] 45 C.F.R. § 164.514(a), (b).
[72] 45 C.F.R. § 164.514(b)(2)(i).
[73] 45 C.F.R. § 164.514(b)(1).

of three different levels of prior patient permission before the use or disclosure.[74] The first use and disclosure requirement allows covered entities and business associates to use and disclose PHI with no prior permission from the individual who is the subject of the PHI—but only in certain situations. That is, covered entities may freely use and disclose PHI without any form of prior permission in order to carry out certain treatment (T), health insurance reimbursement (P for payment), and health care operations (O)[75] activities (collectively, TPO activities).[76] No prior patient permission is required for TPO activities because they are considered essential to the delivery of and payment for health care. One question that has been raised is whether a health care provider may disclose the genetic information of one patient (such as a parent) to a second patient (such as a child) if the child may be at risk of inheriting a genetic condition such as Huntington's Disease from the parent. In preamble language interpreting the HIPAA Privacy Rule, the federal Department of Health and Human Services (HHS) stated that a covered provider may (but is not required to) disclose the parent's PHI to a child for the child's treatment purposes as a permissible treatment (T) activity allowed under the TPO regulation. Indeed, HHS states in the preamble to the HIPAA Privacy Rule that, "We also allow disclosure of protected health information to health care providers for purposes of treatment, including treatment of persons other than the individual [without the prior written authorization of the individual]."[77] This preamble language is not uncontroversial.

Covered entities also may freely use and disclose PHI to carry out certain enumerated public benefit (PB) activities without the prior written authorization of the patient.[78] No prior patient permission is required for PB activities because the interests supported by PB activities are considered superior to the patient's interest in privacy and confidentiality. One example of a permissible PB activity is child abuse and neglect reporting. For example, if a child shows signs of child abuse or neglect, the HIPAA Privacy Rule permits a covered paediatrician or other covered health care professional to report the suspected abuse or neglect to a state authority authorized by law to receive reports of

---

[74]   45 C.F.R. §§ 164.502–164.514 (setting forth the use and disclosure requirements applicable to covered entities and business associates).

[75]   45 C.F.R. § 164.501 (defining treatment, payment, and health care operations).

[76]   45 C.F.R. § 164.506(c)(1) (permitting a covered entity to use or disclose PHI for its own treatment, payment, or health care operations); *id.* § 164.506(c)(2)–(4) (permitting a covered entity to disclose PHI to certain recipients for the recipients' treatment, payment, or health care operations activities, respectively).

[77]   65 Fed. Reg. 82462, 82633 (Dec. 28, 2000).

[78]   45 C.F.R. § 164.512(a)–(l).

abuse and neglect. This report may be made by the physician without the prior written authorization of the child's parents.[79]

A second example of a permissible PB activity is the prevention of communicable disease transmission. For example, the HIPAA Privacy Rule states that a covered health care provider may disclose PHI to a person who may have been exposed to a communicable disease or may otherwise be at risk of contracting or spreading a disease or condition if the covered entity is authorized by state law to notify such person as necessary in the conduct of a public health intervention or investigation.[80] Many state laws contain partner notification provisions that specify a required notification process. For example, Texas law requires health care professionals to notify the Texas Partner Notification Program (PNP) when the health care professional knows the HIV-positive status of a patient and the health care professional has actual knowledge of a possible transmission of HIV to a third party (called a partner).[81] Once a health care professional has notified the PNP, Texas law then requires the PNP to notify the partner regardless of whether the patient with the HIV infection consents to the partner notification.[82] Under Texas law, the PNP is required to notify the partner of the: (1) methods of transmission and prevention of HIV infection; (2) telephone numbers and addresses of HIV antibody testing sites; and (3) existence of local HIV support groups, mental health services, and medical facilities.[83] However, the PNP may not disclose to the partner: (1) the name of or other identifying information concerning the identity of the person who gave the partner's name; or (2) the date or period of the partner's exposure.[84]

Under the HIPAA Privacy Rule's second use and disclosure requirement, a covered entity may use and disclose an individual's PHI for certain activities, but only if the individual is informed (orally or in writing) in advance of the use or disclosure and is given the (oral or written) opportunity to agree to, prohibit, or restrict the use or disclosure.[85] The certain activities captured by this provision include, but are not limited to, disclosures of PHI: (1) from a health care provider's facility directory; (2) to a person who is involved in an individual's care or payment for care; and (3) for certain notification purposes, such

---

[79] 45 C.F.R. § 164.512(b)(1)(ii) (permitting a covered entity to disclose PHI to a public health authority or other appropriate government authority authorized by law to receive reports of child abuse or neglect).

[80] 45 C.F.R. § 164.512(b)(1)(iv).

[81] Tex. Health & Safety Code § 81.051(g)(2).

[82] Tex. Health & Safety Code § 81.051(g)(1).

[83] Tex. Health & Safety Code § 81.051(d).

[84] Tex. Health & Safety Code § 81.051(e).

[85] 45 C.F.R. § 164.510.

as when an attending physician or a hospital social worker notifies a partner or spouse of a patient's death.[86] For example, a covered provider could disclose PHI (including medication information) to a patient's partner if the PHI disclosed is directly relevant to that partner's involvement in the patient's care and one of the following is satisfied: (1) the patient agrees (orally or in writing) to the disclosure; (2) the patient has been given the opportunity to object to the disclosure and has not expressed an objection; or (3) the provider reasonably infers from the circumstances, based on the exercise of professional judgment, that the patient would not object to the disclosure.[87] A provider exercising professional judgment might—or might not—infer that a patient with HIV would object to the disclosure to the patient's partner of information suggesting or stating that the patient has HIV.

The HIPAA Privacy Rule's third use and disclosure requirement—a default rule—requires covered entities and business associates to obtain the prior written authorization of the individual who is the subject of the PHI before using or disclosing the individual's PHI in any situation that does not fit within the first two rules.[88]

Individual Rights

In addition to its use and disclosure requirements, the HIPAA Privacy Rule also contains a second set of sub-regulations designed to establish certain rights for individuals who are the subject of PHI vis-à-vis their covered entities, including the right to receive a notice of privacy practices (NOPP),[89] request additional privacy protections,[90] access their PHI,[91] request amendment of incorrect or incomplete PHI,[92] and receive an accounting of PHI disclosures.[93] The first (NOPP) right is designed to ensure that individuals are notified of how their covered entities use and disclose their PHI as well as the rights that individuals have with respect to their PHI.[94] The second (additional privacy protections) right allows individuals to request and, in certain cases receive, additional restrictions (above and beyond those set forth in the HIPAA Privacy Rule) on the use and disclosure of their PHI. The third (access) right

---

[86]   45 C.F.R. §§ 164.510(a), 164.510(b)(1)(i), 164.510(b)(1)(ii).
[87]   45 C.F.R. § 164.510(b)(1)(i), (b)(2).
[88]   45 C.F.R. § 164.508(a)(1).
[89]   45 C.F.R. § 164.520.
[90]   45 C.F.R. § 164.522.
[91]   45 C.F.R. § 164.524.
[92]   45 C.F.R. § 164.526.
[93]   45 C.F.R. § 164.528.
[94]   45 C.F.R. § 164.520.

gives individuals a right to receive a paper or electronic copy of their PHI when it is held in a designated record set.[95] The fourth (amendment) right gives individuals the right to request amendment of incorrect PHI.[96] The fifth (accounting) right gives individuals the right to receive an accounting (or list) of certain disclosures of their PHI.[97]

Administrative Requirements

In addition to the use and disclosure requirements and the individual rights, the HIPAA Privacy Rule contains a third set of sub-regulations known as the administrative requirements. For example, the HIPAA Privacy Rule requires covered entities to designate a privacy officer who will oversee compliance with the HIPAA Privacy Rule, train workforce members regarding how to comply with the HIPAA Privacy Rule, sanction workforce members who violate the HIPAA Privacy Rule, establish a complaint process for individuals who believe their privacy rights have been violated, and develop privacy-related policies and procedures, among other similar requirements.[98]

Complaints and Enforcement

The remedies available to patients who believe their HIPAA privacy and security rights have been violated are limited. Under current law, no private right of action exists for patients and insureds whose rights under the HIPAA Rules have been violated.[99] Under the HIPAA Rules, an individual who is aggrieved by a privacy or security violation can complain, however, to the covered entity itself,[100] the Secretary of HHS,[101] or a state attorney general who has the authority under HITECH to bring a civil action seeking damages or an injunction on behalf of a state resident for violations of the HIPAA Rules.[102] In response, HHS (and, presumably, a state attorney general) may or will investigate the case,[103] may or will conduct a compliance review of the covered entity or business associate[104] and, if the investigation or review indicates

---

[95] 45 C.F.R. § 164.524.
[96] 45 C.F.R. § 164.526.
[97] 45 C.F.R. § 164.528.
[98] 45 C.F.R. § 164.530.
[99] *See, e.g., Acara v. Banks*, 470 F.3d 569, 572 (5th Cir. 2006) ("We hold there is no private cause of action under HIPAA ... .").
[100] 45 C.F.R. § 164.530(d)(1).
[101] 45 C.F.R. § 160.306(a).
[102] 42 U.S.C. § 1320d–5(d).
[103] 45 C.F.R. § 160.306(c)(1).
[104] 45 C.F.R. § 160.308(a); *id.* § 160.308(b).

noncompliance, may attempt to reach a resolution with the covered entity or business associate.[105]

HHS's resolution options include: (1) the provision of technical assistance by HHS to the covered entity or business associate and compliance therewith; (2) demonstrated compliance (also called voluntary compliance or voluntary cooperation) by the covered entity or business associate; (3) a settlement agreement that includes a settlement payment to HHS by the covered entity or business associate; (4) an agreement by the covered entity or business associate to take corrective action pursuant to a corrective action plan (CAP); (5) the imposition of a civil money penalty; and/or (6) the referral of the case to the federal Department of Justice (DOJ) for criminal action.[106] HHS pursues a combination of the third and fourth options—a settlement plus a CAP—when HHS finds that the covered entity's or business associate's noncompliance was due to wilful neglect or when "the nature and scope of the noncompliance warrants additional enforcement action."[107] HHS pursues the fifth option—the imposition of civil money penalties—when HHS is unable to resolve the matter through technical assistance, demonstrated compliance, and/or corrective action (hereinafter, agreement).[108] If HHS is unable to resolve the matter by agreement, then HHS will ask the "covered entity or business associate … to submit written evidence of any mitigating factors or affirmative defenses" relating to the entity's HIPAA Rules violations.[109] Following HHS's receipt of the requested information, HHS will send the covered entity or business associate a notice of proposed determination (NPD), which announces that a civil money penalty will be imposed on the covered entity or business associate and provides the opportunity for the covered entity or business associate to request a hearing.[110] Depending on the outcome of any hearing, the NPD is followed by a notice of final determination (NFD), which notifies the covered entity or business associate of HHS's final decision to impose a civil money penalty together with information stating when and how the covered entity or business associate shall pay the penalty.[111] Under the current HIPAA Rules, both settlement amounts and civil money penalties are paid directly by the covered entity

---

[105] 45 C.F.R. § 160.312(a)(1).

[106] 45 C.F.R. § 160.312(a)(1).

[107] Office for Civil Rights, U.S. Dep't of Health & Human Servs., Annual Report to Congress on HIPAA Privacy, Security, and Breach Notification Rule Compliance for Calendar Years 2013 and 2014, at 4–5, *available at* www.hhs.gov/sites/default/files/rtc -compliance-20132014.pdf (last visited April 17, 2021).

[108] *See id.* at 5.

[109] 45 C.F.R. § 160.312(a)(3)(i).

[110] 45 C.F.R. §§ 160.312(a)(3)(ii), 160.420.

[111] 45 C.F.R. § 160.424.

or business associate to HHS, not to the individuals harmed by the HIPAA Rules violations.[112] In addition to its civil enforcement of the HIPAA Rules, HHS also refers certain cases that are appropriate for criminal investigation, including those cases involving the knowing disclosure or obtaining of PHI in violation of the HIPAA Rules, to the federal Department of Justice.[113] As of this writing, HHS has referred approximately 1,060 cases to the DOJ for criminal investigation.[114] Although the HIPAA Rules contain no private right of action, some jurisdictions allow plaintiffs to use the HIPAA Rules to establish negligence per se.[115]

DATA PROTECTION LAW

As discussed above, the HIPAA Privacy Rule governs the use and disclosure of PHI by covered entities and business associates. Additional data protection standards, including data security and data breach notification standards, are set forth in the HIPAA Security Rule and the HIPAA Breach Notification Rule.

Data Security

The HIPAA Security Rule requires covered entities and business associates to implement administrative, physical, and technical safeguards designed to protect the confidentiality, integrity, and availability of electronic protected health information (ePHI).[116] In particular, the HIPAA Security Rule's admin-

---

[112] 45 C.F.R. § 160.424(a) (providing that civil money penalties for HIPAA Rules violations are paid to the Secretary of HHS); Resolution Agreement between U.S. Dep't of Health & Human Servs. and St. Luke's-Roosevelt Hosp. Ctr. Inc. (U.S. Dep't Health & Human Servs. May 8, 2017) (requiring St. Luke's to pay a settlement amount (also called a resolution amount) of $387,200 to HHS).

[113] 42 U.S.C. § 1320d–6(a)–(b) (2012) (providing that "[a] person who knowingly and in violation of" the HIPAA Rules uses, obtains, or discloses individually identifiable health information shall be punished in accordance with a three-tiered criminal penalty scheme that includes: (1) fines of not more than $50,000, imprisonment for not more than 1 year, or both; (2) for offenses committed under false pretenses, fines of not more than $100,000, imprisonment for not more than 5 years, or both; and (3) "if the offense is committed with intent to sell, transfer, or use individually identifiable health information for commercial advantage, personal gain, or malicious harm," fines of not more than $250,000, imprisonment for not more than 10 years, or both).

[114] U.S. Dep't Health & Human Servs., *Enforcement* Highlights: Enforcement Results as of March 2021, *available at* www.hhs.gov/hipaa/for-professionals/compliance-enforcement/data/enforcement-highlights/index.html (last visited Apr. 17, 2021).

[115] *See, e.g., Byrne v. Avery Center*, 102 A.3d 32, 49 (Conn. 2014).

[116] *See* HIPAA Security Rule, *supra* note 1.

istrative requirements obligate covered entities and business associates to des-ignate a security official responsible for the development and implementation of the covered entity's or business associate's security policies and procedures. These policies and procedures shall: (1) prevent, detect, contain, and correct security violations; (2) ensure that workforce members have appropriate access to ePHI; (3) prevent workforce members who should not have access to ePHI from obtaining such access; (4) create a security awareness and training program for all workforce members; and (5) address and respond to security incidents, emergencies, environmental problems, and other occurrences such as fire, vandalism, system failure, and natural disaster that affect systems con-taining ePHI and the security of ePHI, among other requirements.[117] In terms of physical safeguards, the HIPAA Security Rule requires covered entities and business associates to implement policies and procedures that: (1) limit phys-ical access to electronic information systems and the facilities in which they are located; (2) address the safeguarding, functioning, and physical attributes of workstations through which ePHI is accessed; and (3) govern the receipt and removal of hardware and electronic media that contain ePHI.[118] In terms of technical safeguards, the HIPAA Security Rule requires covered entities and business associates to implement: (1) technical policies and procedures for electronic information systems that maintain ePHI to allow access only to those persons or software programs that have been granted access rights; (2) hardware, software, and/or procedural mechanisms that record and examine activity in information systems that contain or use ePHI; (3) policies and pro-cedures to protect ePHI from improper alteration or destruction; (4) procedures to verify that a person or entity seeking access to ePHI is the one claimed; and (5) technical security measures to guard against unauthorized access to ePHI that is being transmitted over an electronic communications network.[119]

Data Breach Notification

In addition to the HIPAA Security Rule, which requires covered entities and business associates to implement administrative, physical, and technical safeguards designed to protect the confidentiality, integrity, and availability of ePHI, the HIPAA Breach Notification Rule requires covered entities, following the discovery of a breach of unsecured protected health information (uPHI), to notify each individual whose uPHI has been, or is reasonably believed by the covered entity to have been, accessed, acquired, used, or disclosed as a result

---

[117] 45 C.F.R. § 164.308.
[118] 45 C.F.R. § 164.310.
[119] 45 C.F.R. § 164.312.

of such breach.[120] The notification, which shall be provided without undue delay and within 60 calendar days after the discovery of the breach, shall include: (1) a brief description of the nature of the breach, including the date of the breach and the date of its discovery; (2) a description of the types of uPHI involved in the breach; (3) any steps the individual should take to protect herself from potential harm resulting from the breach; (4) a brief description of the steps taken by the covered entity to investigate the breach, to mitigate harm to individuals whose uPHI was part of the breach, and to protect against future breaches; and (5) contact information sufficient to allow individuals to ask questions or learn additional information about the breach.[121]

When a breach involves the uPHI of more than 500 residents of a state or jurisdiction, the HIPAA Breach Notification Rule also requires the covered entity to notify prominent media outlets serving the state or jurisdiction.[122] When a breach involves the uPHI of 500 or more individuals, regardless of their state of residency, the covered entity is also required to notify the Secretary of HHS within 60 calendar days after the discovery of the breach.[123] Finally, when the breach involves the uPHI of less than 500 individuals, the covered entity is required to notify the Secretary of HHS not later than 60 calendar days after the end of the calendar year.[124]

EXCEPTIONS TO CONFIDENTIALITY

Regulatory Exceptions

As discussed above, the first use and disclosure requirement within the HIPAA Privacy Rule allows covered entities and business associates to use and disclose PHI with no prior permission from the individual who is the subject of the PHI—but only in certain situations. These situations may be understood as exceptions to the default rule of prior patient permission. These situations, or exceptions, include uses and disclosures of PHI for treatment, payment, and health care operations (TPO) activities.[125] Treatment is broadly defined as

> the provision, coordination, or management of health care and related services by one or more health care providers, including the coordination or management of health care by a health care provider with a third party; consultation between health

---

[120] 45 C.F.R. § 164.404.
[121] 45 C.F.R. § 164.404.
[122] 45 C.F.R. § 164.406.
[123] 45 C.F.R. § 164.408(b).
[124] 45 C.F.R. § 164.408(c).
[125] 45 C.F.R. § 164.506.

care providers relating to a patient; or the referral of a patient for health care from one health care provider to another.[126]

Payment is broadly defined as the activities undertaken by a: (1) health plan to obtain premiums or to determine or fulfil its responsibility for coverage and provision of benefits under the health plan; or (2) health care provider or health plan to obtain or provide reimbursement for the provision of health care.[127] Illustrative, but not exhaustive, examples of payment include: (1) determinations of eligibility or coverage (including coordination of benefits or the determination of cost sharing amounts), and adjudication or subrogation of health benefit claims; (2) risk adjusting amounts due based on enrolee health status and demographic characteristics; (3) billing, claims management, collection activities, obtaining payment under a contract for reinsurance (including stop-loss insurance and excess of loss insurance), and related health care data processing; (4) review of health care services with respect to medical necessity, coverage under a health plan, appropriateness of care, or justification of charges; (5) utilization review activities, including precertification and preauthorization of services, concurrent and retrospective review of services; and (6) disclosure to consumer reporting agencies of any of the following protected health information relating to collection of premiums or reimbursement: name and address, date of birth, Social Security number, payment history, account number, and name and address of the provider or plan.

Health care operations is very broadly defined to include, but not be limited to: (1) conducting quality assessment and improvement activities, including outcomes evaluation and development of clinical guidelines; (2) reviewing the competence or qualifications of health care professionals, evaluating practitioner and provider performance, health plan performance, conducting training programs in which students, trainees, or practitioners in areas of health care learn under supervision to practice or improve their skills as health care providers, training of non-health care professionals, accreditation, certification, licensing, or credentialing activities; (3) underwriting, enrolment, premium rating, and other activities related to the creation, renewal, or replacement of a contract of health insurance or health benefits, and ceding, securing, or placing a contract for reinsurance of risk relating to claims for health care; (4) conducting or arranging for medical review, legal services, and auditing functions, including fraud and abuse detection and compliance programs; (5) business planning and development, such as conducting cost-management and planning-related analyses related to managing and operating the entity, includ-

---

[126]   45 C.F.R. § 164.501 (defining treatment).
[127]   45 C.F.R. § 164.501 (defining payment).

ing formulary development and administration, development or improvement of methods of payment or coverage policies; and (6) business management and general administrative activities of the entity, including, but not limited to, customer service, resolution of internal grievances, and the sale, transfer, merger, or consolidation of all or part of the covered entity with another covered entity.[128] Prior patient authorization is not required for these TPO activities because they are considered essential to the functioning of the American health care delivery and payment systems.

Explicit and Implied Consent

To the extent a use or disclosure of PHI by a covered entity or business associate is not for a TPO activity or does not fall within another exception or does not fall within the second use and disclosure requirement discussed in section 5(a), above, the HIPAA Privacy Rule requires the covered entity or business associate to obtain prior, explicit permission—called "authorization"—before using or disclosing the patient's PHI. The HIPAA Privacy Rule requires the written form on which the patient's explicit authorization is obtained to contain a number of core elements and required statements.[129] The core elements include: (i) a description of the information to be used or disclosed that identifies the information in a specific and meaningful fashion; (ii) the name or other specific identification of the person(s), or class of persons, authorized to make the requested use or disclosure; (iii) the name or other specific identification of the person(s), or class of persons, to whom the covered entity may make the requested use or disclosure; (iv) a description of each purpose of the requested use or disclosure; (v) an expiration date or an expiration event that relates to the individual or the purpose of the use or disclosure; and (vi) signature of the individual or legally authorized representative and date.[130] The authorization also must include certain required statements, including statements adequate to place the individual on notice of all of the following: (i) the individual's right to revoke the authorization in writing, the exceptions to the right to revoke, and a description of how the individual may revoke the authorization; (ii) the ability or inability to condition treatment, payment, enrolment or eligibility for benefits on the authorization; and (iii) the potential for information disclosed pursuant to the authorization to be subject to redisclosure by the recipient and no longer be protected by the HIPAA Privacy Rule.[131]

---

[128]   45 C.F.R. § 164.501 (defining health care operations).
[129]   45 C.F.R. § 164.508(c)(1)–(2).
[130]   45 C.F.R. § 164.508(c)(1).
[131]   45 C.F.R. § 164.508(c)(2).

The prior written authorization discussed immediately above is a form of explicit permission. The HIPAA Privacy Rule also contains additional provisions that may best be described as implied permissions. In particular, a covered entity may use and disclose an individual's PHI in certain limited situations, but only if the individual is informed (orally or in writing) in advance of the use or disclosure and is given the (oral or written) opportunity to agree to, prohibit, or restrict the use or disclosure.[132] In situations in which a person is given this opportunity and does not explicitly agree to, or object to, the use or disclosure, the covered entity may proceed as having obtained implied permission in the context of: (1) certain disclosures of directory information from a facility directory; (2) certain disclosures to persons who are involved in an individual's care or payment for care; and (3) certain disclosures for certain notification purposes, such as when an attending physician or a hospital social worker notifies a partner or spouse of a patient's death.[133]

Other Health Care Personnel

Remember that the HIPAA Privacy Rule broadly defines treatment as the

> provision, coordination, or management of health care and related services by one or more health care providers, including the coordination or management of health care by a health care provider with a third party; consultation between health care providers relating to a patient; or the referral of a patient for health care from one health care provider to another.[134]

Remember too that the HIPAA Privacy Rule broadly defines "health care provider" as a "provider of services" (e.g., hospital, critical access hospital, skilled nursing facility, comprehensive outpatient rehabilitation facility, home health agency, hospice), a "provider of medical and other health services" (e.g., physician, nurse-midwife, psychologist, social worker, durable medical equipment, durable medical equipment supplier), and "and any other person or organization who furnishes, bills, or is paid for health care in the normal course of business" (e.g., pharmacist, pharmacy, licensed independent counsellor).[135] The examples provided in the last sentence are illustrative, not exhaustive. If an individual provides health care and is paid for health care in the normal course of business, the individual meets the definition of a health care provider.

---

[132] 45 C.F.R. § 164.510.
[133] 45 C.F.R. §§ 164.510(a), 164.510(b)(1)(i), 164.510(b)(1)(ii).
[134] 45 C.F.R. § 164.501 (defining treatment).
[135] 45 C.F.R. § 160.103 (defining health care provider).

One result of these broad definitions is that many health care personnel, and not just the patient's attending physician, can obtain, use, or disclose a patient's PHI for treatment activities without first obtaining the patient's prior written authorization.[136] A second result is that many different classes of health care professionals (as well as students, interns, residents, and fellows who are training to become health care professionals) can access PHI without patient authorization when, under supervision, they are learning, practising, or improving their skills as health care providers.[137]

Research

The HIPAA Privacy Rule contains an exception to the prior written authorization requirement when a covered entity wishes to use or disclose PHI in certain (but not all) research situations. These situations include when: (1) an institutional review board (IRB) or privacy board has approved the waiver, in whole or part, of the otherwise required authorization; (2) a researcher would like to access certain PHI preparatory to conducting research and the covered entity obtains certain representations from the researcher; (3) a researcher would like to access certain PHI to conduct research on decedents' information; and (4) a researcher would like to use a limited data set (LDS) of PHI and signs a data use agreement (DUA) agreeing to protect the LDS.[138] If a research use or disclosure does not fall into one of these four situations, however, then the prior written authorization of the human research participant or the participant's legally authorized representative must be obtained.

Prevention of Harm to Others

The HIPAA Privacy Rule contains an exception to the prior written authorization requirement when a covered entity, consistent with applicable law and standards of ethical conduct, uses or discloses PHI as necessary to avert a serious threat to health or safety. This exception applies to two different situations. The first situation is when a covered entity has a good faith belief that the use or disclosure is necessary to prevent or lessen a serious and imminent threat to the health or safety of a person or the public and is to a person or persons reasonably able to prevent or lessen the threat, including the target

---

[136] 45 C.F.R. § 164.506.
[137] 45 C.F.R. § 164.501 (defining health care operations to include the training of health and non-health professionals); *id.* § 164.506(c)(1) (allowing covered entities to use and disclose PHI without prior patient authorization for health care operations activities).
[138] 45 C.F.R. § 164.512(i).

of the threat.[139] The second situation is when a covered entity has a good faith belief that the use or disclosure is necessary for law enforcement authorities to identify or apprehend an individual because of a statement by an individual admitting participation in a violent crime that the covered entity reasonably believes may have caused serious physical harm to the victim or when it appears from all the circumstances that the individual has escaped from a correctional institution or from lawful custody.[140]

Police Investigation

The HIPAA Privacy Rule contains an exception to the prior written authorization requirement for uses and disclosures of PHI that applies in six different law enforcement situations. First, a covered entity may use and disclose PHI as required by a law that requires the reporting of certain types of wounds or other physical injuries or in compliance with and as limited by the requirements of a court order, court-ordered warrant, subpoena issued by a judicial officer, grand jury subpoena, and certain administrative requests.[141] Second, a covered entity may disclose PHI in response to a law enforcement official's request for such information for the purpose of identifying or locating a suspect, fugitive, material witness, or missing person, provided that the covered entity only discloses the following information: name and address, date and place of birth, Social security number, blood type, type of injury, date and time of treatment, date and time of death (if applicable), and a description of distinguishing physical characteristics, including height, weight, gender, race, hair and eye colour, presence or absence of facial hair (beard or moustache), scars, and tattoos.[142] Third, a covered entity may disclose, in certain situations, PHI in response to a law enforcement official's request about an individual who is or is suspected to be a victim of a crime.[143] Fourth, a covered entity may disclose PHI about an individual who has died to a law enforcement official for the purpose of alerting law enforcement of the death of the individual if the covered entity has a suspicion that such death may have resulted from criminal conduct.[144] Fifth, a covered entity may disclose to a law enforcement official PHI that the covered entity believes in good faith constitutes evidence of criminal conduct that occurred on the premises of the covered entity.[145] Finally, a covered health

---

[139] 45 C.F.R. § 164.512(j)(1)(i).
[140] 45 C.F.R. § 164.152(j)(1)(ii).
[141] 45 C.F.R. § 164.512(f)(1).
[142] 45 C.F.R. § 164.512(f)(2).
[143] 45 C.F.R. § 164.512(f)(3).
[144] 45 C.F.R. § 164.512(f)(4).
[145] 45 C.F.R. § 164.512(f)(5).

care provider providing emergency health care in response to a medical emergency, other than such emergency on the premises of the covered health care provider, may disclose PHI to a law enforcement official if such disclosure appears necessary to alert law enforcement to the commission and nature of a crime, the location of such crime or the victim of the crime, and the identity, description, and location of the perpetrator of such crime.[146]

PUBLIC INTEREST

The HIPAA Privacy Rule contains a number of exceptions to the prior written authorization requirement that are relevant to the public interest. One such exception applies to uses and disclosures of PHI for public health activities, including the disclosure of PHI to public health authorities that are authorized by law to collect or receive such information for the purpose of preventing or controlling disease, injury, or disability.[147] The HIPAA Privacy Rule specifically states that "the reporting of disease, injury, vital events such as birth or death, and the conduct of public health surveillance, public health investigations, and public health interventions" are activities that fall into this exception.[148] Health care providers that diagnose patients with COVID-19 have heavily relied on this exception during the pandemic. A second illustrative exception allows covered entities to disclose PHI about an individual whom the covered entity reasonably believes to be a victim of abuse, neglect, or domestic violence to a government authority, including a social service or protective services agency, authorized by law to receive reports of such abuse, neglect, or domestic violence.[149] A third illustrative exception allows covered entities to disclose PHI to a coroner or medical examiner for the purpose of identifying a deceased person, determining a cause of death, or other duties as authorized by law.[150] A final illustrative, but certainly not exhaustive, exception allows a covered entity to disclose PHI to organ procurement organizations or other entities engaged in the procurement, banking, or transplantation of cadaveric organs, eyes, or tissue for the purpose of facilitating organ, eye or tissue donation and transplantation.[151]

---

[146] 45 C.F.R. § 164.512(f)(6).
[147] 45 C.F.R. § 164.512(b)(1)(i).
[148] 45 C.F.R. § 164.512(b)(1)(i).
[149] 45 C.F.R. § 164.512(c).
[150] 45 C.F.R. § 164.512(g).
[151] 45 C.F.R. § 164.512(h).

Press Freedom

Under the HIPAA Privacy Rule, covered entities are not permitted to disclose PHI to the press without obtaining their patients' prior written authorization. Indeed, HHS has entered into several resolution agreements with covered entities requiring such covered entities to pay significant settlement amounts to HHS following the unauthorized disclosure of PHI to the media. For example, Memorial Hermann Health System (System) in Houston, Texas, was required to pay HHS $2.4 million following the System's impermissible disclosure of PHI in a number of press releases and media statements made by senior administrators in 2015.[152] Because members of the press generally do not fall within the definition of a HIPAA covered entity or a business associate, their use, disclosure, or publication of PHI is not regulated by the HIPAA Privacy Rule (or similar state health information confidentiality laws that apply to licensed health care professionals and licensed health care institutions).

Audio and Video Recordings

Because patients are not covered entities or business associates, the HIPAA Privacy Rule does not regulate their collection, use, disclosure, or sale of their own health information. Therefore, a patient could videotape or audio record the patient's own conversation with a physician or other health care provider without implicating the HIPAA Privacy Rule. That said, other state laws could be implicated and could render the recording a crime. For example, Oklahoma makes it illegal to record an in-person or telephone communication without the consent of at least one party to the communication, which could be the patient.[153] The Oklahoma law is known as a "one-party consent statute." On the other hand, Pennsylvania makes it a felony to record an oral or telephone communication without the consent of all of the parties to the communication.[154] The Pennsylvania law is known as an "all-party consent statute." In summary, the HIPAA Privacy Rule might not be implicated by a patient's recording of the patient's own communication with a physician but other state telecommunication laws may.

In the United States, some insurance companies have been known to use private detectives to video record patients who are insurance claimants in order

---

[152] Resolution Agreement with Memorial Hermann Health System (executed Apr. 26, 2017), *available at* www.hhs.gov/sites/default/files/mhhs_ra_cap.pdf (last visited Apr. 18, 2021).

[153] 13 Okla. Stat. § 13-176.3, § 13-176.4 (definition and penalty).

[154] 18 Pa. Stat § 5703, § 5704 (definition and penalty), § 5725, § 5747 (civil damages).

to prove that such patients are not injured and, therefore, are not entitled to an insurance payout. Unfortunately, the HIPAA Privacy Rule does not regulate this practice because the HIPAA Privacy Rule only regulates the subsequent use or disclosure of protected health information, not the initial collection thereof. That said, state telecommunication law may apply, meaning that one or both parties to the recording would have to consent depending on whether the state has a one-party consent statute or an all-party consent law.

Other Grounds

The HIPAA Privacy Rule contains a number of additional exceptions to the prior written authorization requirement. Illustrative examples of these additional exceptions include those relating to oversight of American health care system, judicial and administrative proceedings, and state workers' compensation systems. With respect to oversight of the American health care system, the HIPAA Privacy Rule permits covered entities to disclose PHI to a health oversight agency for oversight activities authorized by law, including audits; civil, administrative, or criminal investigations; inspections; licensure or disciplinary actions; civil, administrative, or criminal proceedings or actions; or other activities necessary for appropriate oversight of the health care system, government benefit programs, and entities subject to certain government regulatory programs, and entities subject to certain civil rights laws.[155] With respect to judicial and administrative proceedings, the HIPAA Privacy Rule permits covered entities to disclose PHI in the course of any judicial or administrative proceeding: (i) in response to an order of a court or administrative tribunal, provided that the covered entity discloses only the protected health information expressly authorized by such order; or (ii) in response to a subpoena, discovery request, or other lawful process, that is not accompanied by an order of a court or administrative tribunal, if the covered entity receives certain satisfactory assurances from certain parties.[156] With respect to state workers' compensation systems, the HIPAA Privacy Rule permits covered entities to disclose PHI as authorized by and to the extent necessary to comply with laws relating to workers' compensation or other similar programs that provide benefits for work-related injuries or illness without regard to fault.[157]

---

[155] 45 C.F.R. § 164.512(d).
[156] 45 C.F.R. § 164.512(e).
[157] 45 C.F.R. § 164.512(l).

CONFIDENTIALITY AND GENETICS

The HIPAA Privacy Rule includes genetic information (defined as information about an individual's genetic tests, the genetic tests of family members of the individual, the manifestation of a disease or disorder in a family member of the individual, or any request for, or receipt of, genetic services) within the definition of PHI to the extent such genetic information is identifiable or reasonably could be used to identify an individual.[158] Thus, covered entities and business associates must protect PHI that includes genetic information in accordance with the HIPAA Privacy Rule. In guidance interpreting the HIPAA Privacy Rule, HHS has stated that a health care provider may disclose – without prior patient authorization – a patient's genetic information to another provider if the disclosed genetic information would assist the second provider in treating a second patient. This guidance is controversial among patient privacy and health information confidentiality advocates.

ADULTS WHO LACK CAPACITY AND CHILDREN

When the subject of PHI is an adult who lacks capacity (AWLC) or a child, the HIPAA Privacy Rule allows a personal representative—someone legally authorized under state law—to exercise the AWLC or child's rights under the HIPAA Privacy Rule.[159] For example, a parent has the right to sign a HIPAA authorization form authorizing a paediatrician to disclose the child's PHI to a third party. By further example, an agent named in a health care power of attorney has the right to access an AWLC's medical records to make a health care decision that is within the scope of authority granted to the agent.

---

[158] 45 C.F.R. § 160.103 (defining health information and genetic information).
[159] 45 C.F.R. § 164.502(g)(1)–(3).

11. The obligation of medical confidence in the UK

Nicola Glover-Thomas

INTRODUCTION

Medical confidentiality plays an integral role in the provision and receipt of health care. Without trust that a patient's private medical information will remain protected, necessary information sharing will be hampered. The General Medical Council (GMC) observes that,

> [t]rust is an essential part of the doctor-patient relationship and confidentiality is central to this. Patients may avoid seeking medical help, or may under-report symptoms, if they think their personal information will be disclosed by doctors without consent, or without the chance to have some control over the timing or amount of information shared.[1]

Confidentiality is one of the oldest ethical imperatives in medicine, but it is not, nor has ever been an absolute obligation. The Hippocratic Oath identifies confidentiality as a core obligation and acknowledges the necessity for all of those working within the medical profession to ensure patient privacy is respected and information is kept secret and protected. Yet the assessment of what information 'ought not to be spoken of abroad' is one for the individual doctor. The International Code of Medical Ethics in 1949 also confirms the importance of medical confidentiality and the role of the doctor in determining what information should be safeguarded.[2] The Declaration of Geneva highlights the inherent tensions within the confidentiality paradigm as its wording

---

[1]   GMC, *Confidentiality: good practice in handling patient information*, 2017, para. 1, page 10. Available at: www.gmc-uk.org/-/media/documents/gmc-guidance-for -doctors---confidentiality-good-practice-in-handling-patient-information----70080105 .pdf?la=en&hash=08E96AC70CEE25912CE2EA98E5AA3303EADB5D88 (accessed: 9 March 2021).

[2]   World Medical Association, *International Code of Medical Ethics*, Adopted by the 57th WMA General Assembly, Pilanesberg, South Africa, October 2006.

is more firmly situated within the absolutist narrative. It expresses the obligation of confidentiality in this way: 'I will respect the secrets which are confided
in me, even after the patient has died.'[3] So, does that mean that confidentiality
should be recognised as an absolute obligation?

What is evident is that the conceptual space between the absolute and relative interpretation of the obligation of confidentiality highlights the complexity
of the issues that flow within this debate. Modern medicine strains this once
unbending imperative. Issues with genetic risk, modern medical practices, and
dilemmas regarding the care of those without mental capacity are just some of
the complications of the contemporary health care landscape. Sielger describes
confidentiality as a 'decrepit concept' as he recognises that modern medicine
makes its very difficult for a strictly absolutist approach to confidentiality to
be undertaken. With health care often provided by a team of professionals, the
sharing of information to enable effective therapeutic care makes the process
of controlling the flow of information difficult to contain.[4] This chapter will
consider the complexity that surrounds the obligation of confidentiality and
examine the current legal position within the UK.[5]

BREACH OF CONFIDENCE IN LAW

In England and Wales, the law relating to medical confidentiality has
developed spasmodically over time. In 1981 the English Law Commission
recommended that a separate statutory tort of breach of confidence should be
created, yet this has never been implemented.[6] Over more recent years, efforts
to use the breach of confidence action to form the basis of a substantive right
to privacy in English Law have been made. In actions for breach of confidence,
the courts are concerned to provide a remedy where a breach of trust in a confidential relationship has occurred. In contrast, privacy actions are focused
upon an individual's autonomous decision about what should and should not
be done with information about them. Privacy actions focus on the nature and
control of the information itself. For example, in *Douglas v Hello* the House
of Lords stated, 'the Douglas'... were in a position to impose an obligation of
confidence. They were in control of the information.'[7]

---

    [3]   Declaration of Geneva, as amended 2017 (8th WMA General Assembly,
Chicago, United States, October 2017).
    [4]   M Siegler. 'Confidentiality in Medicine – A Decrepit Concept' (1982) 307(24)
The New England Journal of Medicine 1518–21.
    [5]   This chapter will predominantly focus on the law in England and Wales.
    [6]   See Law Commission Report No. 110, *Breach of Confidence* (Cmnd 8388).
    [7]   [2007] UKHL 21 [118].

There has been some debate about whether a free-standing right to privacy exists. In *Douglas v Hello!*[8] Sedley J indicated that the courts were moving towards the recognition of a right to privacy. It was observed that there is 'a powerfully arguable case that... [the claimants] ... have a right of privacy which English law will today recognise and, where appropriate, protect.'[9] He continued, 'the law no longer needs to construct an artificial relationship of confidentiality between the intruder and victim: it can recognise privacy itself as a legal principle drawn from the fundamental value of personal autonomy.'[10] The courts have since been reluctant to endorse this position, however. In *Wainwright v Home Office*,[11] the court refused to recognise a free-standing tort of invasion of privacy. This position was confirmed in *Campbell v Mirror Group Newspapers Ltd*[12] where Baroness Hale stated that 'our law cannot, even if it wanted to, develop a general tort of invasion of privacy'[13] and preferred instead to develop the law through an expansion of the breach of confidence doctrine. In *Ash v McKennitt*[14] Buxton LJ summarises the current position: 'there is no English domestic tort law of invasion of privacy ... [As a result] ... the English courts have to proceed through the tort of breach of confidence, into which the jurisprudence of arts 8 and 10 has to be "shoe-horned".'[15] Consequently, the courts have thus far not been prepared to use their judicial powers to establish a free-standing right to privacy independent of the action for breach of confidence. Instead, they have contented themselves with redefining the scope of the breach of confidence action, expanding the traditional approach to protect privacy interests through the application of case law and the principles of the ECHR.

DISCLOSURE AFTER DEATH

When a patient dies, does the obligation of confidence cease? The traditional position adopted by the GMC has focused on the importance of maintaining confidentiality even after a patient's death – '[y]our duty of confidentiality continues after a patient has died'.[16] This professional stance is clear and

---

[8]   [2001] QB 967.
[9]   Ibid. [65].
[10] Ibid. [126].
[11] [2003] UKHL 53.
[12] [2004] UKHL 22.
[13] Ibid. [133].
[14] [2006] EWCA Civ 1714.
[15] Ibid. [8].
[16] GMC, *Making and using visual and audio recordings of patients' content*, 2013, para. 47.

chimes with the broader approach adopted regarding private medical information. However, the legal position regarding the disclosure of private medical information after death was less certain until the case of *Lewis v Secretary of State for Health*.[17] Foskett J provided a stronger steer on this issue and stated that 'the "obligation of confidence" is capable of surviving the death of the patient.'[18] It was observed that without the ability to trust that information shared with a doctor remains confidential, even after death, patients would be less willing to share necessary information to aid therapeutic intervention. This reflected the expectations of the public and the profession. With strong public interest policy grounds for upholding the importance of the confidential relationship between doctor and patient, disclosure of information would need to be accompanied by strong justifications. The legal obligation is, therefore, not absolute, nor is it necessarily permanent. How long such information might remain confidential would depend upon the nature and sensitivity of the information and the potential harm to surviving relatives.

EXCEPTIONS TO THE OBLIGATION OF CONFIDENCE – WHEN CAN DISCLOSURE BE JUSTIFIED?

Clinicians can find practical guidance about what information they can and cannot disclose and why from the GMC. The GMC's latest guidance published in 2017, *Confidentiality: good practice in handling patient information* sets out critical directions to clinicians and reiterates that confidentiality is not absolute. Some exceptions provide sufficient grounds for information disclosure.

(a) The patient consents, whether implicitly or explicitly for the sake of their own care or for local clinical audit or explicitly for other purposes (see paras 13–15)

(b) The disclosure is of overall benefit to a patient who lacks the capacity to consent (see paras 41–49)

(c) The disclosure is required by law, or the disclosure is permitted or has been approved under a statutory process that sets aside the common law duty of confidentiality (see paras 17–19 and 20–21)

(d) The disclosure can be justified in the public interest (see paras 22–23)

---

[17] [2008] EWHC 2196.
[18] Ibid. [24].

As identified above, the disclosure of private information requires justification.[19] Where the patient provides a valid, autonomous consent[20] disclosure of information is acceptable. Likewise, where a patient lacks capacity, the decision to disclose information can be undertaken in the best interests of that patient. A statutory requirement to disclose information also exists in certain circumstances thus taking the decision to disclose out of the hands of the doctor. Finally, the decision to disclose can be justified based on public interest. In some jurisdictions it has been suggested that disclosure is of such public importance, that failure to disclose may be actionable in negligence.[21] English law has not adopted such a clear stance; however, it is theoretically possible that the European Convention on Human Rights may impose an obligation in exceptional circumstances to preserve life.[22]

Disclosure with Consent

Where a patient provides valid consent, disclosure of information will be lawfully undertaken. The patient should be provided with all necessary information so that they understand what information is to be disclosed, why the disclosure is necessary and what the implications of this might be. This process of express consent relies on a detailed discussion between the doctor and the patient. In many situations, consent will not be expressly provided. Implied consent can be established on the basis of conduct. For example, the recognition that health care is often provided by a team and medical records will be accessed by several people to provide the necessary care leads to an assumption of understanding that the patient will likely recognise that more than one person will be privy to his medical information. However, to fall within this recognised justification for disclosure all efforts need to be made to ensure the sharing of information is only with health care professionals directly involved in the patient's care.[23] Patient consent does not present universal immunity and care should be taken to ensure appropriate safeguards are in place.[24]

---

[19]   K. Blightman, S.E. Griffiths and C. Danbur, 'Patient Confidentiality: When Can a Breach Be Justified?' (2014) 14(2) *Continuing Education in Anaesthesia Critical Care & Pain* 52–56.

[20]   N. Glover-Thomas, 'Informed Consent: The UK Perspective' in T. Vansweevelt and N. Glover-Thomas (eds), *Informed Consent and Health: A Global Analysis* (Cheltenham, Edward Elgar, 2020).

[21]   *Tarasoff v Regents of the University of California* (1976) 551 p 2d 334.

[22]   *Osman v United Kingdom* (23452/94) [1998] ECHR 101 (28 October 1998). See also, *Selwood v Durham County Council* [2012] EWCA Civ 979.

[23]   *I v Finland* (2008) 48 EHRR 740.

[24]   See K. Adlington, 'NHS News and Notices - Unauthorised Access to Records 05/08/2019. Available at: https://my.dchs.nhs.uk/news/news-articles/post/11005/unauthorised-access-to-records (accessed: 2 March 2021).

Disclosure When the Patient Lacks Capacity

Where a patient can consent and does so (either expressly or impliedly), the decision to disclose is regulated by the rules and expectations outlined above. But what can be done when the patient lacks the mental capacity to give his consent or does not have the ability to understand the nature of the information, why the disclosure is necessary or what the implications of that disclosure might be?

Under the Mental Capacity Act 2005, mental capacity is presumed. The assessment of capacity is undertaken by considering whether the patient is unable to make a particular decision because he cannot understand information given to him, retain that information long enough to allow the decision to be made, be able to weigh up the information, or communicate the decision.[25] The capacity assessment must be rigorously applied and reviewed, with the review being an important part of the assessment process. Mental capacity varies with decisions being subject and time specific. Where a lack of mental capacity has been found, any decision to disclose information about a mentally incapacitated patient must be made in the patient's best interests. If this is done, the health care worker will not face any legal repercussions. The assessment of best interests is assisted with the Mental Capacity Act's best interests' 'checklist'.[26]

The decision to disclose information on the basis that it is in the best interests of the patient must be reflected upon carefully. The need to disclose information should be about medical interests with information sharing being necessary to help the patient in the therapeutic process.[27] Health care professionals who are considering using or disclosing confidential information without the relevant authorisations should consider the reasons for this and what the objective of disclosure is. This process of reflection requires a balancing exercise to be undertaken.[28]

---

[25]   Mental Capacity Act 2005, s. 3.

[26]   Mental Capacity Act 2005, s. 4.

[27]   GMC, *Confidentiality: good practice in handling patient information*, 2017, paras 41–49.

[28]   In the context of suspected child abuse, see *A v GMC* [2004] EWHC 880 (Admin). In this case, Charles J. set out doctors' duty of confidentiality in such circumstances. It was noted that where there are concerns about child protection, it is not necessary to establish that there is 'reasonable cause to suspect that the child concerned is suffering or is likely to suffer significant harm,' before disclosures are made. See also, R. Stretch, 'The Duty to Report Child Abuse in France, Lessons For England?' (2003) 15(2) *Child & Family Law Quarterly* 139.

Compulsory Disclosure

The obligation of confidentiality is recognised as having clear exceptions, and health care professionals have significant discretion as to when disclosure may take place. However, in certain circumstances the disclosure of confidential medical information or the supply of patient medical records is required by law. When this occurs, the doctor has no choice and must comply with the request.

If a doctor is required by a court of law to supply information, he cannot rely on any professional privilege to refuse this request. When subpoenaed to give evidence, the doctor must answer all questions fully though she is not required to volunteer information. While this might require the disclosure of very intimate information about a patient, it is expected that the judge will endeavour to limit the amount of shared information beyond what is necessary.[29] Balancing the need for information by the court with the need to protect confidentiality as far as possible is not easy. Ultimately, a balancing process will be deployed to ensure the fair treatment of competing interests is achieved, but one set of interests will inevitably prevail.[30]

This balancing process between compulsion to disclose and protection within the criminal law can also be seen in relation to the provision of information by the doctor to the court and responding to police questions. The medical profession is not a special professional category that allows doctors to withhold requested information. The Police and Criminal Evidence Act 1984 allows for the police to access 'personal records' which would include medical records and records of counselling (including religious and spiritual).[31] While these medical records must be handed over, if requested, there are some precautions in place. Police cannot enter a doctor's surgery and carry out a search or remove medical records or human tissue and fluids without a search warrant which must be granted by a circuit judge. Typically, police search warrants are granted by lay magistrates, but the important and personal nature of this information requires the additional safeguard. These safeguards were threatened when the Police, Crime, Sentencing and Courts Act 2022 was being debated in Parliament. The legislation was introduced in England and Wales to give more power to the police, and to introduce more restrictions on protests and

---

[29] J. V. McHale, *Medical Confidentiality and Legal Privilege* (Abingdon, Routledge, 1993).

[30] For example, see *D v NSPCC* [1977] 1 All ER 589. See more recently, *Ashworth Security Hospital v MGN Limited* [2002] 1 WLR 2033 and *Regina v Davis (Iain); Regina v Ellis; Regina v Gregory; Regina v Simms; Regina v Martin* [2006] 1 WLR 3130.

[31] Police and Criminal Act 1984, s. 12.

crimes against children, amongst other things. However, a set of Government amendments to the Bill were passed by peers in the House of Lords confirming the Government's commitment that the current rules regarding medical confidentiality would continue to apply where a patient is subject to police enquiries. The original wording of the Police, Crime, Sentencing and Courts Bill allowed for permissive and blanket powers overriding long-standing provisions protecting patient confidentiality. The British Medical Association (BMA), along with the GMC and the National Data Guardian, raised concerns that the original draft of the Bill would place a legal requirement on all clinical commissioning groups and local health boards to share confidential patient information with the police, as well as additional powers to bring forward regulations for sharing this information with a wider list of recipients like councils and educational authorities. However, with the amendments, patients can now trust that the information they share about their health in confidence with their doctor will be protected under existing common law requirements.

Some statutes also require the disclosure of private information. Public health presents particular challenges. Compulsory notification by doctors about patients with highly infectious diseases and venereal disease is required. The Public Health (Control of Disease) Act 1984[32] makes provision for wide-ranging compulsory notification of certain diseases, including tuberculosis, cholera, and a long list of childhood diseases. When faced with a patient with one of these diseases, a doctor must notify the appropriate authorities with details of any infection or contamination that may pose a significant risk to human health.[33] Where infection, and particularly when the contagion is rapid and highly transmittable, public health legislation provides the necessary tools to supress the infection risk. Under the Health and Social Care Act 2008 the remit of compulsory powers to contain contamination risks and health threats has been expanded.[34] The scope of these powers has widened and allows for the legitimate isolation and restraint of individuals and the seizure of property. At the heart of the health protection mandate within the Health and Social Care Act 2008 lies the 'all hazards' approach[35] and the decision to act is now

---

[32]   This has since been amended by the Health and Social Care Act 2008.

[33]   The Health Protection (Notification) Regulations 2010 (SI 2010/659).

[34]   The Health Protection (Notification) Regulations (SI 2010/659) came into force on 6 April 2010 and extends the previous arrangements for statutory notification of infectious diseases in England. The Health Protection (Local Authority Powers) Regulations 2010 (SI 2010/657) and the Health Protection (Part 2A Orders) Regulations 2010 (SI 2010/658), set out the powers and duties of local authorities to take action to protect the public's health from risk of infection or contamination, where an individual does not voluntarily cooperate with necessary precautions.

[35]   Health protection and updating the Public Health (Control of Disease) Act 1984 can be found in Part 3 of the Health and Social Care Act 2008. This change is consist-

determined by the *potential* for a case of human infection or contamination to present a significant public health hazard.[36] In the confidentiality context, this widening of responsibility under the public health legislation potentially extends the extent to which individual patients may legitimately have their personal medical information shared in the public interest.

While the public health legislation applies to specific diseases, and relates to other forms of contamination risk, there has been significant pressure to make other conditions and diseases notifiable and hence, potentially, disclosable. For example, over the years, there has been pressure to make HIV/AIDS a notifiable disease.[37] Threaded throughout the debate surrounding medical confidentiality is how the balance is best struck between protecting an individual's private medical information thus reinforcing trust and confidence in the system while also sharing information when in the public interest. HIV/AIDS has not become a notifiable disease because to curb the spread of the disease patients need to be able to trust their doctor. Furthermore, the disease is not one that is deemed a high contagion risk. HIV, hepatitis B and most sexually transmitted diseases currently remain outside of the scope of the public health legislation.[38]

Disclosure in the Public Interest

The public interest defence in decisions regarding information disclosure often involve the balancing of conflicting rights. In determining whether there has been an unjustified breach of confidence, English law requires a balancing act to be undertaken between public interest claims in favour of keeping information private and a variety of public interest claims which may support disclosure.

Arguments concerning the integrity of medical documents and the relationship of trust between patients and medical practitioners have featured heavily in support of maintaining confidentiality. Judges have been concerned to maintain public confidence that health care professionals will not unnecessar-

---

ent with the International Health Regulations (2005) which help countries collaborate to assist with the international effort to respond to infectious diseases and other health risks. See WHA58.3 Revision of the International Health Regulations at: www.who.int/ihr/about/FAQ2009.pdf. (accessed: 10 February 2021).

[36] See N. Glover-Thomas 'The Vaccination Debate in the UK: Compulsory Mandate Versus Voluntary Action in the War Against Infection' (2019) May *Journal of Medical Law and Ethics* 1.

[37] M. Brazier and E. Cave, *Patients, Medicine and the Law* (Manchester, Manchester University Press, 2016).

[38] M. Brazier and J. Harris, 'Public Health and Private Lives' (1996) 4 *Medical Law Review* 171.

ily breach medical confidentiality. Under traditional equitable principles, once a disclosure of confidential information had been established, it would be for the defendant to demonstrate that the disclosure was in the public interest. In the health context, this requires a balancing act to be undertaken, weighing up the public interest arguments in favour of keeping information confidential and any public interest arguments that support disclosure.

Serious crime

A discernible public interest consideration that would justify breach of confidence is the prevention of serious crime. Doctors may become aware during a consultation with a patient of details of a serious crime or the potential for a serious crime to occur. What expectations should be placed upon a doctor to identify both a crime and any risk associated with it? While there might be a belief that doctors are under a duty to disclose details of a crime, there is no general obligation placed upon the doctor to volunteer information about crime. The courts and the General Medical Council instead ask the doctor to judge the public interest in making the decision. Often disclosure is justifiable to protect others, for example, future victims of gun or knife crime or children at risk of abuse. While a doctor does not commit an offense by failing to inform the police of any evidence that may have come into his possession during his professional capacity,[39] there are several statutes that require doctors to supply information on request from the police, such as, the road traffic legislation and section 19 of the Terrorism Act 2000 which requires anyone to volunteer information about funding terrorist activity. If a doctor or anyone else accepts money to conceal the evidence of a crime, then a criminal offense is committed under the Criminal Law Act 1967.[40]

Serious crime presents two specific issues for consideration: the role of information disclosure to prevent crime and information to detect and prosecute crime. If a doctor has reasonable grounds to believe that his patient or a third party *may* commit a serious crime placing others at risk, the doctor can lawfully contact the police or other appropriate bodies, such as, child services. In *W v Egdell*,[41] W had been convicted of the manslaughter of five neighbours and wounding two others. In support of an application to transfer W to a regional unit, his solicitors arranged for an independent psychiatric report from Dr Egdell in support of this application. But following the examination, Dr Egdell concluded that W was dangerous and manipulative with a psychopathic personality, no real insight into his condition and a morbid interest in

---

[39] Criminal Law Act 1967, s. 5(5).
[40] Criminal Law Act 1967, s. 5(1).
[41] [1990] Ch. 359 CA.

explosives. W's solicitors withdrew the application to the mental health review tribunal and Dr Egdell asked them to pass his report to the hospital where W was detained. They refused, claiming that to do so would be both a breach of confidence and a violation of legal professional privilege. Dr Egdell decided to nevertheless send the report to the director of the hospital where W was detained and agreed with the director that a copy should be forwarded to the Home Secretary. W's solicitors sought an injunction, the Court of Appeal found that (1) Dr Egdell did owe W an obligation of confidence; but (2) the public interest in safety on this occasion outweighed both the public, and W's private, interest in confidentiality.

Where a doctor is in receipt of evidence that a patient has committed a crime, the choice as to whether the police should be contacted largely still rests with the doctor. In the UK, the law does not penalise doctors who choose to maintain the confidentiality of their patients despite clear evidence of a crime being committed. Yet, there remains some debate about whether disclosure of information in this context would amount to a breach of confidentiality.[42] While beyond the medical sphere, disclosure of information regarding all crimes acquired in confidential relationships is seen as in the public interest,[43] the impact of breach of confidentiality within the medical setting may discourage such a broad-brush approach.[44] However, where a patient has been a victim of crime, such as rape, but refuses to go to the police, the doctor may take the view that this could place others at risk. The GMC states that doctors can justifiably disclose information of this nature if they believe others may be at risk from offenders using weapons or domestic violence.[45] Where there is a risk of gunshot or knife wounds, the GMC take a stricter view and requires doctors to contact the police.[46]

The decision to disclose information where a crime has been or might be committed raises tensions for the doctor. Without doubt agreement is universal in that good medical care depends upon confidentiality. When a doctor enforces her duty to her patient it is seen as beneficial to all. Therefore, where

---

[42] *Birmingham Assizes* (1914) 78 JP 604.

[43] *Initial Services Ltd v Putterill* [1968] 1 QB 396 at 405.

[44] The General Medical Council notes that disclosure of crime is justified in the context of serious crime, implying that disclosure of information regarding all crime is not merited. See GMC, *Confidentiality: good practice in handling patient information*, 25 April 2017, para. 63.

[45] GMC, *Confidentiality: good practice in handling patient information* (2017) para. 65.

[46] GMC, *Confidentiality: reporting gunshot and knife* wounds, (2018). Available at: www.gmc-uk.org/-/media/documents/gmc-guidance-for-doctors---confidentiality---reporting-gunshot-and-knife-wounds_pdf-70063779.pdf?la=en&hash=77149AD43F F6F9C89F3DDF2502432E73245EAA92 (accessed: 12 May 2021)

a decision is made to disclose private medical information, sound reasons must be clear.

Communicable disease

Should notification of certain diseases be mandatory? If a doctor had reason to believe that her patient has contracted pneumonic plague, does she have a duty to contact public health officials and prioritise the protection of the community? The Public Health (Control of Disease) Act 1984 (as amended by the Health and Social Care Act 2008) Part 2A and the Health Protection (Notification) Regulations 2010 requires doctors to notify the appropriate authorities about certain diseases.[47] Diseases including tuberculosis, cholera, and a long list of childhood diseases must be notified by a doctor, but notification also more recently requires doctors to notify the relevant authorities of any infection or contamination risk that may pose significant harm to human health. The basis upon which this duty to notify and disclose rests is the protection of the public.[48] It is the risk of harm to others that legitimises the decision by the doctor to disclose confidential information. Key to the justification of placing the public interest over the interests of an individual patient and safeguarding his confidentiality is the belief that significant danger of harm exists.

Where the issue relates to a health care worker with a disease that potentially presents risk to his patients, the GMC obliges a doctor with this knowledge to inform the employer and the regulator if it is believed that the infected health care worker 'places patients at the risk of infection'.[49] In *X v Y*[50] two general practitioners who had tested HIV positive were receiving treatment and counselling from the plaintiff health authority. An employee of the authority 'leaked' the information and the names of the doctors to a tabloid newspaper who planned to publish a 'Doctor with AIDS' story. Rose J prohibited any publication of the story even though the newspaper ultimately promised not to disclose the actual identity of the doctors. There was deemed no public interest in disclosure founded in the protection of others. It was also noted that if health care professionals feared exposure if they sought testing for HIV, they would not come forward for testing and in those circumstances might be more likely to pose a risk to patients. Rose J stressed the public as well as the private interest in medical confidentiality. 'Preservation of confidentiality is the only way

---

[47]   The Public Health (Control of Disease) Act 1984 has more recently been amended by the Health Protection (Coronavirus) Regulations 2020.

[48]   M. Brazier and J. Harris, 'Public Health and Private Lives' (1996) 4 *Medical Law Review* 171.

[49]   GMC, *Supplementary Guidance: Confidentiality, Disclosing Information about Serious Communicable Diseases* (2017), para. 75.

[50]   [1988] 2 All ER 648.

of securing public health; otherwise, doctors will be discredited as a source of education, for future individual patients will not come forward if doctors are going to squeal on them.'[51]

Where the risk of harm might pertain to individuals, such as a sexual partner of a patient who is found to be HIV positive, can the doctor disclose that information? The GMC leaves this to the doctor to decide and states that the doctor[52] *may* disclose (rather than must) where appropriate. In such a case, disclosure of the patient's health status to known sexual partners might be necessary to protect them. Reasonable foresight of harm is the threshold that must be met to justify disclosure and where this is evident, the courts are generally not keen to intervene against a doctor for her decision to disclose. Therefore, the public interest in preserving patient confidentiality should only be supplanted in the face of substantial danger of harm.

Freedom of expression

The exceptional circumstances where a doctor may decide to disclose confidential information about a patient because of communicable disease or risk of harm to others from crime, is justified by common law and Article 8(2) of the European Convention on Human Rights: the right to privacy. However, in some cases a patient's or health care professional's interest in maintaining confidentiality will sometimes be weighed against the right to freedom of expression. Can the media rely upon freedom of expression under Article 10 of the European Convention of Human Rights? And, if so, in what circumstances? How this balance is achieved has been the subject of much judicial discussion. Before the Human Rights Act 1998 came into force the courts had the opportunity to weigh the competing public interests of medical confidentiality and press freedom in several health care cases. In *X v Y*[53] Rose J held that the public interest in maintaining confidentiality outweighed the public interest in a free press. Since the Human Rights Act came into force, the courts have considered the scope of article 10 and what amounts to being in the public interest. In *McKennit v Ash*, Buxton LJ observed that 'what interests the public is not necessarily in the public interest'.[54]

Where disclosure of confidential information leads to the clear identification of an individual health care professional, the courts are unlikely to regard this as being in the public interest. In *H (a Healthcare Worker) v Associated*

---

[51]   *X v Y* [1988] 2 All ER 648 [386].

[52]   GMC, *Supplementary Guidance: Confidentiality, Disclosing Information about Serious Communicable Diseases* (2017), para. 22.

[53]   [1988] 2 All ER 648.

[54]   *McKennit v Ash* [2006] EWCA Civ 1714 [66].

Newspapers,[55] an HIV positive dentist (H) sought injunctions restraining a health authority from conducting a 'look back' exercise and sought an injunction when a newspaper obtained the story and planned to publish. The health care worker wanted his personal identity to be protected, the health authority he worked for and his specialism to remain confidential to ensure he was not identifiable. The health authority was concerned that disclosure of its identity could generate panic in the general population and would necessitate large costs to reassure patients. The Court of Appeal ruled that (1) no details of H's identity should be published as to do so would potentially deter other's from coming forward; (2) the health authority could not be identified as this may equally deter others from seeking treatment; and (3) details of H's speciality could be made public as such a restriction was unnecessary and it would inhibit public debate. Interestingly, in *H*, the court accorded more authority to the right of freedom of expression and the desire to alert the public of the risks and to initiate public debate. The balancing process between the rights set out in Articles 8 and 10 was recognised as a necessity. The Court of Appeal acknowledged the importance of press freedom even in the medical sphere where medical privacy and confidentiality had thus far dominated.

GENETIC INFORMATION AND CONFIDENTIALITY

Can the doctor's duty of confidentiality give way to the interests of a relative who may be at risk from a genetic disease under the guise of the public interest defence?[56] Tests which show that a patient suffers from, or carries a genetic disease, often indicate that other family members could face the same risk of the same disease. The Human Genetics Commission acknowledge that '[d]isclosure of sensitive personal genetic information for the benefit of family members in certain circumstances may occasionally be justified. This would arise where a patient refuses to consent to such disclosure and the benefit of disclosure substantially outweighs the patient's claim to confidentiality.'[57] The GMC further recognises the need to disclose information against the wishes of the patient in rare cases.[58]

---

[55]   [2002] EWCA Civ 195.

[56]   A de Paor, 'Genetic Risks and Doctors' Disclosure Obligations: Revisiting the Duty of Confidentiality' (2018) 25 *European Journal of Health Law* 365–88.

[57]   Human Genetics Commission, *Inside Information: balancing interests in the use of personal genetic data*, 21 May 2002, p.15.

[58]   GMC, *Confidentiality: good practice in handling patient information*, 2017, para. 75. See also, D. Bell and B. Bennett, 'Genetic Secrets, and the Family' (2001) 9(2) *Medical Law Review* 130–36 and L. Skene, 'Genetic Secrets and the Family: A Response to Bell and Bennett' (2001) 9(2) *Medical Law Review* 162–69.

Genetic Privacy

Genetic information brings into stark focus the tensions that exist between the rights of the individual to keep their personal medical information private, and the broader interests of both the public and others directly impacted by another's personal medical information. The Human Genome Project (HGP)[59] was declared complete in April 2003 and this has laid the foundation for an increasing understanding of the role played by genetics in disease. At the same time, this knowledge, and the scope for further knowledge to be gained in the future presents a potential for genetic discrimination to emerge. The right to privacy as set out in Article 8(2) ECHR which seeks to protect against arbitrary interferences with private and family life, home, and correspondence by a public authority[60] is not absolute. Justifications for violating privacy are also set out in Article 8(2) providing scope for others to seek access to genetic test results. Insurers and employers, for example, may argue that knowledge of this kind is essential to defend individual employees or clients, or the health or freedom of others. If access to this genetic information is freely available, the 'life' impact on individuals to find and maintain employment, obtain insurance, apply for a mortgage, and so on, could be significant. While the Human Genetics Commission in the UK was set up in 2000 to develop policy and act as an oversight body to consider difficult genetics-based dilemmas, this quango was disbanded in 2010, producing its final research paper in 2012. There is currently no organisation overseeing these issues so raising considerable concerns about how genetic privacy will be protected in the future.

In *R (on the application of Rose and another) v Secretary of State for Health and another*,[61] an application was made to review the decision not to provide any information concerning two sperm donors, whose sperm was used to produce children. It was argued that the guidance and legislation stipulating anonymity were in breach of Article 8 ECHR, an argument with which the court agreed stating that Article 8 entitles individuals to information about themselves and their origins. The impact of not knowing one's paternity was stated by the applicant as having implications for every area of life. As a result, the Human Fertilisation and Embryology Authority Regulations (Disclosure of Donor Information) 2004[62] now provide that children born from the use of donated gametes after 1 April 2005 can obtain identifying information about the donor once they reach 18. However, in *A v X (Disclosure: Non-Party*

---

[59] Human Genome Project Information Archive 1990–2003. Available at: https://web.ornl.gov/sci/techresources/Human_Genome/index.shtml (accessed: 5 April 2021).

[60] *Libert v France* (Application no. 588/13).

[61] [2002] EWHC 1593 (Admin).

[62] SI 2004/1511.

Medical Records)[63] access to a sibling's medical records was denied to a claimant as this would be an infringement of their Article 8 privacy right. This principle was reiterated in *A London Borough Council v Mr & Mrs N (Foster Carers of the Child and P (A Child by her Guardian)*[64] in which the local authority was held not to have a duty to inform the biological father of a child in foster care that one of the child's foster parents was HIV positive. The risks of exposure were minimal, and consequently, disclosure would be an unjustifiable infringement of the foster parents Article 8 rights.

Up until recently, the legal position was clear. A relative's interests in having access to personal medical information would not erode the doctor's duty of confidentiality to a patient.[65] Yet questions remained as to whether there were any circumstances when a relative who might be at risk from a genetic disease could access information under the guise of the public interest defence?[66]

In 2017, this issue was subject to judicial scrutiny in *ABC v St George's NHS Hospital Trust.*[67] In 2007, the claimant's father, F, was convicted of the manslaughter of C's mother and detained under the Mental Health Act 1983. In November 2009, F was diagnosed with Huntington's Disease (HD). He refused to allow doctors to disclose his condition to his daughter C. C was at 50 per cent risk of inheriting HD from her father. C became pregnant in 2009 and her daughter was born in April 2010. C only learned of F's condition by accident in August 2010. In 2013 C was tested for HD and tested positive thus her daughter was also at 50 per cent risk of inheriting HD from her mother C. C claimed that the failure to alert her to her father's diagnosis was actionable negligence and a breach of her Article 8 right to family life. Had she been so warned in November 2009 she would have terminated her pregnancy.[68] Her

---

[63] [2004] EWHC 447.

[64] [2005] EWHC 1676.

[65] V. Chico, 'Non-Disclosure of Genetic Risks: The Case for Developing Legal Wrongs' (2016) 16 *Medical Law Review* 3–26.

[66] A. Lucassen and R. Gilbar, 'Alerting Relatives About Heritable Risks: The Limits of Confidentiality' (2018) *BMJ* 361. See also, N. Hawkins and T. Hughes-Davies, 'Striking a Balance: Resolving Conflicts Between the Duty of Confidentiality and Duties to Third Parties in Genetics' (2018) 38(4) *Legal Studies* 645–65.

[67] [2017] EWCA Civ 336.

[68] While legally, the 'right to know' has gained some traction, there remains a staunch discourse around the 'right not to know'. Proponents of this stance support the idea that knowledge of a genetic disease is particularly difficult to live with when there is no cure (G. Laurie, *Genetic Privacy: A Challenge to Medico-Legal Norms* (Cambridge, CUP, 2002). But others have argued that when balancing rival considerations about giving or withholding information, a person's 'rights' are more defensible when supporting the notion of 'honest communication ... rather than in defence of ignorance' (J. Harris and K. Keywood, 'Ignorance, Information and Autonomy' (2001) 22 *Theoretical Medicine and Bioethics* 415–36, 432).

claim was initially struck out by Nicol J, but his decision was overturned by the Court of Appeal.[69]

The *ABC* decision places a significant burden on health care professionals. On the one hand there is still an unquestioned expectation that the obligation of confidence between a doctor and their patient remains of primary importance. Yet, at the same time *ABC* formerly acknowledges the possibility of a parallel duty to relatives when genetic risk becomes apparent. In practice what this means is that health care professionals may have a 'legal duty to disclose genetic risks to genetic relatives'.[70] Health care professionals may find that juggling competing interests and balancing the rights of patients and their genetic relatives is difficult, but the task may not be impossible in practice to implement. Dove et al observes that these

> duties can be reconciled ... [as] ... each ... [is] ... focused on the same objective: allowing the implementation of a robust professional assessment of the value of preserving patient confidence and respecting relatives' interests in disclosure, in the context of striving for an outcome that will provide the best clinical genetics service for that family to be implemented, without the fear of legal action.[71]

After losing an initial ruling, which was subsequently overturned by the Court of Appeal, the High Court held a full trial of facts and evidence in 2020.[72] In broad terms, Yip J concluded that health care practitioners did owe a legal duty to ensure the rights and interests of another person were balanced with those of their patient (and the public interest). There continues to be a need to preserve confidentiality, but consideration should be given to disclosure when it could reduce or prevent a significant risk of serious harm, and where the patient has a close relationship with the at-risk person. However, despite this, it was found that in this case, the health care practitioners had undertaken the balancing exercise to determine whether disclosure was necessary. This assessment had met a reasonable standard and therefore, there was no breach of duty. This decision is significant as in the UK health care professionals do owe a legal duty not only a professional obligation, to balance the rights and interests of

---

[69] See, GMC, *Confidentiality: Good practice in handling patient information* (2017) para. 73–76 for guidance on sharing general and genetic information with family members. See also, R. Gilbar, 'Medical Confidentiality within the Family: the Doctor's Duty Reconsidered' (2004) 18(2) *International Journal of Law and the Family* 195–213.

[70] E.S. Dove, V. Chico, M. Fay et al, 'Familial Genetic Risks: How Can We Better Navigate Patient Confidentiality and Appropriate Risk Disclosure to Relatives?' (2019) 45 *Journal of Medical Ethics* 504–07.

[71] Ibid. [506].

[72] *ABC v St George's Healthcare NHS Trust* [2020] EWHC 455 (QB).

at-risk individuals, such as a genetic relative, with those of a patient who has refused consent to disclosure of confidential information. Notably, Yip J. did not confine this analysis within the context of heritable genetic risk. This balancing exercise should be applied by all health care practitioners in relation to all forms of confidential information where disclosure could prevent serious harm, provided there is evidence of a close relationship between the patient and the person at risk. This may open greater discretion for health care professionals in the future is situations where they have felt hampered by the stricter interpretation of medical confidentiality. For example, as considered by Yip J., the duty may apply to psychiatrists if their patient discloses an intention to be violent towards a relative. For GPs who care for several members of the same family, they will now have the discretion to consider disclosure if necessary to prevent harm, for example, where a patient with a new diagnosis of HIV refuses to disclose this information to his wife. In many ways the *ABC* decision encourages the development of a recognisable 'composite duty'[73] which will allow health care professionals the peace of mind to know that the decision to breach confidentiality to genetic relatives will not result in legal action.

DATA PROTECTION LEGISLATION

The EU Regulation General Data Protection Regulation (GDPR) came into force on 25 May 2018[74] replacing an earlier EU Directive on which the Data Protection Act 1998 was based.[75] The 1998 Act is replaced by the Data Protection Act 2018. The GDPR reiterates the right to data protection. Article 1 of the GDPR recites that the Regulation protects the rights of natural persons regarding the processing of personal data[76] and rules relating to the free movement of data. The way in which data in inputted and stored is not relevant, thereby placing automated and manual inputting of data on an equal footing. Under the GDPR, health data is defined as personal data related to the physical or mental health of a natural person, including the provision of health care services, which reveal information about that person's health status.[77] Article 9 of the GDPR creates 'special' categories of personal data which include genetic

---

[73]   Ibid. [507].

[74]   V. Chico, 'The Impact of the General Data Protection Regulation on Health Research' (2018) 128 *British Medical Bulletin* 109–18.

[75]   The impact of Brexit on data protection and data storage remains uncertain. See J. Clark and A. Greaves, 'Brexit: Key Impacts on Data Protection' (2018) 19 *Privacy and Data Protection* 6.

[76]   Personal data has been defined in *Durant v Financial Services Authority* [2003] EWCA Civ 1746 as information focusing on the individual rather than on third parties.

[77]   Article 4(15), GDPR.

data, biometric data, and information about health, with additional protections applying to such 'special data'.[78]

ANONYMISED DATA

Central to the rights and duties of confidentiality is the relationship between the information and an individual's identity. Consequently, controls over information typically relates to identifying information. But, what of anonymised data? Information can be used in a variety of ways and can a provide a valuable contribution to several activities, including clinical audits, epidemiological studies, and secondary research studies. During 2020 and 2021, vast amounts of anonymised data has been collected across the world because of the COVID-19 pandemic. These data have been used in a variety of ways, not least to generate epidemiological models that have led to public-health measures, including testing, isolating infected people, tracing, and quarantining, all of which have been used to try and contain the virus.[79] Anonymised data is used by many commercial organisations for many things. While there has always been a reticence for medical information to be shared with these organisations, recent research has shown that where efforts to inform individuals about how the data will be used, the public are much more willing to be involved for the public good.[80]

The applicational scope of the confidentiality rules in relation to anonymised data was considered in the case of *R v Department of Health, ex parte Source Informatic Ltd.*[81] This case concerned a commercial data collection company that bought anonymised data from GPs to sell to drug companies who were analysing prescribing habits. The Court of Appeal held that anonymised data did not have the necessary quality of confidence. The court observed that the 'patient has proprietorial claim to the prescription form or to the information which it contains ... and no right to control its use provided only and always

---

[78] Article 9(2), GDPR.

[79] Editorial, *Nature*, 27 January 2021, 589, 491–92. Available at: www-nature-com .manchester.idm.oclc.org/articles/d41586-021-00183-z (accessed: 20 May 2021).

[80] V. Chico, A. Hunn and M. Taylor, *Public views on sharing anonymised patient-level data where there is a mixed public and private benefit*, September 2019. Available at: https://s3.eu-west-2.amazonaws.com/www.hra.nhs.uk/media/documents/ Sharing_anonymised_patient-level_data_where_there_is_a_mixed_public_and_privat _Pab71UW.pdf (accessed: 19 May 2021).

[81] [2001] QB 424. See also, HM Government, *Open Data: Unleashing the Potential* Cm 8353 (London, HMSO, 2012). Available at: https://assets.publishing.service.gov .uk/government/uploads/system/uploads/attachment_data/file/78946/CM8353_acc.pdf (accessed: 15 May 2021).

that his privacy is not put at risk'.[82] 'If, as I conclude, his only legitimate interest is in the protection of his privacy and if that is safeguarded, I fail to see how his will could be thought thwarted or his personal integrity undermined.'[83] The *Source Informatics* judgment that a person's privacy can be protected merely by concealing their identity has been criticised on the ground that it removes their right of autonomy to decide what should be done with their information and it ignores a patient's vulnerability when confiding information to health care workers.[84] In the years since the *Source Informatics* decision, considerable infrastructure has been built into the ethical safeguarding of anonymised data. The law concerns itself with information that can only lead to a person's privacy being violated or where their identity can be found leading to serious implications. This approach provides the necessary protection of privacy while allowing sufficient flexibility within the system to enable clinical research, drug companies and other health care workers and researchers to gain from the anonymised information that comes from patients.

ACCESS TO MEDICAL RECORDS

English law acknowledges the use of anonymised data as this information does not possess the quality of confidence. However, there are times when GPs and other health care workers may legitimately share information about patients. In *Health Authority v X*[85] it was found that there can be a compelling public interest in the sharing of pertinent medical records to the General Medical Council if they 'are or may be relevant to the General Medical Council carrying out its statutory duties to protect the public against possible medical misconduct'.[86] Such justification could arise where information is shared to investigate the health care delivery of a GP, to ensure that any practitioners who pose a risk to patients are identified, to protect particularly vulnerable patients from such risk; and to ensure efficient and effective regulation of the profession.

Likewise, the patient himself may wish to access his own medical records. Under current legislation in England, individuals have a right to access their own health records. In limited circumstances they also have a limited right to access information about other people. This right extends to both records held

---

[82]   Ibid. *Source Informatics* [424, para. F].
[83]   Ibid. *Source Informatics* [440, para. D].
[84]   D. Beyleveld and E. Histed, 'Anonymisation is Not Exoneration: R. v. Department of Health, Ex Parte Source Informatics Ltd' (1999) 4(1) *Medical Law International* 69–80. For a more detailed analysis, see D. Beyleveld and E. Histed, 'Betrayal of Confidence in the Court of Appeal' (2000) 4(3–4) *Medical Law International* 277–311.
[85]   [2001] 2 FLR 673.
[86]   Per Cazalet J.

in the private health sector and health professionals' private practice records. Since 2018, access to patient health records is governed by the EU General Data Protection Regulation (GDPR), enacted by the Data Protection Act 2018. Government guidance on access to health records was produced in 2010[87] and covered other legislation that relates to patients' access to their health records, including, the Access to Health Records Act 1990 – which governs rights of access to deceased patient health records by specified persons and the Medical Reports Act 1988 which governs the right for individuals to have access to reports, relating to themselves, provided by medical practitioners for employment or insurance purposes.[88]

While access to a patient's own medical records has become easier since the GDPR, this right to information about oneself is not absolute. In certain circumstances, full access to a patient's health records may be denied. The doctor could invoke therapeutic privilege to deny access to information if it is believed that the release of this information could cause serious harm to the physical or mental health of the patient or another individual. Consequently, while control over what happens to medical information is subject to the obligation of confidence, there are occasions when an individual may also not be able to access information about themselves.[89] The invocation of therapeutic privilege takes the decision out of the hands of the patient and removes the control of information away from the patient.

CONCLUSION

The obligation of confidence in England and Wales derives from an established ethical imperative in medicine. While not absolutist in nature, there are strong ethical arguments for maintaining medical confidentiality as without it, patients will lack trust in the provision of medical care or the therapeutic endeavour. The legal obligation of confidence is derived from the common law through breach of confidence. Efforts to establish a free-standing right to privacy independent of the action for breach of confidence has thus far failed to gain traction. Despite the piecemeal development of the legal framework

---

[87] Department of Health, *Guidance for Access to Health Records Requests* (London, HMSO, 2010). Available at: https://webarchive.nationalarchives.gov.uk/20130103005001/http://www.dh.gov.uk/en/Publicationsandstatistics/Publications/PublicationsPolicyAndGuidance/DH_112916 (accessed: 22 May 2021).

[88] Ibid. p. 8.

[89] E. Parkin and P. Loft, *Patient Health Records: Access, Sharing and Confidentiality*, BRIEFING PAPER Number 07103, 15 May 2020. Available at: SN07103.pdf (parliament.uk) (accessed: 18 May 2021).

governing the obligation of confidentiality, the legal duty to protect patient confidentiality is commonly recognised by health care professionals.

Medical confidentiality commonly presents challenges when competing rights and interests' conflict. It is recognised by the GMC and other professional codes of practice that in certain situations it might be necessary to breach confidentiality. This arises when there is a wider duty to protect the health of others, and when the risk of non-disclosure outweighs the potential harm from breaching confidentiality. Recent legal developments in this area relate to genetic risk and when people share familial genetic information. Overruling a patient's wishes is centred on balancing the duty of care towards the patient versus protecting their relative(s) from serious harm. In the important case of *ABC v St George's NHS Hospital Trust*[90] the Court of Appeal recognised the possible existence of a parallel duty to relatives when genetic risk becomes apparent. For health care practitioners, managing and balancing the competing interests of their patients and their patient's genetic relatives, is now expected, yet in practice it may present a significant burden. 'The scope of the duty extends not only to conducting the necessary balancing exercise but also to acting in accordance with its outcome.'[91] At least in genetic medicine, this is likely to have a profound and critical impact in practice.

---

[90]   [2017] EWCA Civ 336.
[91]   Ibid. [189].

12. Comparative conclusions: towards a global vision of privacy and medical confidentiality?

Thierry Vansweevelt and Nicola Glover-Thomas

GLOBALISATION AND PRIVACY

The contributions in this book offer an insightful overview of a key concept within health law, that of privacy in healthcare. Over time, this concept has evolved considerably both at national level and on the international stage. Privacy has two important foundations: medical confidentiality and data protection. To understand privacy in healthcare, one has to examine both medical confidentiality and data protection. This is very important, because both concepts are different, with different scopes, goals and conditions.

Medical confidentiality has the most ancient roots. It can even be found in one of the oldest documents in history. The (original) Hippocratic oath, written in the fifth century BC, states: 'Whatever, in the course of my practice, I may see or hear (even when not invited), whatever I may happen to obtain knowledge of, if it be not proper to repeat it, I will keep sacred and secret within my own breast.'

Conceptually, medical confidentiality has been embraced around the World. The foundations of the doctrine of medical confidentiality have been reinforced by the adoption of the principle of confidentiality in several international conventions and treaties. The Council of Europe, which includes 47 member states, 28 of which are members of the European Union, has enacted the Convention of Human Rights and Biomedicine, also known as the Oviedo Convention.[1] The Oviedo Convention is an international instrument which

---

[1]   Convention for the Protection of Human Rights and Dignity of the Human Being with regard to the Application of Biology and Medicine: Convention on Human Rights and Biomedicine, Oviedo, 4 April 1997, www.coe.int/t/dg3/healthbioethic/Activities/ Bioethics%20in%20CoE/.

seeks to prohibit the misuse of innovations in biomedicine and to protect human dignity. Article 10 of the Oviedo Convention states: 'Everyone has the right to respect for private life in relation to information about his or her health.'

Likewise, the 2005 UNESCO-Universal Declaration on Bioethics and Human Rights[2] reinforces this approach. The UNESCO counts 193 member states from all over the world. Article 9 of the UNESCO-Declaration stipulates:

> The privacy of the persons concerned and the confidentiality of their personal information should be respected. To the greatest extent possible, such information should not be used or disclosed for purposes other than those for which it was collected or consented to, consistent with international law, in particular international human rights law.

The importance of data and the need for data protection is more recent phenomenon. The arrival of computers, smart devices and the internet has fostered information sharing and mining. The volume and speed with which data is now generated has led to the processing of larger and larger data sets and the emergence of 'Big Data.' The information technology is still growing. To protect people from abuse of their personal data, specific data protection laws are necessary. In order to harmonise the protection of this fundamental right on privacy of natural persons and at the same time ensure the free flow of personal data between states, a regulation on a higher level was necessary. The European Parliament and Council enacted the General Data Protection Regulation or GDPR in 2016.

The principle of medical confidentiality is strongly embedded in historical documents, in international treaties, declarations, charters and conventions. It is a fundamental component of our ethical and legal culture. While medical confidentiality remains a concept, which is variedly interpreted around the world, it is still legitimate to speak of the globalisation of the principle of medical confidentiality. It seems that the same will happen with the principle of privacy or data protection.

THE ROLE OF ETHICS, LEGISLATION AND CASE LAW

The roots of medical confidentiality reach back to the Hippocratic oath. Medical confidentiality was deemed a prerequisite for trust between the phy-

---

[2]   Universal Declaration on Bioethics and Human Rights of 19 October 2005, www.unesco.org/en/ev.php-URL_ID=31058&URL_DO=DO_TOPIC&URL_SECTION=201.html.

sician and patient and thus for a successful medical therapeutic relationship. Medical confidentiality serves dual interests: individual and public health interests.

While medical confidentiality has been recognised and reinforced within international conventions, many countries have rooted the principle of medical confidentiality within their national legislation, in their Constitution, in separate laws on bioethics or patient's rights and in case law.[3]

Although this can have be of symbolic value, it can achieve more than this. By enacting legislation on medical confidentiality, it provides the opportunity to exceed the general principle, which we can find in the international declarations. The legislator can provide greater depth and make concrete the doctor's disclosure duties. This offers greater transparency and clarity for the doctor, the patient and the courts. In the absence of legislation, case-law can and does take over this role in different jurisdictions. While common law systems may experience the disadvantage of less transparency because the duties are not codified in a single text and less certain, it has the added advantage of being more flexible, allowing legal development to more easily take place to reflect new developments or unforeseen situations.

The symbolic value of legislation stretches even more further when the principle of medical confidentiality is adopted in a criminal code. Indeed, the principle of medical confidentiality was regarded as so important, that several countries included the principle in the Criminal Code or in Privacy legislation with criminal sanctions.[4] The healthcare worker who violates his duty of medical confidentiality incurs a penalty and/or imprisonment. Of course, the principle of medical confidentiality has also been adopted in several professional codes of conduct. Regardless of the source of these provisions – Constitution, civil or criminal legislation, code of conduct – the principle of medical confidentiality is interpreted in a largely universal fashion. The scope of the principle of medical confidentiality is broad, applying to all of those involved in healthcare and treatment of the patient. Everyone who has knowledge of personal data of the patient because of his professional activities is necessarily bound by professional confidentiality.

Clearly, the duty of confidentiality is applicable to all healthcare workers, including physicians, in private practice or employed, dentists, pharmacists, nurses, midwives, physiotherapists and paramedics.[5] It is also applicable to other people whose work is necessary to provide these healthcare services, such as students, the administrative staff, the hospital director, the head doctor,

---

[3]   See the introduction of this book.
[4]   Belgium; Canada; Germany; Nordic countries; Qatar; Tanzania; and USA.
[5]   Belgium; Germany; Japan; Tanzania; USA.

the ombudsperson and social assistants.[6] In some countries, the principle of medical confidentiality also covers persons involved in the work of physicians by providing external services, such as accounting, file archiving and IT services.[7] In Canada, and to some degree in the USA, the duty of medical confidentiality applies also to healthcare organisations, like hospitals and retirement homes.[8]

Medical confidentiality is limited to private information. In all countries medical confidentiality applies to the identity of the patient, his health condition, the treatment, etc. But in some countries is also includes the personal, professional, and financial circumstances of the patient (Belgium,[9] Germany,[10] Nordic countries[11]).

The duty to medical confidentiality applies to everyone, even the partner or relatives of the patient.[12] Two cases can illustrate this very clearly. When a physician asks a relative to bring the patient's HIV-medicine to the clinic, where the relative does not know about the patient being HIV-positive, the duty of medical confidentiality is violated.[13] This is also the case when a hospital sends the bill for an abortion accidently to her home email address, instead of sending it to her private address as it was requested, allowing the partner of the patient to acquire confidential information.[14]

But when the partner, relative or friend is the confidant or representative of the patient, confidential information about the patient can be disclosed.[15] In Canada, if not contrary to an express request of the patient, the physician may disclose information to family members with whom the individual is believed to have a close personal relationship.[16]

It is also applicable after the death of the patient.[17] The same reasoning as for the medical confidentiality during lifetime applies. Without the ability to trust that information shared with a physician remains confidential, even after death, patients would be less willing to share necessary information to aid therapeutic intervention. Most countries do not accept a limitation to this obligation of medical confidentiality. But in some countries, such as in

---

6   Belgium; Nordic countries; Tanzania; USA.
7   Germany.
8   Canada.
9   Belgium.
10   Germany.
11   Nordic countries.
12   Belgium; Germany; South Africa; Tanzania,
13   Belgium; Japan; Nordic countries; Qatar; South Africa.
14   Nordic countries.
15   Belgium; Qatar.
16   Canada.
17   Belgium; Germany; UK.

England, the legal obligation is not necessarily permanent. How long the duty the information might remain confidential would depend upon the nature and sensitivity of the information and the potential harm to surviving relatives.[18] In Tanzania it seems medical confidentiality end after a patient has died, so the legal duty of medical confidentiality ends with the patient.[19]

The duty of medical confidentiality is a one-way duty. It is a duty of the healthcare worker. But the patient is free to reveal health information about himself.[20] He can also reveal information about the healthcare worker and record a conversation with his healthcare worker, because he is a party to the communication, and when this is for private purposes or to file a complaint.[21] For European countries the patient must also respect other conditions of the GDPR.

It happens sometimes that private detectives working for an insurance company make a video recording of a patient in a liability case, to prove his/her damage is not that serious as claimed. This would be a processing of personal data and should in European states be in line with the GDPR. It would be justified as long as the video is a recording of a public appearance of the patient[22] and is not made publicly available[23] and is necessary for the establishment, exercise or defence of legal claims.[24] In South Africa a video recording by a private detective may be admissible, if the court determines that such a recording will serve the best interests of justice.[25] But in other countries, like Qatar, the right of privacy is interpreted much more strictly. It is strictly prohibited to use video or audio recordings, regardless whether it is in public or in private places, without the patient's consent.[26]

THE CHALLENGE OF COMBINING MEDICAL CONFIDENTIALITY AND DATA PROTECTION

The second key source of privacy in the health sector, besides medical confidentiality, is data protection law. In Europe this is governed by the GDPR General Data Protection Regulation of 2016. Other countries outside Europe have their own data protection law.

---

[18] UK.
[19] Tanzania.
[20] E.g. USA.
[21] Belgium; Canada; Nordic countries; South Africa.
[22] Belgium; Japan.
[23] Nordic countries.
[24] Art. 9, (2), f GDPR.
[25] South Africa.
[26] Qatar.

In several countries two regulatory systems apply independently, the medical confidentiality rules and the data protection rules, which means that any processing of data is subject to data protection law as well as medical confidentiality.[27]

This coexistence of data protection law and medical confidentiality can cause problems, when the conditions of both regulations do not coincide. In some countries this is the case with the consent of the patient. In Belgium, several authors still defend the view that consent is not an excuse to reveal secret information, but in the GDPR consent is the primary basis for the lawful processing of data. In Germany, implied of explicit consent is sufficient to release the healthcare worker from his duty of medical confidentiality, while the GDPR requires an explicit consent.[28]

COVID-19 AND ITS CHALLENGES

The COVID-19 pandemic has significantly increased the use of virtual healthcare. Many countries have developed virtual care guidelines who describes safeguards to enhance privacy and security in virtual healthcare.[29]

Several countries also introduced vaccine passports to restrict access to flights, railway, gyms, restaurants, movie theatres, etc. Most courts and privacy commissions accepted the necessity of this approach, in view of the health crisis and the urgency of taken measures for the protection of public health.[30] Nevertheless, critical questions have been asked about the proportionality of these measures, when health information would be shared with employers.

In the USA physicians could even report patients with COVID-19 to public health authorities that are authorized by law to collect or receive such information for the purpose of preventing or controlling diseases.[31]

EXCEPTIONS TO MEDICAL CONFIDENTIALITY

The duty of medical confidentiality is not absolute. Disclosure of private information requires justification. All countries accept exceptions to this duty, and they all are quite similar throughout the world, but still some variations exist.

---

[27] Belgium; Germany.
[28] Germany.
[29] Belgium; Canada.
[30] Belgium; Canada; Qatar.
[31] USA.

Statutory Obligation or Authorisation

The most widespread exception to medical confidentiality is, of course, the statutory obligation to disclose information.

In various countries, physicians are obliged to report certain health information to public authorities, for example birth and death,[32] certain infectious/communicable diseases,[33] for example COVID-19,[34] or to notify health insurance funds about the causes of diseases and injuries caused by third parties.[35]

More controversial is the reporting of criminal offences. In Germany, a physician has the obligation to report the risk of an impending criminal offence of a particular serious nature.[36]

Other statutes do not require, but allow physicians to disclose patient data. In case of mental illness, physicians can pass on patient data to courts and road traffic authorities.[37]

Consent

In several countries medical confidentiality is based on the patient's self-determination. It is the patient who decides when, what and to what extent is to be done with his or her data.[38] But the nature of the consent differs in function of the goal of the consent. A patient's data can be shared to other treating physicians based on an implicit consent. To third parties, such as public authorities or private companies, for example insurance companies an explicit consent[39] or even a written consent[40] is required.

The consent needs to be valid, informed, free and autonomous. Several countries have doubts about the free will of the patient and impose additional conditions for such a transfer of patient's data. So, for example, in Germany courts question whether a release from confidentiality can be regarded as an expression of autonomous choice when it is a requirement of an insurance company. The German Federal Constitutional Court has decided that such consent is invalid if it is 'virtually non-negotiable', and the patient is required

---

[32] Belgium; Nordic countries; South Africa; USA.

[33] Belgium; Canada; Germany; Japan; Nordic countries; South Africa; UK.

[34] Germany; Nordic countries (but in Denmark an individual has the right to be tested anonimously).

[35] Germany.

[36] Germany.

[37] Germany.

[38] Germany; Japan; Nordic countries; South Africa; Tanzania; UK; USA.

[39] Canada; Germany; Japan,

[40] Nordic countries; USA.

to consent to disclosure to an unreasonable extent.[41] In Denmark the written consent is only valid for a maximum period of one year.[42]

Emergency Cases

In all countries disclosure of data is allowed in the interest of the patient, when the patient is unable to give his consent, for example in emergency cases because of unconsciousness.[43] The disclosure of data can then be based on the presumed consent of the patient.

Research Purposes

According to article 9 (2), j GDPR processing of health data without consent is possible if the processing is necessary for research purposes which shall be proportionate to the aim pursued, respect the essence of the right to data protection and provide for suitable and specific measures to safeguard the fundamental rights and the interests of the data subject.

Data should, if possible, be pseudonymised, may not be used for other purposes than research, and research projects need an authorisation from a research ethics committee.[44] In the US an institutional review board or privacy board must have approved the waiver of the otherwise required authorisation.[45]

Prevention of Harm to Others

In several countries a physician can violate his duty to medical confidentiality if there is an immediate danger to life or health and this danger can only be averted by a violation of medical confidentiality.[46] For instance, when a physician has serious indications of possible child abuse, he can inform the youth welfare office or the judicial authorities. In South Africa the healthcare worker who makes a report in good faith about a suspected case of child abuse, cannot be liable to civil action on the basis of the report.[47]

---

[41] BVerfG 23 October 2006, *MedR* 2007, 351.
[42] Nordic countries.
[43] E.g. Belgium; Germany.
[44] Nordic countries.
[45] USA.
[46] Belgium; Canada; Germany; Japan; Nordic countries; South Africa; Tanzania; USA.
[47] South Africa.

When adult patient is discharged from hospital, but remains mentally vulnerable, the patient's parents can be informed to avoid exposing them to further distress and harm should the patient go on to take their life.[48]

In other countries, care providers are obliged to report reasonably suspected child abuse or abuse of adults in care facilities.[49] But in some cultures it can be a social taboo to report domestic abuse, because of the moral damage that might cause the broader family. A case of abuse will therefore first be reported to a separate division of the hospital that may liaise with relevant external entities, like a family consulting centre.[50]

Police, Public Prosecutor's Office/Prevention of Crimes

In principle all countries confirm that physicians are bound by medical confidentiality in police investigations and legal preliminary proceedings. However, in practice confidentiality can and does get breached. Some countries provide the right for a physician to refuse testimony in court, and a prohibition of seizure to protect patient information.[51] In other countries the physician cannot rely on any professional privilege to refuse a request of the court.[52]

But, most countries also accept exceptions to this rule. The disclosure of data is allowed when there is an immediate danger to life or health of another person and this danger cannot be averted in any other way. When for example the police are looking for a person who has committed a crime or he is likely to commit a crime or further acts of violence, the physician may inform the police about data of this patient (Belgium, Germany, Nordic countries, UK, South Africa, USA). The decision is with the physician.

Some countries go further by imposing a duty to report planned crimes, when these crimes are particularly serious criminal offences (murder, homicide, kidnapping for ransom and hostage-taking).[53]

Other countries require everyone, including healthcare professionals, to contact the police when a patient has revealed to have committed a crime or whom they for good reasons suspect to have committed a crime, and where another innocent person is at risk of being accused or convicted for the crime (Denmark).[54]

---

[48] Nordic countries.
[49] Canada.
[50] Qatar.
[51] Belgium; Germany; see also the USA.
[52] South Africa; Tanzania; UK.
[53] Germany.
[54] Nordic countries.

Lawsuits

Where a patient puts their health at issue by commencing a lawsuit, for example, a malpractice lawsuit against the physician, relevant information regarding the plaintiff's health is admissible.[55] It is generally accepted that the healthcare worker can breach his duty to confidentiality to defend themselves in court. The right to defence has priority over medical confidentiality.

Media

Disclosure of patient data via the media is delicate. Two rights must be weighed against each other, the right to privacy and medical confidentiality and the freedom of press and information. For some countries if the patient has not consented, the disclosure of data by a physician is unlawful.[56]

Genetic Information

Genetic data are particularly sensitive data, because it retains its importance for a long time, is associated with high predictive potential and may also disclose information about third parties, the relatives.

Some countries have a general prohibition of discrimination because of genetic traits.[57]

The question whether the physician is allowed to inform a relative of the patient diagnosed with a genetic disease is controversial. In some countries the legislator has chosen for the strict protection of genetic data and a prohibition of informing the relatives.[58] In other countries, for example in Norway, the physician may only inform the family with the patient's consent or if the patient is not able to make a decision. In most countries, the physician is allowed to inform the relative after making a proper assessment of whether significant interests of relatives overweight the interests of the patient,[59] sometimes after a mandatory consultation of an ethics committee.[60] This could be the case when the genetic disorder could be prevented or alleviated through regular check-up or early interventions.[61]

---

[55] Belgium; Canada.
[56] Germany; Japan; USA; see also Nordic countries.
[57] Germany; Canada.
[58] Germany; see also Canada (no duty or option to warn family members of serious genetic conditions).
[59] Belgium; Nordic countries; Qatar; USA.
[60] Japan; Tanzania.
[61] Nordic countries; Tanzania.

In the UK a Court of Appeal decided healthcare professionals do have a duty to disclose genetic risks to genetic relatives where there is a serious risk of harm to a relative.[62] The High Court decided it was fair, just and reasonable to impose on the physician a legal duty to the relative to balance their interest in being informed of a genetic risk against the patient's interest in preserving confidentiality in relation to a diagnosis and the public interest in maintaining medical confidentiality generally. The High Court decided the decision not to disclose was supported by a responsible body of medical opinion and cannot be considered to have amounted to a breach of the duty. Significantly, a recent ruling suggests that this duty to others reaches beyond that of genetic risk.

For other countries, there is no duty to inform the relatives about a genetic disease of the patient, even if it could influence the decision to become pregnant or not.[63]

CONCLUSIONS

While there is a common understanding and acknowledgement of the principle of medical confidentiality, this volume highlights the nuances and varied interpretations applied across the continents. While this book has sought to identify and reflect on these differences to enhance our broad understanding of the way in which this concept is interpreted and applied in practice, it is also essential that we readily concede the global shifts that have taken place over the last 25 years in relation to how patients' rights are increasingly being recognised and protected. Medical confidentiality is no longer enough to always protect the patient's privacy. Information technology and big data has made regulation regarding data protection urgent and necessary. There is little doubt that this landscape will continue to evolve; and that this evolution could be rapid. What this volume hopes to do is articulate the variance of approach and the opportunity to learn from around the world while on this path of change.

---

[62] UK.
[63] Japan.

Index